Alexander Graf / Holger Schneider

The E-Commerce Book

This Book was brought to you by Spryker.

Alexander Graf / Holger Scheider

The E-Commerce Book

About a channel that became an industry

ISBN 978-1536937800

© 2022 by Alexander Graf
Heidestraße 9-10, 10557 Berlin
Germany

All rights reserved. This book or parts thereof may not be reproduced in any form, stored in any retrieval system, or transmitted in any form by any means – electronic, mechanical, photocopy, recording, or otherwise – without prior written permission of the publisher.

Translation: Brian Melican, Hamburg, Germany
Cover Design: Grafische Gestaltung Guido Klütsch, Köln, Germany
Type Setting: Fotosatz L. Huhn, Linsengericht, Germany
Project Coordination: Birga Andel, Lektorat & mehr, Rüsselsheim, Germany

Table of Contents

Innovate or Die - Why Composable Commerce is the Key to Building a Digital Platform That Outpaces the Competition

The world of digital commerce is a completely different beast today than it was even one or two years ago. The pandemic has accelerated global digitization by a decade and brought the importance of agility and adaptability to the forefront. Put simply: businesses that could or did not innovate put themselves at risk of extinction. With the competition evolving quickly around us, how can businesses stay at the head of the pack?

Introducing: Composable Commerce.
A term developed by Gartner, Composable Commerce is at its core, the concept that you can custom-build your e-commerce platform like building a house out of Lego - using only the bricks that you want. A composable approach allows businesses to build a highly customized tech stack that enables only the functionalities that serve their unique business requirements and drops the ones that do not.

It's such a vital strategy that Gartner even predicts that by 2023, organizations that have adopted a composable approach will outpace the competition by 80% in the speed of new feature implementation.

A composable platform empowers you to constantly innovate, evolve and grow. It offers the flexibility to try new things, plug components in and out, and play with new technologies all with minimal effort. Composability gives you the ability to continually release exciting updates that provide more and more value to your customers. It also allows you to incorporate customer feedback, to exceed customer expectations, and ultimately garner more and more market share.

Composable Commerce: How Does it Work?

Visualize this: You're given a task to build a home, and for this new home, you're given access to some of the very best contractors, designers, architects, and engineers. The goal is to build a team of experts to ensure that your vision of an ultra-modern home is realized in the shortest amount of time, and all you have to do is simply select the most suitable partners to work with. This is essentially what Composable Commerce is.

Historically, software has been created using a monolithic approach, where platforms are constructed as a single, large, indivisible unit. Imagine monolithic architecture as one large, solid block, cumbersome and inflexible and requiring a lot of work to make any alterations. If changes are made to any part of the platform, all of its software has to be considered and updated. The entire platform is likely to be in downtime when updates take place and adding new technologies must take into account compatibility with the full stack. This requires significant time and costs and often locks out non-tech stakeholders due to complexity.

If monolithic platforms are like a solid block, modular or composable alternatives would be more similar to Lego, as previously mentioned. The most suitable bricks can be chosen to create your final masterpiece, and if one part of the model needs to be adjusted, this can take place with minimal disruption to other blocks.

The same applies to composable enterprise, a modular approach of building software based on separate, best-of-breed services that can easily be individually altered or swapped. Composable enterprise offers faster updates, easier options for tech integrations, and more accessibility to company-wide stakeholders. The result, a highly customized tech stack, is more relevant and agile than off-the-shelf legacy options of past years.

Composable approaches also allow multiple company stakeholders to offer input into the development of the final tech stack. As each service is broken down into an individual item with a specific use case, non-tech employees can more easily speak on and make requests regarding the services they would like to have extended, altered, or updated. In some cases, employees outside of tech entirely are able to make software updates themselves through the integration of plug-in style services.

Meeting Rapidly Changing Customer Demands: The Value of Composable Commerce

As customers demand more functionalities on commerce platforms or across various touch points, businesses need to be exceedingly agile in responding to the ever-changing business environment. Indeed, composable commerce creates room for the much-needed flexibility that an out-of-the-box solution will be unable to deliver. Vendor lock-in can easily be avoided when you have the freedom to replace components as needed.

Composability allows your business to respond quickly to new technologies or functionalities that your customers expect as part of a modern commerce offering, which is key to outpacing your competition. As mentioned right at the beginning, businesses that are able to innovate - quickly - are going to be the market leaders in the years to come.

To sum it up, using Composable Commerce allows you to take offerings from native capabilities, mix with options from the vast external ecosystem and sprinkle in custom components as needed (which can always be swapped in and out on-demand). This approach allows you the greatest flexibility to meet the ever-changing needs of the market and your customer base.

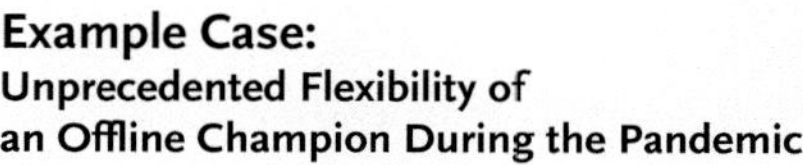

Example Case:
Unprecedented Flexibility of an Offline Champion During the Pandemic

Karls Erdbeerhof, which literally translates to Karl's strawberry farm, is a household name in northern Germany. With a history dating back to 1921, the family business has evolved from a local fruit merchant to a strawberry empire. Today, the company has up to 5,000 employees during peak season, and built up numerous new revenue streams in addition to strawberry sales, most notably their own amusement park "Karls Erlebnishof".

Business challenge:

- Covid hit the company's season start and all their amusement parks had to close
- 5% of the park's area is retail space and 95% adventure space, nevertheless they run their business by those 5%
- Dealing with constant change and unforeseen circumstances that required the rapid development of new business models

Composable solution:

- Going online in no time with little online retail experience, but clear goals and an agile mindset: easy payment processing, clean fulfillment and a functional store
- With a supplier, they seized the opportunity and sold face masks: after two days they had 100,000 orders and many customers ordered jam or sweets in addition to the masks.
- The right test & learn culture, quickly figuring out what (doesn't) work and decomposing or scaling accordingly

> ***"It's all about customer centricity. When customers submit a review on our website, even all managing directors receive a notification. This function enabled us to gain a lot of great insights, identify customer needs, and react to them as fast as possible."***
>
> Robert Dahl, Founder & CEO, Karls Erdbeerhof

Technical Foundations of Becoming Composable

To be truly composable, businesses must keep certain foundational principles in mind. You can think of these technical elements as the building blocks that will determine the composability of any digital commerce platform.

1. Packaged Business Capabilities (PBCs)

Gartner coined the term Packaged Business Capabilities (PBCs) and defines it broadly as "software components representing a well-defined business capability." Essentially, PBCs are an aggregation of independent functionalities presented to business users to enhance speed and agility when handling their digital commerce operations. PBCs guarantee faster time-to-market because each component within a PBC can easily be swapped for another, thereby giving both IT and business teams greater flexibility.

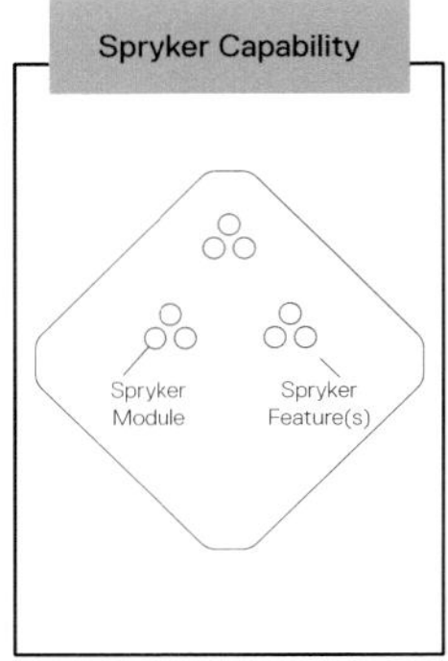

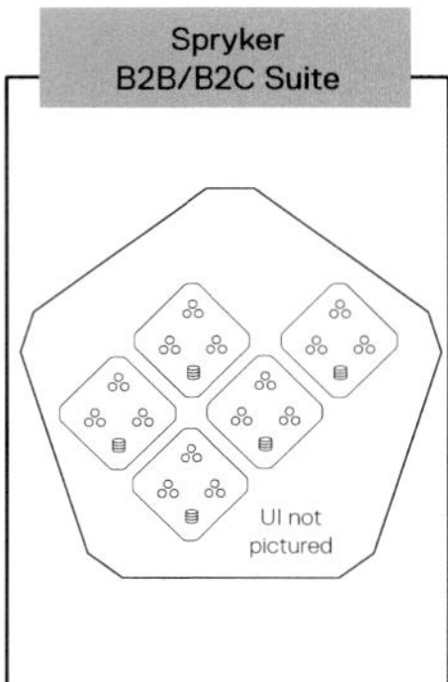

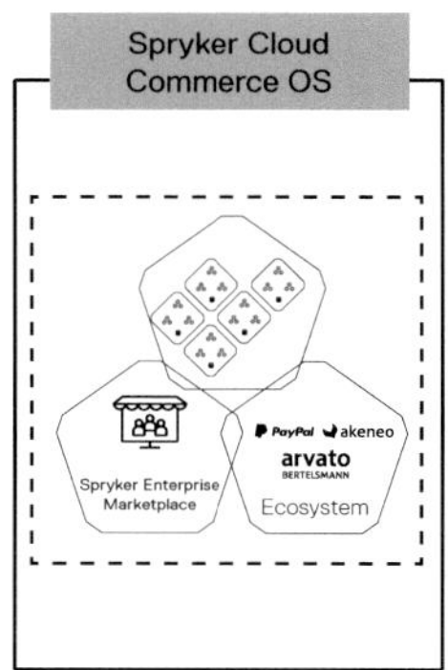

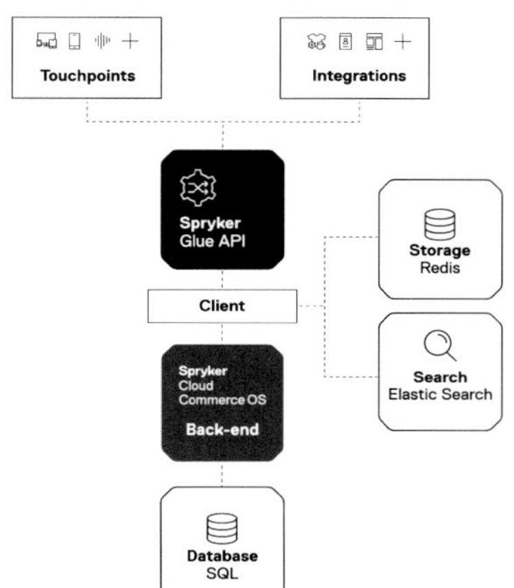

2. Application Programming Interfaces (APIs)

APIs are an important piece when it comes to building a truly composable framework. APIs facilitate the exchange of information between systems. With APIs, you can easily create a unified experience for your customer. Also, PBCs communicate with each other through APIs. The Spryker Cloud Commerce OS works with a GLUE REST API which enables connection between multiple touch points such as mobile, voice, or home devices.

3. Headless Commerce

Headless commerce relies on the use of an application programming interface (API) to connect platforms on the front-end thereby making it easier for developers to create personalized experiences without having to make alterations on the back-end system. Headless systems give room for adaptability by allowing you to reach your customers where they are and creating opportunities for more tailored commerce experiences.

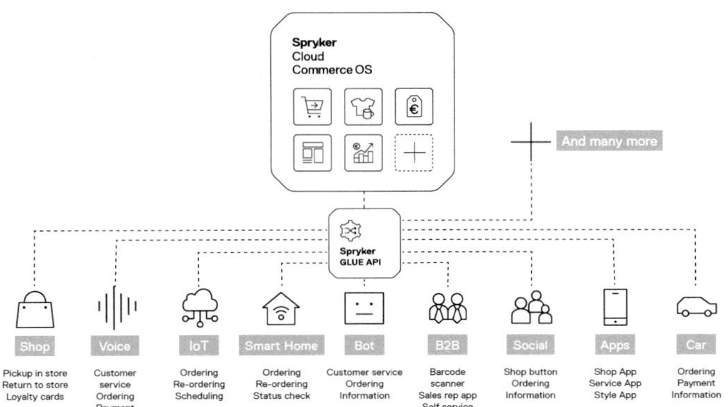

How the Spryker Cloud Commerce OS Enables Ultimate Composability

The Spryker Cloud Commerce OS back-end houses product information, pricing, payments, and all the other management functionalities clustered together and presented as Packaged Business Capabilities (PBCs). It is a Platform-as-a-Service (Paas) solution that helps customers develop, run, and manage their applications without having to deal with the intricacies of building, scaling and maintaining the infrastructure. The initial solution has been modified into a new offering called PaaS+.

PaaS+ is built on providing a seamless process of continuous integration thereby reducing the efforts it takes to make upgrades. It has a quality gate feature which checks the code deployed by a developer to determine if it is indeed quality. When it establishes that the best practices and standard requirements set by Spryker have been observed, the process of automated upgrades will then begin. The automatic upgrade feature of PaaS+ not only heightens security but also increases scalability, because developers have more time to focus on other elements and come up with innovative solutions.

Moreover, Spryker pushes the composability needle by developing an **App Orchestration Platform** which gives businesses access to a carefully curated list of 3rd-party applications that they can try out in one click. Without having to write code, business users can integrate services offered by the best-of-breed 3rd-party providers into their systems. This process eliminates the possibility of vendor lock-in and decreases the go-to-market time for businesses.

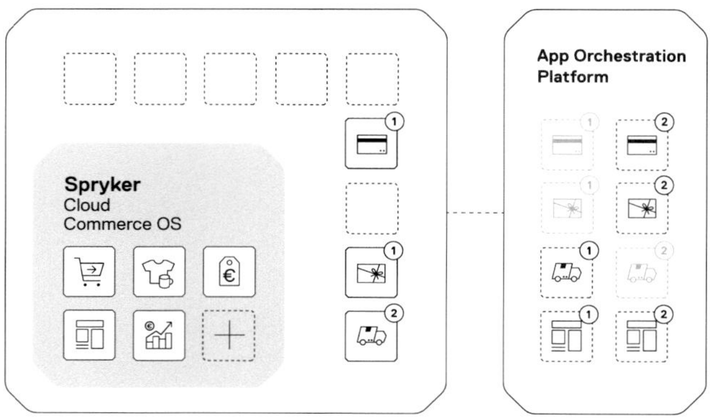

Example Case:
Hornbach Differentiates From Other DIY Stores With Spryker

The German DIY giant and Spryker customer Hornbach has an annual revenue of over €4.4 billion, 160 physical stores and 20,000 employees in nine different countries. They were early adopters of online offerings in their industry, but must always create new ways to stand out despite pandemic restrictions and big-name competition.

Business Challenge:

- With the spread of Covid, just over 60 stores were closed or only open to commercial customers
- Strong competition, especially Amazon, Obi or Hagebaumarkt
- Pioneering work in a previously offline-driven industry

Composable Solution:

- Doubling down on the already significant online presence and technical infrastructure: product range analysis, logistics, scalability - a flexible approach led to 18% revenue growth in the first quarter of 2020 despite the onset of the pandemic
- The Hornbach app: Innovative features such as object recognition, allowing users to scan items with their phone to find out product details and get product suggestions, or to speed up checkout minimizing physical contact
- An outstanding customer experience through unified commerce. Customer needs solved across channels: whether preparing the purchase from home and checking out in the store, assisting on site through the app, or pure online fulfillment.

> ***"We quickly recognized that Spryker is the right choice as it allows us to keep up the speed and flexibility to enter new business opportunities. If you want to offer your e-commerce customers something that goes beyond the standard, you also have to become a technology company."***
>
> Andreas Schobert, CTO, Hornbach

What Customers say About Spryker

G2 bestowed Spryker with the High Performers Europe for Winter 2022 award, which is based on customer satisfaction and market presence.

Trust Radius has announced that Spryker Cloud Commerce OS is one of the top-rated eCommerce solutions of 2022.

8.1/10 score

OMR Reviews awarded Spryker as one of the best shop systems of Q1 2022 for its high usability, fulfillment of customer requirements and customer support.

“We wanted to go beyond the market standard, not just offering a polished e-shop. Our goal was to achieve a one-stop shopping experience for our customers and Spryker delivered on our promise.”

Mark Wever Global Chief Digital Officer
at STAUFF

“Even though we had little time to make a decision, it should still offer a long-term perspective. And it quickly became clear to us that Spryker would provide us with the greatest innovative power and flexibility in the future.”

Daniel Richter Director Multichannel
at Globus

What Analysts say About Spryker

"Major Player in IDC 2020 Marketscape for Digital B2B Commerce.“

Gartner.

"Visionary entrant in the 2021 Gartner Magic Quadrant for Digital Commerce.“

FORRESTER®

"API-led, headlessand highly engaged with partners.“

"Future-focused B2B eCommerce solution.“

Gartner.

"Highest overall growth of any vendor in the Magic Quadrant.“

"Modern, agile and cloud native with Marketplace features.“

1 E-Commerce: The story so far

Since its beginnings around 20 years ago, online shopping has grown from a niche channel into an integral part of today's business and retail structures. Yet still, there are a range of misconceptions afloat about the drivers behind growth in e-commerce and the effects this growth is having. In what follows, we will examine the history of online shopping, going back to its beginnings and tracing its path through to the present day in order to discern the effects the meteoric rise in online sales has had – and is continuing to exert – on various market participants.

1.1 The beginnings of a revolution

The era of e-commerce dawned with the arrival of the first consumer-friendly web browsers (Mosaic in 1993, Netscape 1995) and the development of online payment systems in the mid-90s. In 1995 in a garage in Seattle, Jeff Bezos packed and posted the first order received through his online bookstore (which, back then, was called Cadabra), and started on his course as a pioneer in the industry; three years later, Amazon went public and today is the most valuable retailer on the planet. Similarly, in 1995, Pierre Omidiyar launched an online listing service – legend has it – to help buyers and sellers of Pez candy dispensers transact. His idea quickly turned into the first large online marketplace, which is still relevant today. Yet not every e-commerce pioneer met with the same success as Bezos or the man behind Ebay, Pierre Omidyar. In fact, many of the dot-com doyens disappeared[1] as quickly as they came in the ensuing boom. Nevertheless, established business models were turned upside down, too, as a rash of insolvencies in the mail order sector and the disastrous financial results of department stores such as Sears in the USA or Karstadt in Germany go to show.

1 See "A CLOSER LOOK 2002: The Dot-Com Bubble Bursts", for a few examples.

In this chapter, we will map the course of these developments step by step, using a framework of six distinct business models to determine the winners – and who still stands to lose out. As a part of this analysis, we will be taking a closer look at phenomena such as the growth in e-commerce and the factors driving this growth, changes in the personal purchasing process, and competition in retail. The six business models we distinguish between are: online marketplaces, online retailers, intermediaries, mail order companies, in-store retailers, and (brand) manufacturers.

Online marketplaces offer a platform for multiple third parties to sell goods or services, with the transaction being processed in the online shop of the marketplace operator while shipping and service tend to be handled by the seller. Amazon runs a hybrid system in which it sells products as a retailer on its own marketplace platform and offers shipping and service for third-party sellers. Ebay, meanwhile, is focussed entirely on its role as an online marketplace.

Online retailers are online pure-players (online-only retailers) who offer a product range composed of bought-in merchandise on the internet only; frequently, they are specialised in particular product groups or consumer segments. Examples include online furniture retailer Wayfair (USA), the vente-privée.com shopping club (France) or online fashion store Zalando (Germany).

Intermediaries are aggregators of various online offers, usually applying intelligent search technology to support consumers looking for specific products. This model includes non-sector-specific services such as Google Shopping (international), Shopping.com (USA), and Dooyoo (Germany) as well as industry-specialised intermediaries in areas such as travel which earn commission on sales and bookings made via their websites.

Mail order companies have been a feature of American retail for well over a century now, and also have a long tradition in many European countries such as Britain and Germany. In a manner similar to online pure-plays, mail order operators market product ranges (composed either of their own-brand products, bought-in merchandise, or a mix) directly to home shoppers. Although many have gone insolvent or changed business models, brand names such as Sears, JC Penney, and Bloomingdales (US), Littlewoods, Kays, and Argos (UK) or Otto, Neckermann, and Quelle (Germany) are still indelibly associated with their catalogues.

In-store retailers are the most numerous and varied of the models, ranging from the luxurious Neiman Marcus (USA) to the budget fashion retailer Primark (Ireland, UK, and Europe), from France's chic Galeries Lafayette to Germany's bargain-basement Media Markt. These retailers make most of their sales in their networks of stores, mainly situated in busy town and city centres or shopping centres.

(Brand) manufacturers produce goods for consumers (or B2B customers) and include names such as Samsung, Fossil and Adidas. They require a range of distribution channels as they generally do not have their own retail networks (or only limited elements of one) and make most of their sales through retailers, whether online or offline. Some companies such as Apple and H&M are exceptions to this rule, retaining both production and distribution in-house.

In the following five sections, we will portray the developments and prospects of each of these business models at various points in time over the last two decades; using a "traffic lights system", we will show what the overall mood and situation was among each group of companies in each phase:

Green = **good prospects, confidence**
Red = **poor prospects, anxiety**
Yellow = **no change**

1998: Calm before the storm

The "personal touch" misnomer
"People will always want to buy books in bookstores and never online."
The Riggio brothers (Barnes &Nobles), to Jeff Bezos (Amazon)[2]

It's three years since Ebay and Amazon were founded and e-commerce is still a very young industry. Nevertheless, American customers are quickly discovering the benefits of online shopping: in 1998, online sales in the USA total roughly eight billion dollars; in the previous year, Dell became the first company to turn over more than a billion with online sales[3]. In Britain, too, "e-tailers" – as the jargon of the time has them – are racing ahead. In much of continental Europe, meanwhile, development is slower: under 10% of the population of Germany, for example, even have the internet; e-commerce as a whole isn't even anywhere near the billion mark.

In the States above all, however, Jeff Bezos and his online bookstore Amazon have proved that customers are quite happy to purchase small, standardised items such as books and CDs on the internet and have them delivered to their homes. Indeed, with its huge selection of books and easy-to-use interface, Amazon is already starting to trump the personal touch of in-store consultation and poach customers. 1998 is also the year in which PayPal is born, this far-sighted concept for a standard means of payment online which will soon have established itself as an important alternative to other methods such as credit cards and (this being 1998) cheques.

In these early days of digital commerce, many offline retailers are rather reluctant to pursue an e-commerce strategy that would divert resources and revenue from their dominant in-store sales. This fear of cannibalisation is why Amazon's biggest

2 www.huffingtonpost.com (as of March 2015)
3 www.internetretailer.com (as of March 2016)

rival in books, Barnes & Nobles, remains slow to adapt to the new market segment. Why not let Amazon race ahead, make the first mistakes, and then invest in e-commerce later, when more customers will be online and the market more mature? Bezos is unconcerned about any threat at some point further down the line. When questioned on the prospect of big-name market entries at a later date, he replies: "I think you might be underestimating the degree to which established brick-and-mortar business, or any company that might be used to doing things a certain way, will find it hard to be nimble or to focus attention on a new channel."[4] He will, of course, turn out to be quite right. Meanwhile, Amazon starts gearing up to add more product categories such as toys and electronics to its range.

Prospects in 1998

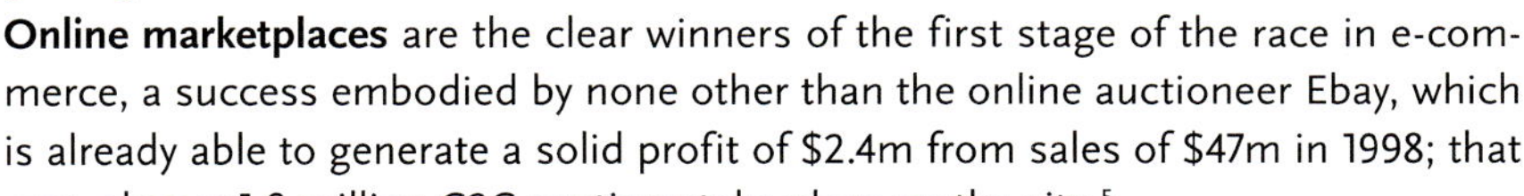

Online marketplaces are the clear winners of the first stage of the race in e-commerce, a success embodied by none other than the online auctioneer Ebay, which is already able to generate a solid profit of $2.4m from sales of $47m in 1998; that year, almost 1.8 million C2C auctions take place on the site.[5]

Online retailers are also profiting from the initial growth in e-commerce: Amazon is, until 2000, solely an online pure-player and will not add a marketplace until 2000. It goes into 1998 with a turnover of $150m from the previous year, growing at an astronomical rate of 800%[6] , and having held a successful IPO on 15th May 1997.[7]

1998 is the year in which the first **intermediaries** appear on the scene: price comparison and product search engines such as Yahoo Stores and Shopping.com make an entrance. Europe, too, sees several comparable sites set up, including Dooyoo (Germany), PriceRunner (Sweden) and Kelkoo (France). They benefit from

4 Brad Stone, The Everything Store, Little, Brown and Company, 2013
5 www.referenceforbusiness.com (as of March 2015)
6 www.wikinvest.com (as of March 2015)
7 www.encyclopedia.com (as of March 2015)

the growth in online-shopping paired with the internet users' pressing need for orientation (Google is not founded until September of that year).

While many of the North American catalogue publishers have already diversified into store outlets, many established **mail order companies** remain unfazed – and unimpressed – by e-commerce. While some have set up websites or even online shops, for most of them the internet is mainly a supplementary channel for catalogue orders – much like fax machines (this is still 1998, after all).

In-store retailers, however, make out a threat in the approaching e-commerce wave, even if few of them are investing in online shopping infrastructure. Barnes&Nobles, for example, recognises Amazon as a serious contender, having tactically filed a lawsuit against Amazon one day before its IPO in May 1997 about this latter's claim to be "the world's largest bookstore". Shakily predicated on semantics ("It isn't a bookstore at all. It's a book broker."), the suit was retracted five months later.[8]

For **manufacturers,** e-commerce is first and foremost a challenge. The prices and services offered by online retailers are almost impossible for producers to keep track of and therefore difficult to set; many fear that they will lose control of where and how their brands are presented. The reputation of Ebay, especially, is at rock bottom among brand manufacturers, above all in Europe.[9] Some are taking their own first steps in direct sales, but the results are often discouraging: B2C is a challenging field for inexperienced manufacturers (user experience is often poor at first) and existing retailers feel snubbed, which endangers sales relationships.

8 www.news.cnet.com (as of March 2015)

9 www.handelsblatt.com (as of March 2015)

A CLOSER LOOK 1998: The rise of Amazon

As far back as 1997, Jeff Bezos has already settled on his long-term strategy for Amazon – a strategy he will continue to pursue over the coming two decades at the helm: move quickly, think long term and always, always put the customer at the centre of your decision-making.

Jeff Bezos' first LETTER TO SHAREHOLDERS, 1997 (extract):

Amazon.com passed many milestones in 1997: by year-end, we had served more than 1.5 million customers, yielding 838% revenue growth to $147.8 million, and extended our market leadership despite aggressive competitive entry. But this is Day 1 for the Internet and, if we execute well, for Amazon.com. Today, online commerce saves customers money and precious time. Tomorrow, through personalization, online commerce will accelerate the very process of discovery. Amazon.com uses the Internet to create real value for its customers and, by doing so, hopes to create an enduring franchise, even in established and large markets.

We have a window of opportunity as larger players marshal the resources to pursue the online opportunity and as customers, new to purchasing online, are receptive to forming new relationships. The competitive landscape has continued to evolve at a fast pace. Many large players have moved online with credible offerings and have devoted substantial energy and resources to building awareness, traffic, and sales. Our goal is to move quickly to solidify and extend our current position while we begin to pursue the online commerce opportunities in other areas. We see substantial opportunity in the large markets we are targeting. This strategy is not without risk: it requires serious investment and crisp execution against established franchise leaders.

It's All About the Long Term: We believe that a fundamental measure of our success will be the shareholder value we create over the long term. This value will be a direct result of our ability to extend and solidify our current market leadership position. The stronger our market leadership, the more powerful our economic model. Market leadership can translate directly to higher revenue, higher profitability, greater capital velocity, and correspondingly stronger returns on invested capital [...].

[...] Obsess Over Customers: From the beginning, our focus has been on offering our customers compelling value. We realized that the Web was, and still is, the World Wide Wait. Therefore, we set out to offer customers something they simply could not get any other way, and began serving them with books. We brought them much more selection than was possible in a physical store (our store would now occupy 6 football fields), and pre-

sented it in a useful, easy-to-search, and easy-to-browse format in a store open 365 days a year, 24 hours a day. We maintained a dogged focus on improving the shopping experience, and in 1997 substantially enhanced our store. We now offer customers gift certificates, 1-Click(SM) shopping, and vastly more reviews, content, browsing options, and recommendation features. We dramatically lowered prices, further increasing customer value. Word of mouth remains the most powerful customer acquisition tool we have, and we are grateful for the trust our customers have placed in us. Repeat purchases and word of mouth have combined to make Amazon.com the market leader in online bookselling.

2002: Intermediaries on the march

The (mis)information issue

"Nobody is going to buy shoes without trying them on."

Silicon Valley venture capitalists (too numerous to count) to Tony Hsieh and Nick Swinmurn, Zappos[10]

Around the Millennium, e-commerce is a dynamic, booming industry, turning over $54 billion in the USA, close to £4 billion in the UK[11], Europe's online shopping pioneer, and managing €5.3 billion in a historically conservative market like Germany.[12] These are the heady years of the Dot-com bubble[13], as the period will later come to be known, and the halcyon days of the intermediaries, which – along with the online retailers – are attracting huge amounts of venture capital. The latter are proving again and again that complicated, emotionally-loaded products such as shoes (Zappos.com) and ladies' lingerie (Victoria's Secret) can successfully be sold on the internet; user-friendly product presentation and a focus on services such as Zappo's free, year-long free returns policy, are attracting customers.[14]

In just a few short years, both the technology and internet users have changed rapidly and are using new means of payment which drive e-commerce growth: PayPal has become a popular method of transferring money and celebrates its millionth user in late 2002. Across all areas of retail, it is consumers who are benefitting from a tangible shift in power as new ways of buying products on the internet overturn existing assumptions.

10 www.businessinsider.com (as of March 2015)
11 SAS Institute, www.statista.com (as of March 2016)
12 HDE, www.statista.com (as of March 2016)
13 See "A CLOSER LOOK 2022: The Dot-Com Bubble Bursts", for a few examples
14 www.zappos.com (as of March 2015)

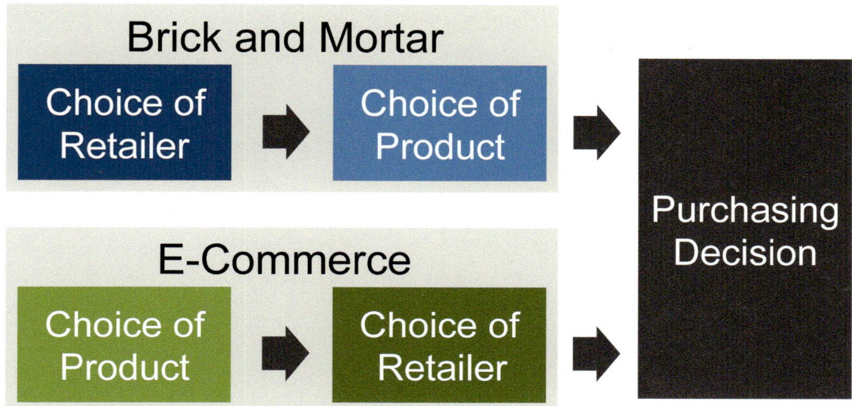

Fig. 1.1: Purchasing process in-store versus e-commerce
Source: B. Schäfers, Social Shopping für Mode, Wohnen und Lifestyle am Beispiel Smatch.com in Web- Exzellenz im E-Commerce, Gabler, p. 313

Traditionally, in the brick-and-mortar world, a prospective customer with a defined interest in acquiring a certain product settles on a retailer and then views the product range provided by that retailer. The investment of time alone and, often enough, the geographical distance between suitable retailers mean that comparing several product ranges across various retailers is seldom worthwhile. On the internet, however, this is no longer the case. In fact, the next retailer is only a click away, while price comparison and product search engines are available to aggregate the various listings, categorising them by price or service level in an at-a-glance format. This often allows customers to cut out several middlemen and opt for the most attractive offer; as such, the consequence of this transparency is that the provider with the lowest price – or the broadest product range at acceptable prices – wins out. In the online environment, the retailer is often reduced to little more than a transaction assistant, earning a lower margin than in other retail situations due to the prevalence of competition by price. The problem, however, is that the retailer's position in the brick-and-mortar world remains by no means unaffected by this race to the bottom if the products it sells are also being marketed on the internet. This effect becomes clear shortly after the Millennium in the consumer electronics segment, in which Best Buy (US), Curry's (UK), or Media Markt (Germany) suddenly find themselves competing with online stores.[15]

15 www.presseportal.de (as of March 2015)

This doesn't mean that everything is running smoothly for the online retailers, though. As the Dot-com bubble bursts in 2002, a range of businesses set up in the euphoria of the late 90s are making such heavy losses that they have to shut down. Amazon circa 2002 is running seven fulfilment centres and makes what will turn out to have been a key decision in concentrating on its in-house distribution structures as its key value driver.[16]

Insight

By 2002, e-commerce has become an important strategic issue for all retailers, yet the switch in the personal purchasing process as depicted in figure 1.1 is still disputed (and remains so to this day) in some retail management circles. Since so many of the existing retail concepts rely on classification systems from the pre-internet era in order to define and understand their target groups, the reality of this new buying process is particularly unwelcome. Offers have thus far been structured for target groups defined by gender, age, income, or consumer preference, and managers who are accustomed to using these kinds of classifications have trouble accepting that these divisions are becoming increasingly meaningless – especially if a large enough proportion of customers in a certain group still appears to be behaving in the way traditional consumer research expects of them. New retail business models, such as the Otto Group's Collins Project, now assume that consumers can no longer be classified by classic market research systems.[17]

Prospects in 2002

In 2000, Jeff Bezos applies the **online marketplace** concept by launching Amazon Marketplace and opening up its infrastructure for third-party sellers. In so doing, he not only secures Amazon an early place in the marketplace segment, but can also offer customers an even larger selection of products and more information

16 Brad Stone, The Everything Store, Little, Brown and Company, 2013
17 www.etailment.de (as of March 2015)

about them. By 2002, Amazon's annual turnover has grown to almost $4b.[18] Other marketplace models develop in Europe, such as Rue De Commerce and Price Minister in France.

Instead of following Amazon into a broader product mix, most **online retailers** are concentrating on conquering specific categories. The current theory is that every product category will soon have a champion that will dominate that part of the market: as such, concepts such as Zappos in the USA, Appliances Online (now AO World) in the UK, and MyToys in Germany are set up to conquer their respective segments.

2002 is the year of the **intermediaries**, with the price-led purchasing patterns of online shoppers fuelling the growth of comparison engines in every category. From six, the German intermediary Dooyoo.de increases its staff to 170 by 2002[19], while Google launches its Google Shopping product search (back then, still punningly known as Froogle).[20]

Mail order companies have finally joined everyone in the new Millennium and are now making substantial – if somewhat belated – investments in e-commerce. In the USA, traditional catalogue publishers had been forcing their expansion into the brick-and-mortar segment, but now start to see the potential synergies offered by adding online retailing operations to their existing catalogue-based home shopping business. In the UK, the Next Directory goes online just before "Y2K", while in Germany, the Big Three catalogue companies Quelle, Neckermann, and Otto all open online operations: in 2002, Otto grows its internet business by 56% year on year to €1.7b.[21]

18 www.wikinvest.com (as of March 2015)
19 www.deutsche-startups.de (as of March 2015)
20 www.google.com/about (as of March 2015)
21 www.heise.de (as of March 2015)

For **in-store retailers**, e-commerce is fast turning from an abstract threat to a clear and present danger. Some larger operators such as Target (USA) and Thalia (Germany) start experimenting with their own online shopping concepts. Others, such as Macy's in the USA, John Lewis in the UK, and Tchibo in Germany have already established their web shops as an integral part of their sales infrastructure.[22]

The pressure on **manufacturers** does not let up. Many of the new sales concepts arising do not suit distribution strategies, while low margins in e-commerce and the loss of control occasioned by the sheer number of online outlets continue to be disruptive: Ebay power-sellers, for instance, hit the wholesalers and offer branded trainers such as Adidas, Nike, Asics on the auctions site at way below normal retail prices; but thanks to their low costs, they still cut a profit.[23] This forces price reductions across the board and poses a serious challenge to brand manufacturers.

A CLOSER LOOK 2002: The Dot-Com Bubble Bursts

As soon as the first major successes become clear in and around 1998, the internet generally – and online retail specifically – begins to attract the attention of entrepreneurs and investors: it's a gold-rush, and just like any boom, the miraculous "New Economy" leads to risky financial decisions. Hundreds of new e-commerce companies are set up and kitted out with huge sums of venture capital – which they promptly blow on hiring sprees, technology development, and, more than anything else, marketing campaigns. Bigger, faster, further, and don't spare the horses! Big-name companies hit the stock market at record speed while still deep in the red and making nine-figure losses.

Investor optimism on the major indexes facilitates this: in 1999, the USA alone records 457 initial public offerings (IPOs), most of which are young tech start-ups[24]. In early 2000, the Nasdaq shoots up to heights of over 5000 points, setting all-time records for the American markets. Yet what goes up must always come down: many of the rising stars start to lose momentum and soon the series of IPOs is turning into a series

22 www.ecckoeln.de (as of March 2015)
23 www.internethandel.de (as of March 2015)
24 www.investopedia.com (as of March 2016)

of Chapter 11s: just one year later, the Nasdaq is lulling at 1962 points (that's a loss of 62%). As the Dot-com bubble bursts, more than 5000 internet companies shut up shop: two of the most high-profile failures are Webvan and Pets.com:

	Webvan*	Pets.com**
Set up	1996	1998
Business model	Webvan sells food online, delivering orders to customers in a 30-minute slot chosen by them.	Pets.com is an online pure-play offering pet food and accessories; Amazon is the majority shareholder.
Growth & IPO	When it goes public in 1999, the company employs 400 people, has $52m paid-up share capital behind it – and turns over a pathetic $395k annually. The IPO brings $375m into the company, which plans to build 28 distribution centres in the coming three years.	Its February 2000 IPO garners this ambitious pure player investment of $82.5m. Yet with a staff of 320 and sky-high marketing spends, the company runs up $147m of losses in just the first three quarters of the Millennial year.
Shut down	By 2000, the company has 2000 employees and turnover of $180 million – but racks up $525m of outlay. You don't need a degree in higher mathematics to see why there is simply no way left around insolvency by 2001.	In 2002, Pets.com shuts down for good. In retrospect, former CEO Wainwright will go on to explain that, at this time, the young industry is still struggling with a range of technological challenges which make scaling up extremely expensive***.

* www.nasdaq.com, www.gartner.com, www.wsj.com and www.cnn.com (as of March 2016)

** www.cnn.com, www.businessinsider.com and www.cnet.com (as March 2016)

*** www.businessinsider.com (as of March 2016)

What is fascinating, however, is that this rash of insolvencies doesn't actually put much of a dent in B2C e-commerce turnover as a whole[25]*. In fact, online shopping continues to grow a rapid pace and will go on to revolutionise the entire retail sector within just a few short years.*

25 de.statista.com (as of March 2016)

2007: Online euphoria

The "retail experience" mirage

"We see that internet and e-commerce is growing, but at the same time, when buying a new bed, a lot of people want to try it first; and if you buy a sofa, you may want to touch the fabric."

Peter Agnefjäll, CEO of Ikea[26]

In the five years from 2002, e-commerce undergoes another growth spurt, expanding to an annual turnover of $136 billion in the USA[27], approaching £14 billion in the UK[28], and €11 billion in Germany.[29] With 60% of consumers now having shopped online at least once, e-commerce has doubled its reach and is showing strong growth in new customers[30]. These customers are ordering more than just books and clothes, too: bigger-ticket items such as furniture and consumer electronics are now being bought online. Detailed product information and advice, as well as increasingly attractive viewing options, mean that customers feel confident spending on more complex items online. 2007 is also the year in which it becomes clear that the internet favours a handful of champions over a broader field as Amazon, Ebay, and Google become increasingly powerful. Amazon, above all, breaks away from the pack, with turnover hitting $15 billion by 2007.

26 www.wsj.com (as of March 2015), although the quote is from 2013, it suits the mood of 2007 equally well
27 www.internetretailer.com (as of March 2016)
28 SAS & Verdict Research, www.statista.com, January 2016
29 BEVH, from www.statista.com, March 2015
30 Based on German market statistics

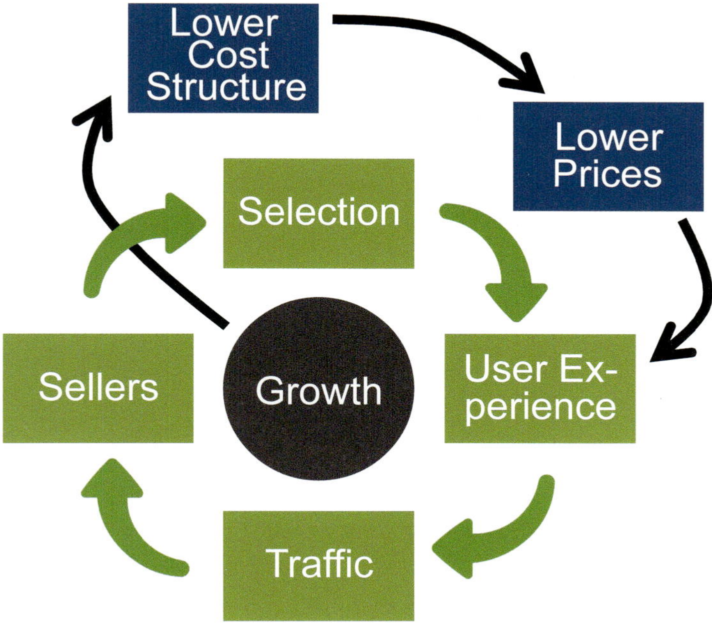

Fig. 1.2: Amazon's virtuous cycle
Source: after Jeff Bezos, 2001

Figure 1.2 shows how Amazon manages to become a lastingly dominant force in the market. The starting point is the broad **selection** of products, which creates a positive **customer experience**, which in turn increases **traffic** as customers return to buy and recommend the site. Amazon's appeal to visitors also makes it attractive for third-party **sellers**, be they merchants or makers, who in turn further extend the product selection. This virtuous circle spins around Amazon's **growth**, which it drives, and while this model can be applied to any marketplace, in the case of the online retail giant, there is an important peculiarity: instead of using its growth to generate high margins and operate profitably, Amazon uses the extremely high volume of sales to **lower its cost structure** and then **lower prices** for customers to the greatest possible extent. This in turn contributes to a positive customer experience and puts even more impetus into the growth cycle. In so doing, Amazon secures itself a permanent competitive edge and is essentially operating as a particularly efficient wholesaler, rather than a marketplace or a retailer. And while this "wholesaler strategy" can certainly work for an in-store retailer in any urban conurbation, it becomes clear that on the internet – with no need for a network of stores to be available to customers everywhere – there is only one top spot to be taken in each country or region.

As if that weren't enough, Jeff Bezos has been keeping another ace up his sleeve, launching Amazon's Prime service concept in 2004. Prime members pay $79 a year (this will later increase to $99) for two-day shipping of all purchases at no further cost; and while Amazon loses around $8 per shipment in logistics costs, Prime soon proves to be one of the greatest drivers of growth for the business. Bezos is typically candid about this: "It was never about the $79. It was really about changing people's mentality so they wouldn't shop anywhere else."[31]

Meanwhile, B2B has become another focus of Amazon's strategy. After launching Amazon Webstore, an e-commerce platform which hosts other retailer's online channels (Target.com uses it for years), the online giant launches its cloud IT infrastructure services AWS in 2006. AWS will continue to grow and become a highly profitable part of Amazon's business model by 2016, while more and more brands and retailers will insource their e-commerce IT as it becomes strategic to their success; Amazon Webstore will announce its shutdown in 2015[32].

The approaching recession of 2007-2009 also works out in Amazon's favour, as a wealth of competitors reduce their investments in view of the downturn and customers become more price-sensitive – and Amazon continues to invest in lower prices and growth.[33]

Insight

A defining element of this phase is the enormous level of investment in what are known as "category killers": every segment, every product group will soon be dominated by a native market leader – or so most investors think. In fashion in Germany, for example, it could be Zalando, with AO.com ruling the regional roost for home appliances in the UK and the US pure-play Wayfair dominating

31 Brad Stone, The Everything Store, Little, Brown and Company, 2013

32 www.internetretailer.com (as of March 2016)

33 Brad Stone, The Everything Store, Little, Brown and Company, 2013

the North-American online furniture market. These projections make sense from a 2007 perspective, with e-commerce sales still split quite strongly across various retail concepts and the eventual dominance of a few marketplaces still hard to see coming. What is more, untapped potential in online marketing and customer relationship management are used to support phenomenal growth projections in the business cases of the time.

Prospects in 2007

Online marketplaces continue to grow, led by Amazon and Ebay. In 2003, Amazon turns its first (albeit small) profit, while country-level market leaders rise to the top of several national markets: Amazon and Ebay win in North America and Europe, Alibaba annexes Asia, Rakuten takes Japan, and Ozon rules in Russia. Innovative new marketplace concepts such as Etsy attract huge amounts of venture capital.

Meanwhile, **online retailers** grow with the market and continue to attract new customers. At the height of their powers, online retail concepts join marketplaces as they draw in investors by the busload, who pour money into new players such as Wayfair in the USA or Zalando in Germany. Some of the most hyped newcomers are shopping clubs such as Gilt, founded in 2007, and the much older vente-privée.com, which starts to attract high value investment that year, too.

For **intermediaries**, meanwhile, the party is over: price comparison engines start to make losses: Dooyoo (Germany) is forced to cut staff steeply from a high-water mark of 170 down to 24[34]; Shopping.com (USA) watches as its growth dwindles.[35] The reason is simple: a few select champions have won the race for market share, above all Google (with Google Shopping and its – then new – Universal Search) and a limited number of travel and finance aggregators. Following its launch in

34 www.deutsche-startups.de (as of March 2015)
35 www.wsj.com (as of March 2016)

2008, the new intermediary concept Groupon seems to be immune from this, forcing its way into the market at an astonishing pace.

Mail order companies, too, are in a funk. The future is looking less and less bright as Amazon and others grab more and more market share. Although catalogue companies' web businesses are growing as a whole, some of the biggest names – above all JC Penney (USA), Littlewoods Index (UK), and Quelle and Neckermann (Germany) – are facing heavy losses, even closure.

Many **in-store retailers** are feeling more bullish about the future: having understood that online retailers are merciless foes, an attitude of "If you can't beat 'em, join 'em!" leads to increased investment in online infrastructure as more and more stores start to integrate e-commerce. The idea is that customers will be able to get "the best of both worlds", but many retailers soon find out that this vision is actually very difficult to make into a reality. In Germany, Media Markt closes its online shop Mediaonline.de in late 2007[36] and announces that it will relaunch with a new concept soon. It will take until 2012 for mediamarkt.de to replace it.[37]

Manufacturers continue to look askance at the developments in the industry. While online distribution is slowly becoming less chaotic as contact to internet retailers is improved and brand-owned shops are set up on online marketplaces, manufacturers remain very much at the beginning of the transition. Many still draw a line at direct distribution or marketplace presence in order to avoid jeopardising existing sales agreements with specialist in-store retailers. Some, however, start their own online shops: hugoboss.com, for example.

36 www.golem.de (as of March 2015)
37 Media Markt press release 01/13/2012

A CLOSER LOOK 2007: Online Zappos shopping for shoes

One of the most exciting e-commerce success stories is that of Zappos. Set up in 1999 as shoesite.com, this pure player is, at first, eyed sceptically by many industry observers: "Shoes are just too personal..." "Customers simply have to try them on before they decide to buy..." "You can't make that work on the internet." Yet founding duo Nick Swinmurn and Tony Hsieh disagree with the naysayers, citing the large number of established mail order companies who have been successfully selling shoes to home shoppers for decades. All that is needed is a mechanism which lowers the various hurdles to the point where customers have no qualms about ordering: Zappos famously offers all deliveries and returns free of charge, gives customers 365 days to exchange unwanted items, and tops it off with astounding customer service (toll-free hotline, no sales script for call-centre staff, no quantitative performance metrics). This customer-focussed approach soon gets people talking and rewards Zappos with a steep growth curve: in 2008, turnover breaks through the billion barrier. The company states that it keeps customer acquisition to a minimum, with 75% of all orders reported as coming from existing accounts. In 2009, Amazon snaps up the online retailer, which is by now selling much more than just shoes, for $1.2 billion.

Here are some clippings illustrating how the press reported the Zappos story:

Inc Magazine. "How I Did It: Tony Hsieh, CEO, Zappos"[38] *(2006)*

> *We all sat around one day talking about what we wanted the Zappos brand to represent. We decided to be about providing the best service; we said, "We're a service company that just happens to sell shoes." But in order for that to happen, we had to control the entire customer experience. We expanded the warehouse to 77,000 square feet and stopped having manufacturers ship directly to customers. It was a scary time--drop shipping was 25 percent of revenue, and we gave it up all at once.*

Internet Retailer. "Repeat customers walk all over Zappos.com"[39] (2007)

> *Online shoe retailer Zappos Inc. has reached a milestone: six million paying customers. Zappos, which is expecting online sales to total about $800 million in 2007, also says that 75% of shoppers who make a purchase each day on Zappos.com are repeat customers. "We continue to grow sales in all of our categories, especially our*

38 www.inc.com (as of March 2016)
39 www.internetretailer.com (as of March 2016)

non-footwear categories of apparel, handbags, sunglasses, watches and other accessories, which are growing even faster than footwear," says Zappos CEO Tony Hsieh.

The New Yorker. "Happy Feet"[40] (2009)

The Customer Loyalty Team, or C.L.T., is the nerve center of Zappos, whose thirty-five-year-old C.E.O., Tony Hsieh, has earned a zealous following by imposing an ethos of live human connection on the chilly, anonymous bazaar of the Internet. He talks about being the architect of a movement to spread happiness, or "Zappiness," via three "C"s: clothing, customer service, and company culture. "Eventually, we'll figure out a way of spreading that knowledge to the world in general, and that has nothing to do with selling shoes online," Hsieh told me after I visited the company over the summer.

2012: The multichannel bubble

Sales talk – but who's listening?

"I believe the death of the retail store has also been greatly exaggerated. The influence of the internet and online sales will continue to increase, but [...] multichannel retail platforms will be the primary beneficiary of this trend."

Bill Bishop, Brick Meets Click [41]

In the five years to 2012, the explosive growth in e-commerce continues, catapulting sales to $227 billion in the US, £31 billion in the UK, and €28 billion in Germany. Innovative concepts emerge such as Etsy, an online peer-to-peer marketplace for handmade products, and the 'daily deal' sites such as Groupon and Fab.com. Founded in 2008, Groupon is the trailblazer: by 2010, Forbes is already titling it "the fastest-growing company ever"[42], and it turns down mega-bucks take-over offers from both Yahoo ($3-4bn) and Google ($5.75bn) before the year is out. Yet just twelve months on, Groupon has become "the world's most controversial company", in no small part due to its bumpy IPO in November 2011.[43] Local service companies, restaurants, and other Groupon merchants begin to realize that an over-supply of offers has decimated prices. Furthermore, the assumption that Groupon customers would become regulars after using a "get to know you" offer soon turns out to be shaky: as it happens, Groupon customers are rarely willing to pay the full price after having received a discount once – and will instead continue to trawl the platform for other one-time offers for similar products and services.

40 www.newyorker.com (as of March 2016)

41 B. Bishop, The MultiXchannel Future of Retail (www.brickmeetsclick.com, as of March 2015)

42 www.forbes.com (as of March 2016)

43 www.businessinsider.com (as of March 2016)

Further e-commerce controversy comes in the form of Fab.com, a flash-sale community launched in 2011 with the goal of becoming the world's largest designer store[44]. In its first year, it acquires one million members, reaching the 10 million mark after another twelve months. This rapid growth comes with a hefty price-tag, though: its marketing spend is out of control at 35% of revenue and yet still, congenitally disloyal online customers prove difficult to keep.[45] The $300m of venture capital it has attracted start to run out ahead of time. By mid-2012, the company is deep in the red and begins shedding employees: the rounds of redundancies don't stop until the staff of 750 has been reduced to a mere 25.[46] Between September 2012 and 2013, Fab.com loses 75% of daily visits year on year[47] and limps on today as a near-forgotten e-commerce irrelevancy.

Fig. 1.3: Revenue distribution between catalogue and online sales over time

Source: Our graphic based on Excitingcommerce.de, Statistisches Bundesamt, BVH, and our own forecasts (linear progression)

Meanwhile, some of the most exciting e-commerce developments are happening in traditionally conservative markets. In Germany, for example, growth in e-commerce has, up until around 2010, mainly come from a reduction in mail order sales: i.e. catalogue customers have been migrating to online shopping (see figure 1.5), leaving in-store retailers more or less unscathed. Overall, the German retail sector

44 www.entrepreneur.com (as of January 2015)
45 www.businessinsider.com (as of January 2015)
46 www.internetretailer.com (as of January 2015)
47 www.businessinsider.com (as of January 2015)

as a whole is – once inflation has been accounted before – barely growing. From 2011 onwards, however, e-commerce breaks away from mail order entirely and its growth curve starts to point ever more steeply upwards. Given the lack of growth in retail as a whole, this means that in-store retailers start to lose between 500 million and one billion Euros to the online competition – every month, with no sign of any deceleration. Already weakened in the years up to 2010, the anaemic in-store retail segment is now bleeding customers and turnover to the fast-growing e-commerce challengers.

In the meantime, in the e-commerce segment itself, both in Western Europe and North America, Amazon breaks away from its competitors. Turnover is driven ever higher by Amazon's resolutely aggressive pricing strategy: the development of pricing robots allows Amazon to monitor competitors' prices and, using algorithms, to continually adapt its own in real time and with the best possible business results. In 2009, for example, Amazon and its rivals Walmart and Target plunge the US bestselling books segment into a controversial price war: in a gruelling campaign of automated attrition, prices drop from $25-30 per book down to under $9 at all three retailers; the American Booksellers Association asks the Justice Department to step in an investigate what it refers to as "predatory pricing".[48]

48 www.nytimes.com (as of March 2016)

Fig. 1.4: Amazon dominates e-commerce

Source: S. Banjo, P. Ziobro, The Wall Street Journal: After Decades of Toil, Web Sales Remain Small for Many Retailers

Price wars are breaking out everywhere. In the German fashion segment, for example, newcomer Zalando is looking to replicate Amazon's ability to slash sales prices using economies of scale. Yet wherever they are, other retailers are playing catch-up with Amazon – and Amazon is breaking away ever further from the pack. By 2012, this dominant market position has become cemented: Amazon's acquisition of Zappos secures its position in the USA as a quasi-monopoly (see fig. 1.3); in Europe, too, its growth cycle just has not stopped turning. In fact, from 2009 onwards, Amazon's sales growth goes into overdrive and leaves competitors shaken – not just direct rivals from the online retail segment, either, who are now themselves experiencing external price pressure for the first time.

As their results take a nose-dive, in-store retailers are desperately trying to pull-up – and the great white hope is a strategy by the name of "multichannel". After all, if offline sales are plummeting, then more online sales will level things out, right? And, what is more, by linking up the various channels, consumers can be reached wherever they are in the personal purchasing process, wherever it suits them best – in the store, on the net, or on their smartphones... There's nothing wrong with the idea, of course, but most traditional in-store retailers have trouble offering customers a real value-add with their new strategy: services such as click and collect – which allow customers to order online and pick up in-store – or accepting returns of goods bought online in store are all well and good, but when customers are searching for a product on the internet, these aren't decisive criteria at all. As it turns out, retailers have to offer customers a genuine reason to buy in each channel on its own terms; and simply hooking up existing channels does not, in and of itself, do much about the fact that brick-and-mortar stores are serious costs factors.

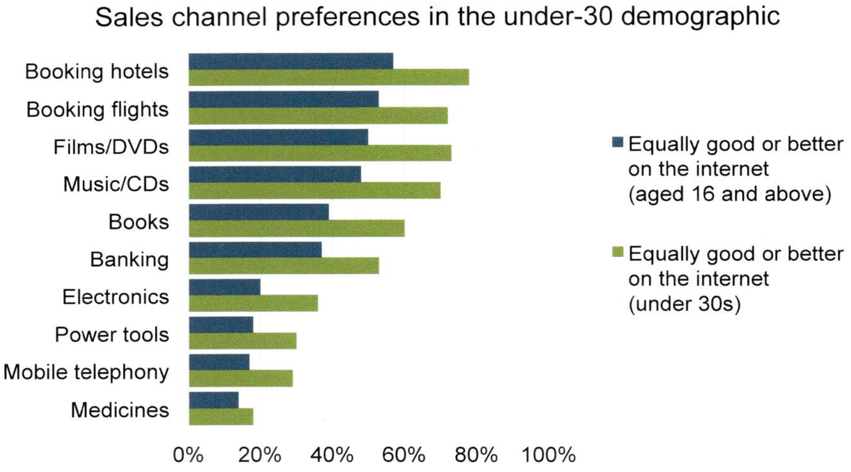

Fig. 1.5: Sales channel preferences per age bracket

Source: Prof. Dr. Renate Köcher, ACTA 2012, (www.ifd-allensbach.de/fileadmin/ACTA/ACTA_Praesentationen/2012/ACTA2012_Koecher.pdf)

Overall, in 2012 there are still clear differences in customers' channel preferences: while more than 60% of younger German consumers, for example, prefer the internet as a sales channel for a range of product categories (e.g. travel, entertainment, books), the overall preference for online in the population as a whole is closer to 45%. The trend towards customers doing their own research on the internet is far more visible among younger consumers (for whom the word "digital natives" is coined around 2010), and is a factor in pushing sales of ever more complex and information-heavy product segments over the internet. From 2011 to 2012, online sales in (frequently pricey) product categories requiring high levels of consumer engagement such as furniture (+58%) and cosmetics/perfumes (+67%) post hefty growth figures, albeit from a low base-line[49]. This development is supported by customer ratings, recommendations from online merchants, product comparison sites, and the growing availability of product information provided by manufacturers. This trend is made clear by a survey in Germany comparing online and offline buying habits[50], in which consumers explain why they, for example, ended up purchasing in store after having researched online: 57% of those surveyed explained that they wanted to touch and feel the product before buying, while 44% cited a lack of immediate availability on the internet; only 27% gave the opportunity of talking to a salesperson in an actual shop as their reason for having gone in store. In other words, almost three quarters of those surveyed did not see sales talk as a key reason to make a purchase offline. Coming at the issue from the opposite angle, the survey also asked about consumers' reasons for buying on the internet rather than in store: 48% cited a fast, easy online ordering process, and 44% said low prices were a reason. Hence, the combination of good online information and advice, fast-track ordering processes, and competitive pricing, can convincingly explain the success of e-commerce concepts such as Amazon, Ebay, and Zalando.

Insight

Back in 2012, retail companies with their roots in brick and mortar still saw serving customers on all channels as the *non plus ultra* for holding their own against the likes of Amazon, Wayfair, and Zalando. The idea driving this "bricks and clicks" strategy was that there was a sufficient level of loyalty to retail brands such as Macy's and Sears (US), BHS and Boots (UK), or Douglas (Germany) to draw customers from their physical into their online stores, which were then simply named after the time-honoured brand: barnesandnoble.com, bestbuy.com, karstadt.de. Yet this customer relationship promise has, by and large, failed to materialise. In fact, a wealth of studies and other evidence shows that customer loyalty to retail brands is practically non-existent.[51]

49 www.bevh.org (as of March 2015)

50 ECC Köln, Cross-Channel-Einkaufserlebnis (www.ecckoeln.de, as of March 2015)

51 z. B. OC&C, Wenn zwei sich streiten… entscheidet der Kunde (www.lebensmittelzeitung.net, as of March 2015)

Prospects in 2012

Now an **online marketplace** as much as anything else, Amazon dominates and the numbers of competing portals is thinning out. Yet the disappearance of smaller marketplaces does nothing to stop the overall growth in the segment and, by creating something of an oligopoly in marketplaces, influences all of the other business models.

The rash of previously promising **online retailers** are losing increasing chunks of their market share to Amazon and others; any new market share they acquire to stem their losses is bought with sky-high marketing spends and wafer-thin margins: the pressure is growing. The German fashion pure player Zalando, for instance, expands by an astonishing 125% in 2012 to turn over €1.159b – and loses €90m in the process[52]. In the USA, it's a similar story for pure-plays such as Wayfair and Zulily.

By 2012, almost all **intermediaries** have been driven out of the market for good by Google and a handful of segment-specific leaders. This leaves Google Shopping, Kayak.com, Booking.com and few others as the only operators of importance; meanwhile, Groupon has established itself, but failed to live up the sky-high expectations voiced in its 2011 IPO (the largest since Google's in 2004). The prospects for those intermediaries left – and anyone looking to enter this part of the market with a new concept – are poor.

Mail order companies are still in trouble. While there was still online growth to be had back in 2007, figures are flat-lining now that most existing offline customers have migrated to the catalogue publisher's websites. Through to 2012, several big

52 www.excitingcommerce.de (as of March 2015)

names leave the market: Sears had already killed its catalogue in 1993, and now JC Penney follows in 2009 as Eddie Bauer files for chapter 11 – again (2005 being the first insolvency). In Germany, former titan Quelle folds in 2009, with Neckermann following in 2012.

Among **in-store retailers**, the multichannel mythos keeps spirits up: Home Depot and Macy's invest decidedly in their multichannel offering, while in Germany, Media Markt has a another go at an online shop. Other retailers in Europe's biggest economy put internet terminals in their shops (Conrad) or develop apps for smartphones. Yet the signs of trouble ahead are hard to ignore: big-name insolvencies like those of Sears (US), HMV (UK), and Karstadt (Germany) hang over the segment like the sword of Damocles.

Conditions for **manufacturers** finally take a turn for the better: e-commerce has become dependent on professional partnership with brands and so producers have every reason to be confident going into online retail. They are gaining an ever better understanding of how to make marketplaces work for them, using their own brand stores to increase sales and profits. Some manufacturers such as Adidas and Asics, however, keep a very tight rein on online retailing of their brands, and try to block merchants from selling on Amazon or Ebay[53]; the aim is to maintain control of the brand image, product presentation, and – of course – the retail prices, but they often run into problems due to competition law. The path most brands take is therefore to start their own direct sales operations online, allowing them to keep control of the brand without missing out on online sales. What is more, direct customer contact allows manufacturers to gather valuable feedback for further product development.

53 www.internetworld.de (as of March 2015)

A CLOSER LOOK 2012: Death of the Catalogue Salesmen

In 2012, the bells toll for Neckermann, the last of Germany's traditional mail order companies. Like erstwhile rival Quelle, which gave up the ghost in 2009, Neckermann was unable to replicate its catalogue orders success story on the internet. Otto, the third of the once mighty mail-order trio, is still standing, but only because it has become an online retailer: its catalogue business has withered away. In the USA, too, the catalogue is dead as mail order companies such as JC Penney have stopped printing them altogether.

Welt.de. "Now it's official: Neckermann is broke"[54] (2012)

Simply put, Neckermann got caught sleeping. "It's always the same story: the managers at the top get to make business mistake after business mistake – without any consequences (and on pretty good remuneration packages, too) – and, when it all goes wrong, it's the employees who get the raw end of the deal," commented trade unionist Thurner. Industry experts are almost unanimous: the classic catalogue company was not able to transform itself into an internet retailer as several changes of ownership and management prevented important investment into crucial areas such as IT.

Dallas News. J.C. Penney is turning last page on its Big Book (2009)[55]

The Internet has made the 1,000-page shopping venue obsolete, and printing and transportation costs have been rising annually. The move also improves Penney's environmental footprint, reducing its catalog paper use by 30 percent next year.

"It became a very ineffective way to communicate to our customers," he said (Mike Boylson, Penney's chief marketing officer). "It forced us to bring product in too early and locked in pricing. It was an outdated way of shopping and the last big book in America."

Exciting Commerce. Is this where the future of home shopping in Germany finally starts? (2009)[56]

The Quelle insolvency is more proof, if needed, that the German home shopping segment is on its knees. As an industry, it has stayed stuck in the 1970s and has

54 www.welt.de (as of March 2015)
55 www.dallasnews.com (as of March 2016)
56 www.excitingcommerce.de (as of March 2016)

completely lost all connection with the international reality over the last fifteen years, remaining utterly unable to gain so much as a toehold in any of the future markets (...) Things look even worse for German home shopping companies, by the way, when you limit the focus to nothing but future business models: once all of the various moribund shop and catalogue concepts are stripped away, there is little left.

The dominance of Otto, Quelle, and Neckermann and their legacy of market power in Germany has led to a situation in which it has hardly been possible for new business models to arise: this means that all of the innovations now come from the USA or, increasingly, from France.

2015 In-store retail in crisis

Just another brick in the wall

"I believe the rebirth of retail will come as developers, retailers and cities understand the retail paradigm of the future is based on something timeless and enduring."

Rick Caruso, CEO Caruso Affiliated[57] in a press release[58]

57 Caruso Affliated is one of the largest owners of US retail real estate

58 Caruso Affliated press release 01/12/2014

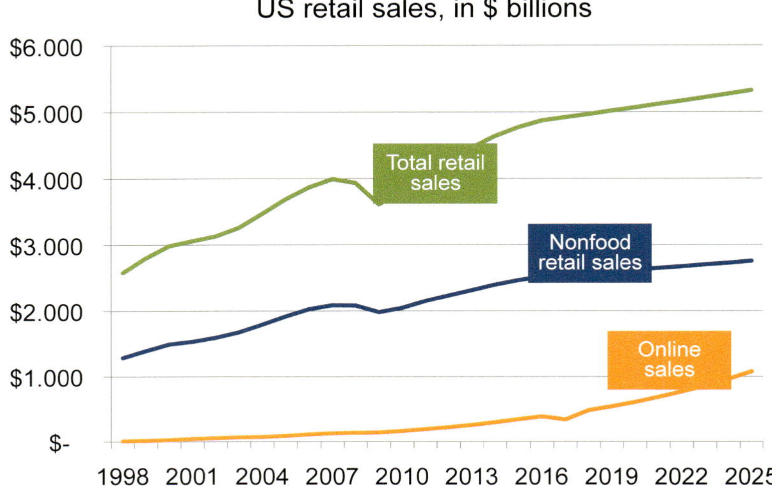

Fig. 1.6: Annual e-commerce revenue, USA

Sources: US Department of Commerce, eMarketer, Internet Retailer, Statista Market Outlook de.statista.com/outlook/243/ecommerce

In 2015, e-commerce sales total a record-breaking $349 billion in the USA, smash the £43 billion mark in Britain, and hit €47 billion in Germany: this is just another instalment in an almost decade-long story in which e-commerce growth is outpacing that of the retail sector as a whole. In the US, growth in B2C online sales is – depending on which measure is applied – running at somewhere between 11% and 15%, while overall sales growth is only 3.7%[59]. If these growth rates continue in a linear fashion[60], that will give e-commerce a 39% chunk of the US market[61] in 2025; in Germany, online shopping will grow to over 38% of sales while Britain – currently topping the European leagues with over 14% in 2015 – looks set to break the 33% mark by 2020.

59 www.bloomberg.com (as of March 2016)

60 See chapter 4 why we believe the growth will actually be accelerated, bringing the e-commerce share to 30% by 2020.

61 As percentage of the non-food retail, excluding groceries, automotive sales and gasoline.

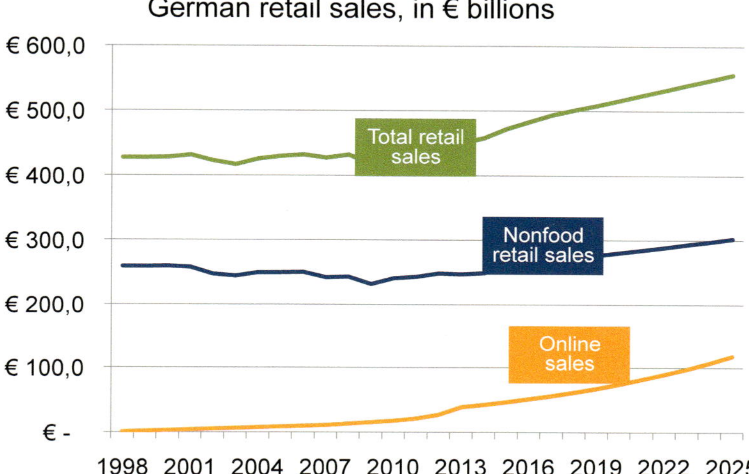

Fig. 1.7: Annual e-commerce revenue, Germany

Sources: BEVH, Statista Market Outlook de.statista.com/outlook/243/ecommerce

The shift in the market towards e-commerce can also be read out of the sinking foot traffic figures being posted by stores in recent years. In the USA for example, footfall in brick-and-mortar outlets has dropped by 6.5% – in just the most recent four quarters (see figure 1.8). In Germany, the IFH trade research body is forecasting that 30% of all retail stores will close by 2020 and categorises another 40% as having an uncertain future ahead unless they are able to adapt their business model to suit the new realities on the market[62].

62 www.wiwo.de (as of March 2015)

Fig. 1.8: Quarterly year over year change in in-store foot traffic, USA
Source: S. Banjo, The Internet Can't Save Retail, www.bloomberg.com

At the same time, it has become clearer than ever that the retail shift is happening under the shadow of one towering giant: Amazon. E-commerce solutions provider Channeladvisor reports that Amazon books somewhere between 40% and 60% of online sales in the US market,[63] while figures for Germany suggest it takes between 30% and 50% of turnover online[64]. In the US, the combined sales volume of the 20 next-biggest online retailers is still lower than Amazon's[65]. This development has a lot to do with new patterns of consumer behaviour, which we will be referring to in what follows as "Amazon Commerce". It is a phenomenon that is being pushed strongly by Amazon itself and describes a completely new way of purchasing consumers goods which is no longer orientated towards specific products, but towards the actual point or use of the item desired. The typical Amazon Commerce customer is, for example, one of the more than 50 million Amazon Prime customers, many of whom buy products based on utility via Amazon often without even checking the prices and service levels offered by other providers; it is a pattern of consumption that becomes particularly visible in low-emotion categories such as technical/tools and everyday consumer goods.

63 www.retailgeek.com (as of March 2016)
64 www.kassenzone.de (as of March 2016)
65 www.bloomberg.com (as of March 2016)

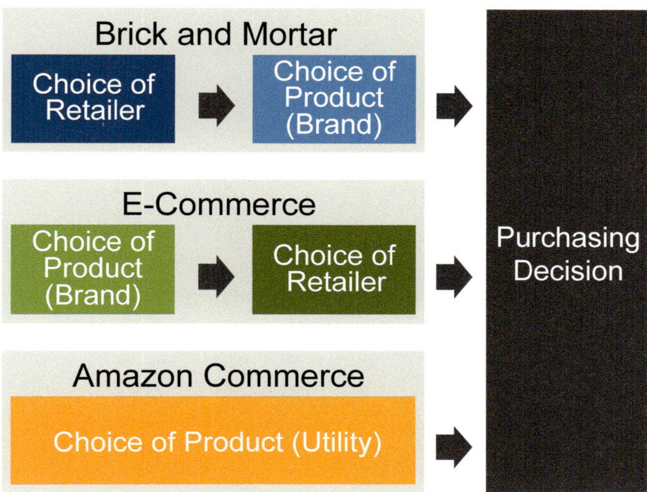

Fig. 1.9: Purchasing process in-store versus e-commerce versus Amazon
Source: Our graphic in reference to B. Schäfers, Social Shopping für Mode, Wohnen und Lifestyle am Beispiel Smatch.com in Web-Exzellenz im E-Commerce, Gabler, p. 313

From today's perspective, there seems to be nothing which can stop Amazon, and the stock market seems to think so too, with Amazon valued higher than the gigantic Walmart since July 2015. Yet it is not only Walmart which is fighting for its share of the market: whether offline or online, Amazon is squeezing everyone. BestBuy, for example, while increasing online sales to just under 9% of its total revenue[66], is bleeding total turnover in 2015[67], while the Gilt Group, a former unicorn (i.e. once valued at over a billion dollars) has been bought up by Hudson Bay Company for a knocked-down $250m, as has German retailer Kaufhof following poor results. In Chapter 4, we take an analytical look at Amazon with a view to what its development means in strategy terms both for retailers and manufacturers.

2015 has also been the year in which several other developments triggered by the 20-year-old phenomenon which is e-commerce have become clearer than ever:

- The increasing price pressure which online business models exert on other market participants has led, as in previous years, to sinking margins. Above all, in-

66 www.internetretailer.com (as of March 2016)
67 www.marketwatch.com (as of March 2016)

store retailers are losing price-sensitive target groups; in 2014, 71% of customers were already convinced that the best prices are to be found on the internet[68].

- One key development is direct sales from manufacturers and brands to consumers. More and more of the makers are clearing the hurdles in their company and distribution network structures and using e-commerce to open their own online shops, and direct online sales are showing themselves to be an excellent way to complement turnover on third party platforms and provide customers with a positive brand experience – all the while increasing margins. Through to 2015, a long list of formerly sterile brand presences on the internet have been transformed into very competent online shops: the Swiss furniture-makers Vitra or the luxury Burberry brand are typical of this development. Customers enjoy the wealth of information about the products and access to the complete selection – and put their money where their mouths are.
- The rapid growth in mobile sales ("m-commerce" in the current argot) is, however, still being underestimated in 2015. Studies have revealed that up to 45% or digital sales are already taking place on tablets or smartphones, and this development has significant technological effects for a range of online retailers, who are investing in improving their mobile user experiences.

Insight

By 2015, almost all participants in the market have become acutely aware of the explosive potential of the current situation; stable strategic decision-making has become almost impossible. As growth in e-commerce accelerates from what was already a high rate of expansion, legacy companies look on as entire sectors change shape: neither Barnes&Noble in the USA nor Thalia in Germany seem to have a plan in the book trade, and it is difficult to make the kind of investments urgently required without a coherent vision for the future. Moreover, for many retailers, that ship has sailed: it is already five minutes before midnight when it comes to setting up the kind of innovation structures which can make a company agile enough to keep producing new business models. In Germany, the Otto Group looks likely

68 www.mashable.com (as of March 2015)

to be one of the few who has made the transition in time, building the innovative fashion platform Collins (About You), investing in the Project A incubator, the e.ventures venture capital organisation, and the Liquid Labs accelerator[69].

Prospects in 2015

At present, the biggest **marketplaces**, Amazon and Alibaba, are unchallengeable and are even beginning to eliminate national champions such as Rakuten in Japan. Ebay, too, the former marketplace pioneer, is feeling the pressure from Amazon as customers and merchants migrate to the rival; partly because products are difficult to locate on the platform, and partly because merchants are becoming less inclined to pay for listings (something they originally did unquestioningly), Ebay is having trouble keeping its figures up. At the same time, the marketplace is making headlines for splitting up with PayPal after 13 years of corporate marriage.[70] What is more, Amazon offers merchants potentially higher turnover while reducing their logistics costs – and was able to capture an overall turnover of $107 billion in 2015. At the same time, the question of how and when Amazon turns off the growth expressway and into profitability is still open: for the moment, the marketplace-cum-retailer is still reinvesting every cent in its push for continued growth and expansion.

For **online retailers** besides Amazon, the situation has changed little since 2012: competitive pricing is keeping margins puny and ever more pure-plays are feeling blue compared to the euphoric mid-2000s. According to the German IFH research body, by 2020, almost 90% of those currently active will have shut down[71]: the institute cites the "merciless price war", increased online marketing expenditure, and high costs for product returns. At the same time, some exciting niche shops are seeing impressive growth and innovative concepts can still cut a path to profitability.

69 www.kassenzone.de (as of March 2015)
70 www.cnbc.com (as of March 2016)
71 www.wiwo.de (as of March 2015)

Many **intermediaries** have already disappeared; Google is now all-powerful in this segment. Erstwhile rivals such as guenstiger.de in Germany ("cheaper.de") have hit an all-time traffic low. Only the large, well-established travel and finance portals remain – and are unchallengeable in their areas. Groupon remains, but is diversifying rapidly away from its intermediary business model of offering cheap deals, acquiring several smaller online retailers and moving into fresh foods delivery.

By 2015, **mail order companies** have become more or less a thing of the past. In the USA, most have spent years focussing on brick and mortar and e-commerce, but the catalogue concept has run its course. What is probably the largest traditional mail order company, Sears, is now the fifth largest online retailer in the USA – but only books 18% of its sales on the internet, is losing offline sales, and has gone on a quest to shrink back into profitability in 2015[72]. Other catalogue businesses, such as electronics discounter TigerDirect, suffer the same fate. In Germany, the remaining mail order names such as Bon Prix and OTTO are, in all truth, no longer catalogue companies, but simply companies with catalogues while web shops generate the vast majority of their turnover. Then again, it has been exciting to see traditional US catalogue publishers such as J. Crew, Bloomingdales and Williams-Sonoma investing in the concept once again in 2015; even some digital retailers such as Bonobos are printing catalogues. These appear, however, to be more lifestyle magazines than traditional mail order publications[73].

Declining turnover and failing growth now characterise swaths of **in-store retailers**: Nordstrom, Sears, JC Penney, Kaufhof, Esprit are suffering, as are those who invested so heavily in multichannel infrastructure such as Walmart, Macy's[74] and Thalia[75]. There is no shortage of insolvencies either: to Eddie Bauer and Karstadt

72 www.nytimes.com (as of March 2016)
73 www.marketwatch.com (as of March 2016)
74 www.bloomberg.com (as of March 2016)
75 www.buchreport.de (as of March 2015)

come Radioshack, Praktiker, and Schlecker among others. As such, confidence in the sector is – quite justifiably – low, and only a small number of accompanying online concepts and strategies seem to really make an impact on the market: Bonobos, Warby Parker, John Lewis, and Home Depot, to name some. Some of the traditional brick-and-mortar retailers like Staples have been able to grow significantly online while closing more and more stores.[76]

The winners of 2015 include the **manufacturers**, who now have enough know-how and e-commerce staff to really take their destiny into their own hands. In order to get out of the downward price spiral, for example, Hugo Boss delists its range from Zalando in 2013 and concentrates on its own web shop and premium online retailers. Meanwhile, anti-trust legislation is making life difficult for brands such as Adidas and Asics looking to keep tight control of their online distribution: since 2012, much jurisprudence has gone against them[77]. Adidas, for example, is forced to comply with German competition overseers in 2014 and loosen distribution restrictions on marketplaces such as Amazon; this development may limit the strategic flexibility of manufacturers in future[78]. Yet by taking the right action, many can use this state of affairs as an impetus to go on the offensive and start actively working on marketplaces themselves[79].

An international comparison reveals very quickly just how differently e-commerce has developed in various countries to date – and where a lot of potential remains untapped. In view of these imbalances, the story of e-commerce in China in 2015 makes an interesting field for a more detailed examination.

76 www.multichannelmerchant.com (as of March 2016)
77 www.bundeskartellamt.de (as of January 2015)
78 www.handelsblatt.com (as of March 2015)
79 Alexander Graf & Nils Seebach, *Knut geht baden* (www.etailment.de, as of March 2015)

2015	online shopping penetration	revenue per user	total revenue (in millions)	growth rate (year on year)
USA	63%	$1,757	$287,392	11%
UK	77%	$1,630	$66,721	11%
Germany	71%	$1,145	$57,330	9%
China	35%	$626	$247,036	25%
Japan	72%	$966	$75,937	10%
France	60%	$1,227	$40,304	10%
Brazil	35%	$350	$19,217	13%
Australia	60%	$977	$11,085	12%
WORLD	36%	$740	$ 1,035,029	15%

Fig. 1.10: International comparison of key market statistics
Source: Statista Market Outlook de.statista.com/outlook/243/ecommerce

2020: The winners and the losers of e-commerce

"Mummy, can you print me a new toy truck, please? I broke the one from yesterday."

Welcome to the future. It's 2020 and, in case you missed any of the intervening years, here's a run-down of how e-commerce looks now.

1. E-commerce kept growing at similar rates and now turns over $612 billion in the US, £72 in the UK, and €77 billion in Germany. The online retail growth is headed for a market share clearly north of 30% of all non-food revenues by 2025. For one, this is because of the continued growth in various e-commerce sectors. Secondly and equally impactful, offline retail is going through a significant market adjustment, with several large retail chains losing more and more sales to Amazon and other online category leaders. This has lead to a retail growth rate equal to the inflation rate, leading to a net zero growth in overall retail sales.
2. The trends we saw around 2015 have become even more pronounced: broad swaths of the e-commerce market are oligopolies, securing economies of scale for a select few organisations who use them to produce growth; smaller online

retailers fall by the wayside. In-store retail, too, is in terminal decline and more and more manufacturers are selling straight to consumers.

3. Continued growth in e-commerce is coming both from increasing numbers of intensive online shoppers and from the rising availability of new, previously off-line product groups on the internet.

4. Mobile commerce is more relevant than ever, and many mobile-first concepts are now dominating consumer segments, especially among younger target groups.

5. Changes and ruptures in the market of the immediate future look set to come from innovations such as 3D printing.

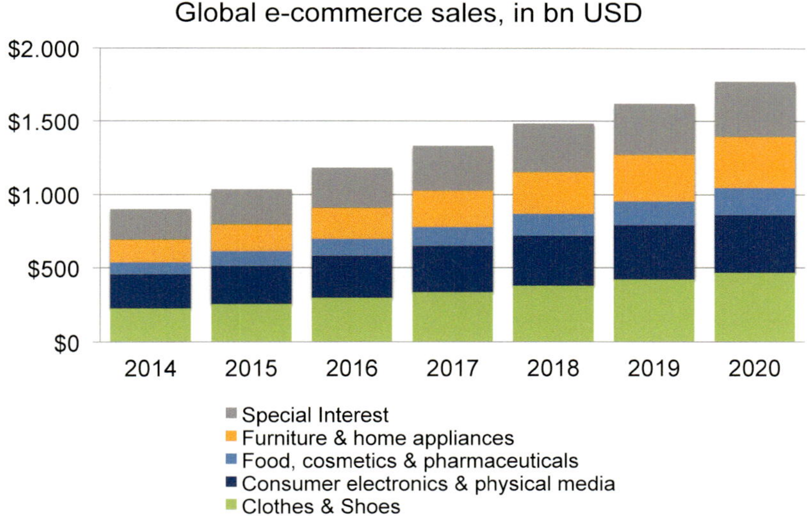

Fig. 1.11: Annual e-commerce sales forecast over time

Source: Statista Market Outlook de.statista.com/outlook/243/ecommerce

Prospects in 2020

This is where we get our crystal balls out: while anyone who claims to be able to see the future is lying, we're relatively certain the following will apply in 2020.

Established **online marketplaces** and their "wholesaler for consumers" approach continue to flourish. The **winners** are Amazon, Alibaba, and other select national champions.

Online retailers are forced to grow at exponential speed in order to defend their niches, and the only way the market can allow them to do so is by consolidating them. Some new specialists will become category killers: and only category killers will remain immune from the effects of other market participants. The **winners** are the largest of the segment-specific retailers, providers of niche product ranges, and new concepts such as Modomoto and Blue Apron.

Intermediaries have been completely obliterated – either by Google or by one of the other consumer relationship brokers such as Facebook, Apple, and Amazon. The **winners** are therefore Google, Facebook, et al.

In most segments and target groups, **mail order companies** cannot survive from catalogue business alone. Catalogues have become little more than an additional marketing channel, but – due to the strong competition for consumer attention online – a very attractive one at that. In this area of the sector, there are **no winners** (and no participants, as the survivors are now no different to online retailers).

Those **in-store retailers** whose business is primarily composed of selling third-party brands are under extreme pressure to invent and implement new business models which make sense in a segment rocked by wave after wave of big-name insolvencies. The only growth is coming from chains with business models based on vertical integration, meaning that the **winners** include names such as Asos, Zara, and Primark.

Manufacturers with an understanding of balancing in-store and online distribution to retailers with their own direct sales approaches will be among the **winners**. Expect brands such as Hugo Boss and Samsung to still be doing well.

Don't just take our word for it, either. In Germany, the IFH institute forecasts for online sales (figure 1.7) tell a similar story:

1. Web shops run by erstwhile mail order companies continue to lose market share.
2. Internet pure players (i.e. including marketplaces) continue their growth – growth driven above all by national champions and large marketplaces.
3. The online channels run by in-store retailers are growing due to heavy investments in omni-channel activities, but remain overshadowed by online pure players.
4. In-store retailers continue to lose sales dollars to e-commerce. By 2020, the IFH predicts e-commerce to make up 25% of all non-food retail in Germany.

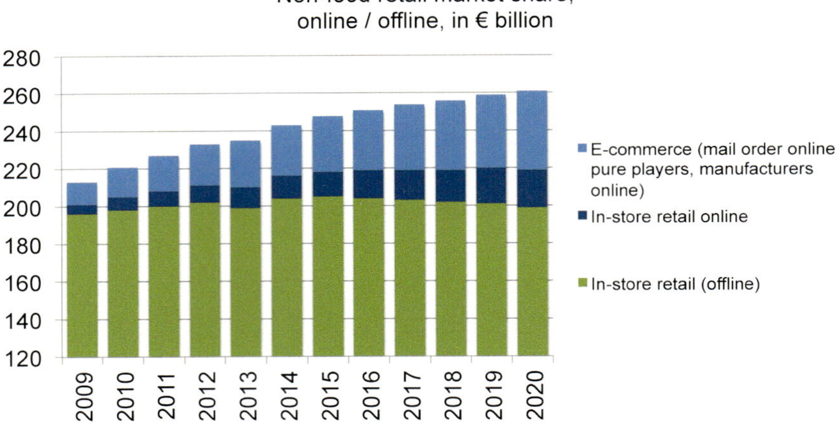

Fig. 1.12: Sales distribution in the non-food segment, Germany
Source: Branchenreport Online-Handel, IFH-Köln, 2015

Conclusion

E-commerce today is more complex and more competitive than at any point in its existence to date. Trends in the market in recent years are set to intensify, leading to an increasingly polarised landscape of winners and losers. The strong growth in online shopping will continue, but will only be of real benefit to internet market-places, niche providers, and manufacturers; by and large, retailing non-proprietary brands will prove no longer sufficient to sustain a business model in the era of e-commerce.

	Market-places	Online retailers	Intermediaries	Mail order	In-store	Manufacturers
1997	+	+	+	~	–	–
2002	++	++	+++	+	~	– –
2007	++	++	~	~	+	–
2012	+	~	–	~	++	+
2015	+	~	– –	~	–	++
2020	Winner	Displaced	Displaced	Displaced	Displaced	Winner
Winners in 2020	**Winner: Oligopolies**	**Winner: Nicheproviders**	**Winner: New models?**	**Winner: Category leaders?**	**Winner: Vertical models**	**Winner: Manufacturers**
	Amazon E-Bay	*Etsy Modomoto*	*About You Google*	*Otto Zalando*	**Asos Primark**	*Samsung Hugo Boss*

1.2 E-Commerce in China

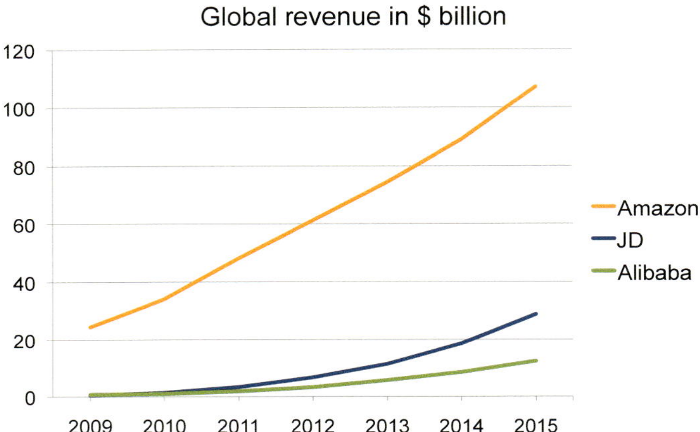

Fig. 1.13: Global revenue comparison Amazon, JD and Alibaba, in $ billion
Sources: phx.corporate-ir.net, wikinvest.com, finanzen.net, marketwatch.com, forbes.com, de.statista.com

Why China matters

If you have China pegged as the manufacturing powerhouse of the world, but not much of an e-commerce innovator, then think again. China's e-commerce story may have started a few years later than the West's, but it's certainly catching up quickly. Not only does the current and projected e-commerce market in China exceed its counterpart in the US, but the two largest Chinese e-commerce companies have joined the 10 largest e-commerce companies worldwide by revenue.[80] Clearly, rather than simply imitating US models, China has developed some e-commerce superpowers of its own.[81] Here's how it happened.

80 www.statista.com (as of April 2016)
81 See Chapter 3 Alibaba, Ali Express, JD.com, Tmall, Xiaomi, Vipshop

China's e-commerce giant takes its first steps: The rise of Alibaba

While Amazon is already turning over $610 million in revenues in 1998[82], China is just starting its e-commerce journey as Alibaba, Tencent and JingDong (today known as JD) are launched. And the timing is certainly no coincidence: new policies and government reforms[83] are laying the foundation for a less bureaucratic, less corrupt business environment, fostering economic growth and supporting the penetration of internet usage in China. But even though, by the end of 1999, Chinese internet users have more than doubled from 4 million to 9 million[84], this number is clearly dwarfed by the roughly 100 million internet users in the United States in the same year[85].

One of the most influential figures in Chinese e-commerce is Jack Ma. In 1999, the schoolteacher-turned-entrepreneur, working with 18 others, founds Alibaba, a marketplace which connects manufacturers from China to (mostly wholesale) buyers from around the world, while outsourcing most of its logistics operations to third-party vendors. Alibaba has early international ambitions and, in the same year, opens offices in the U.S. and Hong Kong, which mostly focus on customer acquisition. Yet growth doesn't go quite as planned and a few difficult years follow as the dot-com bubble bursts. As a result, Alibaba shifts its global strategy down a gear and focusses more on the domestic market. By 2003, the company is back to posting strong growth and returns to its global vision.[86]

82 www.ecommercetimes.com (as of March 2016)

83 www.theconversation.com (as of March 2016)

84 USA International Business Publications, China E-Commerce Business and Investment Opportunity Handbook, 2009

85 www.indexmundi.com (as of March 2016)

86 www.technode.com (as of April 2016)

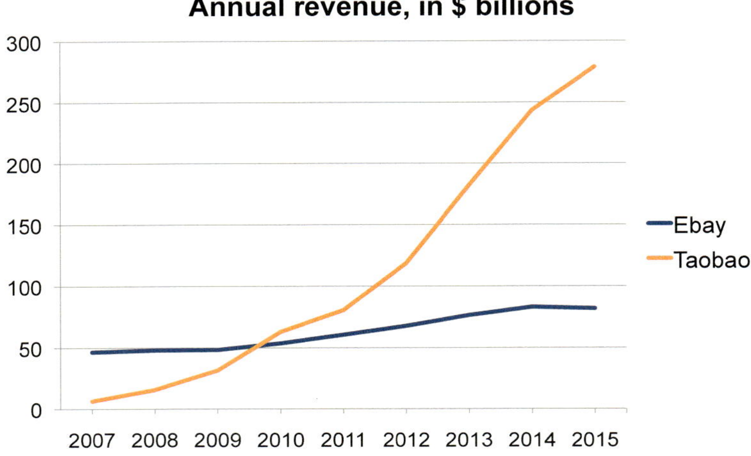

Fig. 1.14: Ebay and Taobao annual revenue 2007–2015

Sources: Ebay's total gross merchandise, Statista, de.statista.com/statistics/242276 and Taobao's gross merchandise volume, Statista, de.statista.com/statistics/323075, chinadaily.com.cn

In that same year, Ma launches his next billion dollar e-commerce business: Taobao, a peer-to-peer auction site[87]. Ebay had just entered the Chinese market the previous year, but Taobao is able to outgrow the competitor from America quickly with a home-turf advantage and a much deeper understanding of Chinese consumers. For instance, the company uses effective TV marketing campaigns and offers instant mobile messaging as, at this point, Chinese consumers are still less accustomed to using the internet than their Western counterparts.[88] On the seller side, Taobao offers free product listings and adopts a business model based on advertising rather than transaction fees.[89]

Alibaba's next coup is launching Alipay in 2004, an online payment platform which starts off as an integrated service at Taobao. Again, Alibaba does not simply copy the American model Paypal, but adapts it to Chinese consumer habits by adding an escrow service[90] to protect consumers from paying for the counterfeits so prevalent in the market, especially in the luxury goods segment. Alipay is quickly adopted across the board, becoming a stand-alone product supporting the entire Alibaba ecosystem.

87 Taobao translates to "digging for treasures"
88 www.businessideaslab.com (as of March 2016)
89 www.forbes.com (as of April 2016)
90 www.chinainternetwatch.com (as of March 2016)

Finally, Alibaba ventures into the B2C sphere with Tmall in 2008. With many brands staying away from the C2C site Taobao due to concerns about counterfeiting and brand image, Alibaba can now tap into higher-quality brands[91] and skim the growing Chinese middle class market. The marketplace model is based on transaction fees plus a one-time security deposit and an annual fee for merchants and brands[92]. It is split into a domestic marketplace for Chinese companies and a global portal on which foreign brands and retailers sell. Alibaba offers Cainiao, its in-house logistics platform, to global marketplace sellers, while third-party logistics and delivery companies handle fulfillment and delivery for domestic sellers. Today, even Amazon can be found on Tmall Global with its own flagship store.[93] Throughout the years, Ma has skillfully built an e-commerce giant of impressive scale, and all without owning warehouses or holding inventory for its domestic operations. Operating margins and profits are much higher compared to its competitors JD.com in China or Amazon in the US, and the group's ecosystem is further supported by features such as a search engine, a cloud-data service platform, a financial environment, and strategic partnerships for logistics.[94] In 2014, Alibaba stages the biggest IPO in history.[95]

A second giant emerges – and this one has a big brother: JD.com and its ties to Tencent

Parallel to Alibaba's rise, JD.com (formerly jdlaser and 360buy) is founded by Liu Qiangdong in 1998, but doesn't really take off in the early years. Starting off as a brick-and-mortar electronics retailer, Qiangdong doesn't begin selling online until 2004. However, in 2006, his company secures US$10 million in funding and sees a massive e-commerce sales lift in 2007[96]. The investment is used to expand its product portfolio and develop new software and systems for its nationwide fulfillment infrastructure. In 2015, JD Worldwide is launched, a cross-border platform which enables foreign companies to sell in China without a legal entity there; sellers have the option of letting JD handle fulfillment and customer service. Today JD.com is a typical online pure player, curating products, holding inventory, and re-selling

91 www.multichannelmerchant.com (as of March 2016)
92 www.investopedia.com (as of March 2016)
93 www.multichannelmerchant.com (as of March 2016)
94 www.techinasia.com (as of April 2016)
95 www.forbes.com (as of March 2016)
96 www.nytimes.com (as of April 2016)

brand goods to shoppers. By owning all the products being sold, JD can guarantee high quality and consumer-friendly terms, which helps counter the widespread mistrust among Chinese consumers due to the prevalence of counterfeited products. Insourcing its fulfillment infrastructure in 2007[97], JD fully owns the customer experience and today controls its supply chain from the supplier to the customer, with more than 100 warehouses and thousands of delivery vehicles which also handle returns[98]. By becoming a full-service retailer, JD.com has gained the trust of the growing, consumption-orientated Chinese middle class, making it China's largest only pure-play retailer with US$ 28.0 billion in revenue in 2015.

Yet JD's story is not complete without examining its ties to Tencent, China's largest technology company. Tencent started off in 1999 with a focus on social messaging and gaming – and with, as it seemed, no clear business model. Its ICQ messenger copycat "OICQ" (which would later be renamed to QQ due to legal dispute with ICQ) got more than a million users in its first year, but struggled to find a way to cover its fast-rising costs; yet a US$32 million investment from Naspers, an ageing local print business, in 2001 gave it the space it needed to find and implement a business model. (As an interesting side note: largely due to this acquisition and its subsequent good performance, Naspers is now the biggest media company in Africa). With enforcement of intellectual property rights in China weak, Tencent made a lucrative habit of imitating successful technology companies, mostly from abroad, and adapting them for its Chinese user base. Consequently, launching various ventures ranging from a search engine to online games, from internet retailers to social networking services, and then mobile internet[99]. Impressively, it made these models stick as, in the West, companies such as Netscape, MySpace, and ICQ were either swallowed up or brushed aside by more innovative competitors. In 2015, Tencent generated US$ 15,8 billion in revenues[100], catching up with companies like Facebook, which reported US$ 17,9 billion in revenues for the same period[101]. While about half of its revenue come from sales of mobile games, Tencent is following a strategy similar to Alibaba. Expanding its general user base also boosts Tencent's online payment service Tenpay, which is available on WeChat. Its ambition is confirmed by Tencent's many investments in e-commerce businesses across China in recent years[102]; the aim is to convert customers to Tenpay users. It is worth noting at

97 www.chinainternetwatch.com (as of March 2016)
98 www.phys.org (as of March 2016)
99 www.chinainternetwatch.com (as of March 2016)
100 www.tencent.com (as of March 2016)
101 www.investor.fb.com (as of April 2016)
102 www.fortune.com (as of April 2016)

this point that, shortly before entering into partnership with Tencent, JD.com ended its cooperation with Alipay and another third-party payment provider.

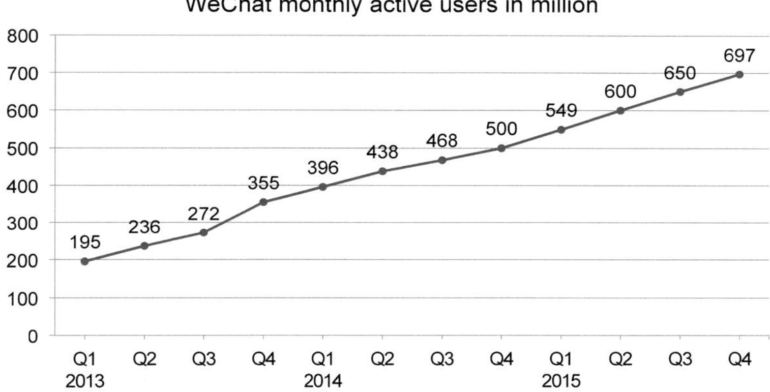

Fig. 1.15: Monthly active users, 2014 and 2015

Source: S. Millward, WeChat still unstoppable, Tech In Asia, techinasia.com/wechat-697-million-monthly-active-users

Tencent has focused more and more on the mobile sector. And for good reasons: due to the late start of digitisation in China, smartphones arrived relatively early in its evolutionary cycle, meaning that many consumers more or less skipped the PC phase. In line with this development, Tencent launched the instant messaging service WeChat, the mobile version of QQ, in 2011. In under two years, WeChat had 100 million users, rising to about 450 million active users in 2014 (that compares to about 500 million WhatsApp users worldwide).

In 2014, Tencent and JD.com enter a strategic collaboration. For a 15% stake in JD, Tencent injects its e-commerce businesses PaiPai (C2C), QQ Wanggou (B2C), and parts of Yixun into JD.com in order for it to become a more equal competitor to Alibaba[103]. JD.com leverages Tencent's WeChat as a mobile online store platform while Tencent increases user numbers for its gaming business; further gains are made as its online payment service Tenpay is integrated into WeChat.

When JD.com launches its shopping channel on WeChat, mobile e-commerce sales already account for nearly 40% of all sales in the Chinese e-commerce sector. In order to take advantage of the development, the two companies transform WeChat

103 www.bloomberg.com (as of March 2016)

into a platform to connect businesses and end-consumers[104]. Next, WeChat adds a peer-to-peer payment system as well as "City Services", which allows consumers to "pay electricity bills, handle transportation booking, pay traffic fines, book doctor appointments and more"[105]. The e-commerce ecosystem that JD & Tencent have created is in direct competition to the Alibaba Group's offering: JD.com competes with Tmall, and WeChat competes with Alipay.

Battleground of the giants

In recent years, the competition between Alibaba and JD has made the Chinese market highly competitive as the two e-commerce giants vie to extend and secure their vast market shares. The competition looks, in many ways, like a duopoly: for instance, aiming to create more closed e-commerce ecosystems, both Taobao and Tmall block Baidu, China's largest search engine, from indexing them. At the same time, JD.com blocks Alibaba's product search engine from indexing its website and WeChat blocks all traffic towards Alipay, Taobao, and Tmall. Consequently, both companies force their customers to access their shops directly and thereby increase the relevance of their internal search engines. Merchants can place their ads in these engines, similarly to SEA on Google, resulting in e-commerce ecosystems which are, to all intents and purposes, closed to the outside[106].

Meanwhile, the mobile payment war continues: JD blocks Alipay from its site in 2013. Shortly after, JD teams up with Tencent and focuses its payment services on Tenpay as well as its in-house offering, JD Finance. Alipay then goes on to add peer-to-peer payments and social messaging in 2015, and on top of that, launches mobile payments for offline commerce. By the end of 2015, WeChat is set to reach the 200 million users mark in its payments service, while roughly to 350 million users are registered at Alipay in mid-2015[107]. However, the online B2C market is still dominated by Tmall, with 54%, followed by JD.com with 23.2% market share (Q3 2015)[108].

104 www.recode.net (as of March 2016)
105 www.walkthechat.com (as of March 2016)
106 www.investopedia.com (as of March 2016)
107 www.techcrunch.com (as of March 2016)
108 www.chinainternetwatch.com (as of March 2016)

E-commerce in China today

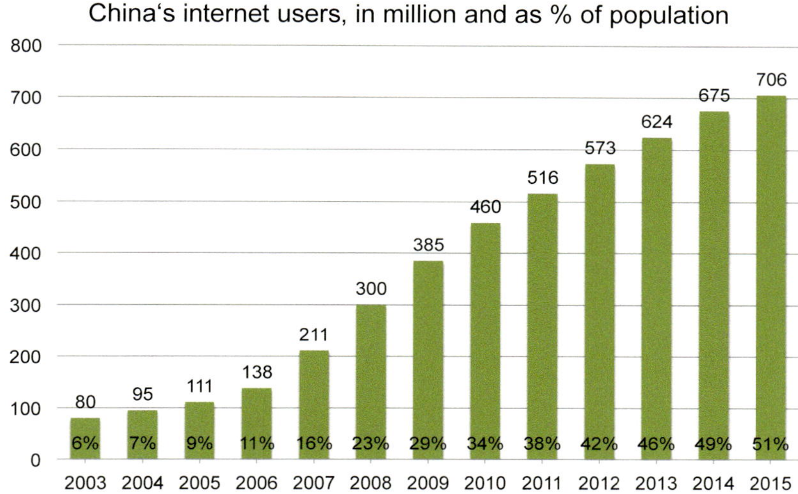

Fig. 1.16: Growth of Internet penetration in China since 2003
Source: internetlivestats.com/internet-users/china/

In 2015, Chinese ecommerce sales surpass US ($300 billion) and European ($370 billion) sales to reach $417 billion[109]. Yet, with 700 million internet users[110] and so far only 10% of retail sales generated online, there remains plenty of space for growth. So far, e-commerce consumption had been driven by the "connected spender" demographic, a relatively young group of consumers which, as of 2014, makes up 27% of the Chinese population, but accounts for 44% of total consumer spending. Even though their buying power in no way compares with that of their US counterparts, population growth and increasing wages make for huge growth potential; these "connected spenders" are expected to account for about 60% of total consumer spending in China by 2025.[111]

One example for the sheer mass of people and their willingness to shop online is Singles' Day, a Chinese online shopping promotion on 11th November marketed by

109 www.asia.nikkei.com (as of April 2016)
110 www.edition.cnn.com (as of April 2016)
111 www.businessinsider.com (as of April 2016)

Alibaba Group: it is the largest single online shopping day in the world and, in 2015, broke all records, with Alibaba online sales alone surpassing Black Friday ($2.74bn) and Cyber Monday ($3.07bn)[112] in the US to reach $14.3 billion[113]. The phenomenon saw such growth that it hit its own sales volume of the previous year within just 12 hours; by the end of the day, Alibaba and subsidiaries had processed goods with a total value of $14.3 billion on the day (60% more than Single's Day 2014)[114].

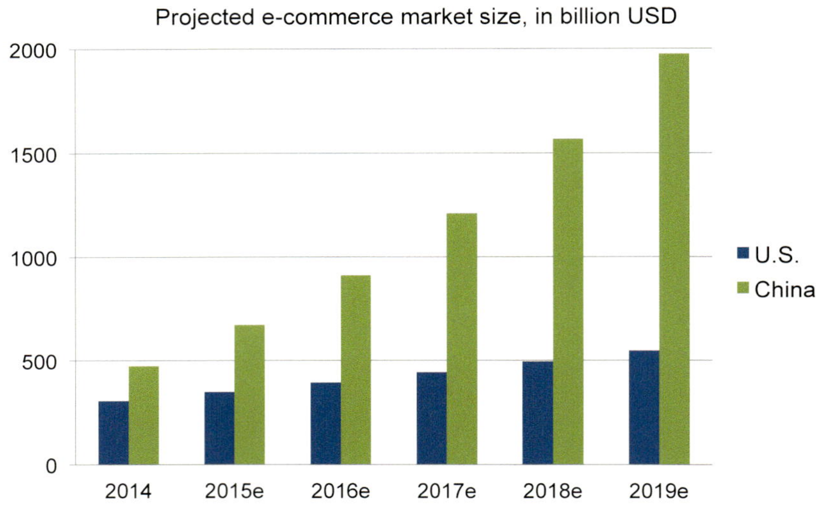

Fig. 1.17: E-Commerce market size USA vs. China
Source: *ar.alibabagroup.com/2015/china-context/index.html*

Despite all of this, the background rates of economic growth in China have been declining as the country shifts from an investment-driven to a demand-oriented economy and wages increase. Consequently, all major e-commerce players are now striving for more independence from the Chinese market; a popular target for these companies is India.

112 www.techinasia.com (as of April 2016)
113 www.practicalecommerce.com (as of April 2016)
114 www.asia.nikkei.com (as of April 2016)

Things to consider when entering the market

China is the largest e-commerce market in the world and still growing. It is therefore no surprise that it is increasingly attracting foreign companies. Yet new entrants must consider a multitude of issues when eyeing up the Chinese market.

1. **Consumer Behaviour**
   The most underestimated aspect of selling in China is the stark difference in consumer behaviour compared to what companies encounter in the West, which is why demand cannot be predicted by reference to the home market. Firstly, Chinese consumers are highly brand conscious and will ultimately seek the product with the highest value for them (and not necessarily the best quality); in fact, many believe that higher prices correlate with better quality. Therefore, the corporate identity needs to be in line with branding, pricing, and promotions. In turn, it is not the product itself which necessarily needs to be adjusted to the market, but the way it is presented. Secondly, the customer journey often begins with customer service (typically chat based), which makes service a pre-sales channel. JD.com, for example, offers to take on customer service for sellers; Tmall, meanwhile, does not. At the same time, many Chinese consumers buy based on word of mouth, which is a strong form of recommendation in China.

2. **Entry via marketplaces/Indirect market entry**
   E-commerce in China happens almost exclusively on marketplaces which offer an almost identical user experience, but often quite different services on the seller side. JD.com and Tmall are the two largest B2C marketplaces in China; both offer a domestic as well as a global marketplace. Only foreign companies may sell on the global marketplaces, whereas the domestic marketplaces are reserved for those who have a legal entity in China. Hence, the global marketplaces appear more trustworthy to Chinese consumers with regard to the absence of counterfeited products. In the consumer's mind, foreign sellers are guarantors of authenticity and so the global marketplace enjoys much higher conversion rates and basket sizes. Furthermore, logistics can be handled by third-party providers or, in the case of JD.com, by the marketplace operator itself. Brands such as Burberry or Estée Lauder, as well as retailers like Macys and even Amazon, are opening flagship stores on these platforms to tap into the Chinese market. However, Amazon is, for example, using its own warehouses and handling its own logistics in China. Yet smaller marketplaces may offer advantages, too, due to lower levels of competition. Leveraging the high usage of WeChat is unfortunately only possible for companies with a legal entity in China.

Another way to enter the market indirectly is exhibited by Windeln.de, the German pure player selling baby products online. The company today generates about 50% of its revenue in China, predominantly by selling milk powder and thereby exploiting the trust issues with regards to product quality. Selling to Chinese consumers is tacked onto this in two ways: on the one hand, third-party freight forwarders from Europe (usually Chinese start-ups or CEOs) buy on behalf of Chinese customers after registration at windeln.de. They own warehouses and take care of fulfillment services; on the other hand, Windeln.de offers direct B2C delivery to China, which makes up about 70% of the order volume to China today, and improves delivery time and costs for their customers.[115]

3. **Direct market entry**
   It is not advisable to pursue a direct market entry as a first step because building a brand and attracting customers present a high barrier to entry. The existing large-scale players take care to make sure that customers access their marketplaces directly, forgoing search engines such as Baidu (the dominant search engine in China). Anyone opting to go for a direct entry nonetheless must identify if the market is open to them and what restrictions apply: many foreign companies find themselves forced to enter the market through a local partner as it is not always possible to set up a 100% foreign owned company.

4. **Product import**
   Importing goods to China can pose a serious challenge. Laws may or may not be applied in the way they are written, which is why each entry point for goods can present different obstacles. Furthermore, registration processes are difficult and it is hard to keep track of products in country. Merchandise may be returned to the seller by the authorities if they do not comply with regulations, and compensation may be levied, too. Experienced freight forwarders such as Windeln.de are an easier way to kick off operations in China than going it alone.

5. **Government intervention**
   While Chinese e-commerce has been growing thanks primarily to the rise of a free-spending middle class, the government's role as a protective market force is not to be underestimated. Government officials aspire to be the governing force for the development of the internet, meaning that trade and media must be in line with the values advocated by the Party. For instance, in 2010, the Chinese government banned Google as the company refused to censor search results following Chinese hacker attacks. Similarly, the government is restricting

115 www.corporate.windeln.de (as of April 2016)

market access for foreign investors, limiting the share they are allowed to hold in Chinese internet companies to a maximum of 50%[116]. However, it is not only foreign companies have to keep an eye on state interventionism: the government goes as far as locating police stations inside China's biggest internet companies in order to keep their grip on virtual China.[117] Ultimately, interventionism by the government is leading to the isolation of the internet in China. Notably, the failure of companies like Ebay, Groupon, and Paypal in China and the state interventionism which companies like Google, Facebook and Twitter have faced is keeping foreign companies from taking large risks[118]. Yet it is important to note that these high-profile missteps are often also the result of companies underestimating the differences in Chinese consumer preferences and behaviour, not simply regulatory and political hurdles.

116 www.freshfields.com (as of April 2016)
117 www.techinasia.com (as of April 2016)
118 www.technode.com (as of April 2016), www.technode.com (as of April 2016)

2 The Topography of E-Commerce

With the proliferation of articles and books about the "tectonic shifts triggered by e-commerce" and the "creative destruction" it is wreaking, it is no surprise that many see online shopping as a new and frightening world of chaos. And while, in view of the scale of the changes which are occurring, e-commerce undeniably is a new world, it would be wrong to see it as a purely destructive free-for-all; rather, e-commerce is simply replacing familiar structures with different, albeit slightly more complicated ones. Indeed, in many cases, the structures in the new online world are, on closer examination, actually analogue to those of the old offline lands, as our detailed exploration of the topography of e-commerce in this chapter will make clear.

The seven links in the value chain

In the beginning, there is the product – the product which is to be sold, at the end, with value added. The first link in the chain of value-creating steps which retailers provide is **procurement** and purchasing: which products sell well on the internet and how can an attractive product mix best be compiled? Customers then have to view the products offered, meaning that the second link in the chain is **product presentation**.

The third and fourth links are **marketing** and **distribution**, both of which are central to online shopping and closely linked at several points. The internet is an extremely dynamic, highly promising, and – more than anything – very complicated marketing environment which is moving at a faster pace and in more unpredictable dynamics than any other area of e-commerce; most importantly, online marketing offers the most attractive prospects for lasting increases in turnover – many of which, however, are mirages. In terms of distribution, online structures very quickly become all-encompassing issues for merchants and manufacturers alike: how can the closest contact possible to customers be maintained without relinquishing control of the core business to the e-commerce behemoths? Which channels make the most sense in a multichannel context?

If the marketing and distribution links provide traction, then customers buy: the next point at which online retailers add value is therefore by handling **orders and sales** on their sites. The most important issue in this area is making sure that customers do not abandon their purchase at this stage.

Once orders have been received, they must be processed from bytes into bits, transformed from electronic data into physical packaging – and that needs to happen as quickly as possible. This is where **logistics**, the sixth link in the chain, adds value for customers by delivering (and often picking back up) their orders to their doors.

The seventh and last element in this chain is **customer service**; and while it is the last link, it is by no means the least important. In fact, it often joins up to other links in the chain as it can both support marketing activities and act as a valuable source of feedback for purchasing.

Links in the chain, or cast as a ring?

While the various activities with which online retailers add value to their products may, for our purposes, best be described as links in a chain, it would be foolish to take this metaphor too literally as, in fact, many of the links cannot actually be decoupled from one another: they couldn't back in the offline world, either, but on the internet, identifying where good product presentation stops and where marketing activities start, is harder than it ever was – and often simply a matter of opinion.

At the same time, many processes stretch over the entire chain of value creation: web analytics and business intelligence, for example, are so important at every stage of e-commerce than they must be seen as the gearwheels over which the chain is spanned, not one of its links (see 4.1 and 4.2, Strategy Development and Benchmarking, and the interviews in Chapter 3 for more); what is more, the actual architecture of an e-commerce platform is the structure overshadowing every other process.

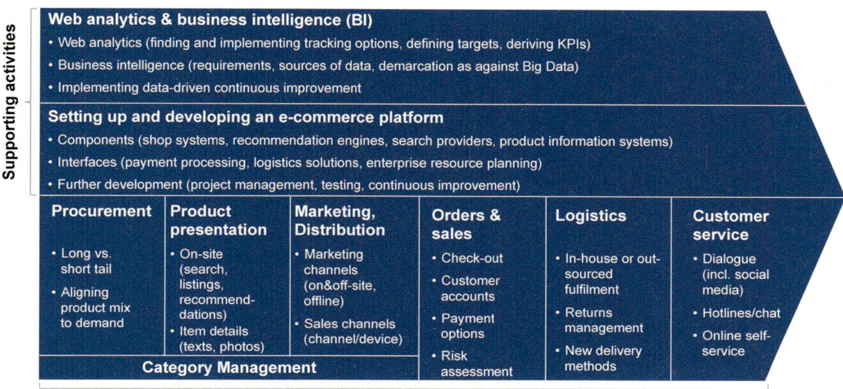

Fig. 2.1: The value chain in e-commerce

Source: Our graphic, with reference to Michael E. Porter (2004), Competitive Advantage

This is because the "platform" is not simply the shop system, but encompasses all of the component parts of the online shop experience such as recommendation engines and search providers, as well as the interfaces which connect up the shop to inventory control systems, payment providers, and logistics (see 4.3 and 4.4. for shop systems and product information management). Figure 2.1 shows how the links in the chain are organised and how they relate to accompanying processes and secondary activities.

In the following chapter, we will take a detailed link-by-link look at the e-commerce value chain, starting with procurement and finishing with customer service. In order to make our topography easier to follow, we will frequently be visualising the "digital high street/shopping precinct" as a thought exercise which shows the parallels, interfaces, and differences between traditional in-store retail and mail order models as opposed to internet retail. Are you new to e-commerce? Join us for a stroll down the digital high street and through the links in the value chain. Are you an expert on internet shopping? Then please feel free to go on ahead at a faster pace, perhaps stopping to look at some of our more specific definitions or case studies.

2.1 Procurement

Introduction

The effects of e-commerce on how products are procured are fundamental and can be described in three processes: **specialisation** in products, **orientation** to the customer, and continued **optimisation** of the product range. These processes are driven by dramatic changes to the timescales in which inventories need to be sold, the new precedence afforded to customer wishes, and the imperative of adapting inventories to suit customer preferences faster and more consistently than ever before.

The challenge

The factor driving these shifts is remarkably simple: customers on the internet expect more. Consumer expectations online are easier to sum up than to fulfil:

> *"I want everything, and I want it right now, whenever I decide and wherever I am."*

And while getting products to customers as quickly as possible and delivering them to wherever they currently are is a (thorny) matter for distribution and logistics, offering everything and offering it all the time is the poisoned chalice that falls to procurement managers. Successful purchasing in e-commerce is not simply, as it so often was in pre-internet retail, a question of buying as much as possible of a high-selling item quickly and then selling it on even more quickly; to the contrary, the principle of buying for internet shoppers is to offer a broad selection of attractive, perhaps very specific products so that people can find what they are looking for – and don't disappear off to the next, better-stocked competitor (who is, of course, only ever one click away).

The solution

Fortunately enough, online retail also creates the framework required for the ever more varied product range it demands. After all, if bricks-and-mortar buyers want to double the range of products they are stocking overnight, they had best hope their neighbours give up their lease – and soon. Online shops, meanwhile, can simply list the new product and hire more warehouse space. What is more, it has never been easier to adapt purchasing planning to the wishes and needs of customers, and to keep improving it consistently: webshops, after all, provide not just detailed sales information, but also show precise search requests almost in real-time. Customers are more transparent than ever for buyers who know where to look.

All of this means that, while retailers may need to take their buying policies back to square one, they could potentially reorganise their procurement to be more precise and thus more efficient than ever before. In what follows, we will examine the theory behind **specification**, **orientation**, and **optimisation** in online retail.

Specialising products: From short tail to long tail – or: "Every little bit helps"

"The long tail" is one of those concepts that you're bound to have heard about, even if you've had little or nothing to do with e-commerce until now. Popularised by Chris Anderson, editor in chief of *Wired*, in his 2006 book *The Long Tail: Why the Future of Business is Selling Less of More*, the revolutionary power of the concept is still often underestimated, even more than a decade after the book's release. In some ways, the term has become a victim of its own success, as many consider it a vacuous business buzzword.

Yet the concept is remarkably simple and describes a mechanism so fundamental that it has a proverb:

"Every little bit helps."

Classic retail theory, of course, states the opposite when looking at buying patterns: a product is put on the market and, very shortly afterwards, reaches its sales peak. After this high-point, sales decline drastically and eventually, the product in question is only shifting at a very slow rate: it becomes a shelf-hugger; and because shelf-space is a limited commodity, it must be removed so has not to become a shelf-blocker – i.e. a poor seller which takes up space which could be put to better use displaying the next sales blockbuster. That, in a nutshell, is the **short-tail** approach.

The **long-tail** approach, by contrast, is interested in what happens after the sales high-point – or indeed in what happens if there never really was much by way of a high-point. A long-tail product mix is not just about generating hit sellers, but about cultivating niche products, collector's items, and things of very limited interest to the general consumer – and about offering such a depth, breadth, and variety of these specific products that they, as a group, produce more sales than stonking sellers.

So if products are taken into the mix which are, at first sight, unattractive to retailers due to their low sales volumes or limited niche appeal – or if products are not removed from the mix once their sales figures start to decline, but kept on sale – a back-catalogue of shelf-huggers develops. These products, however, do eventually let go of their grasp on the shelves are do get sold, but over a longer period of time; the larger this selection of low-selling products, the higher the proportion of turnover their sales generate. This is important for online retailers because typical brakes on sales space such as shelving space and shop size are removed. While costs for compiling digital product data and presenting items online (see 2.2. Product presentation) are not to be underestimated, and while large storage inventories certainly tie up capital, the costs are far lower than in a classic retail situation with high rents for sales space and high wages for staff; in fact, in many online retail business models, these costs can be outsourced wholesale to third parties (see below). Meanwhile, items such as MP3 songs or e-books can be stored and sold digitally to an almost unlimited extent.

Case study: Music in classic and online retail

The first place in which the effect of the long tail in consumer behaviour could be documented was the music industry; even today, music sales remain the clearest example and so, in this brief case study, we will look at specific sales figures from long and short-tail retail concepts which date back to the beginning of the 2000s and, in our analysis, show how they provided proof of concept at an early stage.

> In 2006, *The Long Tail* author Chris Anderson illustrated his theory by comparing the structures of Walmart and Rhapsody sales in the music segment: at that time, superstore giant Walmart was the US's biggest seller of music in CD format, while Rhapsody was the leading provider of legal MP3 downloads and music streaming.
>
> Walmart stores had a defined music sales space and, as soon as a given album stopped selling fast, it would be removed to make space for a faster-selling one. This concept saw Walmart listing around 4,500 CDs with a total of roughly

25,000 song titles; of this product mix, 200 top-sellers generated around 90% of Walmart music sales.

Rhapsody, meanwhile, offered 4.5 million single song titles, meaning that it "stocked" 180 times as many as Walmart. Now, at Rhapsody too, the most popular songs generated the lion's share of the turnover, but what was interesting about the portal's sales figures was that a significant proportion of sales was nevertheless provided by songs which had never been top of the charts. What is more, another chunk of turnover came from songs which had once been high-sellers, but had slipped far down the charts since their peak. Overall, more than 15% of the total value of sales was generated by songs languishing between numbers 100,000 and 800,000 in the rankings.

It's easy to miss the true significance of this, so let's rephrase it in the following terms: by and large, Walmart was not offering any songs that weren't in the "top 25,000" tracks; Rhapsody, meanwhile, was making money with songs which were below this popularity threshold – far below it, actually, to the point that it was earning on songs which were four or even six times less popular than the top-selling tracks.

What follows from comparing Walmart and Rhapsody is that ...

... the vast majority of products that are not among the top sellers make as much money as the tiny minority that are at the head of the rankings.

The long tail of products was therefore important because it encompassed a huge amount of products – albeit each a poor seller on its own terms. If one thousand products are each sold 100,000 times over, they generate 100 million sales: if 100,000 products are each sold only one thousand times over, they generate exactly the same number of sales.

Yet if the maths is so simple, why is the idea so recent?

E-commerce is about the longer tail

The answer is of course that the idea isn't as recent as all that, but that it was impossible to implement on this scale before the advent of online shopping. After all, the long tail sales approach is by no means new to music: although Walmart, as a general stockist, was ruthless about weeding out music which was not making enough money in its limited retail space, it is not as though the US market was undersupplied with retailers who specialised in music and attracted customers interested in older or less popular records. In the 1980s and 1990s, there was a broad spectrum of specialist music stores, from the encyclopaedic racks at Tower Records through to the proliferation of shops run by owners enthusiastic about specific genres or promoting local, underground sounds, especially in big cities. These record stores tended to generate a lot of their turnover from tracks which were definitely outside of the short tail.

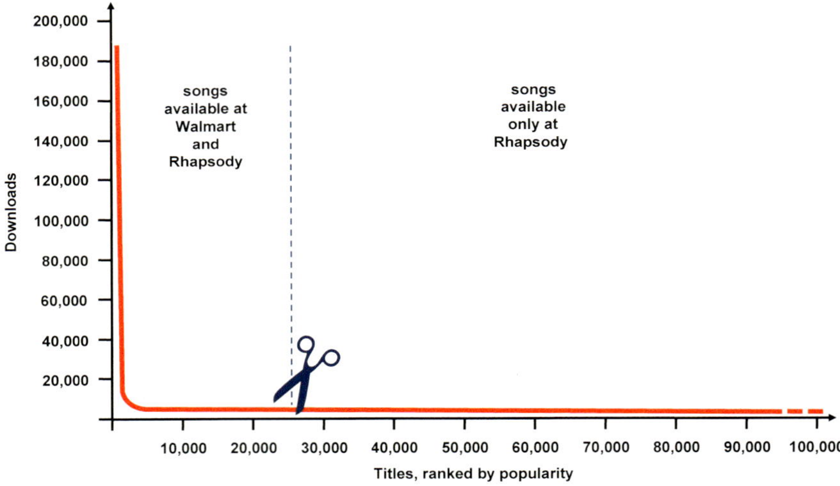

Fig. 2.2: Download rankings of individual songs on Rhapsody

Source: based on Chris Anderson, The Long Tail, Random House Business Books (2009) P,25

Nevertheless, such stores' long tail was clipped halfway at best, with a range of limitations meaning that even specialist stockists have always had to draw the line somewhere. First and foremost, the **profitability of retail space** imposes its own logic on what can be kept on display and what has to disappear: vinyl, cassettes, CDs are all physical distribution items which require square footage, and even the biggest music store chains have never had unlimited budgets for rentals; similarly, shopping centres have never had space that can be extended at will. Furthermore, stocking large numbers of titles ties up capital, as shops have to buy and pay for products before selling them; and then there are staffing costs, which are high in music stores, as well as the actual location of the shops – especially chain stores have tended towards to prime-segment, pricey rentals.

Meanwhile, while neighbourhood record stores may be located in cheaper parts of town and have less expensive staffing costs, they too have to turn a profit and could never stock every title which a customer might want. Nevertheless, for many years, the ace up their sleeve was music that could only be bought there: in the 80s and 90s, mixtapes made by musicians operating under the commercial radar could often only be acquired from smaller, owner-run shops. Yet this **exclusivity and rarity** too had certain limits, as the artists producing underground music nevertheless needed the resources to record and reproduce their music – in however amateurish a fashion – and then had to convince the owner to free up shelf-space for their efforts.

Moreover, besides the limitations to the breadth and depth of their product ranges, both chain and neighbourhood stores had geographical barriers: the very last copy of an old vinyl record made by a long-forgotten rock band from the 70s was of no use to a fan desperately searching for it in Seattle if it was slumbering somewhere on the shelves in Boston. What is more, until our Quixotic fan found out that the record was in Boston and had made it there to purchase it, it had been nothing but a burden to the retailer.

In short,
supply and demand were not properly connected.
The long tail was stubbed.

Then, of course, the internet came along – and with it, portals such as Rhapsody, then later iTunes and Amazon, selling music. They replaced shelving space with server capacity and were therefore able to start offering everything: unpopular, forgotten, amateur... Even musicians who had never had the opportunity to put anything out before were suddenly able to bypass discouraging record executives and stubborn store-owners and just start listing their tracks: in the virtual Rhapsody music shop, there was nothing to stop anyone and everyone having a listen, whether they were in Boston – or in Seattle, Rhapsody's home-base.

As such, the story about how Rhapsody made money with the long tail is part of a far larger overall shift – which is most advanced with media content – from limited, strictly-guarded means of production and distribution through to democratic structures in which anyone can become a producer or a retailer at any moment.

This is a decisive development for e-commerce inasmuch as a business which enables producers to contact customers and allows customers to find what they are looking for can earn money even in the furthest, thinnest extents of the long tail.

The long tail was first documented with Rhapsody and is still at its most visible in electronic media: Amazon, iTunes, and Netflix all rely on business models which would not work without the long-term, drip-drop sales of millions of niche or dated books, songs, and films, primarily in electronic form. Nevertheless, the principle can easily be applied to other product segments, even if the scale and numbers involved are smaller as, even in cheap warehouses out in the sticks, clothes or home furnishings are products which, by their very nature, require space and bind up capital. What is more, these and many other segments have short product life-cycles: in consumer electronics, for example, the rate of innovation is extremely fast and each new model relegates its predecessor to the bargain basement or, worse, the trash heap, within a matter of months.

Notwithstanding, in e-commerce the sales hit might not be a thing of the past, but it is by no means the be-all-and-end-all it once was.

From "or" to "and": long-tail procurement

The shift in weighting on the internet becomes particularly clear when e-commerce models are compared to classic retail sales breakdowns and analysed on the relationships between **products**, **turnover**, and **profit**: put simply, the old "80:20 rule" of thumb is replaced by three thirds.[1]

Let's assume that, in an in-store retail situation, 20% of the products in the range generate 80% of the turnover. It therefore follows that 80% of the products are only contributing 20% to total sales; worse, once all of the store's costs for maintaining sales space are deducted, these 80% are not adding anything to profits at all: 100% of the result is coming from those 20% of items that are generating 80% of sales.

A long-tail, fully-digital model, however, turns these figures on their head:

- The product range encompasses ten times as many items, meaning that high-selling articles are only 2% of the total number of items stocked – and not 20%.
- Consequently, the 80% of products which sell less well are now only 8% of the product inventory.

1 Chris Anderson, *The Long Tail, Random House Business Books (2009)*

- 90% of the products are in the long tail of extremely low-volume sellers, but contribute one quarter of sales.
- Another quarter of sales is generated by the 8% of items which are not top sellers.
- A full half of turnover is generated by the 2% of top sellers in the product range.
- One third of profits is made up by each of the three segments in the product range.

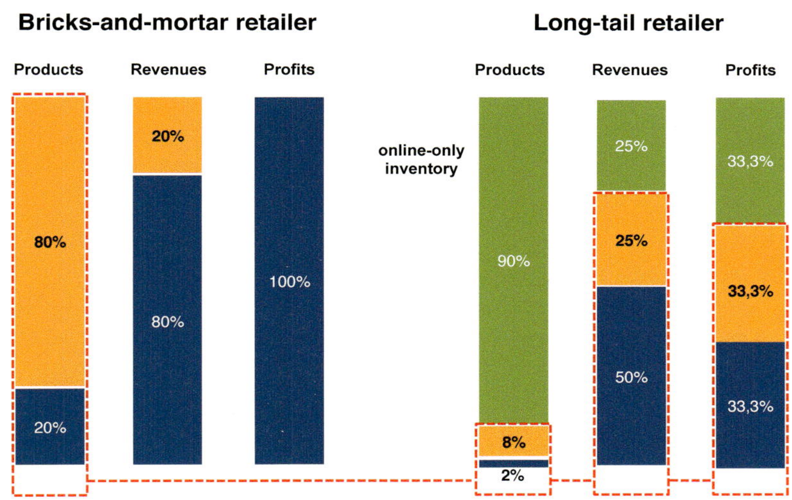

Fig 2.3: Turnover and profits comparison between in-store retailers and long-tail models

Source: based on Chris Anderson, The Long Tail, Random House Business Books (2009) P. 132

Some interesting conclusions can be drawn from these model calculations. Firstly, in a store in an average shopping street, around four fifths of the products stocked are not sold at a profit; but at the same time, they must be kept in stock in order to attract customers into the shop – so that they then buy items from that one fifth of the range that does make profit.

What is even more notable, however, is that top sellers are even more important in the long-tail sales structure: the top 2% of sellers generates a half of the turnover.

Yet in the third stage, when it comes to assigning shares of profit, this importance is trimmed back down as each segment of the product range contributes roughly a third to the final result. What this tells us is that the difference is in the costs: in an inventory stocked entirely with virtual products – e.g. the back-catalogue of a music downloads provider – storage costs per unit are so low as to almost be incalculable; commercial store rent is replaced by cheap digital storage space; staff costs are negligible. In this environment, the margin generated on each individual product is more or less immaterial; in fact, it is perfectly acceptable for the major sellers generating half of all turnover to be strongly discounted and to then only contribute 33% of the profit. Why does it matter as long as sales are high – and the other segments of the product range are pulling their weight?

In order for this long-tail approach to work, though, the range of products offered has to be as broad as possible – and accessible to customers.

Expanding the product range is the work of procurement, and the challenge can be summed up pithily as "make everything available". Buyers who are still using the word "or" when listing products to order should be switching to "and". Then again, even in a low-cost environment such as a fully digital e-commerce concept, making an all-encompassing product range available to consumers can be a costly exercise. The whole long-tail equation only works in favour of the seller if the inventory can be stored cheaply, and in terms of storage costs, there is a broad spectrum of intensity from digital music archives (which require only cheap computer memory) through to petrol-driven lawn-mowers (which take up several cubic meters of space, and which start to deteriorate in storage). Whatever the segment, for procurement the lesson is clear: inventories need to either be able to be stored for almost nothing, or be stored on the cheap, preferably using outsourcing.

Amazon shows how this works. In contrast to digital-products-only outfits such as Rhapsody and iTunes, Amazon's aim is of course to sell everybody on the internet everything they could ever want, and it therefore needs a lot of physical storage space. The online retail giant's answer is to create this space away from major cities in economically depressed areas where site rent is cheap, local politicians roll out the red carpet for new business (and make sure the planning permission is not a problem), and staff are willing to work on the lower end of the wage distribution.

Then again, there are only so many costs savings that can be made by relying on out-of-the-way greenfield locations and weak local labour markets, as Amazon has discovered in Germany, where broad public support for strikes in the company's warehouses served as a reminder that many Europeans will only tolerate so much hire-and-fire-'em capitalism. Then again, Amazon's story in Germany also shows that it has actually been able to increase pay and reduce staff harassment, all the while extending and deepening its product range in the country.

How? Besides the products which Amazon itself offers, it also allows third-parties to list products on its site using the Amazon Marketplace. This allows the company to cement its position as the shop that has everything for everyone: Amazon can offer products in its shop that it has neither paid for up front nor paid storage costs on – and can take up to 20% of the sales price in commission. That's not a bad margin for a product in which it is the seller who ties up capital and invests in storage costs up to the time of sale.

It therefore comes no surprise that other online retailers have discovered the use of supply chain management when it comes to expanding their product range, listing items held either by the manufacturer, a wholesaler, or another retailer and using drop-shipping to transfer customer orders straight to them. The online retailer doesn't need to put up any capital, and can only be forced to do so if sales are so good that the third-party supplier's negotiating position becomes stronger and they can threaten to de-list their strong seller unless the retailer buys it in – in which case the retailer knows it is onto a sure a thing. Successes can be bought in after failures have been weeded out.

Orientating to the customer: From push to pull – pulling the right strings

Not all online retail outfits, however, have an automatically dominant position in the same manner as Amazon and are thus able to expand their product range at will, often getting others to finance the expansion for them. In fact, what works like a dream for Amazon might sound more like a nightmare to a classically-trained store buyer, who now has to, just to keep up, offer all things to all customers. After all, the presence of giant operations such as Amazon who do just that has raised consumers' expectations almost beyond recognition and created a self-perpetuating spiral in which the increasing availability of everything means that consumers' requirements grow ever more specific and ever more immediate. Conversely, the old purchasing methods of buying products and then pushing them into the market is no longer effective; instead:

Procurement must allow itself to be directed – pulled – by customer requirements.

In other words, in the old world, buyers tried to predict demand and then put products into shops based on these predictions; now, consumers buy a product and send a signal back up the supply chain. Manufacturers used to be at its beginning, but are now also at its end.

Indeed, in industry, many manufacturers are old hands at using pull processes to minimise the storage space required in factory halls: car-makers, for example, took their lead from Toyota which, with its *Kanban* system, surpassed others by allowing workers at the end of the production line to "pull" it onwards when they were ready to proceed, rather than having models "pushed" into their finishing area regardless of how much capacity they had; this stopped productivity-sapping blockages all the way back down the line. In the retail sector, the company which showed how this switch from push to pull could work was the fashion chain Zara.

Case study: Fast fashion, from Zara to Zalando

At the turn of the Millennium, the fashion chain Zara made waves by combining supply chain management and consumer-orientated procurement in a completely new way. Beyond logging every single sale in its stores and sending the data straight to headquarters in real time, the company took a bold step by defining the entire product range based on sales. Zara, in contrast to many other chains, had kept most of its production in house, and so was able to react to peaks in demand for specific items by producing more of the same, or similar articles, at speed. The advantages of this way of working soon became clear.

> Several times a week, Zara stores across the world place orders at headquarters in Spain and receive delivery of their stock in a matter of weeks. Coupled with a high degree of in-house production, this efficient, rapid, and centrally-organised supply chain opens up a new world of possibilities: Zara can, for example, produce new pieces in small batches and place them in stores to test demand. If the new items sell well, production is ramped up and the next batch is in stores just weeks later. Only articles which sell well over extended periods of time are outsourced from production sites around headquarters in Galicia to nearby

Morocco or Turkey, while nothing more than absolute basics such as t-shirts and underwear are outsourced further afield to Asia. Zara's costs are therefore higher, but the company is happy to pay them because in its experience, Western consumers are decidedly trend-sensitive, unpredictable customers and inter-continental supply chains are simply far too sluggish to allow for a fast response to fluctuations. What is more, Zara has discovered that consumers are actually perfectly happy to pay a premium for pieces which are just becoming fashionable, and this premium compensates the costs incurred by more flexible, agile supply arrangements. Zara is therefore unperturbed by the ever speedier cycles in fashion: in fact, if styles were not to change so quickly, the company would be stuck with an expensive procurement apparatus that offered it no commercial advantage.

To sum up the Zara system in a deliberately provocative, culturally critical way, we might ask if Zara responds to fast fashion trends or if it actually develops them itself with its agile procurement processes. Whatever the answer to this chicken-and-egg conundrum, however, Zara has been so successful with this strategy that competitors such as H&M, Topshop, and Forever 21 have actually altered some of their production processes: while few are in-sourcing back towards their core markets, they are coupling production far more tightly to sales. In today's fashion business, sales figures aren't just passed up the chain of command from the stores through the buyers and then into management, but are transmitted in real time to all departments – above all to the next warehouse in order to make sure that stock is distributed to where it is needed, and to headquarters so that the product range can be adapted to match actual sales.

While Zara's success was achieved in a traditional in-store retail context, it was nonetheless a result of methods which pre-figured what was beginning to happen in e-commerce:

Real-time analyses, rapid logistics reactions,
and centrally-managed agility.
These technological processes are all to be found
in the DNA of the internet itself.

While Zara starts by producing small batches of new designs in order to test the water, Google and Facebook improve their high-performance algorithms in a similar form of trial and error by testing modifications as beta versions for small numbers of users. Anything that doesn't work here doesn't get shipped in the next big update; it's a system in which risk is all but eliminated.

What is more, in retail terms, it's a system that only reaches its full potential in an online context. While Zara's efficient consumer response approach was something a revolution on the high street, the German online clothing champion Zalando shows how the model can be taken even further – in the fast-forward mode so characteristic of the internet and with the extreme pressure that comes with the territory in e-commerce.

This pressure comes from outside. While Zara is weeks ahead of its bricks-and-mortar rivals, a week is several months in online shopping time; customers on the high street are still limited by the good old laws of time and space, but on the internet, the brakes are off. If an online store doesn't order enough of a popular item, then the warehouses run out and customers on the website immediately see that the item isn't available; their reaction is to simply click onto the next online shop, and the next, until they find one that has what they want in stock; it's even worse if the online store doesn't stock what they're after at all. Click, gone.

So like Zara, internet fashion store Zalando tests products in small batches: if the piece in question sells well, Zalando registers this immediately and can order more of the high-seller before the last one has been snapped up. What is more, just like Zara, Zalando has started to create its own brand early, the margin on bought-in ranges being – even with a large-scale network of cheap, efficient warehouses – simply too thin in the long term: given the omnipresent possibility that the customer will notice a difference in price and click onto a website selling the product more cheaply, pricing on the internet is, quite simply, a ruinous race to the bottom.

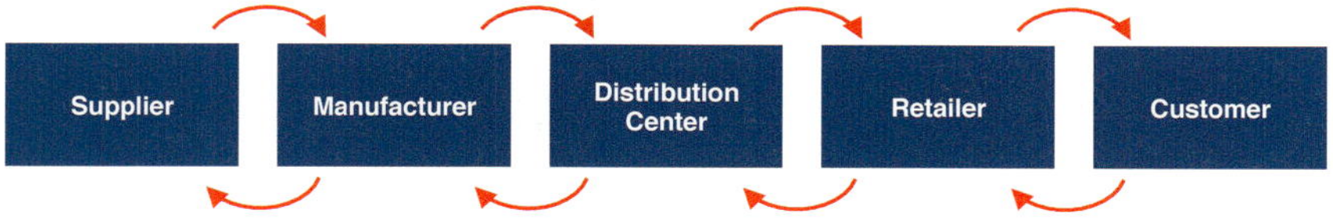

Fig. 2.4: Schematic comparison of push and pull supply chains
Source: with reference to Michael Levi et. al, Retailing Management, McGraw-Hill, 2013, p. 261

The shift toward own-brand clothing on Zalando is also an important evolutionary development inasmuch as it lays bare another mechanism in e-commerce procurement: online retailers collect a huge amount of data about both big sellers and items that are being searched for by large numbers of customers. So if Zalando sees that boots made by a certain brand in a certain look are selling well, it can take off its Merchant Hat and put on its Manufacturer Hat, using its proprietary footwear brand Stups to produce a similar boot. An even richer field for this kind of *jeu double* is data about expensive brand items that customers regularly view without actually buying. An experienced fashion buyer can see that there is demand, but at another price-point, and then order in a cheaper version from the in-house designers.

Amazon has become notorious for this form of cherry-picking on its marketplace as, if an item listed by a third-party retailer is selling well, it – or a carbon-copy version – suddenly crops up in Amazon's own range. For Amazon, it's a no-risk approach: no capital outlay during the test phase and when it places its own order later, it knows it's got a guaranteed sales hit on its hands. It should therefore come as no surprise that Amazon too is now placing increased emphasis on developing its own-brand product ranges, with Amazon Basics already offering products as diverse as electronics accessories and camera tripods and its Pinzon brand selling a range of home fabrics (see 2.4.2, Internet distribution channels, for more).

Customer-orientated procurement on the internet is, in essence, data analysis. Gut feeling about what customers "may" want has little place here. What is more, e-commerce favours retailers who also have their own production capacities over pure-breed resellers, as merchant-makers have the kind of sales data that other manufacturers are often lacking. Nevertheless, this data advantage also exists for retailers unwilling or unable to enter into their own production activities.

Optimising the product range: Minority report – the pull effect online

In a bricks-and-mortar retail concept – even an agile one such as Zara – product range optimisation does not start until a customer has bought a product: that is the point at which demand for the product is recorded. In online shopping, however, demand for a product is visible a long way before any money changes hands. Due to the fact that they have to express their wishes in writing electronically, customers – or rather, potential customers – have become more transparent as, both in a webshop and on the internet generally, consumers feel their way towards products they want to buy, leaving a trail of traceable search entries behind them. So even if a customer does not buy a product straight away, there is a clear expression of interest on the internet that is plain for all to see. For procurement, this means that optimising a product range is a process which starts the very second that range is made available and continues right through to concluding sales analyses.

In the following section, we will go through the individual tools which can be used to optimise e-commerce product ranges. These methods can broadly be classified into three categories:

- **off-site:** online tools outside of the shop
- **on-site:** online tools inside the shop
- **classic:** traditional analyses of the kind also used for in-store retail

By combining these tools, procurement professionals in e-commerce can create an optimised information flow which gives them up-to-the-minute information about how the current product offering is faring, as well as indications about how this range could or should be altered and extended.

Off-site: listening to white noise

We'll start with off-site optimisation tools since off-site is the area from which prospects arrive in a webshop. Before the advent of the internet, retailers and manufacturers were heavily reliant on market research and surveys in order to find out which products might turn prospects into paying customers; today still, wholly-offline operations have little other way of getting hard-and-fast information about what consumers might like to buy. The only other way to find out, of course, is experimentation: on the high street, shop managers put new products in the window and use a process of elimination to find out which ones are drawing people in.

Moving into the new world, we can imagine Google as a shopping precinct and a webshop as a real bricks-and-mortar affair. Now, in the analogue high street, you watch crowds of shoppers going past the window, and every now and then one stops and peers in; some even come in, and even fewer buy something. Yet until someone does buy something, you have very little information about what it is they were after in the first place, or at the very least – assuming that not all shopping is purely needs-driven or can be controlled by the actions of retailers – what they were willing to spend money on at that particular moment.

In the digital high street, however, things look a bit different. Customers are also streaming past your window, but – what's this? They all have little cardboard signs hanging around their necks with a list of things they are looking for: a dress, a television, a lamp. When they stop to look in your window, you've got time to have a look at these lists and note some of the details: the dress needs to be long and red; the television they want has a 50" screen; the lamp must have a touch-sensitive dimmer function. The prospect doesn't see you looking at the list, mind, because they're too busy looking at all the things you've put in the shop window.

The digital shop front has a buyer hidden in plain sight taking endless reams of notes about the written customer wishes.

This is why **keyword analysis**, i.e. analysing which words people put into search engines, is such an important aspect of e-commerce procurement. Looking at Google Trends, a free tool which offers information about search terms entered into the Google search engine, is essentially a way of reading consumers' minds as they hurry down the digital high street: on what dates do people most look for X? Where are these people when they search? Is X a fixed term or is it part of a range of words used? Now, since Google is not going to give away highly detailed information for free, many have to make do with the entry-level version of search analysis featuring indexed figures and very approximate graphs, but these are still enough to go on for many procurement professionals.

Case study: lederhosen and dirndls

The fact that demand for lederhosen, dirndls, and other Bavarian fashion items jumps around the Munich Oktoberfest ought not to surprise anyone, but a closer keyword analysis on Google Trends is by no means superfluous and is a good example for beginners in the field as it shows very clearly how off-site tools can be used to improve product ranges.

Our keywords are "lederhosen" and "dirndl". We start by seeing how frequently these items are searched for and get shown a graph detailing the development since 2010. The first thing that strikes us is, as expected, the peaks in searches during the months of September and October around the Munich Oktoberfest and other tribute events worldwide; what is more interesting, however, is to have look at searches in specific countries. In Germany, for example, we can see that dirndl dresses get searched around ten times as often as lederhosen, while in the US, it is lederhosen that is the leader between the two, being searched for twice as often as dirndls. Comparing the US to the UK, we see another difference: while searches for dirndls in the US are quite stable, in the UK there is a sharp increase from September 2012 onwards which recurs every autumn. Globally, however, we see that dirndls are still some way ahead of lederhosen as keywords because dirndls are searched for five times more often in Germany than in the US, and it is of course in Germany that the lion's share of Bavarian clothing searches happen.

Things get even more exciting for buyers when we look at the related search terms: Google offers up "lederhosen costume" as an example, alongside "damenlederhosen" (ladies' lederhosen) and "lederhosen trachten", the German word for traditional Bavarian fashion. Yet while "lederhosen costume" is almost never searched in Germany, this is a very common combination in English-speaking countries. Germany, however, has a near monopoly on lederhosen searches involving the keyword "trachten", as well as other German compound nouns such as "damenlederhosen".

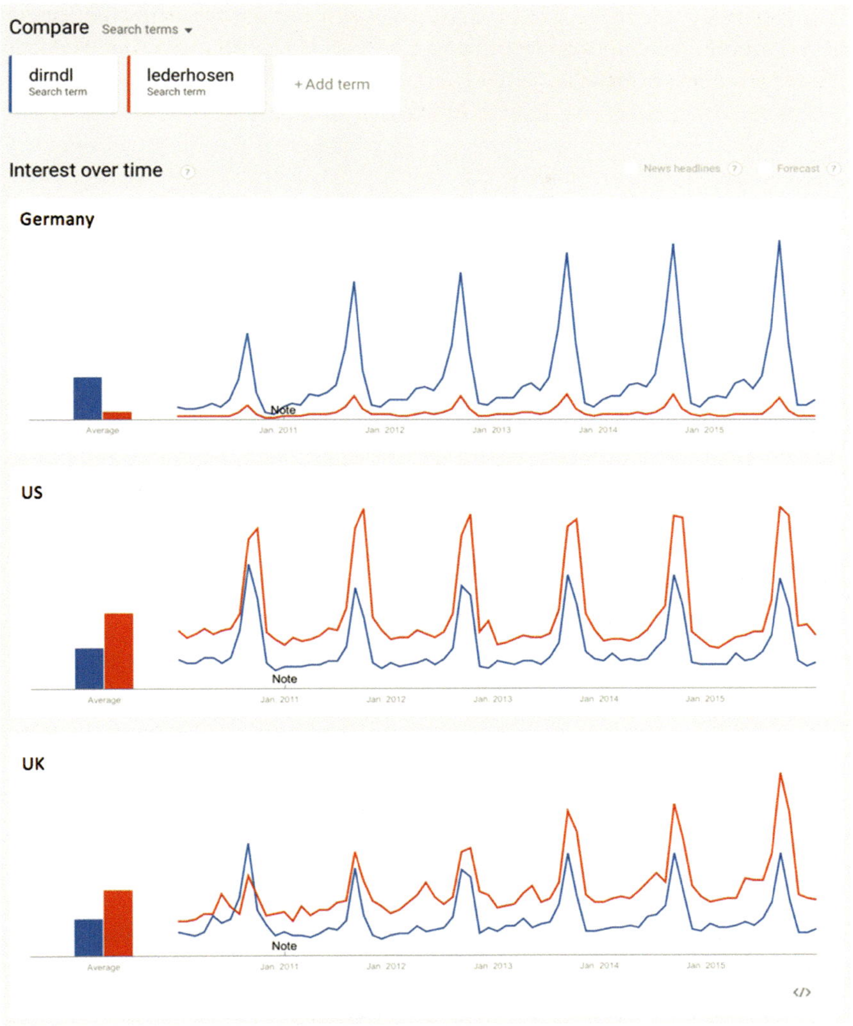

Google and the Google logo are registered trademarks of Google Inc., used with permission.

Fig. 2.5: Google Trends Screenshot

Source: Adapted from https://google.com/trends

This large amount of freely available information allows us to draw some fundamental conclusions about the worldwide market for Bavarian clothing which are of importance to anyone looking to sell it. First off, in Germany the biggest search demand is for women's dirndl dresses, not lederhosen. If lederhosen are searched, it is very often as ladies' lederhosen, a relatively new development in the market. In summary, anyone selling Bavarian clothing in Germany is selling first and foremost to women.

Anyone selling to English-speaking countries, however, will be selling primarily to men: most of the searches there are for lederhosen, and very often for costume lederhosen. In the USA, demand for dirndls online is low, but consistent; in Britain, demand for dirndls is rising year on year, suggesting a trend.

Anyone setting up an online shop selling Bavarian outfits would be able to use this information to gain insights about what product range to offer, and where. In selling to the US market, they would need more lederhosen than anything else, and specifically, they'd need lederhosen that make a good costume – i.e. not the most expensive hand-made ones, indeed maybe with less real leather to make them cheaper to send, and perhaps more colourful or whimsical than traditional models. If, however, they intend to sell more to the home market, Germany, then they would need the genuine article, high-quality leather breeches that customers will wear again and again, as well as a range of lederhosen for ladies – not to mention piles of dirndls of all shapes, sizes, and colours.

Researching keywords forms part of search engine marketing, or SEM, which is about leading consumers into a webshop by using specific terms that they search for.

SEM in turn breaks down into two different disciplines: search engine optimisation (SEO) and search engine advertising (SEA): the former covers measures which web-shop operators themselves can take to get a top position in search rankings for various keywords; the latter is about paying for adverts which are displayed to consumers searching for particular keywords and link to the shop.

Both SEO and SEA are not just marketing tools (see 2.3 and 2.4 about marketing and distribution respectively), but are also useful in procurement and buying. After all, in order to get a high ranking for a specific keyword, a shop operator first needs to know what is being looked for, and this knowledge should exercise influence on what is bought.

Web-shop operators who have a Google AdWords account can get their procurement team even more information about searches as well as tools and analyses which present searches made on Google in hard figures: how many searches for which exact sequence of letters? When and from where? This level of detail allows search keywords to be checked for their precise relevance, and Google also suggests related or improved keywords.

Anyone currently running a campaign in Google AdWords can also see how many conversions are being made: i.e. how many orders are being generated by the adverts they have bought – and which precise keywords triggered the advert to appear. In the world of the analogue high street, that is roughly the equivalent of a customer walking straight into a shop with a sign around their neck saying "I am looking for X" and then saying "I saw your advert for X and would now like to purchase this product in your establishment". On the internet, this level of transparency and traceability is the norm, not the exception. Now the procurement professional knows that the product is not a casual buy, but one which is searched for and in demand; and if there are similar keywords among the Google AdWords suggestions, then it might be advisable to provide corresponding products.

On-site: eavesdropping on the customer

As soon as a customers are inside an online shop, they start to leave very obvious tracks, often in writing as keywords. In the analogue world, this would equate to having the shop buyer following browsing prospects around, cunningly disguised as a shop assistant and peering over their shoulders as they look at products. Yet what would of course be considered an invasion of personal privacy – and a decidedly creepy experience to boot – in the real world, happens on the internet without customers realising.

> *When customers use the shop's own search function, for instance, to see whether you stock a particular item, you can see exactly what they are looking for.*

If they haven't already made that abundantly clear by coming onto the site as a referral from a Google search or clicking on a Google advert, this is in fact your first chance to get a look at that cardboard sign around their necks with their shopping list written all over it. What is more, you'll get a very detailed look at that list now that they're in the shop, because once customers are already in a shop environment, the search terms they enter will be specific: "red evening dress" or "jeans, 32w 34l, blue" will be far more frequent than "dress" or "men's fashion".

This means that the online search function of a webshop is one of the most interesting places to get a feel for what customers really want – even if they don't find it and leave the shop. After all, if customers are looking for something on site and not simply on Google, then they must imagine that they have a fair chance of finding it in the shop. If they don't – and if the customer isn't clearly deranged and looking for "monkeys" or "missiles" – then it may well be that there is a gap in the product range that procurement needs to think about filling.

Even customers who don't come into a webshop via a keyword, but simply "drop in to browse", don't disappear again without a trace. Whether tempted in by a particular product or advert or simply "walking in" (i.e. typing the shop name into the URL box), each visitor to a website leaves footprints. Analysing user behaviour – often called **behavioural analytics** in e-commerce – can provide another rich source of information for procurement and purchasing:[2]

- **Length of visit:** Did the customer stay long? If they clicked away again almost immediately, this could be a sign that the product offering was not attractive to them: why was it not? Was the keyword that bought them in wrong or misleading? Did the products stocked not suit the search? If not, then this is an issue for procurement.
- **Depth of visit:** How far into the shop did the customer get? Did they just look at product category overviews or did they get down to detailed views of specific products? The deeper the visit, the more interested the customer was in the products stocked. In the old world, this kind of behaviour is expressed by picking up and touching items, while a shallow visit is more comparable to someone eyeing up a few isles and then leaving the shop – i.e. an indication that the products were not of interest to them.
- **Navigation path:** Which path did the customer take through the shop? Did they use the navigation bar, moving from "men's fashion" through the "trousers" page and then down into jeans, before clicking on a colour and size to reach a selection? Or did they just go straight to the site search and put in "blue jeans, 36w 34l? Did they use any other links on the site such as the product listings or even the sitemap?

2 With reference to Hassler (2011), Web Analytics

- **Clicks/path analysis:** How can we visualise the customer's path through the shop? By applying path analysis techniques, we can either follow a specific customer through the shop, or look at individual pages and see where customers came from and where they move on to. Where this kind of mapping gets interesting for procurement is when, say, a product page gets a particularly high amount of traffic from another product page, or if it sends on a large number of visitors to another specific product; another pattern to watch out for is a well-trodden path which runs from a specific product to the shopping basket.

By combining these subsets of behavioural analytics, a set of accurate conclusions can be drawn about what brings customers into the webshop and whether they liked the product range. Specifically, this kind of data can be used to judge whether products have earned their place in the offering; one way to do this is buy using a product performance matrix which combines a range of behavioural and usage indicators to show what various products in the range contribute to overall turnover – or, as we like to call it, a "4Hs analysis", the Four Hs being: Hits, Hypes, Hideaways, and Horrors.

Products which are entry pages or receive a large amounts of traffic from within the site – and are then sold – are patently **hits**. It is obvious that these products should be retained and advertised.

If analysis of clicks and visit depth show that a product receives an above-average number of visits and is often looked at in detail, only to not make it into the shopping cart, then it's a **hype**. Although it would be foolish to remove this head-turner from the range, the fact that it isn't being sold should make procurement people sit up and listen: do we have enough of this product or is it consistently "currently not available"? Is there something obviously faulty about the item? Or is it a compelling article, but simply too expensive for most customers?

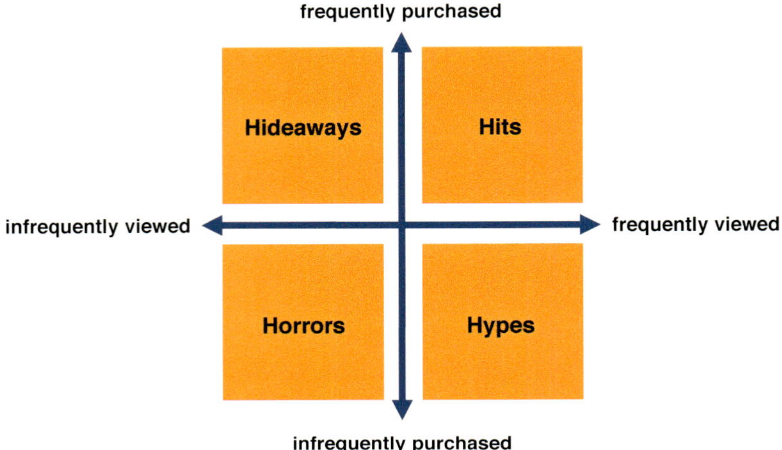

Fig. 2.5: Product performance matrix: the 4Hs analysis

Source: With reference to a blog-post by etracker, www.etracker.com/blog/web-controlling/optimiertes-categorymanagement-eine-fundierte-datenbasis-fuer-alle-entscheider-teil-3 (as in March 2015)

On the other side of the matrix are the products which receive below-average numbers of visits. If, however, a low-frequency item makes it into the basket whenever it is clicked on, then buyers should give themselves a pat on the back – and then call people in marketing and sales to make sure that this **hideaway** gets put in the limelight.

It's a different matter if the product not only receives a low amount of traffic, but also doesn't get bought: then it's clearly a **horror** and a case for procurement, who should try and examine why it is performing so poorly. Has it simply been sold-out for too long to be of any interest to anyone, or is the product itself genuinely poor? If it is, it needs to be delisted.

As a general rule, behavioural analytics should be regularly applied to online shops and procurement should draw its conclusions from the results.

Is a specific product page suddenly bouncing visitors *en masse* after having been a good seller? If so, it might have sold out or a competitor may be offering it at a noticeably lower price. Or is there a sudden hype around a product which, up to now, has had low sales? If so, then it might simply be a matter of improving the product presentation to create a new sales hit that buyers will soon be ordering by the bucket-load.

In the longer term, procurement should also be taking a close look at **visitor statistics**: on a monthly basis, web analytics should be used to find out how many of the visitors are new to the shop, how many are returning after a previous visit – and how often they return. This kind of regular analysis would reveal any strong drops in repeat visits, for example, which could be an indicator that the site is losing customer segments it previously had because it no longer offering them products they need or want. While it would not be practicable to try and orientate entire product ranges entirely to the ups and downs of visitor behaviour, sustained declines in keyword referrals combined with a high bounce rate across a range of product pages and dwindling repeat business would certainly pose serious questions about procurement decisions in recent months.

Of course, there are quite direct ways of getting answers to questions about product ranges. Simply because digital consumers are walking around with public wish-lists hung around their necks, it doesn't mean that digital sales assistants shouldn't be trying to get into conversation with them. It might be, for example, that not all of the items on the wish-list are particularly well described, or perhaps the customer means one thing but thinks it is called another. Surveys can be a useful tool to find out if customers like the product offering: while only a tiny minority of those asked to on a website will ever fill out a survey, participation rates can be increased by offering discounts or entries into prize draws; then questions can be asked such as "Did you find the product you wanted to buy in our shop?" or "Did you like X?" Combined with the broad statistical analyses, these individual responses can provide valuable insights.

Social media is another channel for this kind of direct feedback – whether the shop in question wants it or not. Users on Facebook, Twitter *et al* like nothing better than expressing their opinions about products and services and don't wait for the company concerned to ask: so if your shop is represented on these channels, expect direct feedback on your product range – and take the opportunity to contact users in an informal context (see 2.7.1 for more about using social media interaction from a customer service perspective). Social media also offers statistical, quantitive feedback in the form of the Facebook Like or Pinterest postings, so it is always a good idea to include these buttons on product pages; products receiving a lot of likes and other social media attention is the digital equivalent of word-of-mouth. Besides this, offering customers the ability to rate and review products can also open up channels for quantitive and qualitative feedback respectively on specific articles.

Classics: last, but definitely not least

At the end of the process, it's time to apply the classic analysis tools which have been the bread and butter of procurement departments for decades: sales data analysis, ABC analysis, and supplier analysis. In **sales data analysis**, the aim is to see whether sales are progressing as planned, and this weekly exercise is to be recommended whatever the online retail concept being applied: have we sold our stock? When are we likely to do so on current projections? Do we need to order in – or indeed: produce – more? And by when?

Meanwhile, **ABC analysis** remains one of the key techniques in retail, whether off or online. In fact, it is more important on the internet than anywhere else due to the price pressure and rampant discounting endemic to this environment. Not only sales figures, but margins and return on investment are of interest here. If, for example, a 4Hs analysis revealed a hype product that was strongly discounted to turn it into a hit, then the ABC analysis will be required to work out what the effect on the margin was and what conclusions can be drawn for planning the product range in future.

The importance of **supplier analysis** remains unchanged: do products made by specific manufacturers and brands sell well and at what price points and conditions? Was the shop able to sell them for their full margin? Was demand high? This form of analysis is particularly important for webshops run by generalists and category killers, but less so for specialists and – obviously – the online stores of individual manufacturers or brands, or stores which resell only one make.

In these issues, the work of procurement professionals in online retail is by and large the same job as they have always done in traditional retail, albeit with different numbers.

The long tail, for example, makes it quite acceptable to sell some products for a lower margin and over a far longer period on the internet than in a bricks-and-mortar shop; products can be "archived", for example, and no longer advertised, but still sell. This depends on the segment, of course: fashion products simply must be sold while they are still on trend, on the internet as in stores, and if it takes an eyewatering price cut to shift them, then so be it. With expensive, hand-made furniture, however, the figures look quite different.

There are also big differences in procurement for online mass-customisation business models such as personalised cereal creator mymuesli.com or t-shirt-printers Spreadshirt, which require a certain amount of "raw material", i.e. oats or blank t-shirts – much like a supermarket or a classic clothes shop respectively. Yet at the same time, the customisable extras offered need to be examined continually based on their profitability: procurement would need to look at sales and earnings before deciding whether to continue providing users a specific, expensive ink or a muesli ingredient that is perishable. As with high street stores, buyers here have to ask themselves what they need to make sure customers come into the shop, and how much margin they can sacrifice to this end.

Conclusion

So even in an online pure-play concept, there is no shortage of age-old procurement and buying questions; yet these questions often have different answers now that consumers have got used to getting everything everywhere anytime. This means that, whatever the retail approach, on the internet, it is about keeping up availability at all times and making sure that the product range is either sufficiently broad or sufficiently deep: breadth is for category killers (e.g. Zalando) and multi-category killers (Amazon), while depth is about giving consumers access to, say, the full range offered by a particular brand. The next shop will only ever be one click away in the digital high street, so availability simply has to be guaranteed.

Depending on the business model applied, procurement professionals need to think about how they can make everything available anytime on the internet – and have been given a whole digital toolbox to do this. As for everywhere, that is a matter for distribution (see 2.4) and logistics (2.6).

2.2 Product presentation

Introduction

As varied as business models in e-commerce may be, online shops share a relatively standard set of functionalities, especially on what is referred to as the front end (i.e. what the customer sees). The homepage which appears when the webshop's address is entered and the opening app interface for smartphones and tablets must offer certain core functionalities and, as there are only a limited number of ways of producing these, the structures used are relatively standardised.

It has ever been thus. In high streets and shopping centres, all stores have display windows, doors, shelves or product vitrines, and a salesperson; how much produce is stored in the stockroom, who delivers it, or whether it is actually fabricated out back is all secondary. Whether it's a café whose owners hand-make their sandwiches every morning or a multi-storey destination store offering the latest in entertainment electronics imported from Asia, almost every shop implements a broadly standardised concept. When, after all, is the last time you went into a shop without windows and without even a single member of staff? Or a shop that did not display any products on sale there on shelves or in cabinets? In classic retail situations, it's almost impossible to imagine how a store would get by without these elements.

It's no different in e-commerce: whether it's Zalando with its endless parade of mass-produced t-shirts from low-wage countries or Spreadshirt, which offers customers the opportunity to have each and every t-shirt customised in Germany, the front-end areas of these online shops have the same key features and offer similar functions. For all the depth of in-house production and the overall size of the companies may differ – from global giants such as Amazon down to dwarves turning over less than a million dollars a year, from brand-owned outlet webshops through to marketplaces for anything and everything such as Ebay – the way e-commerce websites are structured is very similar, both on PCs and on smartphones. As different as mobile shops may look to classic browser versions, they too tend to apply standards to surmount the challenges posed by small screens and exploit the benefits offered by multi-touch input technology.

The building blocks

Besides actual product presentation, the following five functions constitute the core of any e-commerce front-end:

- Product catalogue/categorisation
- Search
- User/customer account
- Shopping basket/cart
- Recommendations/adverts/teasers

Each of these five key components is essential to an online store: a webshop without a link to the shopping basket – usually accompanied by an icon based on a standard real-world basket – would be like a supermarket without trolleys and baskets next to the entrance.

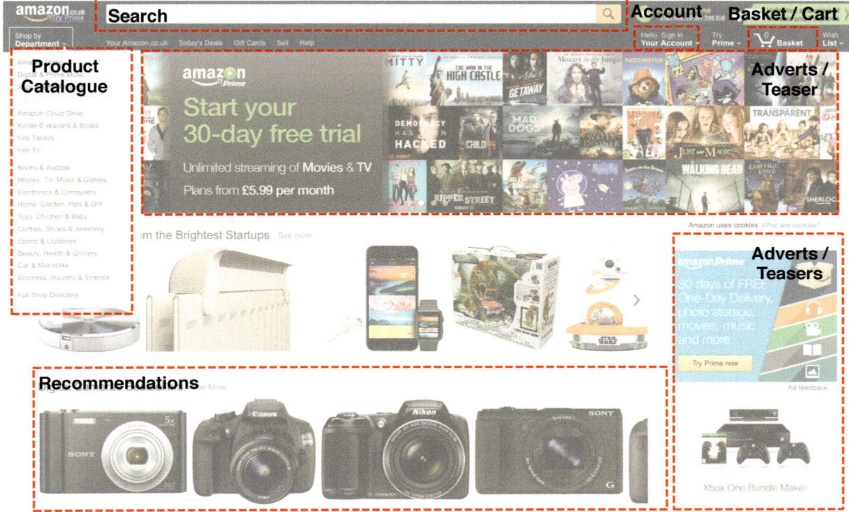

Fig. 2.6: Typical components and features of an online front end

Source: www.amazon.co.uk (as of March 2016)

These elements can be provided either by using all-in-one shop software solutions or by using one of the widespread modular structures; the latter relies on components from a range of providers which are combined using interfaces to offer the consumer a fully-functional front end. As an example of how this kind of patchwork shop is put together, external search technology is quite common (e.g. provided by Google), while advertisements and recommendations are also generated and served by external engines using customer data – or indeed third-party records. Customers using the front ends don't usually see the joints, and should be able to use the shop with all the same functionality in their PC browsers, mobile browsers, and smartphone apps.

This chapter is about how, using catalogues and categories, search functions, and adverts or recommendations, customers are guided to the right products – and about how these products are presented on their individual pages.

Guiding users on site

Users typically begin their visit to online shops either on the homepage/mobile start interface or, following a Google search or a click on a Facebook link, on a specific page – usually a product page or specially-designed landing page. As a general rule, the visit will then progress hierarchically rather than asymmetrically through the site: whether on the standard homepage or a landing page, the product search and product categories are visible, the former generally at the top of the page and the latter usually on the left-hand side; visitors who are new to the shop tend to recognise the structure immediately, find their bearings quickly, and instinctively progress using the navigational behaviours they generally use.

Operators of online shops can be very sure that almost every other site will display the same range of front-end tools in roughly similar positions. There are four standard tools which allow users to navigate through from the page on which they have entered the shop down to the product in which they are interested:

- Product categories/catalogue
- Filters
- On-site search
- Links, adverts, and recommendations

In terms of speed, the slowest way for the user is to progress through product categories and catalogues: it may take several clicks and a comparatively long period of time spent navigating until a specific product page is reached. The fastest way is to click on adverts or recommendations, as these generally tend to move users directly to a product page. We will now examine these four methods, looking at how often they are used, the level of technical complexity behind them, and what they say about customers' wishes and goals.

Product categories and catalogues

Data structures used to organise products stocked in webshops are, more often than not, complex issues: classifying items is no easy matter and immediately raises questions about how many classes of product there should be, with how many levels of sub-classes, and what to do with products which span two or more of the classes set up.

Yet while the systems used to classify products vary in terms of their applicability to various areas (i.e. what works for MP3 songs might not work for lawnmowers), there simply must be a unified structure in which products are organised on the basis of their commercial descriptions or technical features. These structures are generally comparable with file trees, branching out into boughs and ending with various groups of products at their tips.

With an MP3 song, for example, a genre is defined, then the performer, and then the album from which it is taken. If the song is not being sold on a specialised music portal like iTunes but in a generalist shop such as Amazon, then further classification is required back down the tree towards the roots: before "genre" comes "MP3" and the product group "music".

With a lawnmower being sold by a garden machinery manufacturer, the overall class "garden machinery" would not be required; classification would start with "lawnmower" and could continue with the motor – i.e. petrol-driven or electric? Each of these two classes might then be further subdivided by revs and wattage respectively. Beyond this, classification could continue using the dimensions, weight, or blade size of the devices.

This strict product **classification** as a way of structuring data stands in contrast to the looser system of product **categorisation**; this latter is particularly important from a front-end navigation point of view because a product may well belong to several categories and consumers are well within their rights to expect to find them there. Customers are, quite rightly, uninterested in the class to which the product they are currently searching for belongs as far as each stockist is concerned: customers want to find the product where they might logically assume they will find it.

The class/category problem can be illustrated by taking a pair of men's brown leather boots; fashion especially has many competing classification structures. One possible classification tree might split at the trunk into men's and women's fashion; on the men's side, the trunk would branch off into classes such as trousers, shirts, and shoes while, on the women's side, there would be trousers, shirts, shoes, and skirts. Then again, the tree could also be structured in an entirely different way, branching out first into trousers, shirts, skirts, and shoes and only later into men's and women's (or indeed, with unisex products, not branching out on gender at all).

Homepage | Sale | Categories | Shoes | Men | Shoes | **Reduced men's boots**

Homepage | Sale | Categories | Men's fashion | Shoes | **Reduced men's boots**

Homepage | Men's fashion | Categories | Shoes | **Men's boots**

Homepage | Shoes | Men | Men's shoes | **Men's boots**

Fig. 2.7: Example of product categorisation
Source: our graphic

Product categorisation is how this contradiction is resolved: products can only ever belong to one class at once, but may form part of several different categories simultaneously; this in turn allows products to be reached using various paths. As a consequence, good navigational structures follow categories and not classifications, opening up click paths through "men's fashion" or "shoes" to our hypothetical brown leather men's boots.

What is more, in contrast to classes, categories can be time-limited: a clothes merchant may well introduce a category like "Ready for winter" featuring items such as overcoats, gloves, and leather boots in autumn, and then transfer the contents to the "Sale" category in summer when demand for such items is at its low. It is therefore entirely possible that our boots would be present in three categories at once: Men – Shoes – Boots; Shoes – Men's – Boots, and Sale.

This example shows just how many categories addle the fixed classification structure. Swimwear can be both its own category as well as subcategory of women's and menswear; poolside fashion might also first appear in a "New!" category and then, towards the end of its sales cycle, find itself reduced in the "Sale" category.

This kind of multiple categorisation for product range navigation purposes can be the result of automated processes or manual choices. In the latter case, the webshop manager might decide to add individual products or whole categories to various keywords in the navigation menu; sellers on Ebay especially should make sure to manually list their products across all relevant categories since the marketplace software automatically assigns the listing a class.

The larger the shop, the greater the importance of automating this process; the most common way of doing this is to use attributes in product data. In a men's/women's-based classification, our men's boots would be categorised using the rule that all products with the attribute "footwear" are also assigned to the "shoes" category. If the classification is structured differently, however, with classes such as shirts, jackets, and shoes, then all products with "men's fashion" as an attribute would also be added to the "men" categories. Another rule for the "Ready for winter" category, for example, would be that all products with the attribute "boot" are included, but not those with attributes such as "sneakers" or "shoes".

This is why a well-kept product database is of the utmost importance: only on the basis of strong data can various categories be tested and amended reliably.

All product data – including series numbers and other forms of alphanumeric identification – must be entered into the database so that if, for instance, a particular manufacturer offers a time-limited discount on their products, this can immediately be transferred into a matching category using the manufacturer's name or product identifiers. Another possible source of categorisations are business rules: i.e. every time a product is reduced, it should automatically be listed in the "Sale" category. All of this is predicated on product databases and all other sources of information being kept up to date at all times.

Filters

This kind of good information practice also forms the basis for a successful filter navigation function: filters are a popular method for many consumers on e-commerce platforms, especially once they have reached a specific product category or class, or entered a preliminary search term, at which point filters can be applied to adapt the results shown to their own personal needs. With our hypothetical men's boots, for example, the most useful filter would probably be "shoe size", allowing a user to click "size 10" and then only view articles which are available in that size. Ebay, Amazon, or John Lewis show how intuitive and visually attractive filter navigation structures can be applied, using small squares to represent the colours of clothes and shoes.

Fig. 2.9: Example of filters

Source: www.amazon.co.uk (as of March 2016)

These kinds of techniques allow e-commerce to play its strong hand: while browsing and rummaging might feel like typically analogue activities in which customers gain a swift visual impression of the product range available in a shop and examine individual items, the ability to apply a filter which immediately removes irrelevant items such as shoes which are not available in the customer's size is something the in-store experience cannot offer – and is a key feature of the long-tail approach to stocking an online shop (see 2.1 Procurement).

The long-tail strategy is, after all, predicated not just on making everything available, but on helping people to find it: given the sheer number of items and permutations that the long tail entails, filters are needed to help customers pick the needle they want out of the digital haystack.

This targeted search, however, is not the only reason that consumers actually spend time looking around in online shops; some like to click through product categories or apply filters to gain a general impression of the shop and the number of products available, just as customers might wander around a bricks-and-mortar store.

Search

Nevertheless, the search function is generally more popular than other forms of navigation in most shops: almost every second visitor on average heads straight for the search. In the offline world, this is the equivalent is walking into a shop and immediately finding a sales assistant to ask questions of. This is the key characteristic of consumer behaviour when there is concrete intent to purchase, and online shopping portals are far better able to deal with it than traditional retailers: the online search box is always ready to listen, while shop assistants are not always available. For a large chunk of consumers, the on-site search actually replaces search engines, too: around a third of online shoppers don't look on Google for new boots, but go straight to Amazon *inter alia*; the crucial role the search box plays is made clear by its positioning in the shop, with Amazon having programmed it to dynamically increase in breadth with the browser window if it is made larger, for instance.

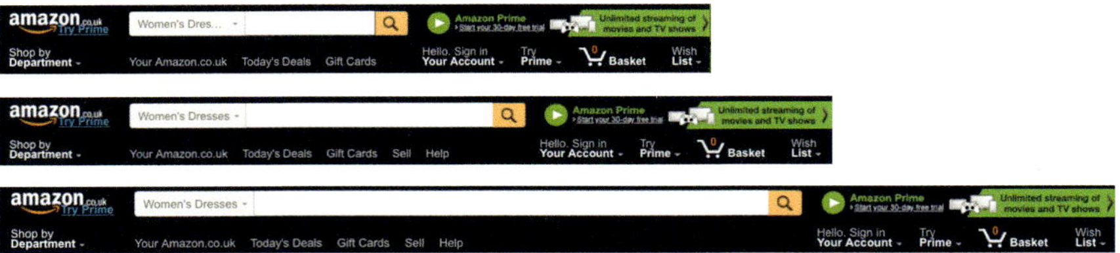

Fig. 2.10: Example of dynamically resizing search box
Source: www.amazon.co.uk (as of March 2016)

The prevalence of users who head straight for the search function on online shops indicates a high level of intent to purchase for concrete products: this level of focus has to be matched by the performance of the search engine, which should lead customers straight to the product they are interested in acquiring. Despite this importance, however, in many online shops the search function feels like an afterthought.

Searches should, however, be an integral part of the shop system – and not least because the search terms entered are of particular importance for devising the right product mix (see 2.1 Procurement). Shop search engines must, as well as examining the entire product stock within nanoseconds, be able to take the customer straight to the right product.

This is where functions such as **category selection** take on a key role: if a customer on Amazon searches for a musician, product categories such as "MP3" and "CD" are suggested. If the artist in question has also bought out filmed concert performances, then "DVD" is also shown. In this way, the customer is able to immediately select the right category and can save themselves a few words and further search requests.

Other forms of auto-complete can also be useful. If you type "jeans" into the John-Lewis.co.uk search, it immediately shows "Men's jeans", "Women's jeans", and "Armani jeans", and this form of **suggested results** pioneered by Google is particularly valued by customers looking for items with long designations, customers who do not type regularly, and customers browsing on small mobile devices. Search suggestions are also useful tools for removing doubts about spelling: anyone unsure of which way round the I and E in "Klein" go, for example, will be delighted to see the word suggested after typing in the far easier "Calvin".

This is another important characteristic of a good search: **tolerance**. A good e-commerce search adapts to the input errors its customers most often make, rather than rapping them on the knuckles for poor spelling. After all, the internet isn't an English class, and many customers aren't bothered about orthography when typing; others make classic "form/from" switch errors or simply do not care about how words are spelled in general. Typical mistakes which are the bane of teachers everywhere ("bicicle" or "appliences", and much worse besides) simply have to be accounted for; the search engine should make suggestions using the proposed, correct spelling either as the user is typing or, at the latest, shortly after they have finished.

Search functions must also be set up to deal with the bewildering variety of words which is the hallmark of English, especially in view of its use across the globe, as well as the fact that many products go by more than one name: you say "blazer", I say "jacket" (tailors know the difference, but customers often don't); meanwhile, Americans wear drawers under their pants and the British put on pants under their trousers. Search functions which only shows products with the attribute "blazer" and don't display are range of men's smart jackets are unnecessarily limiting the choice offered to the customer and possibly hiding from them the items they are looking for.

This means that a fully comprehensive list of synonyms which learns from user input is utterly essential.

A good search will, within the space of a few clicks, either have directed customers straight to an article or at the very least to a selection of products of interest to them; selections can then be further pared down using filters (see above) or the search can be made more exact. The assumption to work on is that customers who use the search and do not find what they are looking for fast will switch to another site rather than try out lengthy navigation paths through product categories; they are, after all, looking for a specific item and want to find it fast. This means that, even if there are no exact matches in the shop for the search at hand, showing the customer messages like "No matches found" should be avoided as much as possible: displaying "We didn't find quite what you were looking for, but how about..." is the better strategy. The products shown could be from the recommendation engine (see below) or just similar items; after all, something else might actually do the trick, or the user might be tempted to try another search. Students tend, quite early on, to grasp this key piece of exam technique: not answering is a guaranteed

"O marks", while attempting an answer based on what they do know – however adventurous or ill-informed – automatically increases their chances of getting at least a couple of points.

Links, adverts, and recommendations

The only method of navigation which leads visitors deeper into the shop than the search – and does so more speedily – is a link straight to a specific product, or product category page. This type of link is generally presented as an advert or a recommendation: this latter was pioneered by Amazon, with the phrase "Customers who bought this item also bought..." headlining a carousel underneath the product purchased; this reel features links directly to other products frequently bought by other customers in combination with the same item, or previously bought by the same customer.

Advertising starts, however, on the homepage or start screen of an online shop, which might be compared to the display window of a classic store: i.e. the place to hawk big sales, new deliveries, or seasonal products. Amazon's browser home page, for example, provides space both in the centre and to the right for a range of advertisements; Zalando, too, offers its brand partners "window space" on its homepage and also uses it to promote clearance sales, while a carousel in the centre of the page automatically displays the day's most popular items (a clever application of that cast-iron rule in the fashion business that most customers are not so much buying clothes as they are a sense of belonging and acceptance).

On the level below the homepage, too, in search results, category, and product pages, adverts are, more often than not, part of the picture: small top-right banner ads, for example, or pop-ups which direct customers to completely different areas of the shop – and are, of course, frequently clicked away by frustrated customers, or nipped in the bud by their ad-blocking software. Indeed, partly for this reason, e-commerce invests far more resources in trying to recommend customers products that will suit them and cross-sell them matching products once they have made their selection.[3]

3 In reference to Müller (2005) – *Kundenbindung im E-Commerce*

Personalised recommendations in online shops

Generating this kind of personalised recommendation is a complex process composed of several distinct steps, the first of which is **identifying the customer**. Next up is **collecting customer data** in order to **create a customer profile** which can be used as a basis for **generating recommendations** and **addressing the customer personally**.

Identification

There are several ways to identify customers; as a general rule, they fall into one of two categories – passive or active identification.

Passive identification takes place when customers "get identified": on a PC, this might be achieved by reading their IP addresses or using cookies; session cookies or specific URL extensions are used to track customers as they visit the site, while persistent cookies make it possible to re-identify the same customers when they next visit the site. Hardware and software features of the computers customers are using (i.e. processor, network card, screen resolution, plug-ins installed) can be added into the mix to support identification, and indeed since a growing number of internet users regularly delete cookies or adapt their browser settings to delete them automatically on exit, this form of recognition using device configurations – often termed "digital fingerprinting" or "forensic tracking" – is becoming increasingly important.

Another priority area here is identifying users on mobile devices. Here too, there are a range of options depending on how the user accesses the online shop: mobile browsers, for example, also support cookies which can be used for recognition; tablets and phones also offer shopping apps, which are often a more comfortable way to browse and buy on smaller screens. Both Android and Apple mark each users with an alphanumeric identifier so that they can be recognised every time they use applications – Google calls its "Advertising ID" and Apple uses the acronym IDFA ("Identifier for Advertisers"); in contrast to cookies, these identifiers cannot be deleted and therefore allow permanent identification of users throughout the entire applications landscape. This means that users of the OTTO, John Lewis, and Amazon apps can be tracked through their use of other apps on the same device, and while this, in theory, means complete and continuous recognition, it is of absolutely no help in identifying the phone or tablet owner if they switch back to the browser to access the online shop. The result is that many users are in fact doubles because they are identified as one user via browser cookies and once more with their app ID.

Active identification is what happens when customers "identify themselves", e.g. by creating a user account, for example, which generally happens directly before a purchase as it is usually not mandatory, but certainly more comfortable, to buy from an account than as a guest. When customers then return to the site, they can use their account data to log back in and actively identify themselves; many then use the "Remember me" or "Stay signed in" functions and remain permanently identified from that point on. Mobile devices also offer users the opportunity to stay signed in and therefore access their accounts and information more easily. Another permutation of this form of active identification is the Google or Facebook single sign-on (SSO), in which users stay logged into these services and allow apps on their devices to access their user profiles.

Data collection

Nevertheless, whether users register or not is of relatively little importance for collecting data on them: after all, while some types of data must be made available by users explicitly, many other chunks of are collected with implicit consent. Users who access Amazon, for example, can be passively identified by the retailer regardless of whether they log in or buy something: data about their internet access and approximate location are given the second they reach the site. Any searches users then carry out are logged and connected to this passive identification profile, as are product pages they view. Unless users then delete cookies or switch devices, they can be re-identified when they next head to the site – which in turn allows the retailers to present products they searched for or viewed on the last visit. Zalando, for example, uses this data to make a call on whether to show men's or women's clothing on the homepage when it identifies a returning visitor.

Yet precisely in this instance, the limits of implicit data collection become clear: it is difficult to make the right call in this instance if several users – male and female – are using the same device; some data, meanwhile, can only be gathered with explicit consent. So while search behaviours can provide indicators about, say, roughly what age the passively identified user might be, the actual age, as well as gender, marital and familial status, precise address, and a range of other demographic data can only be gathered by explicitly asking for it – or from user profiles in social media which users have agreed to make accessible.

Profile generation

The user data collected both explicitly and implicitly, and any available information about customer preferences (e.g. what users have looked at, or perhaps even purchased), is already enough to generate a simple user profile. This is achieved using a matrix which produces a mathematical rating for each customer per preference element.

This means that it is easy to recognise that customer A – female, under 30 – is unlikely to have a high level of interest in men's boots; the more this person buys in this profile, the more information is gained e.g. about her size, the colours and cuts she likes, and her price bracket.

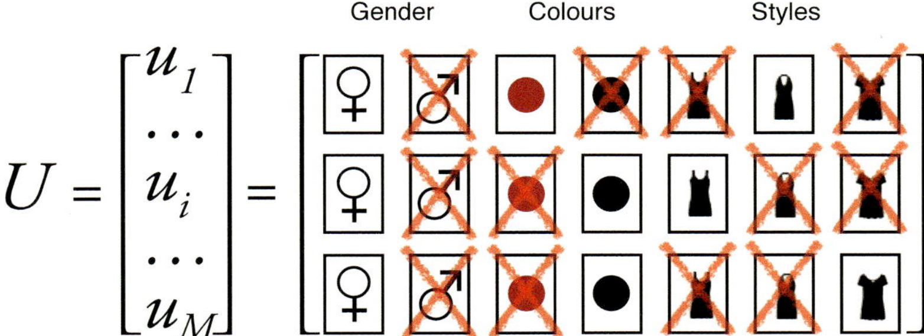

Fig. 2.11: A rating matrix, illustrated
Source: our graphic

Nevertheless, this type of data, collected by online shops as a matter of course, can be quite one-dimensional: clicks and buys; portals which do more than simply offer products to look at and purchase offer far more opportunities to collect quality data. Facebook, for example, collects a whole range of data both directly and indirectly: it knows its users' age, roughly where they live, and what they look like; and while online shops can only compare customers if they have similar buying patterns, Facebook knows which users are connected and can even draw conclusions about how well they know each other. On top of this, the network also gathers data about events, books, music, and films which users show interest in, which in turn allows for accurate predictions about which products such users might prefer in other areas. This not just exciting in terms of generating recommendations, of course, but for advertising on the internet generally (see 2.3 Marketing).

What is more, although the precise value of a Facebook Like is not always entirely clear (what does it mean when a user "likes" a report about an outbreak of a deadly disease or the damage caused by a hurricane?), it is generally unambiguous when applied to a product. Items which a user likes will generally be of interest to them, and this kind of data is, in commercial terms, gold dust: customers become transparent, walking up and down the digital shopping street with a big sign saying what they want to buy next (see 2.1 Procurement).

Websites connected to Facebook and apps on mobile devices can, as long users agrees to the data being shared, access Facebook profiles and use the information stored there outside of Facebook; in connection with what the user then looks at themselves on the website or in the app, a relatively complete picture of personal preferences can be created. Those online retailers which get access to this kind of data and know what to do with it therefore gain a massive leg-up on competitors who don't, viz. a much more comprehensive user profile as a basis on which to generate recommendations which may lead to sales.

Recommendation

Regardless of the extent to which customer profiles have been completed, there are two primary approaches to generating recommendations: **content-based filtering** and **collaborative filtering**; a third approach is using **machine learning** to create rules for producing recommendations from patterns in customer profiles and user behaviour.

Content-based filtering is about applying rules which can use data available out users' preferences to produce recommendations. Even after just a few purchases, a simple matrix is enough to start recommending products which could be of interest to a particular user. Nevertheless, choices still need to be made about which recommendations to show (you can't ever show them all!), and so the most common rule used in this approach is, phrased somewhat unmathematically: "Show the customer the element which has the highest preference value." Following this basic rule, several others can be added, such as business rules which are more about the company's bottom line (return on investment, brand of product) and can stop products being recommended which the customer cannot buy immediately (availability, inventory levels). Nevertheless, this approach always begins from the profile of each individual user, meaning that users can fundamentally only ever be recommended either what they have already bought, or similar items. Perhaps a man who bought boots in winter might want sandals in summer? With this process, there is no way to find out until he buys sandals. Nevertheless, his shoe size and preferred colours are already stored, and can thus be used to offer slightly personalised search results even at this stage which, for example, removes shoes not available in his size from results presented.

With **collaborative filtering**, various user profiles are compared, meaning that recommendations are generated based on similarities between the preferences of different customers, not on the basis of each user's profile alone. If customer A and customer B have similar preferences, then "gaps" can be filled: i.e. if customer A has bought products X, Y, and Z, but customer B has only purchased X and Y so far, then it would a good bet to recommend customer B product Z. The only precondition to this process is that there are overlapping rating vectors between some elements of the product range offered: the degree of similarity between two or more users or their rating vectors can be determined using mathematical processes such as Euclidean distance.

The strength of this approach is that documented past behaviour can be used to create a proactive system which points to the next purchase in the future.

The weakness, however, is that this system requires a basic stock of data about preferences before it can start to compare profiles, an issue known as the "cold start problem"; another weakness is that each customer will only ever acquire an infinitesimal percentage of the products made available by an e-commerce provider, meaning that purchase data is, compared to the whole product range, sparse.

A way to get around these issues is to combine the two approaches into a **hybrid recommender system**, using elements from both content-based and collaborative filtering along with other data which may have been collected. The cold-start problem, for example, can be circumvented by applying rules-based matching to customers for whom there is still too little by way of data for a collaborative approach; this allows recommendations to be generated from the fist purchase on and is even more effective if the customers can be persuaded to share their age and place of residence, or if this information can be garnered from their Facebook profile.

Beyond the cold start – and especially for shops with a high number of daily clicks – **machine learning** can lead not only to better recommendations, but above all to slimline, time-saving processes. While defining business rules, for instance, remains the preserve of humans, getting a machine to compare them with data collected about the search and buying behaviour and characteristics of users, and then refine the rules according to the data, can save a huge amount of time – and allow shop operators to buy in the mathematical and business knowledge needed to carry out this kind of in depth analysis without labour and wage costs. The only prerequisite is that the webshop feeds in the correct data into the machine learning system (which can, of course, also mine external datasets, too) and soon enough, it will soon be churning out personalised results – which it in turn independently refines even further as long as data keeps being fed in.

Pro tip

Information about users' ages, and what to do about this, throws up a whole range of interesting questions for professional sales strategists. In women's fashion, for example, a given customer's strong preference for extra-tight, bright-pink jeans may lessen with increasing age and maturity: tastes change, and it might well be an accurate reflection of reality to delete information about this kind of purchase from profiles after a certain period of time has elapsed to make sure that recommendations don't start to jar.

A step further, however, is to not apply, but retain such data and use it to produce sophisticated personalisation results based on life-cycles: if a women's fashion customer regularly orders babyclothes and nappies in increasing sizes, this information might be used to start recommending toddlers' and then children's clothes at a certain point in the future.

In the streaming business, however, no data about previously viewed films and programmes is ever deleted. Why? Because if a subscriber has, say, spent years watching horror films and then suddenly switches to schmaltzy rom-coms, it is probably not a sign that his or her tastes have changed, but that he or she is now living with someone. If, however, in a few years, a horror film suddenly crops up again – either due to a relationship breakdown or simply because the most intensive part of the cocooning phase has passed – the streaming service still knows precisely what kind of horror films used to be the customer's favourite and can start recommending these again.

Personal address

Once recommendations have been generated, they need to be shown to users as soon as they are identified in the shop. This might happen quite blatantly on the landing page, a portion of which can be reserved for the "Our recommendations for you" carousel; recommendations can, however, be served in far more subtle ways, too. The actual layout of the website, for example, can be changed to suit the user based on recommendations generated, making sure that each user gets shown the most relevant categories; a slightly less all-out approach is to modify navigation aids in order to direct users away from areas of the webshop for which they are unlikely to show interest.

Conversely, users may actively request recommendations: anyone who willingly links their Amazon and Facebook accounts is most likely doing so in the knowledge that Amazon can access more data for its recommendation engine and in the hope that this will lead to more useful suggestions. Joining the two can provide customers with a genuine value-add inasmuch as Amazon begins to generate recommendations which are not just personalised, but relevant to the present moment: i.e. a Facebook friend's birthday might lead to a gift idea being served. Recommendations can be addressed to customers outside of the network and shop sphere, too, serving as the basis for targeted online advertising (see 2.3 Marketing).

Then again, whether in the shop or "out in the wild", recommendations are something of a double-edged sword.

While even a rudimentary recommendation engine can remember more faces and recall more preferences than the best of human sales assistants, what the machines cannot do is reliably recognise whether their suggestions suit the context at hand – or whether they are perhaps too accurate. After all, if a given recommendation really suits the customer, it is quite likely that he or she may have already acquired the item in question elsewhere: in fact, he or she may even be wearing or using it as the recommendation is served. Or perhaps the recommendation is accurate, but so blindingly obvious that it needn't be suggested, meaning that the customer sees it as uninteresting or, worse, unwelcome spam. Taking the leap from precision to empathy will be difficult for the engines, but whether they manage it or not, they can certainly already produce predictions about potentially interesting products that are by no means devoid of value and certainly lead some customers to click on the product page in question – and make a purchase.

Product pages

There are range of functions which are at once essential for product pages and difficult to execute in e-commerce; for while online shopping may make it easier for prospective customers to locate and compare items at speed, what it cannot do is offer them physical products to try on or try out.

This makes it all the more necessary for product pages to offer as much easily accessible information as possible and to use photos, videos, and interactive functions to make sure that any uncertainty users have about the item is removed: nobody likes to buy sight unseen. This means that all of the key product data – i.e. the specification, dimensions, notable features – must be provided in as **comprehensive**, **comprehensible** a way as possible with a maximum of **multi-media** presentation.

Product texts

Written statements about products must achieve several goals at once, informing users quickly and effectively about the product in question while also taking into account search engine optimisation concerns (SEO, see 2.1 and 2.3) as search engines – Google above all – still rely mainly on text.

SEO best practice for written texts is an issue for a whole range of industries. Besides e-commerce professionals, online media outlets spend a lot of time thinking about how to write and structure texts on their websites in such a way as to gain a high degree of visibility in organic search results. For many years, the prevailing opinion across all sectors was that each article should revolve around a defined keyword and that this word should be worked into the writing as much as possible – which was all very well in principle, but was nigh-on the exact opposite of what makes writing worth reading. A text about lamps, for example, in which every second world is "lamp" is horrible to read and by necessity uninformative, and the ease with which this kind of second-rate copy could climb in the search results spurred Google on to make changes to its algorithms – and even intervene manually – to push this kind of material back down the rankings. Today, Google recognises and punishes overly-strong keyword density and is generally better at distinguishing between texts produced for its readers' and texts produced for its own sake.

This is good news for copywriters, who can now go back to writing for readers without worrying that this will put their material at a competitive disadvantage. In terms of SEO, the principal concern today is simply to make sure that each product has its own text; even if there are only minimal differences between the various versions of a given product, each page for each version must have a text which is different to all the others, as search engines recognise duplicate content and rank the pages with it lower. What is more, two different texts are always better than one as they increase the sheer amount of words listed and therefore the chances that words will be included which users enter into search machines. If several pages do have to carry identical content, then this should at least be marked as such so that search engines do not automatically downgrade the material.

Customers, meanwhile, do not want texts stretched out beyond their natural length.

Each and every sentence should be checked for what information it is actually offering about the product in question. Moreover, texts should always be considered in combination with the standardised lists or tables which are often provided (e.g. size and colour for clothes and shoes, or package size and weight).

Actually describing what makes a product text good is very difficult, of course: you know one when you read it, but writing one is no easy feat. Nevertheless, the pitfalls to avoid are quite clear; and a product text which avoids making any the following five common errors will generally be well produced.[4]

1. **Excessive focus on (frequently fallacious) facts:** A product text is more than just a list of facts, especially if these facts are abstract qualities. A light-bulb which has a lifespan of 10,000 hours means very little to the average consumer, who might prefer information about its average length of service in standard household usage.

2. **Excessive superlatives:** While some words might be perfect in a spoken conversation between a salesperson and a customer, they can quickly rob a written text of its credibility. On the screen, words like "brilliant", "top quality", or "best value" are revealed for what they are: empty window-dressing. Customers would like to assume that everything they are offered is of good quality and value: saying something about the specific product is far more convincing.

3. **Excessive (nice, special, luxury, exclusive, select) adjectives:** The same principle applies to adjectives which often find their way into product texts: it ought to go

4 www.t3n.de (as in March 2015)

without saying that everything on sale has been selected for its special qualities. Adjectives have their place, but only when describing an actual attribute of the product which is not obvious, either from the visual material or the standard product information.

4. **Insufficient personality:** None of this means that product texts should be boring – far from it! Interest and character, however, don't come from empty words, but from imagining the customer who will be reading the text and responding in it to questions they are likely to have after having read the standard information. Any text which doesn't address issues customers might still be pondering – or have suddenly thought of – after going through the product data might as well be canned completely.

5. **Insufficient proofing:** Although customers generally don't check the dictionary before entering search terms (see above), they do expect people writing product descriptions to have done so. Every product text should ideally be proof-read by a fresh pair of eyes before going live: the advantage of having a second person check the text is not only the ease with which another reader can spot spelling mistakes, but also that this first reader can play the role of the user: is this text answering my questions? Is it interesting and informative? The reader is better at this kind of feedback than the writer.

Product photos and videos

In many product segments, however, product texts pale in importance next to product photos and videos: fashion items, for example – which make up the lion's share of all e-commerce sales, by the way – are almost always bought on the basis of the photo. Not just in clothing, images of products have the dual role of triggering the "Want!" buy impulse and also providing information in much the same way as text, and these two tasks can be divided into two visual areas: while the whole-product shot needs to produce the "Wow!" factor, detailed close ups with powerful zoom functions can be used to inform. If this latter function is neglected and customers are not offered high-resolution images from a variety of angles and perspectives, they feel limited in their ability to examine the product and begin to have doubts: is there perhaps a small detail somewhere I won't like, but won't notice until I get the product? A customer who has had to return a jumper they ordered precisely because it looked simple, mono-coloured, and smart, only to discover that it featured a loud "designer patch" or some supposedly amusing morsel emblazoned across the shoulders ("So *that's* why there was no photo of the back!"), will be unlikely to make that mistake again. Trying to sell products with a lack of photos is simply asking for cost-sapping returns (see 2.6) – and a real turn-off to savvy customers.

With fashion items, for example, a large photo featuring a model should be used to show the piece to its best advantage as part of an outfit – whose other components of course make great recommendations (see above) – to generate immediate user interest. Detailed shots of the product without a model, and/or super-zoom on the main image allow prospects whose attention the item has caught to examine it in more depth, ideally down to the last millimetre: what do the seams on those jeans look like up close? Do I like the decorative pattern on that belt buckle? Shoes, especially, require a range of shots from various perspectives: what is the sole like? How does the shoe look to the person wearing it when it is on the foot? 360° imaging can be used to offer as complete a view of the product as possible, while films offer the best way to demonstrate products which having moving parts or are made to move or be used in motion.

Technical progress is making this kind of advanced product presentation ever more broadly applicable.

Automatic photo production[5] is opening up perspectives such as "clothing" stock-photos of models: ten years back, shooting the entire season's collection would have taken several days, various live models, stylists, and photographers in a studio or on a location hired specifically for the purpose; today, the collection can be shot with two stylists and a mobile mini-studio in under 24 hours. So it's goodbye to all those oh-so-stressful long-haul trips to sun-drenched sandy beaches that photographers, models, and stylists alike used to complain about so loudly and hello to dramatically lower costs for manufacturers and merchants. It's the solution that suits everybody, right?

The next step in online clothes shopping will be the ability for customers to virtually "try on" individual pieces and whole outfits, and simpler versions are already a reality. OTTO in Germany has tested a system in which users can select a model to "put on" the clothes they are interested in in various colours and sizes; a range of models is available, meaning that most users can find a roughly suitable alter-ego for the purposes. The same software used for automatic photo production is

5 www.looklet.com for instance (as in March 2015)

then applied as customers select the clothes they want to "take into the changing room". It won't be long until this concept is developed further into real augmented reality, allowing customers to create avatars with their own measurements and photos; the virtual versions will then show customers exactly how a specific size or cut fits their own body. The changing room and the mirror held up by the shop assistant are about to go digital.

Preventing returns

While this may read like needlessly expensive, somewhat self-indulgent technical finery or, depending on your politics, part of the broad-fronted assault on paid employment, this kind of virtual testing will actually be decisive in turning low-margin online-shops profitable – not only, but especially, in fashion. At the moment, returns are a serious issue: some customers will buy the same t-shirt in three sizes so that they can try it on in their very own "changing room" in the comfort of their own homes. Once they've got the right size, they return the other two to the retailer, who – in most cases and in most territories – is obliged to accept the return and, often enough, to cover return shipping costs, too. This state of affairs is due to a complex mixture of consumer behaviour, statutory regulations, and market competition: customers cannot be entirely sure of what they are buying online and so will often want to able try things on/out at home with a money-back guarantee before they place an order; because of this, the US, Europe, and many other jurisdictions accord consumers statutory rights in home-shopping situations that they do not have in store.

And with online pacemakers such as Amazon offering exceptionally generous goodwill returns policies, consumer expectations are high.

In Germany, for example, home both to the language which is said to have a word for everything and to Europe's highest percentage of online returns, there is even a compound noun specially for what happens when clothes customers order the same item in a range of sizes: *Auswahlbestellung*, or "selection order"; UK retailers refer to the phenomenon less precisely as "overbuying". Yet whatever it is called and whatever the precise conditions offered, the widespread prevalence of easy, quick returns eats into profit margins like little else and simply cannot continue at current rates if many online retailers are ever going to turn serious profits. What is more, questionable returns – while perpetrated by a minority of customers –

are a genuine issue: fashion retailers trade war stories involving tuxedos returned with noticeable stains and crumpled wedding invitations in the inside pockets and cocktail dresses which come back in, more cocktail than dress, because they "didn't fit right" (see 2.6 Logistics).

Away from the darker sides of fast-fashion and consumer culture, returns in other segments such as furniture or home entertainment can be even more damaging for retailers: flat-pack furniture bought online is generally assembled before the home shopper, spanner in hand, realises that it isn't quite right for the room. Once the wardrobe, sideboard, or chest of drawers in question has, however, been delivered, put together, taken apart again, and returned, most of it can't be resold and gets taken to the Big Wood-Chip Shredder in the Sky. Yet any company looking to sell furniture online has to come up with serious alternatives before it can even think of restricting its returns policy, which explains why some in the industry are developing their own augmented reality solutions which insert the piece into a photo of the space for which it is intended, showing the customer exactly what it will look like before it is bought and assembled.

While this kind of technical advance must clearly be the path of choice , allowing retailers to use multimedia, customisable solutions to reduce costs without castigating their customers, until augmented reality becomes, well, reality, there are low-tech sticking-plasters: customer reviews, for example, especially written in response to descriptions and photos. After all, a customer who bought a product in an online shop based on the information found there with a specific set of expectations is one step ahead of the customer considering a purchase and can alert other prospects to unexpected features or gaps in the product information, allowing them to gain a "customer-eye view" of the product as well as the sales text (see below).

Dynamic information

Besides key product data and information and images, online shops also need to offer up-to-the-minute dynamic information which may vary strongly hour for hour or, in larger operations, even in a matter of seconds.

The most important non-static items of information are as follows:

- availability
- delivery time
- price (and any discounts)
- shipping costs
- customer ratings/reviews (if applicable)

Making sure that this kind of fluctuating information is shown in real-time is of the utmost importance: there is no other way to show availability accurately than to link the front-end to the inventory control and ERP systems; if this interface is lacking or faulty, then the classic "waiter-kitchen problem" is bound to rear its head – who doesn't get annoyed when they've ordered a dish only to find out is off the menu for the rest of the day, but not until the waiter comes back to the table after passing on the order? Customers are, however, less piqued if the lack of availability is communicated before they place their orders. Yet making sure that this occurs is a thorny issue for larger online shops and, above all, multichannel systems with various stocks and shops. If a stationary store is also serving as the warehouse for online sales, then the online availability must be updated with every sale; for larger operations such as Amazon, Otto, or John Lewis, a specific challenge arises in showing accurate availability in the front end without the product pages having to send sustained requests to the back end; this volume of internal traffic could lead to a slowing of processes and loading speeds.

Showing accurate delivery times is another tall order which entails further complexity inasmuch as it is not simply an internal inventory matter, but dependent on external factors: systems for producing delivery schedules must be able to understand whether the item can be express-dispatched with existing logistics suppliers – and at what cost. Furthermore, used cleverly, the delivery time can generate an order even when the item is not actually available: if the retailer has been caught short and needs to order in more, or if the manufacturer is not able to supply at the rate required, being able to at least put an exact date on a future delivery is often enough to reassure a prospective customer, who will then place an order and be prepared to wait. Even for items which can be dispatched immediately, the more exact the delivery date, the better, since customers need this information to plan – and perhaps even alter their working times – to be at home to receive goods; they are understandably nonplussed if the information given about delivery turns out to be inaccurate. In fact, dependability beats speed in a majority of cases: many customers would rather get their package in two days' time – but actually get it then – rather than be told that it might come tomorrow, only for it not to arrive.

The price, too, should be linked up to the ERP system to make sure that any discounts or increases are reflected immediately in the online shop. Discounts should, for obvious psychological reasons, be displayed next to the original price (this latter preferably crossed out in red) while shipping costs should also be displayed, but not included in the headline price, also due to sales psychology considerations.

Customer ratings and reviews

On a large number of online shops, ratings and reviews by customers are now standard features of product pages; while ratings are quantitative and generally displayed as 1-5 stars, reviews are qualitative, i.e. written texts about the customer experience.

The popularity of this user-generated content among webshop operators is due primarily to the results of a range of studies; these have shown not only that online shoppers see them as more credible sources than either advertising or e-mail newsletters, but also that positive reviews produce noticeable increases in prospects' probability of buying.

The high level of trust users place in other users' opinions is only assured, however, if these opinions have patently been written by *bona fide* customers: nothing looks more suspicious than 5 out of 5 stars all the way through and a litany of lackadaisical praise: "Absolutely brilliant!" "Fantastic!" "Just what I was looking for!" What customers like are detailed reviews based on other customers' experiences: *why* was the product good? Was there anything unexpected that the customers writing didn't notice until they got the article? Do they still like it now that they've been using it for more than a few hours? Does the product wear well and stand up to everyday use? The only way to offer this kind of content is, of course, to let customers write it. This, however, solves one issue and then opens up another can of worms: how can customers be motived to rate and review products? How can external, non-professional content be produced in such a way as it is of use to others? How can reviews be checked for unfair, unjustified, or – in the worst case – plain insulting content?

This is an area in which Amazon shows everyone else how it is done. Quantitive feedback with 1-5 stars is visually simple and allows the user to gain an immediate impression of the popularity of the product. The reviews then provide more detail and, crucially, other users can rate reviews on how helpful they were: this is an important meta-level which saves both Amazon and users time by promoting reviews which are good and flagging up problematic content or abuse; this in turn increases the trust users place in the reviews to an even greater degree. Users who consistently write reviews others consider helpful are then offered Vine membership, allowing them to get free products from partner retailers or manufacturers who want their products reviewed. Reviews and ratings can, however, be elicited without freebies simply by inviting customers to give their opinions in an e-mail after their purchase – and by then making it as easy as possible for them to enter text.

None of this makes the question of what to do about poor ratings or negative reviews any less delicate. As long as they are not in the majority, however, the best course of action is to keep calm, both in order to uphold the trustworthiness of the review system (users see if their bad feedback has been deleted – and then get *really* mad) and as part of an overall customer-focussed approach. After all, whether good or bad, reviews are actually valuable personal feedback which online shop operators – never actually seeing their customers – do not otherwise get.

> *Pro tip*
> Requests sent to customers asking them to review products should include the 1-5 star selection or a "top/flop" thumb icon in the actual e-mail: if the user clicks on a star or the thumb, this can directly be tracked and, that way, even if the user doesn't follow the link to the landing page and start typing away, the e-mail has still provided a rating if nothing else.

2.3 Marketing

Introduction

In e-commerce, the marketing as a discipline takes on a far higher importance than in classic retail models: after all, an online shop gets no "footfall" simply by opening its doors. On the digital shopping street, customers may be numerous and their needs may be more visible than ever before (see 2.1 Procurement), shops may be more customer-friendly and more systematically structured than ever (see 2.2. Product presentation); but on the down-side, customers don't simply walk past and take a look in the shop windows. In fact, they don't even notice that there is a shop there unless someone points it out to them.

In the bricks-and-mortar world, it's often a question of "location, location, location": a newsagents will do better if it is situated in a railway station or on the corner of a lively residential street than if it is, say, halfway down a little-used roadway in the middle of nowhere. For this type of stationary retail space, the number of people going past who suddenly feel the need for a can of coke or a bottle of water is the decisive factor. If, however, you are looking to sell drinks on the internet, you can't do this "in a residential area" or rent a profitable outlet at a busy railway station: there are plenty of websites for rail operators and stations, but none of them are in the business of selling refreshments.

As recently as ten years ago, there was still no shortage of people who thought that there would eventually be a kind of "map" on the internet based on domain names and URLs representing certain products and services: in the boom years, domainers could make big money by speculating on "cyber real estate", registering everything kind of generic name with various country code top-level domains (shopping.com, shopping.co.uk, shopping.de), later "flipping" the addresses to companies looking to open up online shops. Yet as it turned out, customers didn't automatically type "shoes.com" into their URL bar when looking to buy shoes online, but instead went to shops that attracted customers on the internet in other ways – and often had names that were exotic or even utterly made up: Zappos.com, later Amazon.com have knocked shoes.com, bags.com, and pretty much everything-else.com into a cocked hat. In fact, Amazon has made itself into the railway station of the internet inasmuch as merchants selling products there are counting on "footfall" due to the site's enormous visitor numbers.

Nevertheless, even on Amazon, customers don't just "drop in"; merchants and, especially, online shop operators need to take their store to the customer.

Fortunately, however, it is easier to contact and address customers on the internet than ever before – and yet, by the same token, far more complicated. This paradox is due to the increasingly **multi-optional** nature of the purchasing process: 20 years back, anyone who needed a television would go to their preferred electronics retailer and search the limited range of sets on offer, selecting the one that best meet their needs; this is a **linear** purchasing process. Anyone looking for a flat-screen television today has a far broader range of options which are continually re-sorted according to the customer's requirements, location, and the degree of urgency; these options include online, offline, and mixed-channel processes.

This change from a **linear** to a **multi-optional** personal purchasing process has a range of effects on each link in the value chain. In the good old days, branded goods were sold by first making consumers aware of them: they would then go into a shop (there was little choice regarding which one) and see the product next to various competitors on the shelf. If the product happened to be the best choice for them, it was sold. If the product kept its promise and was right for consumers, they might well become loyal customers. This is, of course, a very schematic, simplified depiction of how things were: prospective buyers could always compare various shops and their prices, and could gain information from friends and acquaintances or the media and consumer literature. Yet making an informed choice required considerable effort, and consumers were unwilling to go to these lengths for anything other than larger purchases (and, even then, many were astoundingly unconcerned about comparing options). As a general principle, every time they wanted to buy something, old-style consumers entered a funnel in which their choices were limited to an ever greater extent the deeper they got inside: 1) Which shop? 2) Which product in this shop? 3) Buy now or leave this shop and start again?

Nowadays, however, consumers may well be "in the funnel" in a shop and then decide that nothing on the shelves is really what they are looking for – or that it is all too expensive by half. What is more, they don't even have to exit the store to find out what else is out there: a smartphone is their window back into the outside world. In fact, they may well buy a produce from a competing online outlet from inside a legacy store. Or, turning this on its head, consumers may well spot a product online and then find out that it is currently available in a nearby shop, or in a competing online outlet – and on offer. Ten minutes later, and the purchase has already been made or, respectively, order has already been placed.

From the sales point of view, any brand looking to win over this new type of consumer needs to make sure that their products are available both on and offline. Similarly, retailers need to make sure they can be reached via the internet and on the high street. Both need to market products in such a way as the number of touchpoints is expanded as exponentially as possible. It is simply no longer enough, as it once was, to scattergun consumers with brand advertising in the mass media and then back this up with in-store offensives in order to finally sway the customer and decide the battle at the last minute: for starters, the average consumer watches less television, listens to less radio, and reads fewer newspapers than before. He or she is spending the time that frees up on the internet – and in online shops.

Whether they are in town, at work, or on the couch: consumers today want everything, anytime and anywhere – and want to use the channel that suits them to buy it. In terms of distribution (see below, 2.4), this means offering everything on every conceivable channel; for **marketing**, it means being ready to reengage and win over consumers at every possible time and place.

Marketing in e-commerce: decisive or irrelevant?

The changes brought about by the way e-commerce broadens options make themselves felt everywhere in the marketing mix; but they are not equally pronounced in each area. While each of the 4Ps of classic marketing activity – 1. **Product**, 2. **Price**, 3. **Promotion** and 4. **Place** – is affected, e-commerce has far lesser effects on product policy than it does on pricing, promotion, and placing practice.

Above all, online shopping revolutionises place (P4). As sketched in simplified terms above, existing geographical assumptions about points of sale, sales systems, and sales channels are not valid in e-commerce; in fact, these assumptions are pretty much reversed, and this will be the topic of the following section, 2.4, in detail.

In terms of promotion (P3), the internet adds new instruments to the existing mix which are of interest even to wholly non-digital bricks-and-mortar operations and are therefore central priorities for all online or multichannel business models: social media, direct marketing, and e-mail, communication which is personal – and personalised. At the same time, e-commerce also leads to a decline in the overall importance of promotion as against the other elements of the marketing mix as, the more transparent the market becomes, the more irrelevant communication about products becomes. After all, with differences in price and service levels now clearer and easier to access on the internet than ever before, any slippage against a competitor – who is only ever one click away – cannot be masked by product promotion. Put simply, consumers cannot be duped – and are far less loyal to specific outlets than they were (or were assumed to be) in the pre-internet era.

This is why e-commerce has had tangible effects on pricing policy (P2) – and will only continue to increase the pressure on this area of marketing. Winners to date have been those who have been able to extract the maximum amount of leverage out of the five pivots of price, discount, bonuses, delivery, and payment. Amazon, Zalando, and OTTO, for example, with their strong discounts, low or no-cost delivery, and extremely customer-friendly terms of payment, are setting the tone for the industry; and now that consumers are better informed than ever – and just as price conscious as ever – other providers have no choice but to follow suit unless they are happy to see potential customers clicking away to the cheaper competition. The fall in prices has been made even more precipitous by dynamic pricing, an automated process by which prices on one portal are matched to a field of reference prices offered by competitors or adapted to user behaviour (e.g. frequency of visits to product page prior to purchase); other factors, too, such as time and weather, can be included, to make sure that prices are always competitive. The goals include increases in turnover, better profitability, or stocks clearance; the dangers, however, are damaging levels of price volatility triggered by sales initiatives among competitors which all too frequently hoover up any remaining profit margin.

The only providers unaffected by this veritable price vortex on the internet are outlets selling products which are personalised, limited, or exclusive in some other way.

For everyone else, the transparency of the internet and customer behaviour on it have made keeping a tight rein on costs and sitting on a prices a matter of sheer survival. This, by extension, has an interesting effect on product policy (P1) inasmuch as innovation, niche product ranges, and improvements to product mixes show a path out of the pricing abyss: while the market for ubiquitous standard goods is a race to the bottom, exclusivity allows products to be sold at a premium.

The other key effect of online shopping on product policy is the possibility of collecting data about which products are most popular, allowing merchants to consider manufacturing items that sell well themselves (see 2.1 Procurement).

The myth of customer lifetime value

This new state of affairs sweeps away many of the existing articles of faith with regards to the interaction between transactional and relationship marketing. The goal of **transactional marketing** is to get customers to purchase a single item: it works on short timescales, is limited to a specific product, and is successful if it does not eat away too great a portion of the margin on the product sold, giving a positive return on investment (ROI). In **relationship marketing**, however, the aim is to create a lasting bond between the customer and the company. This means that no single product is advertised, but rather a whole product range along with all the accompanying services and, in some cases, more abstract arguments such as corporate values. This is a far more costly approach and, in terms of ROI, can only be a success if it generates enough sales from the target customer during a customer life-cycle to make a positive contribution to the margin overall.

This is summed up by the idea of customer lifetime value: a consumer who gets linked to a company over a longer period of time creates profit, becoming a regular customer – i.e. returning to buy at shorter intervals and less likely to switch to other providers than another – and thus justifying the high acquisition costs (especially since, if the approach works, less transactional marketing is needed).

The only snag is that customer lifetime value is seldom achieved in e-commerce. Those offering specific products to a large "fan base" may well see a return on their investment: their customers have a high intrinsic motivation to purchase the goods in question and can therefore easily be tied to one of the few providers using relationship marketing. Private shopping clubs, for example, such as vente-privée.com or brands4friends.de, are not unwise to assume that they will see customer lifetime value: they thrive on offering products which are limited in number, have high levels of attractivity, and yet are comparatively cheap for their members; and not only are customers delighted by this opportunity, but also have the warm, fuzzy, "in-crowd" feeling of being in a limited group – a feeling which these clubs communicate in relationship marketing.

Yet in other areas, the transparency of the market and the venality of consumers as described above are more than enough to ruin marketing bottom lines for companies selling average, unspectacular products, but intending to attract and retain customers on a relationship level; promotional activities (P3) prove to be a particularly spectacular waste of money. To put no too fine a point on it, shops can send out all the personalised e-mails they want and re-target customers in every last corner of the internet with the latest technology but, if the same product is available on Amazon for £3 or $5 less – and there are no shipping charges – then they are pouring money down the drain.

Having said that, it is, of course, by no means the case that Amazon is neglecting relationship marketing: quite to the contrary. The crux of the issue is that, for a retailer the size of Amazon, relationship marketing cannot be divorced either from product or price policies (P1, P2) or from trouble-free logistics and polished customer service (see 2.6 and 2.7 for more on this). The resources Amazon devotes to developing and defending its advantage in these areas constitute, in effect, the best relationship marketing investment there is. What you won't see, however, is Amazon launching a range of expensive customer acquisition drives: the positive experience and the ease of buying on Amazon, or loyalty programmes such as Prime with its free-of-charge, next-day delivery, are the Giant's methods of choice when it comes to customer retention. In actual fact, Amazon has squared the proverbial circle and can even let its pricing slip in some areas as, eventually, customers do become creatures of habit – even on the internet.

From fulfilling demand to creating demand

It is not just the habit of buying from Amazon instead of from another provider which eventually becomes anchored, but the habit of buying from Amazon – period. While the early years of e-commerce were marked by consumers going online to fulfil specific needs which they had already formulated and considered, there has recently been a notable increase in the importance of spontaneous purchases and impulse buys on the net.

Amazon today is, more than ever before, able to trigger unplanned purchases from existing customers; this was unthinkable in the technical environment of the 1990s, in which it was nigh-on impossible to present products on the internet in an attractive, informative manner. This meant that customers tended only to buy products online which were easily identified and utterly standard: it was with books and CDs that Amazon grew in its first ten years, as books could be identified by titles, author names, and ISBN – even without pictures, if not available or accessible – and CDs could be bought without any concerns about whether they fit and whether that red is little *too* red... Customers had a very clear idea of which items they wanted to acquire; the most they could be upsold was another couple of books or another album – there was no question of selling them a pair of jeans while they were at it.

As the years went on and the connections got better, this kind of target first-time purchase was joined by target replacement purchases: if the TV was broken or the washing machine was on its last legs, consumers were happy to order a replacement online. After all, dimensions and performance were easy enough to present online even without super-high-resolution images; many customers were already in the habit of showrooming (i.e. viewing products in stores before buying online) by this point in any case; furthermore, consumers had gained experience of the previously unknown, somewhat faceless shops on the internet and now trusted them enough to spend three-figure sums there for household appliances, too.

Now, of course, consumers are in the habit of buying all sorts of product categories online which would have been considered impossible to sell on the internet a decade ago: there is no longer any inhibition about ordering big-ticket items off the net, and the continuous improvements in product presentation (see 2.2. Product presentation) and favourable returns policies (see 2.6 Logistics) make it quite possible to offer products online which are more specific to customers, more personalised, and require more sales consultation than, say, books and fridges. What is more, the advent of social media means that friends don't just go shopping together on a Saturday afternoon, but post their purchases during the week. We are now on the threshold of a new era of e-commerce in which online shops will be able to pull off a trick formerly the preserve of high street shops and supermarket check-outs: websites will soon reliably be able to provoke a spontaneous "want" feeling, i.e. generate an impulse buy.

This means that e-commerce must start to concentrate on **creating demand**, rather than just **fulfilling needs**, all the while making sure not to neglect **brand awareness**; and while it certainly may have lost its potency as compared to other marketing instruments (see above), promotion (P3) must not be ignored. After all, those price, product, and sales policies won't communicate themselves.

Nevertheless, the mix of communications tools
is more diverse than ever:
with the purchasing process
moving from linear to multi-optional,
the promotional accompaniments have also become
multi-modal and multimedia.

The internet has opened up an array of new marketing channels that are enough to give old-school marketing managers who already had trouble keeping track of newspapers, broadcast media, flyers, billboards, and mailshots panic attacks. Not that any of these "old media" channels is "dead", by the way, as digital evangelists like to claim – even online pure-plays such as Zalando can be found printing catalogues and paying for poster boards – but their role has be relativised by the proliferation of new forms of advertising on the internet.

The pace of change is relentless and the confusion sown palpable. In academic research groups and marketing departments across the sector, classifications for these new channels are designed, implemented, and then consigned to the waste-paper basket: some like to organise the various instruments by their role in brand as against performance marketing, while others prefer to distinguish between online and offline marketing tools, which are the subdivided into on and offsite as against radio, TV, and out-of-home respectively. Yet whatever the categorisation approach used, the borders are porous: location-targeted marketing on consumer smartphones may strengthen a brand while triggering an impulse buy as it goes – where does the brand awareness campaign end and performance marketing on a transactional basis start? And what to make of guerrilla marketing offensives which are decidedly offline – i.e. happen on the street – but don't unfold their real potential until they "go viral" on YouTube?

The increasing level of blend between formats became clear in 2010 with the "Old Spice Guy" Isaiah Mustafa. Remember him? You might not, but with a series of eccentric, mildly amusing videos featuring him and his chest, shot to cinema-trailer quality, Old Spice managed to rack up eight-digit viewing figures on YouTube. What is more, the campaign allowed viewers to ask Isaiah questions on a variety of social media platforms, turning him into a popular expert on men's grooming (and broader issues of "manliness"); once the initial buzz on the web was established, the material was available for TV commercials and posters to boot. Right from the beginning, this "viral video campaign" was in fact the overture to a far broader marketing initiative covering a range of media[6].

Half a decade into this kind of environment, the only means of categorising promotional activities which really retains any usefulness is one working with aims, not formats: while some of the YouTube viewers back in 2010 *might* have rushed out to the nearest drugstore to buy and try a bottle of Old Spice – and other existing customers might have been reminded that they needed to go stock up – the overall aim of the

6 See socialfresh, https://www.socialfresh.com/old-spice-viral-videos/ as of March 2016

campaign was to increase **brand awareness**. Many of the other follow-up adverts featuring Isaiah, however, such as online advertising across the web, were more intended to **create demand** while specific point-of-sale measures with his impressive torso were orientated towards customers looking to **fulfil demand** that was already there.

Pull-marketing: fulfilling demand

Nine times out of ten, online customers who already have a good idea of what they would like to buy will open a browser window and head for their favourite search engine (and that is still very likely to be Google). Their first priority is to get basic information about the product they want and find out where they can buy it. If it turns out to be available on the internet, there is quite a high chance that they will either buy it immediately, or return later on to make the purchase. Even if the product in question isn't available online or they don't want to buy it online for other reasons, customers will now be better informed about it if they come across it in the high street or at the mall.

Of course, this account only applies when we are talking about an existing requirement: the customers in question have demand and have gone to their computers and smartphones looking to fulfil it: this is classic "lean forward" behaviour, and while customers are actively searching on the internet, there is a range of marketing instruments which can be applied which either draw them straight into the shop of a specific provider or, at the very least, increase the chances of them noticing it.

Search engine marketing: SEO & SEA

Search engine marketing (generally abbreviated to **SEM**) is about reaching potential customers when they are searching on Google, Bing, and – increasingly – site-internal engines such as Amazon's A9 for a specific product or service. SEM subdivides into two disciplines: **search engine optimisation** (or **SEO**) and **search engine advertising** (**SEA**).

In the case of **SEO**, the aim is to achieve the highest position possible in the organic search results: customers should, when they enter a specific product into Google, see the shop in question on the first page of the search results (the top spot being, of course, the holy grail). A huge amount of effort is poured into achieving this aim – and quite rightly so, as users will only click through to the second or third page of the search results if they do not immediately find something remotely approaching what they are looking for on page one. Put bluntly: a shop on the second page will lose trade to a competitor placed on the first.

As a discipline, SEO covers all measures which can be taken to improve this organic ranking and is defined against SEA inasmuch as the advertising boxes are placed next to, above, or between the organic results and are reserved for fee-paying clients who book them with the search engine operator (see below). That doesn't mean that SEO is free, of course, but costs for it occur within the company or are paid to service providers; no money changes hands between the company looking to optimise and the company running the search engine.[7]

The core task of SEO is therefore to understand how the algorithms in search engines run in order to adapt websites to them.

And this is no easy task: the major search engines' algorithms are protected from competitors and the public in the same way as Coca Cola's secret recipe. Yet some things are obvious from examining a glass of Coke, while others have seeped through into the public domain: certainly, cinnamon, ginger, and citrus flavours are key ingredients. The same is true of Google inasmuch as, for all the actual algorithm may be a secret and will always remain one, there is no shortage of conclusions which may be drawn about it.

One of the things that has been common knowledge for years is that, between two pages which contain the same search term, Google ranks the page with more links from third parties higher: Google sees links to a website as proof of interest in it and, by extension, of relevance to the person initiating the search enquiry. It is also well known that Google works with keywords: a keyword is a word which is in the search entered (the search may even consist in it) or which Google assigns to the search; pages featuring this specific keyword several times are listed above sites on which it is less frequent. Beyond this, Google evaluates its own search results by tracking whether the user returns again a few seconds later: if they do, the algorithm notes that the site, despite having a high density of the keyword searched, did not carry content of interest to the person searching, and ranks it lower next time. This process is one reason why "keyword stuffing" – a practice which includes everything from disfiguring copy with excessive use of the same keyword to including it one hundred times over in a specific box rendered invisible by making the text small and matching it to the background colour – is no longer effective. A whole range of other measures of website quality, including the regularity with which content is changed and the date of the most recent update, is also included in deciding the order in which search results are displayed.

7 Kreutzer (2014), Praxisorientiertes Online-Marketing

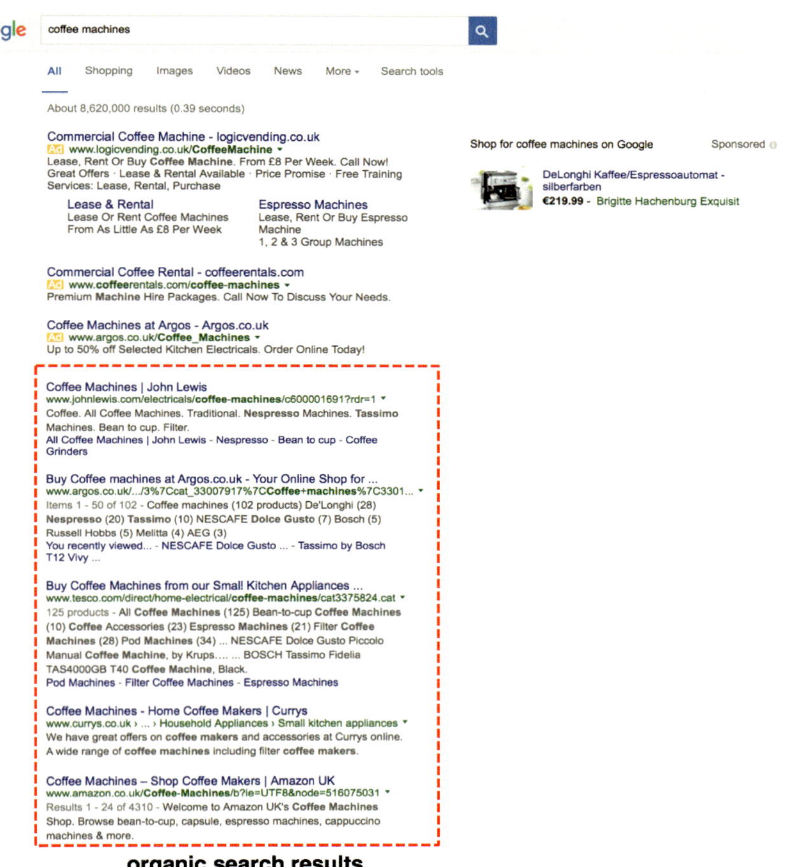

Fig. 2.12: Screenshot showing organic search results (SEO)
Source: www.google.co.uk (as of March 2016)

Measures derived from what is known about how search engines work can be sorted into a pyramid of priority (see figure 2.13). At its base, it rests on quality content: texts which the site operators have created, not ripped from elsewhere; a clearly structured set of URLs and pages which are interlinked and lead the user through the site. The first thing that becomes clear is that even the best agency in the world cannot do much with a site built on sloppy or copied content and lacking a clear structure. Keywords are only important in the second step in the pyramid: the challenge here is to identify the keywords which are important and then to integrate them into the right part of the site at the right rate. Step three is about links: who can be persuaded to include a link to the site and how? The tip of the pyramid is social media: i.e. if all goes well, content which spreads around Facebook or circulates on Twitter and which draws in links back to the website.

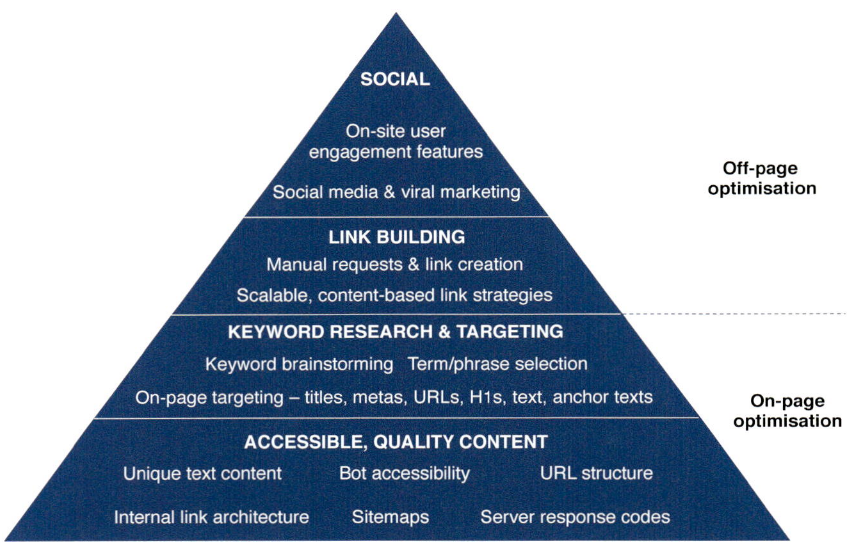

Fig. 2.13: SEO pyramid (on-page and off-page optimisation)
Source: with reference to moz.com/blog/whiteboard-friday-the-seo-fundamentals-pyramid (as in March 2016)

The exciting news for website operators is that each of these four elements in the pyramid can perfectly well be achieved without advertising agencies. While it might pay to consult with experts about keywords and the precise density of them required, this isn't always necessary either. On the downside, however, SEO is a process, not a campaign: if new products or new pages are added to an online shop, then these too must have texts optimised with the right keywords so as to be easily identified by search engines, and must also be conceived to be attractive in a social media environment.

This means that there is never an end to SEO – and even if a website never changes, the rules of SEO always do, so that existing texts must be re-examined recurrently to make sure they conform to the latest standards. Google, above all, continually amends its algorithms both as part of its never-ending quest to provide search results which customers want and, not least, in order to make sure that no one site can optimise its way to the top spot and then make itself comfortable. Changes to algorithms are therefore a way of stopping webshop operators relying too heavily on specific SEO strategies: quite simply, Google doesn't want to be gamed.

Another challenge is not just the search engine itself, but the competition who, generally, will have access to roughly the same information about how the algorithms are currently operating. This levels the playing field and allows even complete newcomers to knock old hats out of the top ten if they have better optimised content and manage to weave a broader web of links. What is more, the "top ten" in Google terms is actually now more like the "top three", because the Universal Search approach now includes results from Google Maps, video, and even ads from paid-for Google Shopping: while once displayed on their own discrete pages, they are now taking up space on the headline search and putting the squeeze on classic, organic search results. The competition for the top spaces has never been so intense.

So shops looking to achieve and/or defend a high Google ranking need to devote corresponding resources to the job. On the plus side, however, the long-term nature of SEO as a discipline means that the costs, however high, remain stable.

In the discipline of **search engine advertising (SEA)**, however, it is quite the contrary: since advertising space for keywords is auctioned off online, paying for ads to be shown next to the organic search results for popular keywords can be a very pricey and highly unpredictable business; the more competitors on the word in question, the higher the price tag.

While successful SEO can place a shop higher up in the results for specific searches in the long term and make it generally easier to find on the internet, SEA is more about achieving short-term gains, generally for specific products or sales drives. Both for this reason and due to the high costs, especially in competitive product segments, SEA campaigns tend to be run for defined periods of time with one specific goal in mind: upping traffic to a shop overall, for example, or getting customers to buy a certain product in the online shop; in some cases, the advert might even be for an bricks-and-mortar store. This means that the core tasks of SEA are defining relevant keywords and developing the relevant advertising for it, then setting the maximum spend and the timeframe of the campaign, as well as deciding which search engines should be included.[8]

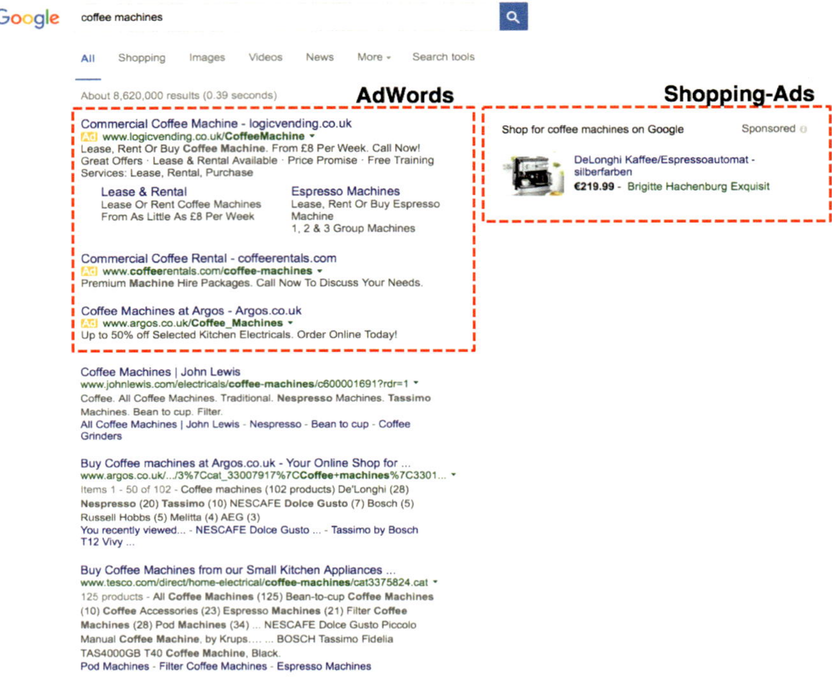

Fig. 2.14: Screenshot showing search engine adverts (SEA)
Source: www.google.co.uk (as in March 2016)

In terms of selecting keywords, the craft is to weigh up the relevance of search terms from the points of view of the person searching, the company selling, and the competition. Ideal keywords to pay for are those which are searched for by potential customers, are relevant to the company's product range, and have thus far been neglected by competitors. Keyword adverts then need to be designed to actually get prospects to click on them: they are, after all, not the organic search results most users focus their attention on and therefore need to do the running.

8 Lammenett 2012, *Praxiswissen Online-Marketing*, p. 124 ff.

This means making sure that an advantage to the customer is made immediately clear: "Full range of...", "Great prices on..." It is also important to communicate any time-limits in play as a psychological trigger: "Only one day left get your 10% discount!" An intelligent ruse is to develop several different versions of a specific advert and test them out against each other, noting success rates. Nevertheless, search adverts should never be *too* creative: Google, for example, carries out regular quality checks to make sure that adverts accurately reflect the contents on the page linked to. If users bounce straight back to Google from an advert, the algorithm will flag this and questions will be asked.

The trickiest part of SEA is budgeting. The most attractive parts of the search engine page with the highest click rates are auctioned off to the highest bidder: companies looking to book these "hot spots" generally enter the maximum amount they want to pay the search engine per user click, and this means that an area of the page with a lot of clicks can very quickly make for sky-high bills if the price at auction was high, too. It is therefore key to set daily or weekly budgets and to monitor these, as mistakes or mis-estimations can lead to eyewatering invoices for companies booking search engine advertising: a worst-case scenario is an advert attracting far more clicks than planned and tearing through a budget not defined tightly enough, yet without generating any noticeable increase in turnover in the webshop. This makes it essential to carry out regular evaluations of all adverts booked, the maximum bids entered, and the budget burn-rate and reach ROI-based decisions.

Push-marketing: creating demand

Away from search engines, the aim of online advertising is to reach consumers while they are enjoying – not searching for – content; while reading online news media or watching YouTube, for example, consumers are in "lean-back" mode, having found what they are looking for and relaxing into their desk chairs or sinking into their sofas.

Online advertising: display ads, affiliates

Not, of course, that advertisers are happy to leave them that way. Google AdWords, for example, doesn't just sell space on the Google search engine page, but also offers its clients the option of advertising elsewhere on the internet; a lot of websites sell space for **online advertising** in the form of banners, rectangles, or background wallpaper to Google and other providers such as Tradedoubler or adconion. From hobby blogs who, on a very good day, might make a hundred dollars through to major international news media websites looking to finance a big chunk of their activities with the takings, the advertising networks are composed of a broad spectrum of websites on which they can place clients' **display ads**, whether static, animated, or even in full video form with accompanying audio.

Another form of online advertising is the **affiliate marketing** model, in which a shop operator produces adverts for its sales partners for them to place on their websites, include in customer mailings, or even include in their own keyword ads. The sales partner then receives commission if a customer comes into the shop through the link the partner has advertised.

In fact, this type of performance-related payment is a key feature of online advertising, whether in its affiliate or network form.

Costs are not generally incurred until a user has clicked on the advert displayed and entered the shop (cost-per-click model) or, in some cases, until a user has made – and then not later cancelled – a purchase (commission model). In between and beyond, there are a range of remuneration practices, from sales commissions through to overall turnover shares, from provision on second-time purchases through to a fee for each new customer registration in the webshop or each new newsletter subscriber; the overall aim of the advertising initiative – e.g. whether it is transactional or brand-orientated – is often the determiner of which precise arrangement or combination of arrangements is made.

What all of the models have in common is that, in comparison to classic print advertising or TV commercial slots, they are cheap. Actual click-through rates, especially on standard display ads, are remarkably low – and is anyone surprised? Who out there hasn't been driven to distraction by areas of animated advertising which, even in this age of broadband and 4G, are enough to slow down loading times or even crash a browser? And then there's everyone's favourite, the pop-up ad, pouncing on unsuspecting users in a new browser window, often with obstreperous music or an annoying voiceover... This kind of spamming has made online advertising one of the most hated forms of publicity on the internet: while search engine advertising is at least shown with a clear link to whatever it is that users is currently looking for and – placed next to the actual results in low-key text boxes – does not distract them, display adverts elsewhere on the internet are generally unbearably intrusive and bear scandalously little relation to the needs of the individual user.

The original idea was that, similarly to viewers of advertising-funded television channels, internet users would willingly enter into a sort of trade-off in which they would enjoy content free of cost and expose themselves to a continuous stream of advertising in return. The problem, however, is that they won't. Internet users have an almost unlimited selection of content at their fingertips, just a few clicks away, and so are able to select between sites overloaded with advertising and webpages which are more considerate of their needs; more radically, they can simply download an ad-blocker and enjoy whatever it is they wanted to read without any of the annoyingly loud, frilly window-dressing.

*Rightly or wrongly,
users are by and large
simply unwilling to accept online advertising
unless it is suited to their needs.*

The average TV viewer is in "lean back" mode (see below) and so might turn a blind eye to the odd commercial for incontinence pads and cholesterol-lowering margarine (regardless of their state of his or her own bladder or heart respectively) so that the show can continue; what is more, if the advert really is annoying, he or she can simply switch channels or go and get something to drink. Anyone in "lean forward" mode looking for information in a browser is going to be far less receptive to unsuited advertising.

The hope for online advertising therefore lies in improving its targeting processes. After all, contrary to television channels or newspapers, ad-servers such as Google AdWords are well positioned when it comes to their ability to show different adverts to different users. In fact, why display one ad to all users at all when each and every user provides sufficient data to allow educated guesses about their interests? The idea isn't revolutionary, of course: Google had it ten years ago with its search engine adverts, hypothesising quite correctly that, if a user is searching for something, this is a hard-and-fast indication of what his or her interests might be. The key was using the short delay between the search term being entered and the search results being presented to find and serve a suitable advert: Google mastered the challenge and now **real-time bidding** allows whole advertising networks to recognise user input and data and offer the advertising space on the site to companies with an interest in advertising there; these companies will have set their maximum bids beforehand (just as Ebay users do), and the ad space is auctioned off in a matter of milliseconds. The winning company's ad reaches the user in real time.

In the following, we offer an overview of the tracking and targeting methods used to deduce what users may be interested in[9].

The most rudimentary or methods such as **geo-targeting** or **technical targeting**, in which information which is automatically transferred to a website by a visitor or third-party services are used to determine the location of the user and the hardware they are using. This method makes it possible to tell Mac from Windows users, for example, meaning that a MacBook user from San Francisco and somebody soldiering on with a mid-2000s Dell in Liverpool can be served adverts for suitable computing services in their home city.

Another of the simpler targeting methods is **context** or **content targeting**, allowing car advertising to be shown on pages about cars, for example; this form of targeting is agreed on between the advertising network and the client before the campaign starts. **Semantic targeting**, meanwhile, is what the network uses when it decides to match the adverts it displays to users without the involvement of the client: the content of websites it its network is scanned and machine-classified.

Tracking methods become more complicated as they zero in on individual users as opposed to user characteristics such as hardware or content being visited.

Users who can be clearly identified provide a rich source of information about themselves, of course: Facebook or registered Google account users often reveal their age, gender, and occupation. If these users then surf the net while continuously signed in to Google (SSO), or if the advertising networks in question have access to Facebook user profiles, then advertising can be served using **sociodemographic targeting** (i.e. no more incontinence pad adverts for the under 60s – unless, of course, they happen to work as carers in an old people's home...). A particularly close form of observation involves analysing the user's actual history and searches in order to target advertising: in **behavioural targeting**, for example, networks place tracking cookies on users' computers in order to log the sites they

9 Kreutzer (2014), *Praxisorientiertes Online-Marketing*, p. 175ff.

visit (the data is stored anonymously). Advertising is then shown to users based on their behaviour on the internet to date and, since this technique relies solely on cookies, users do not even have to be unambiguously identifiable by being logged in to Facebook, Google, or anything else. A step further is **retargeting**, a process by which online sellers follow users who entered their shops with cookies activated around the internet and show them advertising; the users, however, don't need to have bought anything in the shop beforehand. In fact, if a user was on the point of buying something and then aborted the transaction, the operator of the shop has good grounds for surmising that the user is interested in the product in question and can keep advertising it to them full blast.

That is how Amazon shows many customers hitting its homepage a range of articles they searched for and viewed on their last visit before they've even logged in; what is more, these products are also promoted to users by Amazon in the spaces in the shop it reserves for ads; should customers leave Amazon again, it continues to show them the products in banner display adverts on other websites. Yet this approach is, for all its technical sophistication, also a liability. One the plus side, retargeting tailors online advertising to users: anything which is genuinely unsuitable can be avoided and many such adverts rely on actual purchases in the past. Precisely this aspect, however, reveals a weak point: the server will never know why a user terminated a transaction at the last minute. Was that pair of jeans too expensive after all? Is the user ashamed of having to buy incontinence pads? Did his or her partner return with the item in question just before they pressed the order button, rendering the purchase superfluous? In any of these cases, persistent advertising of the product in question may be an annoyance more than anything else. Furthermore, servers aren't (yet) capable of distinguishing between products which consumers may well need to buy regularly and items which fulfil a specific need well for the foreseeable future. What is more, purchase-frequency is, in many respects, a matter of user psychology: while some consumers who have just bought a bathing suit may well be delighted to see an advert for more designs from the same brand, another might be less happy: "Really? They expect me to buy another pair of swimming trunks this year? The same brand and a similar colour? Do I look like a schmuck?"

To counter this issue, advertisers are increasingly placing their hopes on the next step, **predictive behavioural targeting**. The idea here is to categorise user profiles into broader user groups according to their surfing and searches thus far: the behaviour of the target group as a whole should then allow reliable hypotheses about what individual users in that group might do next; this would, in turn permit recommendations outside of areas already tracked in an approach similar to collaborative filtering (see 2.2 Product presentation). In the case of swimsuits, for example, predictive targeting would show what other users in the same target group who had also bought swimwear from the brand in question went on to look at; this is certainly a more promising route for advertisers looking not just to bombard consumers with the same products, but rather to inspire them and, perhaps, awaken their desire for a complimentary product – or even a completely different one.

Consumers are more receptive to this kind of unplanned purchase, of course, when they are not in "lean-forward" mode on the look-out for a specific product, but rather in "lean-back" mode – i.e. ready to just browse.

That is why, up to now, creating demand has been seen as the strong-point of the stationary shopping experience, with bricks-and-mortar stores considered the best environment in to surprise consumers: window displays, shelf placement, and the notorious check-out area promotions are the perfect ways to draw in customers off the street, show them new products in the shop, and get them to make unplanned purchases using children's "pester power" respectively.

Mobile ads

Recently, however, the lightning expansion in mobile technology penetration has started to rob highstreets and malls of their consumers, who are increasingly to be found using their smartphones and tablets after work and at the weekend – and using them quite differently to PCs or laptops. They might be in their armchairs or lying on the sofa, browsing through articles, dipping in and out of videos, or listening to podcasts in a more leisurely and comfortable fashion than before, when they would be stooped over a glaring computer monitor. Social networks such as Facebook and Twitter, too, are increasingly being accessed from mobile devices – often from public transport or from out on the street. In these environments, consumers are much more receptive to unsolicited advertising, as long as it is embedded in a suitable form.

Mobile ads are **display ads** served to mobile devices: banners are the simplest, downsized from stationary browser dimensions to fit the mobile versions of websites, designed for smaller screens on smartphones and tablets. Just as in PC and laptop browsers, however, display ads on mobile devices are certainly not among users' favourite parts of the mobile internet experience; then again, they do have an ace up their sleeve inasmuch as tablets and, above all, smartphones tend to be more closely tied to one single specific user. Display ads on the good old family computer in daddy's study or on a laptop shared by a couple have always been something of a loose cannon: what if, for example, dad and kids had conspiratorially gathered round to book a surprise holiday for mum – who sits down the next day only to be bombarded with adverts for cheap flights to Rome? If her husband then tells her she should make sure she's not doing anything for the week after her birthday because he's got a surprise in store, then the cover is all but blown... Mobile devices, however, are heavily personalised; the only communal mobile devices are family iPads in the living room – and these, too, are fast diversifying into individual-use tablets as prices fall.

Besides this kind of safe targeting environment, mobile applications also offer a range of advertising possibilities which are more strongly anchored within the user experience. Advertising is often inserted into audio apps such as TuneIn or Spotify feeds as **pre-stream or in-stream ads** without users aborting in any great number. Learned behaviour from the days of broadcast radio seems to have stuck as users have transferred to streaming radio stations and music on their mobiles: users are happy to accept short advertising slots if they can continue to use audio content free of charge. When linked up to targeting and real-time bidding (see above), this is a promising way of serving users adverts in which they may be interested without them resenting the intrusion.

The principle also seems to be extending beyond mobile audio onto the whole device environment: in the market for mobile apps, there is a growing consensus that users are happiest when given a choice between the option of free content with some advertising or a premium, commercial-free service for which they pay. Whether streaming services such as Spotify or newspaper and magazine apps, the model is becoming increasingly common – and, as such, increasingly tolerated by users, as long as the user experience offers a real improvement in the ease and speed of access as compared to an independent search for free content using the browser.

Social media marketing

The ultimate environment for creating new desires, however, is not tied to a specific device: social networks such as Facebook and Twitter can be accessed from PCs, tablets, and smartphones, and users make full use of this cross-platform flexibility – with an increasingly strong tendency towards mobile use, however. What is interesting about this development is that the variety of advertising formats is increasing and that advertising receives a far better entry into the user experience in this environment, too. Facebook, for example, serves classic **display ads** which, with the astronomically high number of users and the long hours they spend in the network, have a very high theoretical potential. Besides display advertising, companies may also weave their messages more closely into the fabric of the network using **sponsored content** posted to users between updates from their friends and funny cat videos; Twitter offers something similar in the form of "sponsored tweets". What is more, companies can, of course, set up their own profiles in these networks and use their **own social media presence** to present their content and messages, too.

Nevertheless, caution is advised: firstly, the vast majority of social media users is there in a personal capacity and, what is more, social media is a two-way street in which users can – and do – talk back. This means that an "advertising for content" approach is only applicable to a certain extent; users, after all, produce the lion's share of social content themselves and are therefore quite correct in viewing their social networks partly as their own turf. It may be the operators of the networks who provide the infrastructure, but it is the users who actually breathe life into it – and these users have no qualms about moving on to the next network when an existing one is no longer hot (see MySpace, MSN, and a range of defunct national champions such as the German StudiVZ for proof). On the other hand, users are not *per se* against commercial presence in the networks; many, in fact, positively expect it. They want companies to be contactable where they are – even if it is only for the purposes of publically rubbishing them when their order goes wrong (see the section on multichannel sales below and 2.7 Customer service for more).

What is more, the wondrous targeting potential offered by Facebook makes a one-size-fits-all "public address approach" to advertising seem ridiculously outdated to anyone who looks twice: users, after all, implicitly allow companies to analyse everything they post publically and then move around the network openly and identifiably: when a Facebook user "likes" something, this is a public expression of interest. A user may, for example, dispense a Like both to the Facebook page of a webshop and to a post from a friend of hers about buying a specific pair of trousers there; once this is coupled to the socio-demographic data that she has disclosed to Facebook, her Like history over the last year, and – perhaps most importantly – interactions on other sites and in other apps which the user has accessed while logged in to Facebook, an astonishingly detailed profile emerges on the basis of which advertising can be precision-targeted. The adverts might be streamed into the user's timeline in an unobtrusive fashion, popping up among posts by friends and various media outlets or other organisations the user engages with on the platform. In this relaxed, "lean-back" context, unplanned purchases on a whim are just as easily provoked as in a shopping centre or a high street.

Indeed, Facebook has now recognised the extent to which its treasure-trove of consumer data can be used to target advertising not only within its platform, but on the internet more broadly; the network's proprietary Atlas advertising network aggregates user data and makes it available for off-platform advertising, too.

Amazon, which of course holds a comprehensive purchase history for millions of customers, is not far behind, having introduced its own ad network. What is more, the company has long been tracking customers elsewhere on the internet in order to target them with advertising and get them back buying; it was a logical next step for the company to offer this to others as a paid service. It's still a smooth move, however: a retailer has started to earn actual money with the data it collects on customers and, rather than simply pushing its own products, is now selling advertising space.

This represents a highly sophisticated hybrid approach born of social and predictive behavioural targeting processes (see above), and it is difficult to see there being much more theoretical advance on it – not without direct access to users' neurones and Orwellian levels of profiling, that is.

There is simply no better way of calculating how receptive someone may be to a specific advertising message and how likely they are to buy a certain product than accessing and analysing their purchases and behaviour on social networks – provided, of course, that they use social networks. Those who do, however, are generally not against being advertised to there: surveys show that roughly one third of female Facebook users in the USA, for example, uses the network to garner recommendations and inspirations for products to purchase; on Pinterest, a pictorial posting site, almost 50% would be prepared to make a purchase based on interaction with the network.[10]

Open commerce

Yet if friends post their new purchases to each other and comment on them in groups, if Pinterst provides the equivalent of a digital corkboard full of things people might want to buy when decorating their homes, putting together an outfit, or making models with their kids, then there is a clear benefit to, as a business, simply building up a convincing presence in these networks and leaving it at that. After all, advertising – even if it is targeted to a pinprick and slipped into a newsfeed as a sponsored post – is still advertising, i.e. an intrusion; in fact, some users may even experience overly-targeted advertising as "stalking".

What follows on from this is a new approach: rather than penetrating into user environments, why not actually create an environment to which users come of their own accord in order to talk about products and then potentially buy any they happen to like? Rather than assuming that customers will come looking for the right product, this kind of environment can push the right products down the road towards customers.

Case study: Collins

A blueprint for this approach is the Otto Group (Germany) Collins platform, an exciting blend of online shops, magazines, apps, social networks, and online advertising payment models.

> What Collins offers are fashion product ranges in online shops and a technical infrastructure supporting external apps: what merchants, manufacturers, and media have to contribute is creativity. These latter produce apps which may be of interest to users and entice them into shops, in which they find products selected for their target group. **aboutyou.de**, for example, is a shop for the 20-40 age bracket embedded in a web of apps about fashion; these apps include dress code guides for various clubs in major cities as well as get-the-look engines with photos of Hollywood stars. Younger consumers, meanwhile, are targeted by **edited.de** (no affiliation to Edited.com) which offers an online magazine with

10 www.eMarketer.com (as in March 2015)

a range of articles and galleries as well as social content. New apps can be designed by third parties and docked into the environment; if they generate turnover in the shops, the developers get a share.

A shoe manufacturer might, for instance, create an app which is successful in the Collins environment and in this way rake back in some of its marketing spend. At the same time, however, a group of e-commerce or information technology students might build a suitable app instead, in which case the money goes to them. Whatever the case, if the approach proves to be a success, the Collins projects will have to spend less on customary forms of advertising than in a traditional business model; the commission it pays for apps, content, and networks which generate turnover will be the major expense. It is an advanced form of content marketing: rather than forcing its way into consumers' lives between other items of interest in magazines or websites, the seller actually becomes the item of interest and the transition from messing around in an app to actually spending money becomes so smooth the customer barely notices.

Brand awareness: the "old spice" of life

Even without a direct segue into a shop environment, content marketing can draw its legitimacy simply from contributing to the overall brand awareness of a manufacturer or merchant. As far back as 1900, tyre manufacturer Michelin printed its first handbook for drivers with recommendations for restaurants along major routes; nowadays, aftershave producers are producing interactive comedy content about male grooming. Neither approach, however, has even the slightest aim of triggering an immediate purchase:

> *The overriding aim is simply to inform or amuse, and anchor the company name with this experience.*

Online shops, especially newcomers, should take the importance of brand awareness to heart. The success of companies such as Amazon and Zalando, or even pre-internet convertees such as John Lewis and OTTO, is in no small part built on their names. As such, these established companies can be less concerned with search engine marketing than new shops: after all, they have themselves to some degree become customer's product search engines of choice. Why go to Google and type in "black leather boots" when you've worked out that Zalando always has several hundred of them – on a well-organised, nicely-illustrated results page and at a good price, too? And if you already have an account there, that's one less reason to look elsewhere first.

Classic channels

Nevertheless, five years ago, few of Zalando's millions of customers across 14 European countries had any idea who or what it was – and it didn't make a name for itself by luck alone. As well as investing in distribution and logistics that could compete with Amazon, Zalando and owners Rocket Internet didn't blink when it came to marketing budgets and booked TV commercial slots in every new market it entered: the company's adverts are popular – generally featuring long-suffering men bemoaning their partners' addiction to buying shoes or clothes on the platform or, in Germany, women screaming hysterically in incongruous situations when their new dream-dress arrives – and enjoy a profitable post-broadcast second career on YouTube, where the Zalando Facebook and Twitter pages can link to them; this campaign was rounded off with billboards in European public transport system and, especially in the early days, aggressive Groupon discount offers.

So while classic advertising in print and broadcast media or out-of-home contexts is no longer central, it is a tool which still has its place in the box. In fact, its effect can even be improved when fused with new impulses such as online couponing, guerrilla advertising initiatives, and viral marketing. Yet this kind of cross-media, non-transactional campaign based exclusively on upping brand awareness and, regardless of whether the consumer is leaning back or forward, with no direct purchase pathway is not within the means of every online shop. In fact, the kind of campaigns described above can generally only be financed with record sums of venture capital not available to most retailers; in Europe, it is almost certain that there will be no second Zalando, especially since each market segment can only really accommodate one or two online shops whose name is almost synonymous with certain product ranges in the way that Zalando stands for "shoes" in Germany and Amazon for, well, pretty much everything everywhere.

Each market segment can only really accommodate one or two online shops whose name is almost synonymous with certain product ranges.

One moral of the story, however, is clear: a unified, coordinated brand campaign across all channels can generate genuine buzz. Zalando has made it onto Germany's DAX index and become one of Europe's largest fashion retailers in under a decade – and this is in no small part due to its dominant market position, however high the price Rocket Internet paid for it.

Coordinated approaches, constant monitoring

Whether aiming to reach category killer status like a Zalando or going for a niche area with little potential upwards of seven-figure turnover, anyone in e-commerce with an advertising budget will have to re-evaluate the aims of their spending at ever shorter intervals in the coming years, especially in the transactional marketing area as opposed to overall brand awareness. Yet e-commerce also offers better information about the effectiveness of advertising than ever before inasmuch as it allows shop operators to track customers' paths into and through the shop, revealing more about the costs and benefits of specific advertising measures. A visualisation of how all advertising channels contribute at various stages of a purchase on the internet in the form of a conversion funnel is a helpful way to approach important overall questions with regard to marketing: Where do customers come from? What do they look at? When do they leave?

While data about from where customers have come into an online shop can be complicated to gather (and will never be entirely comprehensive), there is no shortage of it. Tracking cookies and codes can be used to identify visitors from affiliates or who have accessed the shop through search engine or display adverts – and to find out whether they buy or not. Alternatively, the links used in SEA and display ads can go to a dedicated landing page, allowing the shop operator to see who is entering the shop thanks to these marketing measures. This same technique can also be applied to e-mail newsletters and even print mailshots, flyers, and adverts thanks to QR codes: users can scan them with their smartphones and be directed straight to a landing page, offering the clearest metric possible of genuine interest in the advert. For the vast majority of visits, however, looking at referrers – i.e. sites from which users come from – is the only option, and yet can also be revealing: if there are noticeable numbers accessing the shop from, say, a brand video of YouTube, then this is a clear indication that this form of brand awareness without transactional intent works for the company in question and may even have a direct effect on turnover.

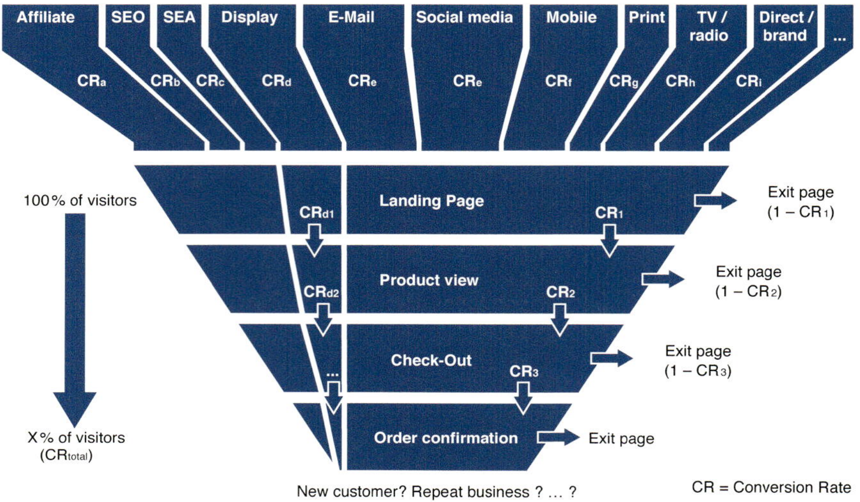

Fig. 2.15: Multichannel conversion funnel
Source: Extended graphic based on Marco Hassler, Web Analytics, mitp, 2012, p. 201ff.

Once on the site, visitors can be tracked as they move through the shop and either leave it or make a purchase. The resulting data can be used to produce solid statistics about the efficiency of a range of marketing measures, often in the widespread cost-per-click (CPO) metric. While this kind of price is difficult to calculate down to the penny for overall brand awareness marketing, there is certainly mileage to be had in examining figures for connections between marketing spend and turnover over longer timeframes: in some cases, effects are visible immediately, as traffic peaks to a webshop after a television advert has been broadcast can be identified against baseline fluctuations ("white noise"). While this is not a user-by-user list of who came to shop because of the TV ad, it can certainly be used to evaluate the statistics of a broadcast media campaign overall. What is more, there is nothing to stop shop operators carrying out their own market research during the order process by including a "How did you hear about us?" question.

Nevertheless, even this kind of specific query can never produce genuinely hard-and-fast answers as to the overall effectiveness of the marketing mix used: did a large number of customers click through from the e-mail newsletter primarily because they had seen a range of display and search engine ads and been "prepped" by a radio campaign in the background? And which of these various other activities did the most running? Or did a YouTue video conceived as part of a light-touch image campaign tip the balance when Mr. Joe Bloggs finally decided to make that purchase? And if so, by how much did it tip the balance, and when? Before he got to the site or at the check-out? Did one of the various marketing tools do more than the others to anchor the brand in his mind? Or did advertising not influence him until later, while he was already thinking of a specific product? Or did he not even see any adverts for the brand until he had already decided to buy a specific product? At which point, precisely? Right before he got out his credit card and sat down at the computer? All of these questions are what customer journey specialists try to answer, looking at how and when the prospective customer became a "conversion", as the old-school gamer-style jargon of e-commerce would have it.

Fig. 2.16: Customer journey
Source: our graphic

Where do what measures have an effect – and how much of an effect? This quest for an overall understanding of what contribution each marketing and communication measure makes to the goals a company sets itself is the discipline of attribution. Since this can never be a wholly exact science – not every marketing measure offers metrics – the aim is to continually refine more and more hypotheses out of the information available to gain a maximum amount of insight into the workings of the marketing activities undertaken. As there will never be answers such as "X customers came to us as a result of Y with no influence from any other channels at all", the key is not simply to collect data and measure results, but to optimise and tests various approaches and activities and then look for changes in statistics.

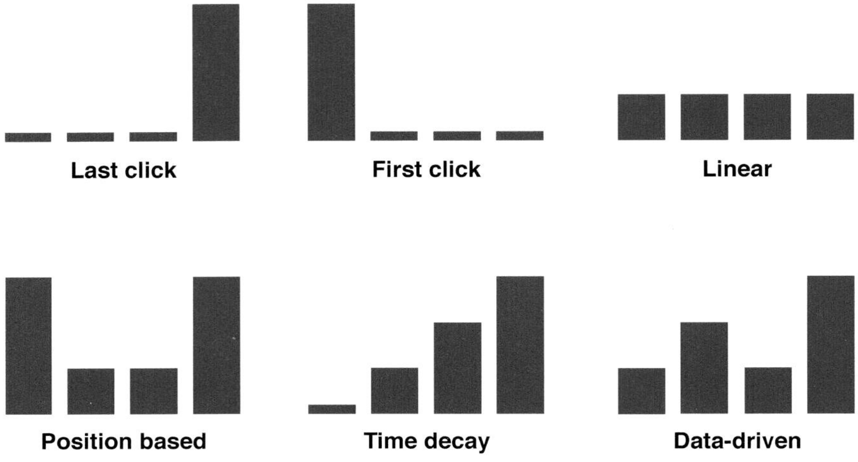

Fig. 2.17: Attribution Models
Source: our graphic

Moreover, there are always competing approaches to interpreting the same sets of data; applying two or more can help to distil a hypothesis on a case-by-case basis. The last-click approach, for example, assigns the full credit for each conversion to the last click the customer makes before buying – e.g. the click into the online shop from an affiliate; the first-click approach, meanwhile, frontloads credit onto the first click which brings the customer into the shop – from a display ad, for instance – regardless of whether a conversion follows or not. Other attribution models are more complex, using mathematics to distribute the credit across several channels and give a more realistic picture as a basis on which to make base marketing decisions. Dynamic attribution models, created by analysing individual points of contact using processes such as Markov chains, can provide this fuller picture, but are resource-heavy and only apply once large numbers of cases can be fed into the models; their application is therefore limited to larger online shops.

In addition to this, there is a range of other possibilities such as the linear approach, which divides credit up equally between the channels, and the time-decay approach, which draws in the time elapsed between channel contact and the conversion itself. Whatever the approach used, however, the end result is generally comparable to a football match: the team's star striker (i.e. a successful channel) may well score all the goals, but without the passes beforehand and the other players in the team (i.e. preceding advertising contact), that strikers would never have even got the ball. Legendary goal-scorers are always as much the product of a well-functioning team as anything else.

By this stage, two fundamental insights become very clear. Firstly, marketing channels and their objectives are getting increasingly difficult to compartmentalise – and the categories are likely to become increasingly porous. This means that efficiency calculations and costs-benefits analysis are to be taken with a pinch of salt: the more closely interwoven the various marketing activities become, the harder it is to unpick and remove one particularly unprofitable measure. What if customers would have been unwilling to subscribe to the newsletter and click through to the check-out without the expensive brand marketing campaign with the big-budget commercial and the pricey guerrilla initiative?

*The effectiveness may, in conversion-funnel terms,
be clearly assignable to e-mail marketing;
but without a strong brand,
the e-mail subscriber list might well have remained anaemic.*

Furthermore, marketing in online shopping is not only a string of tightly-woven threads, but one which is increasingly wrapped around other activities such as distribution. To take the weekly e-mail newsletter as an example: it may have begun life as a brand marketing initiative that, due to the well-chosen selection of products it offers, attracts an increasing number of spontaneous conversions; this transforms it into a transactional marketing activity which targets customers in a relaxed, lean-back setting – and, in some respects, into a sales channel in its own right, as some customers may now only enter the shop at all through the newsletter.

2.4 Distribution

Introduction

In a multi-optional environment in which customers switch merrily from in-store to online-shops and back again, from smartphones to tablets and back to PCs, the border between marketing and distribution becomes blurred. Marketing activities such as an e-mail newsletter can soon become "fixed" sales channels in the distribution structure while printed catalogues are fast losing their original function as a channel for orders – precisely as they start to become an interesting vector through which to deliver consumers visually attractive marketing material they can hold in their hands. When does marketing become distribution; when is selling already sales?

To take H&M as an example: with its dense network of shops, its webshop, and its home-delivery service, the Swedish fashion chain has established itself as a successful multichannel operator worldwide. One of the key elements which holds the channels together is the H&M catalogue, an expensively produced, high-end full-colour glossy which is sent to millions of subscribers several times a year. Having flicked through the various looks, styles, novelties, and staples of the season, customers can then decide which of the various H&M channels is the best for them at that point: there are order slips which can be filled out and returned by post, or customers may chose use their ballpoints to put crosses next to the items they are interested and head to the store; others might immediately log on to HM.com on their computers, smartphones, or tablets. This is a multichannel approach which has been so successful that even online pure-player Zalando is now producing printed catalogues, too; then again, the Zalando book is much closer to the lifestyle magazine produced by Airbnb – i.e. a marketing activity through and through. After all, Zalando is about as ready to open its own network of high street shops and mall stores as Airbnb wants to have the trouble of actually running its own hotels.

It is as well to remember this whenever yet another media hoax does the rounds about Amazon's plans to open bricks-and-mortar stores across broad swathes of the Western world. While Amazon has indeed opened customer stores – the first one debuted in Seattle in 2015 and a bookstore will be hitting Berlin and other European capitals soon – the online retail giant has absolutely no plans to weave a dense web of actual physical shops through the towns and cities of America and Europe: why would it create that kind of cost factor in expensive rental locations?

When Amazon does move into urban areas (something that is currently a definite trend), it is doing so in order to improve its core strength, logistics, not to compete with the heritage leaders it is beating quite nicely – and risk losing for the first time – on their home turf. Amazon's big-city presences are smaller warehouses which allow it to offer Super Prime service (delivery within two hours) to an increasing slice of urban America and, soon, Europe. The few bricks-and-mortar stores it will go on to open will be little more than impressive monuments to the Giant in physical space; more marketing than distribution channel.

A fun example from Hamburg, that musical metropolis where the Beatles once honed their skills, shows that not just Goliath, but David too, can turn the tables of established concepts. The Hanseplatte record store so beloved of the city's hipsters kept going through its turbulent early years with a witty, urbane e-mail newsletter which reminded music fans of the serendipitous joy of browsing through the racks and got them coming in and buying records of a Saturday morning; some clicked straight through to the store's online shop, too, and bought their indie rock albums there rather than at Amazon. The newsletter proved so popular in and of itself, however, that the shop owner eventually decided to bring it out a Best Of compilation of his funniest missives as a book – and sold it, of course, on Amazon. So what started as a marketing initiative became a distribution channel and then ended up as an actual product.

While bricks-and-mortar stores are setting up on the internet, online giants are moving into the stationary sphere with the aim of reaching consumers wherever they are and counting on cross-fertilisation between distribution channels.

This is by no means an ungrounded assumption, either: already, around a quarter of all purchases in store have been preceded by a search for information in online shops; about a third of all sales in e-commerce, meanwhile, happen after the customer has been into stationary store location. A similar merry-go-round effect can be shown with printed material as a means of accessing information and other methods of actually ordering products. What is more, whether online or in store, an increasing amount of product research and comparison leading up to a purchase is taking place on smartphones[11].

11 ECC/IFH Köln (2013), research on cross-channel buys of branded goods

More than a decade into widespread e-commerce, consumer expectations have grown considerably. In a range of spot surveys, "loyal offliners", i.e. consumers who move through the entire **linear** buying process and do so in bricks-and-mortar shops, are now in a minority, with only one third of consumers avoiding the net[12]. Nevertheless, the proportion of "pure onliners" is actually smaller, with only 8% of consumers getting information, comparing products, and then purchasing online without at least one visit to a real, live store. By implication, this means that 61% of consumers are to be found both online and offline – and give increasingly short shrift to heritage companies who are not also to be found on the internet. Yet how do manufacturers and retailers deal with the fact, given this prevalence of **multi-optional** buying behaviour, one single sales channel is unlikely to be enough in the future?

Online strategies

Online strategies for manufacturers

For manufacturers of branded goods, building up a customer base on the internet is absolutely essential. Even though figures for sales through stationary retail may not look particularly bad, the only reason for this is that they are stagnating at a very high level. Wherever in the developed world retail analysts look, the story is the same: progression in bricks-and-mortar sales figures is low – sometimes below inflation – while e-commerce rockets ahead. In the US in the years through to 2015, overall growth B2C sales has been running at about 3.7%; e-commerce growth, however, hovers between 11% and 15% year on year. In Germany, meanwhile, heritage retailers are growing thanks to a strong economy – at rates of around 1% or 2%, which means that they are losing market share to strongly-growing online shopping operations; in 2012, a particularly striking year, stationary retail in Europe's strongest economy grew by a billion Euros, or 0.25% percent, while online retailers surged from a turnover of €21.7 billion in 2011 to €27.6 billion, booking seven times the growth. By conservative estimates, German e-commerce will already be worth €100 billion by 2020; its bricks-and-mortar competition could, by this stage, be flatlining at €300 billion. In Britain, online shops are already cruising towards a 20% share of consumer spending after what looks to have been a bumper 2015.[13]

12 Björn Schäfers in G. Heinemann & A. Haug (2010), *Web-Exzellenz im E-Commerce*

13 See also Chapter 1.1 for market development overview

While legacy retailers may well be happy to stay at their current (large) sizes, sales growth for manufacturers is only to be had by engaging with e-commerce.

Any manufacturer without a coherent online strategy has slim chances of remaining in the market in the long term.

Not that online shopping is a cake-walk for manufacturers, however, especially those with large existing offline sales. How can they start selling their products on the internet without jeopardising their relationships with in-store retailers? Is it worth manufacturers' while setting up their own online operations when, in the worst case, they may end up cannibalising turnover away from existing sales channels? And should manufacturers allow their existing networks of retailers to sell their products on Amazon and Ebay – or attempt to fill out the space in these channels themselves at the risk of getting themselves involved in a price war?

In view of the figures from the overall retail landscape, there is no choice for manufacturers to getting onto the internet: the details of how they do so are very much dependent on their product segment and long-term brand strategy. Manufacturers of luxury goods, outsized products, or items which require extensive sales consultation are dependent on their networks of retailers to stock and deliver products, and to advise customers, and must therefore adapt their online strategies accordingly: Rolex, for example, has an internet site which offers an introduction to the brand and its products – a kind of online shop window. Customers may browse and add articles to a shopping list, but are then fed into the store locator and pointed in the direction of the nearest stockist, where they can have their watches customised before collecting and paying for them there. This strategy has the advantage of preserving Rolex' status as a genuine luxury product – i.e. one which is intricately tied up with personal service and not available around the clock – all the while not neglecting customers whose journey starts on the internet. Meanwhile, while it delivers smaller items to home addresses, caravan and gardening manufacturer AL-KO has a concept similar to Rolex for its larger items such as petrol-powered lawnmowers, unsuited to home delivery as they are: customers can order products to listed AL-KO partners and pick them up there, the only difference being that they pay AL-KO directly. Rolex does not take any money online, but receives its payment from the stockist; AL-KO inverts the process and disburses commission to the shop offering the service (see 2.5 Orders and sales).

For manufacturers of more everyday consumer items, of course, things look slightly different.

Is this a brand which is aiming to stay in an upper segment or is the aim to offer it in as many possible outlets at the best possible price? In short, how much control over the product is the manufacturer looking to retain as it moves down the value chain towards the consumer? Manufacturers who, in the days before e-commerce, turned up their noses at the Walmarts and Tescos, at the JC Penneys and John Lewis' of this world will get the same feeling when they look at Amazon and its fierce discounting policies today. Others, meanwhile, will see nothing but a huge sales opportunity. Deciding in which direction to take a brand is especially important for online sales channels such as marketplaces, where used or strongly-reduced surplus items may crop up as retailers try to offload: is this something the brand is happy to see on the internet?

Another question is the cost issue: how many costs generated at various points in the value chain is the manufacturer willing to start dealing with? Makers who have thus far distributed their stock exclusively to merchants and are now looking to start selling directly to consumers on the internet will be throwing themselves into a steep learning curve: direct consumer engagement means not just opening an online shop (see 2.2.), but also processing orders and payments – and absorbing the risks that come with the territory (2.5.2), as well as taking care of logistics (2.6) and customer service (2.7). Building up this infrastructure can easily require a seven-figure investment. Then there is always the danger that the existing network of retailers will feel as if it is being undermined and, in the worst-case scenario, retaliate by delisting the manufacturer; turnover missing will now have to be generated by the online shop – and fast.

Nevertheless, manufacturers are in the stronger position as e-commerce and multichannel wreak havoc with stationary retail models: it remains quicker and faster to open an online shop than it is to open a chain of own-brand stores in a major consumer economy. Makers today have the opportunity to sell straight to customers and can decide how they want to weight various distribution channels; the only prerequisite is that the strategy and mix they opt for means that their products can be found in online shops.

Online strategies for retailers

For retailers, the switch to distribution on several channels is a far more delicate situation. Say a manufacturer who has, to date, only distributed to a network of bricks-and-mortars stockists decides to open its own online shop, and say this shop starts to channel existing sales into this own-brand store, then, although there is clearly cannibalisation – and not growth – taking place, the turnover being cannibalised still ends up with the manufacturer. In fact, once the costs for its new sales channel have been deducted, the manufacturer may even break even and has the potential to increase its sales in the new shop. The retailer, however, is left with nothing.

Things also look bad for in-store retailers who, with their comparatively high fixed costs, end up in a price war with the King of Cost-Cutting, Amazon. While the manufacturer will sell at a similar price to both, the retailer has to watch as its margins are squeezed more and more by the price pressure Amazon exerts. To add insult to injury: new growth is happening online, meaning that the in-store retailer can't even compensate for reduced margins with increased sales. And most terrifyingly: the younger the consumer, the higher the proportion of goods and services he or she buys online. Any in-store retailer who does not find a way of dealing with this shift onto the net is on a one-way street to closure; it is a question of when, not if.

Again and again, retailers looking to react to the threat and take the e-commerce plunge are faced the same set of decisions. Most importantly, they need to answer question of whether the existing retail brand can work on the internet – i.e. whether it can find its target group there and deliver them what the brand promises using the internet. If the target groups on the high street and in the online shop diverge too greatly, or if it becomes clear that the prices the retailer is used to charging are not competitive enough for the online environment, then there are very coherent arguments for opening up online under a different brand.

This kind of dual-brand strategy has the virtue of avoiding cannibalisation between channels if, for example, prices need to be set lower in the online shop in order to be competitive.

Yet the disadvantages of a dual-brand approach are manifold: a range of structures are duplicated because both marketing and customer communication activities need to be kept separate. This acts as a brake on synergies and prevents the kind of positive exchange between channels set out above; the overall risk is that, in the long run, both the bricks and the clicks fail to reach their true potential in the market. For this reason, one approach is to limit e-commerce engagement to being present and easily located online, but to reserve actual sales activity for stationary stores. If the in-store infrastructure has been sufficiently digitised, it is quite feasible to serve Google shopping ads showing which products are on sale where – even with price and availability on a per-shop basis in real time, given a suitable interface to enterprise resource planning systems.

The path of choice, however, remains a **single-brand strategy** which, for example, allows addresses and other personal customer data gathered in the online shop to be used in advertising initiatives for the physical store, sending flyers and coupons to customers at home. What is more, orders can be placed online and picked up in store ("click and collect") if that suits customers better; another plus is that returns can be handled using the bricks-and-mortar network, which can save the merchant costs – and the customers time spent in post offices or waiting for parcels couriers. Then again, the retailer's infrastructure must be developed to the point where these benefits can be reaped: customers will be confused if a merchant is present on and offline using the same brand, but does not offer the same service level across the two channels. "Oh, you mean you bought this in our webshop? Well in that case, I'm afraid we can't take it back for repairs here..." A customer confronted with this kind of casuistry is one who won't be coming back anytime soon. Differences between the channels can only be justified – if at all – by differences in prices, which of course leads us back to the issue of cannibalisation, only worse: customers buying cheap on the net and receiving a lower level of service are both spending less than they would have spent in store and are less likely to be satisfied with the service they receive. This is a double-jeopardy situation in which a retailer is potentially losing money from existing customers – and losing the customers themselves – and should make merchants consider this kind of "online outlet" with due caution. In many cases, the best option is to keep prices and service levels as constant across channels as possible.

Online sales channels

Proprietary shops and marketplace presences

Below the overarching distinction between bricks and clicks, online subdivides into an array of channels which in turn pose questions for both manufacturers and retailers with regards to the extent of special offers or other divergences from a unified brand presence: in most cases, a **proprietary online shop** is, although central, only one plank in the overall online strategy, flanked by **one-stop shopping** and **marketplace** presences (both for makers and merchants) and **brand shops** (mainly makers). These channels open up the possibility of reaching customers at larger online retailers such as Amazon, John Lewis, or OTTO and, after having sold to them on these platforms, bringing them into the proprietary web store.

One-stop shopping is the process by which products listed in a proprietary online shop are automatically entered onto third-party platforms. On retail platforms which offer this form of integration, the listing customers see is the same, regardless of whether it was created by the retailer or by a third-party retailer or manufacturer; the customer pays the platform for the product, which in turn deducts its commission before forwarding the funds to the originator of the listing.

A similar approach is to list products on marketplaces as a seller; while this form of integration can also be automated so that listings in a proprietary online shop are synchronised onto other retail platforms, there is an important distinction inasmuch as customers enter into a sales contract with the seller, not the platform. Consumers are made aware before ordering that they are not purchasing the product in question from, say, Amazon, but from a third-party seller – often a manufacturer or a retailer – who has listed the product on Amazon. In the days of Ebay dominance, sellers would pay to list products, but with Amazon, the sales commission model has become widespread here too.

Besides one-stop shopping and marketplace integration, some online retailers also offer third-parties brand shop presences on their platforms. Generally intended for manufacturers rather than other retailers, these shops-within-shops are used to show whole product ranges in greater-than-usual detail in an on-brand visual environment within the infrastructure of a larger shopping platform such as Amazon. The concept is comparable with the old store-within-store agreement under which brand manufacturers would rent space in department stores in order to reach greater numbers of customers than they could with own-brand shops limited entirely to their proprietary product ranges; the store-within-store concept was also intended to increase brand awareness among shoppers.

Although technically undemanding, these channels pose an almost unresolvable dilemma to companies considering using them: on the one hand, Amazon and several other platforms offer a low-effort, low-investment opportunity to increase reach and sales; on the other, there is a serious risk that customers will migrate to the platform – taking turnover with them. It is not overstating the case to call it a Catch 22. While Amazon especially has customer numbers and click statistics so high that a successful platform integration is almost guaranteed to increase sales, as a quasi-monopolist, Amazon dictates the rules of the game and does not offer this kind of potential without taking its tribute. In the early years when it was still concerned with increasing its reach and gaining new customers, Amazon offered unprecedentedly advantageous conditions, especially to manufacturers in its vendor programme, from whom it would buy in goods at the same price as other retailers and, for a small discount, throw returns and customer service into the bargain; many larger vendors were even given free brand stores on the site, too. Meanwhile, marketplace sellers were tempted away from Ebay with low listings fees or commission.

This latter initiative was of particular importance as, thanks to Marketplace, Amazon has now surrounded itself by an ecosystem in which almost every imaginable item Western consumer society can produce (and some unimaginable ones) is available to be found and sold.

*By attracting so many third-party sellers,
Amazon has achieved its "abracadabra" status
as a kind of Google for products
without actually tying up much by way of up-front capital in products
and without entering into any serious business risks.*

The result is that many Amazon customers no longer think of looking elsewhere for anything.

Given this kind of power, of course, Amazon no longer has any need to attract manufacturers as vendors and other retailers as sellers: Amazon customers are large in number and unswerving in loyalty, and are being tied ever closer to the company (see below). The result is that Amazon now takes a very confident, some might say robust approach to the large numbers of makers and merchants dependent on its platform for large chunks of their sales. The time of gifts is long gone. Brands looking to build up an attractive presence on Amazon now pay for the pleasure – for instance to input extended product texts only a few characters longer than standard entries – and anyone who, in Amazon's view, isn't pulling their weight – i.e. doesn't offer discounts or cut Amazon a good deal on its buy-in – gets tortured into submission. The range of implements the Giant keeps handy is sobering: uncooperative providers' product pages get branded with banner adverts such as "View similar products with better customer ratings" leading to competing items from more pliable partners; the arbitrariness of "better customer ratings" is well documented, but Amazon insists that these adverts are served on a completely automated basis...

Retailers especially can end up on the rack without actually having done anything to displease Amazon: it can, in fact, be enough to simply provide the Giant with a big Markeptlace seller which it then recognises as such; cue banner links to its own-brand products of a similar nature or, if it doesn't yet offer the item in question itself, a direct supply contract with the manufacturer. When presented with the choice between a third-party seller and Amazon itself as seller, customers will generally select Amazon and its guaranteed service level – and even pay a few pennies more to do so. The retailer goes home empty handed as Amazon muscles in with aggressive pricing and – judge, jury, and executioner all in one – uses its control of advertising and search results on its own platform to channel sales towards itself.

Amazon is, however, constantly striving to shut manufacturers and not just retailers out of the relationship with the customer, too, as became clear in the product segment on which the Giant once cut its teeth: books. Nowadays, Amazon is not just a bookseller, but a publisher too: it knows from sales figures exactly what sells, so why wouldn't it try and swallow up the margin where it can by producing its own content? Amazon's tried-and-tested method is to approach successful self-publishers using the platform with contracts in which Amazon becomes the publisher. Given the Giant's history of applying what works in the books segment to other product categories, it won't take long for Amazon to start producing in previously unthinkable areas of the market. The Amazon Basics range of technical items and home appliances is just a warning – and one that is keeping Panasonic, Philips, and Ikea managers awake at night in the same way as the Amazon Elements set of home essentials is giving supermarket retailers cold sweats.

*So it is not just retailers, but manufacturers,
who must examine their situation and weigh up
the chances of marketplace operators
such as Amazon becoming their direct competitors.*

The lesson is that sales made directly through a proprietary online shop offer both a higher, commission-free margin, and come with data – data that Amazon, OTTO, Zalando, and whoever else the digital middleman may be would love to get their hands on. Companies lacking their own dedicated online channel and only selling via marketplaces, or those generating a significantly higher proportion of their sales from third-party platforms than through proprietary channels, are much more vulnerable. Not that a strong own-brand presence in search engine results or elsewhere on the internet is easy to achieve; in fact, outside of niche segments, the online marketing investment can be enormous (see 2.3.1, for example).

Retailers selling products not found widely or in possession of exclusive re-sales deals with specific manufacturers have a better chance of working with the larger online retailers as partners, as do genuinely innovative manufacturers. Any company dealing with standard, mass-market products – whether as a maker or a merchant – must steel itself before approaching Amazon and be aware that it may well be undermining its own position in the (not so) long run. The Catch 22 situation remains unresolvable inasmuch as online shops opened by this kind of company will never be able to compete with the big internet retailers: thanks to their reach and size, they can run a ruinous "pile 'em high, sell 'em cheap" race in which they can subsist on wafer-thin margins (and isolated losses in particularly competitive product segments) until everyone else has collapsed from exhaustion. In this environment, legacy retailers would be wise to think twice before adding an expensive, complex proprietary online shop to their existing, not inconsiderable costs structures. The key is to be visible online – not necessarily to sell through an online shop.

Mobile devices: responsive design, apps

Mobile technology is the next sales environment in which leaders like Amazon will be unfolding their advanced innovative advantage in a battle the likes of which e-commerce has yet to see: in 2015, smartphone penetration was, depending on the source running at between 40% and 80% in major markets such as Germany, USA and UK; most importantly, in most developed countries, more 90 of 100 new mobile phones sold are smart devices with internet access. As such, by 2020, it is highly likely that the role of old-style Nokia handsets will be limited to that of museum exhibits (alongside video recorders and Minidisc players). The vast majority of consumers will be using devices with which they can go online and make transactions – and research shows that they have nothing against doing so. Surveys from 2014 show that almost 60% of US and German smartphone and tablet owners[14] had already used their devices to make a purchase (in Germany, this was up by half in just three years).

The trend towards using mobile devices such as smartphones and tablets not only changes existing online channels, but also adds a new one: online shops need to be adapted so that they are displayed optimally on a range of device types and sizes (**responsive design**) while the mobile operating systems offer a new, exciting channel in the form of dedicated shopping **apps**.

There are many similarities between responsive websites and applications. The goal of both is to offer consumers an easily navigable, speedy path through an online shop and towards a purchase on devices which often have very small screens and are reliant on rather imprecise finger jabs as opposed to precision mouse operation; meanwhile, despite improvements in mobile internet speeds, responsive designs and apps are still reliant on a method of transmission which is frequently patchy. This means that key design features of both are easy touchscreen usability – zooming in an out, for example, needs to be easy using finger movements – as well as simplified layout without any unnecessary graphics or text as a space-saving measure both from a visual design and a data loading point of view. In an app, for example, the search function may occupy a fifth of the screen at any one time while it takes up less than 5% percent of the total surface of a webshop as viewed on a PC monitor. In this and other design issues, it is relatively immaterial whether the shop is delivered to a device as a responsive, browser-based website or as a dedicated application; nevertheless, from a technical point of view, it is far harder to reduce loading times in a responsive solution than in a native application.

14 Source: US, Placeable (digital marketing consultancy); Germany, BEVH (Federation of E-Commerce and Mail Order Companies)

Fig. 2.18: Example of amazon.co.uk on desktop browser, iPad & iPhone browser as well as apps

Source: www.amazon.co.uk (as of March 2016)

The difference between the solutions is more a matter of the possibilities they offer in respect of identifying consumers, advertising to them, and making them into regular customers. Anyone browsing a product range in an application can, for instance, be identified immediately. A user on a mobile version of the online shop, meanwhile, needs to be identified using cookies if he or she is not logged in (see passive and active identification, 2.2.2); as soon as the user activates cookie blockers or aborts a purchase before logging in, data is lost which could have been of interest from a marketing perspective (see retargeting, 2.3.2).

What is more, a shopping app is closer to the user, who can navigate to it on a touchscreen with one or two taps of the finger; mobile sites are more complicated as users have to open a mobile browser, tap on the URL bar, wait until the keyboard function has been activated, and then enter the site address by hand. The Amazon app for the iPhone, meanwhile, shortcuts logging in by allowing the customer to identify themselves and validate purchases with their fingerprint: no more fiddling around typing long passwords on small smartphone keypads. Then again, applications will not be replacing mobiles sites entirely any time soon: not every customer – and, above all, not every prospective customer – is happy to simply install an app provided by an unknown company on a no-questions-asked basis; many will still want to try the shop in a non-committal context like their mobile browsers first. This makes a well-optimised responsive website a must even for companies placing the emphasis on a shopping app, even if it is only as a shop window; then again, there is no reason not to go the whole hog and allow users to buy using mobile browsers, too, as anyone who can search for and view a product should be able to purchase it without a break between channels.

With its easy access and high speed,
the app is more of a customer relationship tool
for repeat business and, above all, intensive users.

Once they have started buying using shopping apps, customers tend to grow used to the direct access and clean look of the software and the chances that they will abandon the company operating the app for another decrease further. What is more, apps also allow for push messages advertising specific sales initiatives to be displayed to customers, who only need to tap on the missive to access – and purchase – the products in question.

Adjusting product mixes to suit channels and devices

The differences between the various distribution channels can make it necessary to adapt the product mixes sold on each one. As an overall channel, online sales allow for a considerable amount of price flexibility: figures can be dropped overnight, announced as a lightening sale, and then cranked back up a few hours later. Among online booking platforms for plane tickets, for example, this kind of time-limited price shift is very widespread: lead ticket prices are often lower over the weekend, when the vast majority of customers are booking flights for personal reasons; when business travellers hit the office again on Monday morning and start booking, the figures take off again. In contrast, other product prices and, more than anything, other channels, require months of planning and are then set for a long period of time (catalogues are the most extreme example); on the other hand, these channels offer a completely different range of presentational and promotional activities.

Just as the in-store retail channels requires managers to set the focus differently at various locations, online sales channels need to be adapted to various devices. For the majority of manufacturers and retailers, their proprietary online shop may be considered the "flagship store" in this channel, featuring the whole product range; at the other end of the spectrum, third-party marketplaces may only see individual products as being bait in attempts to build a broader customer base without exposing the entire product range to marketplace operators' gaze – and rendering the proprietary shop pointless. There is often a difference between manufacturers and retailers here, with manufacturers dictating to retailers where their products may be sold; many, for example, do not want to see their goods being sold on marketplaces – or would rather keep this channel under their own control. Mobile shops, whether as responsive websites or apps, can generally display a full range of products.

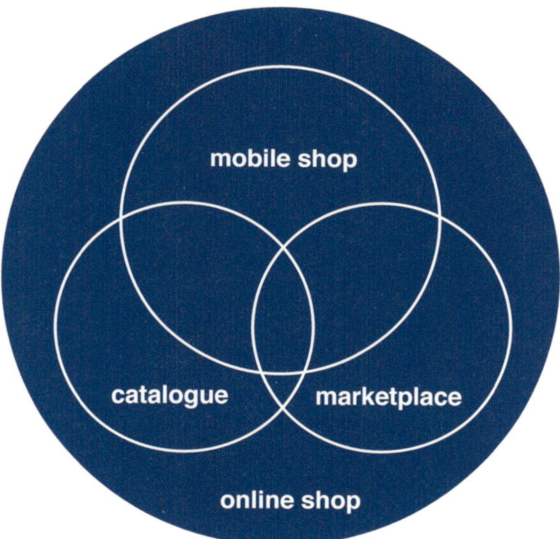

Fig. 2.19: Product range per distribution channel
Source: our graphic

Moreover, the new variety of distribution channels opens up room for experimentation. With their large screens, tablet computers, for example, offer an ideal sales and marketing space: when using tablets, customers tend to be in relaxed, "lean back" mode, generally at home or using a stable broadband wireless connection. These parameters mean that special sales initiatives, specific areas of a product range, or thematic selections can be prepared in a visually attractive, data-heavy way and served to customers as a sort of "digital catalogue": in view of this, many progressive multichannel retailers have taken to kitting out their bricks-and-mortar stores with iPads which can display items that are currently out of stock in store – and which allow customers to place an order immediately, before they resort to their own devices (in Germany, according to BEVH, a quarter of smartphone shoppers consult their devices when in physical stores; in the US, marketing experts put the figure at a third. Over a half of mobile shoppers in the UK compare in store).

Multichannel strategies

How much of the product range should be available in each channel? What level of service is required for each channels and how can this be technically implemented? The answers to these questions vector manufacturers and retailers to one of the following three strategies: **lead channel**, **multiple channel**, and **seamless commerce**.[15]

In a **lead-channel strategy**, the focus is very clearly on one central channel; all other are supporting channels or feeders. This is a model frequently applied by legacy market leaders in the retail sector as well as manufacturers with the aim of generating growth with existing networks. In this approach, an online shop might be more of a catalogue than anything else, or offer the chance to order some parts of the product range (often for customers to collect in store). While this is an easy solution to implement as it entails no change in logistics and customer service, it comes at the price of higher opportunity costs: if customers see a shopping basket-shaped icon, only to realise later that they are, in fact, not using a full-service online shop, many will abort before ordering; any competitors who do dispatch to customers at home are, of course, only one click away. This strategy is also often hampered by systems focussed on the lead channel which are difficult to synchronise; hastily-erected online shops run by external agencies, for example, are often unable to dovetail into enterprise resource planning environments, and this leads to work being replicated.

With the **multiple channel strategy** approach, customers are served on two or more channels all offering a broadly similar product range, generally at a constant level of service; nevertheless, the two principal channels – generally one brick and one click channel – run parallel while others are not yet fully developed and only offer support functionality (mobile devices are often neglected here). In evolutionary terms, this approach is one step further along from lead channel: customer contact, pricing, and branding are coordinated across platforms, as are customer data and information. This exchange between channels relies on hybrid systems which, while saving money as opposed to the lead-channel strategy, can never be fully integrated; this often leads to problems in synchronising ERPs. Many specialised retailers with a heritage brand are currently at this stage of development.

At the end of the evolution process is **seamless commerce**, also referred to as **no-line commerce** or the **omnichannel strategy**: customers can buy more or less the

15 In reference to Heinemann (2012), *Cross-Channel-Management*, p. 52.ff.

entire product range in all channels and on all devices; the channels are all served by fully integrated systems, which represents a considerable technical and financial investment in the short-to-medium term, but is a long-term saver of time and cash costs. A single ERP system and one CRM system avoid duplication and can easily encompass new channels. Customers learn that they can always access the company's products at all points in time and have far less incentive to keep looking for alternatives. This full-blooded approach to commerce is the most promising for the future, and it is no surprise that innovative companies like Apple have implemented it wholesale.

No-line, no limits

For most companies with bricks-and-mortar heritage, a shift to seamless commerce is a decade-long challenge with a multitude of uncertainties. German e-commerce expert Gerrit Heinemann has defined no less than seven factors which are crucial if this kind of transformation is to be a success.[16]

Firstly, the company must offer genuinely **multichannel services**. This means making sure that customers can make appointments in physical stores online or by telephone, or handing out coupons for the online shop to customers who visit a bricks-and-mortar store. What is more, the majority of the overall product range must be available in most of the channels. **Mobile services** are the second key features: location-based services, for example, in which customers are served offers close to their current location in a fitting context. Another important characteristic of no-line commerce is that the smartphone becomes the hub for customer relationship management. Moreover, a **multimedia, crossmedia, social media concept** is required to ensure a unified brand presence across all marketing and communications channels: whether it's targeted advertising or quick access to help and support, customers get what they need in the best channel for them.

The fourth factor is **multichannel customisation**, by which services, products, and advertising can be adapted to customer needs in each channel. Personalisation is also the key to keeping a hold on costs in this process: customers make a contribution by telling the company what they need from which channel. A fifth matter of importance on the issue of costs is defining a clear **business plan** relying on modelling to show which channel combinations work in which order and how sales and delivery processes need to be arranged. Next, the revolution should lead to a genuine **multichannel organisation** in which core business areas such as finance,

16 In reference to Heinemann (2012), *No-Line-Handel*, p. 150f.

purchasing, marketing, and internal auditing are placed above individual distribution channels in the hierarchy. Lastly, no-line commerce can only be implemented on the basis of a **strong IT infrastructure**: whether various existing ERP and CRM systems are being combined or a new, unified system is being set up, the degree to which processes are covered, integrated, and standardised is key.

Failure in any one of these seven points can turn a promising seamless strategy into a sales disaster of the first order: in the worst cases, customers of an existing channel are dissatisfied with changes and switch to competitors while implementation in other channels crawls forward at snail's pace; meanwhile, a lack of channel-hopping options – or poorly implemented interfaces – leads to confusion as uncoordinated marketing activities and CRM systems see customers being inundated with the same message across several channels until they cut all ties. The gamut of risks runs from embarrassing PR fails through to serious drops in sales.

Companies which do, however, master all of the factors in no-line success, are rewarded many times over.

Increased customer reach and better market coverage over a range of target groups often rejuvenate the brand in passing as unified systems and the synergies they offer lead to improvements in profitability and a better understanding of customer needs thanks to the customisation initiatives; truly no-line companies also enjoy a decrease in risks as their dependence on one particular channel becomes less pronounced.

Case study: Apple

A shining example of how no-line commerce looks when it is done well is Apple. With the Apple website as the core element of the system offering a range of information and detailed, self-service support for its own products, Apple also runs a responsive-designed online shop offering most of its products in a range of configurations and with suitable accessories recommended, too. The store finder on the website allows users to make appointments in physical shops, which are of course used to display products in a strongly branded marketing environment; by offering training and customer service, they also serve functions beyond sales. On iPhones and iPads, the Apple store app offers a shopping experience conceived for no other device that Apple's own, closing the circle. Customers are hooked up to their local store using location-based services, meaning that appointments can be booked at the shop nearest to the customer in the app (the time and date is, of course, directly transferred into the customer's diary). The app can also be used in store to receive contextualised information and even to pay for other products purchased. As such, Apple has developed a full ecosystem which is so all-encompassing that existing customers above all have no need to leave the Apple universe in order to continue buying Apple products.

Without a doubt, Amazon has observed and understood the importance of the Apple approach: not only does Apple sell products, but it sells products with which customers are uniquely identifiable – and which they can use to make other purchases. Anyone who owns an iPhone can use it to buy music, podcasts, films, software, and a range of other items form iTunes – and then get a new iPhone in the Store app at a later date. By this point in time, the company knows the customer's tastes almost as well are he or she does; this, in turn, makes it easy to generate suitable recommendations. And so the Apple circle of life is shut (the ring-shaped design of the company's new headquarters is no coincidence).

The success of Apple's approach explains why, in 2013, Amazon developed the Kindle reader into the Kindle Fire multimedia tablet (i.e. an iPad competitor) and even tried, in 2014, to place its own smartphone Fire on the market. Even though it didn't catch on, what Amazon was aiming for was clear: customers were to be given a device with which they could then buy everything else from Amazon. The company has, after all, produced almost every conceivable add-on conceivable to turn smartphones of all stripes in Amazon buying-machines: the Flow app, for example, allows Amazon to recognise products from videos made by the phone, which customers can then go on to order – using Amazon's own payment system, of course.

Not that Amazon has given up on the idea of placing its own devices – such as Amazon Dash, for example, a scanner which US customers can use to make easy follow-up orders for a range of household products. Run out of coffee? Scan the empty packet and order straight on Amazon. April 2015 even saw the launch of Dash buttons which can be stuck onto cupboards and walls next to where products are kept: all the customer needs to do is push the button to place a follow-up order. Run out of coffee again? Just tap on the button stuck on the side of the coffee tin.

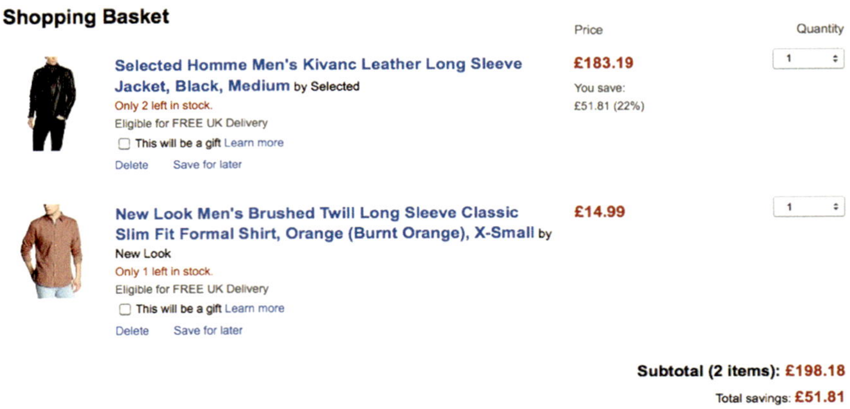

Shopping Basket

	Price	Quantity
Selected Homme Men's Kivanc Leather Long Sleeve Jacket, Black, Medium by Selected Only 2 left in stock. Eligible for FREE UK Delivery This will be a gift Learn more Delete Save for later	**£183.19** You save: £51.81 (22%)	1
New Look Men's Brushed Twill Long Sleeve Classic Slim Fit Formal Shirt, Orange (Burnt Orange), X-Small by New Look Only 1 left in stock. Eligible for FREE UK Delivery This will be a gift Learn more Delete Save for later	**£14.99**	1

Subtotal (2 items): £198.18
Total savings: **£51.81**

Fig. 2.20: Amazon Dash Button
Source: https://www.amazon.com/dashbutton (as of March 2016)

There's no let-up, either, with the Amazon Dash replenishment service now entering the next generation as part of the internet of things: as of January 2016, the first machines to automatically re-stock on consumable supplies are on the market. A printer by Brother, for example, independently orders ink from Amazon, while a new GE washing machine makes sure it never runs out of powder; there's even a smart blood sugar test pack by Gmate.[17] So it shouldn't be long until the coffee-maker starts ordering its own coffee without the owner needing to do anything. Amazon can sell this kind of product as a loss-leader, subsidising customers to buy it as long as they accept that Amazon will be supplying them the material. It's a classic lock-in effect.

For customers who baulk at relinquishing this level of control over their spending to Amazon – or who simply would prefer a different coffee machine – the retail giant also has something up its sleeve: how about Amazon Echo, a small voice-recognition device which acts as a kind of stock-room secretary and answers to the name Alexa. "Alexa, I'm out of coffee" is sufficient for the device to order coffee from Amazon. The particularly advantageous conditions at which the device being sold to customers is an indication of how highly Amazon rates the sales potential.

17 cf. http://phx.corporate-ir.net/phoenix.zhtml?c=176060&p=irol-newsArticle&ID=2130275 (as of January 2016)

It's a very clear approach:
Amazon is aiming to be there
whenever the need to purchase something arises.

It is, after all, already the top search engine in the US when internet users are looking for products; the next step is to extend its reach into items required on an everyday basis in the household for which no consumers would even consider searching on Google. Thanks to its long-tail approach to procurement (see 2.1.), Amazon and its Marketplace now offer almost every imaginable article, and customers note that they can find everything on Amazon. If Echo always happens to be nearby, ears open, then the customer has yet one reason less to look for products he or she needs elsewhere.

So customers really do not just "drop in" to online shops. But, so it would seem, online shops do drop in to see customers.

2.5 Orders and sales

Introduction

British people fresh in America are often pleasantly surprised by the presence of dedicated baggers at supermarkets: what, you mean there is someone employed specifically to pack my groceries into shopping bags for me? How luxurious! In the UK, customers are used to performing an odd kind of dexterity test as they use their right hands to stuff their purchases into various receptacles and their left to manipulate the keypad on the card machine, smiling apologetically at the customers waiting patiently – and yet clearly impatiently – behind them. It's a uniquely British mixture of politeness, genuine embarrassment, and passive-aggressive defiance. Americans who come to the UK are reliably shocked by the stores' lack of customer care – and by just how strong the British stiffer upper lip really is. Their own impulse is turn to the person behind them and let rip: "Think you can bag my groceries any faster, wiseguy? Huh?"

In Germany, however, Brits or Americans hitting any of the country's supermarkets and drugstores have to master a far more challenging showdown at the check-out: from the second the cashier touches the first item on the conveyor, time speeds up as the produce flies over the barcode scanner in a multi-coloured blur of bananas, breakfast cereal, and beer cans. Before the customer can even make it to the other side of the check-out, the shopping has piled up into an unsightly mess and, as the smoke clears, the till operative is already asking "Cash or card?" while the bewildered Brit and amazed American are still looking around for a bag. Germans – not famed for tact – quickly become visibly, audibly impatient: there is much clicking of tongues and expelling of air through nostrils in the queue; the cashier can barely disguise her disrespect for anyone unable to keep up with the mean pace she sets. As far as Germans are concerned, at the check-out, it's all business. Only the couple behind the Brit and the American in the queue has a momentary flash of tolerance, sympathy even: in a matter of seconds, they too will be struggling to bag up their groceries while the merciless check-out Olympian bombards them with their own produce. He squeezes her hand and, swallowing audibly, motions her forward.

Despite these amusing, often infuriating cultural differences, check-outs in all three countries mentioned do have an overarching objective in common: speed.

That's one reason American stores go to the trouble of employing professionals to bag groceries: they are not only more experienced in packing, and consequently swifter than customers, but also free up hands to root around for cards or cash. It's also the reason why British supermarkets keep a huge amount of check-outs in operation (often 20 simultaneously for a medium-sized, suburban store) and are investing considerable sums in self-check-out tills: although customers often need a few moments longer to scan their own shopping, a supermarket can fit between four and five self-service check-out stations in the same space as one conventional till, which in turn keeps queues down. Germany, meanwhile, the home of hardcore fiscal probity, has gone a different route: supermarket chains there are mean with human resources – a store which would have double-digit staff numbers in the UK or the US will frequently be run on a skeleton crew of three-to-five employees in Germany – and instead train their cashiers to keep the pace at the tills up, transferring those who consistently dawdle to the stockroom or, not infrequently, firing them. Stoic German consumers have, thus far, been happy to play along with this unpleasant game, pearls of sweat on their foreheads, as the process keeps queues moving while guaranteeing low prices.

Whatever the approach, supermarkets worldwide know that nothing kills sales like slow check-outs. A customer who dropped in for a bottle of wine to take to a dinner party and then got upsold to three bottles on a "buy 2, get 1 free" deal must be put through the till quickly before they run out of time ("7.30pm tonight. Please don't be late or the sauce will spoil!") or start to reconsider their purchase ("Do I really need *three* bottles? And does it really work out that much cheaper...?"). If they are in line for longer than three or four minutes, they may well think better of the whole enterprise and leave the basket orphaned next to an unstaffed check-out.

In e-commerce, processing orders and sales is, as in many other areas, analogous to the offline retail world – and yet completely different at the same time. Similarly to in bricks locations, in the clicks world, speed is of the essence: if a webshop starts to load slowly at the wrong moment, users will start to abort purchases. They will also drop their baskets if the purchase process drags on through several stages, even if each page in the chain loads at lightning speed.

In contrast to offline retail situations, however, customers can abort their purchase at literally every single point in the process.

A user may well spend half an hour clicking their way through the webshop and adding items to their shopping cart, have reached the pay-screen, and even have inputted their address and credit card number – until he or she clicks on "order" and actually enters into a contract, he or she can always simply close the browser window. Purchase aborted. This kind of behaviour would clearly be unacceptable in a physical shop location: just imagine somebody allowing a trolley full of food or a basket full of clothes to be scanned, inserting their card into the terminal and then – without warning – walking off, card in hand, saying "Sorry, not right now!" Yet what would be considered pathological in an interpersonal interaction is an everyday occurrence when people are accessing webshops: as soon as something jars or if any last-minute doubts about the purchase surface, customers reach for the "Eject!" button.

And why shouldn't they? They haven't spent waiting time in a queue or troubled a member of staff for a personal sales consultation, so they don't feel as if they are wasting their own time – or anyone else's – by aborting a purchase. What is more, if they then decide to return and actually buy, they know the shop will still be open and ready to take an order – even at 4am, if they want. The delivery won't reach them for two or three days, either, so there is very little advantage to be had in placing an order now as opposed to some point later in the day. Or tomorrow. Only products which are in demand (or sold as such: "5 other users are currently viewing this hotel room!") create any sense of urgency. For anything not needed immediately, tomorrow is as good as today. Then again, next week is too far off: can they really not dispatch faster? Abort. Tomorrow? But look at those shipping costs – that's extortionate! Eject. Amazon's cheaper on shipping, right? Let's just compare that..." Purchase cancelled.

In fact, given just how diverse the motivations for not completing a purchase online are, it should come as no surprise that, in America for instance, almost 70% of all shopping carts filled in webshops don't actually make it to check-out.[18]. Excessive shipping costs are the number one kill-factor[19], with 44% of those surveyed saying that this was the reason they aborted their purchase. Another 41% didn't end up placing their order because, quite simply, they weren't ready to buy the product(s) in question. The third cause of what are often referred to "orphaned baskets" is that around one quarter of customers use the function as a shopping list rather than an actual shopping cart. Meanwhile, 22% ejected at the last minute because

18 www.baymard.com (as in 2015)
19 www.seewhy.com (as in 2015)

no shipping costs were displayed: this probably makes the deal look too good to be true and, by extension, dubious; customers are wary online and don't want to get a nasty small-print surprise further down the road. Another four common causes of cancellation before purchase were the obligation to create a user account (this scared off 14% of those surveyed), concern about a complex-looking check-out area (11%), the lack of a preferred payment option (7%), or delivery dates too far in the future (6%).

In view of this broad spectrum of reasons to abandon carts, there can be no doubt that rates of non-completion will remain high in e-commerce. Yet this is not as disastrous as its sounds: after all, not every customer who goes into a department store just to have a look around or kill some time walks out with bulging bags – and it is not this behaviour that is causing bricks-and-mortar stores their problems. What is more, some of the highly frequent causes of cancellation tend to indicate that filling up and not purchasing an online shopping cart is often actually just another stage in the customer journey towards a purchase. Only 25% of those who abandon a cart in a webshop will never return; the other three quarters will come back to the shop where they left the "orphaned basket"[20]. After all, users who aborted because they were simply not ready to buy the product and those who just use their cart as a shopping list have, in fact, revealed a relatively concrete intent to purchase – and can be reminded of this intention using retargeting (see 2.3.2). From a sales perspective, this kind of behaviour is actually very beneficial: if a woman stops by a premium department store every couple of weeks and longingly fondles a pair of expensive designer shoes, no-one in the marketing department knows where she lives or how to contact her. Yet if the same woman also keeps a basket full of un-bought fashion items at an online retailer, she will almost certainly have divulged her IP, perhaps even her e-mail address, and given a comprehensive list of all the products she has been eyeing up.

Nevertheless, there are specific steps which can be taken to improve the online orders process and reduce the numbers of purchases interrupted for the wrong reasons. If, for example, shipping charges are too high or delivery times too long, there should be a concerted examination of how they can be cut down (see 2.6 Logistics). Meanwhile, if customers show a reluctance to register in order to make a purchase, or if they want other payment options than those offered, then changes must be made to order processing; the same goes for overly-complex, intimidating check-out areas.

20 Research: *Gesamtkosten von Zahlungsverfahren*, www.seewhy.com (as of March 2015)

Shopping baskets and check-outs

How can digital shopping baskets be designed to that customers who have decided to buy immediately do not put them down until money has changed hands? It's a simple question – and one that has very clear answers. There are a range of specific measures which can be implemented to make sure customers do not get cold feet, most of which revolve around offering them as much transparency as possible and in strengthening the decision to buy and confidence in paying by underlining the legitimacy of the shop. And whatever happens, the contents of shoppers' carts should always be stored – just in case the customer does interrupt the purchase to return later. Finally, there is nothing wrong with adding a few tried-and-tested favourites from every salesman's box of tricks ...

In what follows, we offer an overview of shopping-basket best practice which will help make sure that the contents of online carts make it through check-out with increased regularity[21]. If you're an already an expert, none of this will be new to you; yet it is always astonishing to note just how often many of these basic rules are broken when digital shopping baskets are designed.

Avoiding the basket case

A good digital shopping basket always shows customers how many steps are left until their purchase has been made: standard steps from basket to check-out are customer address, selecting delivery options, and making payment. These stages need to be depicted as a kind of **roadmap** in a way that makes them look as simple as possible. A popular way of doing this is to use four or five arrows across the top of the screen to show progress: Cart, Address and Delivery, Payment, Order. These steps can also be displayed as chains or lines along which the user advances: Amazon, for example, moves a cart icon through the steps to indicate to the user where they are in the process, with steps completed shown behind the icon in corporate orange and the stages to come in light grey. This kind of overview should always be placed near the top of the page to assure visibility and underline its status as a navigation tool (which, on almost every site, is towards the top of the page and therefore where users instinctively look).

21 www.konversationskraft.de (as of March 2015)

Shopping Basket

		Price	Quantity
	Selected Homme Men's Kivanc Leather Long Sleeve Jacket, Black, Medium by Selected Only 2 left in stock. Eligible for FREE UK Delivery ☐ This will be a gift Learn more Delete Save for later	**£183.19** You save: £51.81 (22%)	1
	New Look Men's Brushed Twill Long Sleeve Classic Slim Fit Formal Shirt, Orange (Burnt Orange), X-Small by New Look Only 1 left in stock. Eligible for FREE UK Delivery ☐ This will be a gift Learn more Delete Save for later	**£14.99**	1

Subtotal (2 items): £198.18

Total savings: **£51.81**

Fig. 2.21: Example of a Shopping Basket
Source: www.amazon.com (as of March 2016)

In terms of **information**, the number of items in the basket should be emphasised, followed by an overview of the individual products; to keep the contents easy to view at a glance, there should not be too much detail here, but all of the key points should be visible so that customers can check at any point that they have the right items: product name, a short description, and the price are essential, as is the number of each item in order to avoid the kind of unintentional double-ordering so common when users stock up a basket over several sessions or navigate away from the basket to the product and back during a single session.

Notifications about dispatch and shipping should also be shown here: customers should get as much information about current availability as possible, including the estimated date of delivery and any shipping costs levied (or *not* levied, as the case may be). This prevents unwelcome surprises and confusion later on in the check-out process.

Nevertheless, the precise order and way in which this important information is divulged may vary from shop to shop, depending on its circumstances. An overall rule is that products currently unavailable must be shown as such in the basket at the very latest (better on the product page, to avoid that annoying "restaurant experience" when the waiter has to go to the kitchen before coming back to say that a dish is off the menu; see 2.2 Product presentation), yet how the emphasis is placed depends on whether most of the goods in the shop is always available or not. In shops which have generally high availability, "In stock now" should be posted next to all products; if a shop's range is different and only a small number of products is continually available, the "In stock now" notification would only be displayed for a minority of items in most baskets, which would in turn make all of the other, later delivery dates – however close they may be – look poor.

The precise point at which to notify customers of shipping costs is often, simply put, a matter of trial and error. Shops which do not charge for delivery should definitely make sure this is prominently communicated in the basket: this reminds the customer of the competitive advantage and makes sure they don't wrongly suspect foul play and a nasty surprise later on in the order process. The same is true for shops which have special no-delivery-fee offers or which drop them from a certain spend threshold: any offer in which delivery fees are waived should be announced in the basket.

Beyond this, however, different shops' customer bases have different overall reactions to how shipping costs are displayed. Some customers like to see the end price they will be paying very early on in the order process and get cold feet when they see messages like "not including delivery" next to the price of their goods in the basket. Others, however, rely on this delay as a kind of psychological crutch which gets them moving towards the check-out: the price looks pretty cheap still, right? If a shop doesn't display shopping costs early in the basket and suffers from high rates of abandonment at later stages, then it might be advisable to try front-loading the notification; if there isn't an improvement in completion rates, then the issue may be the price of the delivery costs (see 2.6 Logistics), not the positioning of information about them. However it is done, delivery costs must at least be mentioned in the shopping-cart phase before check-out: any other approach looks like attempted deception – and may even be investigated as such by the relevant authorities.

Not that **sales psychology** doesn't play a key role in online shopping baskets: price discounts should be shown at all stages – just like they are on a product in a physical shop – in order to keep reminding customers that they are enjoying a price cut and underline the wiseness of their decision to buy. An even more effective tool is limitation: baskets should be linked with the electronic inventory system to make sure that it is always made clear when there are only a few of a given item left in stock. In online clothing retail, sentences such as "Only 1 left in this size/colour" are one of the strongest buy-triggers there are.

Another key psychological factor is the feeling of **security**: online shops which are not yet widely known or are new to the market are often greeted with suspicion and must do everything they can to allay customer fears. After all, in e-commerce, customers are lacking physical contact with the product and often not entirely surely if what they are buying will be right for them; if they are also unsure about who the seller is and whether the purchase will ever reach them, they are highly unlikely to take a risk.

This is one reason to offer a range of payment options, perhaps including the ability to pay on delivery, or at least involving trusted brokers such as PayPal – and to make sure this range of payment options is communicated early in the basket so that customers know they will be able to pay with their preferred method. Customers who don't find a payment option they like often abandon their carts (see below), and the same goes for the delivery options: customers who've recently spent a fruitless morning waiting for DHL or UPS will be happy to see other choices.

As a general rule,
customers – quite understandably –
need a lot of reassurance in the shopping basket
and as they move towards the check-out.

Trust-building measures such as the "Trusted Shop" safety badge should be placed in a clearly visible way, as should any signage about safe SSL data transfer so that customers know that not every spotty teenage hacker this side of China will be able to read their credit card details. Information about returns policies, too, can help to build trust at this stage, as can a reminder of any environmental certifications the shop has or carbon-neutral services it uses (DHL offers carbon-neutral shipping, for example, complete with a badge for online shops). Contact details should also be displayed in shopping baskets, too: a telephone hotline number with opening hours as well as an e-mail address should be offered; although almost no-one will ever call it, the telephone number does a huge amount to create trust – most customers who have questions about their order, however, are likelier to write an e-mail. First-time buyers especially, meanwhile, like to be able to buy without having to open a customer account: anyone who has been using the same e-mail address as a username for online shopping accounts for five years or so will only have to look at their own inbox to see just how difficult it can be to avoid unwanted or overly-frequent newsletters, sales adverts, and the like. Offering the option of a guest order can be a good way of signalling to customers that the first priority is to serve them in their specific wish now, not to try and milk them for every spare penny they have further down the line. What is more, an increasing number of internet users are becoming concerned with data protection; while still a minority, those prospective customers who see being forced to set up an account as an imposition on their privacy are more likely to abandon their cart than to complete the purchase.

Any niggling doubts which remain can be allayed by reminding customers that, even in the shopping basket, they retain the ultimate control over the process. Including buttons such as "Continue shopping" leading back into the shop leaves a back-door open which lets consumers retreat from their cart without having to flee the shop entirely. Users subconsciously register the absence of pressure and feel comfortable on the site.

Light at the end of the check-out tunnel

Although not pressuring customers into purchasing is important, it is equally important to make sure that, once they have decided to go to the check-out, nothing else gets in the way. The principle behind this is called "tunnelling": once they make the decision to purchase, customers enter into a tunnel from which they can only retreat by clicking the back button or by, ideally, emerging having checked out. Navigation options are limited so that all forms of distraction are removed: category bars, product search fields, and all forms of advertising should be removed; even the site logo at the top left which, in almost all standard web designs, takes the user back to the homepage, can be made inactive. The reason for removing all these other navigational options is to make sure that customers concentrate fully on entering their address and payment data – and that they don't click on something else and forget their immediate intention to purchase. This is in no way coercion: customers who decide, even at this late stage, that they really don't want to buy now, can always simply close the browser or application.

If a customer does indeed do this, the basket they were moving towards the check-out with should not be deleted: many customers, in fact, are counting on the "eternal shopping cart" retaining the products they almost-nearly-bought because they are using it as a form of digital list. Above all, baskets belonging to any customers who have actively identified themselves (see 2.2. Product presentation) should never be emptied, even after long periods of inactivity; this data is stored in the customer account as a matter of course – as is the customer's e-mail address. The items in the cart can therefore be advertised directly to the customer's inbox, and studies show that this form of specific advertising can be well worth the investment: customers who are successfully lured back into a shop in which they abandoned a purchase often go on to spend up to 50% more when they do eventually go ahead and place an order.[22]

Even if the user in question does not have an account, passive forms of identification can be used to pin abandoned baskets to specific profiles or, at the very least, cookies; using display-ad retargeting (see 2.3.2), customers can then be reminded of precisely the items which they left in the basket and, if the user re-accesses the shop using the same device, the basket can be reloaded in a matter of seconds – hopefully for the customer to take with them on the next approach to the check-out.

Payments

Once customers place orders, the next big hurdle is payment – and it can, in fact, be one of the hardest to clear. A lasting mismatch between the methods of payment an online shop offers and the methods its customers are willing or indeed able to use leads to less orders being placed; in markets with strong payment preferences, a significant proportion of users will abandon a purchase if they cannot make the payment using their preferred method (in Germany, for example, one in five customers retreats and a whopping 67% consider cancelling the purchase)[23]. At the same time, many forms of payment come with their own risks for shop owners and may lead to serious liquidity issues. From the customer point of view, a new and untested shop may make them unwilling to use certain forms of payment they might be happy to use elsewhere.

22 www.forrester.com (as of January 2015)
23 www.ecckoeln.de, access through www.docplayer.org (as of March 2015)

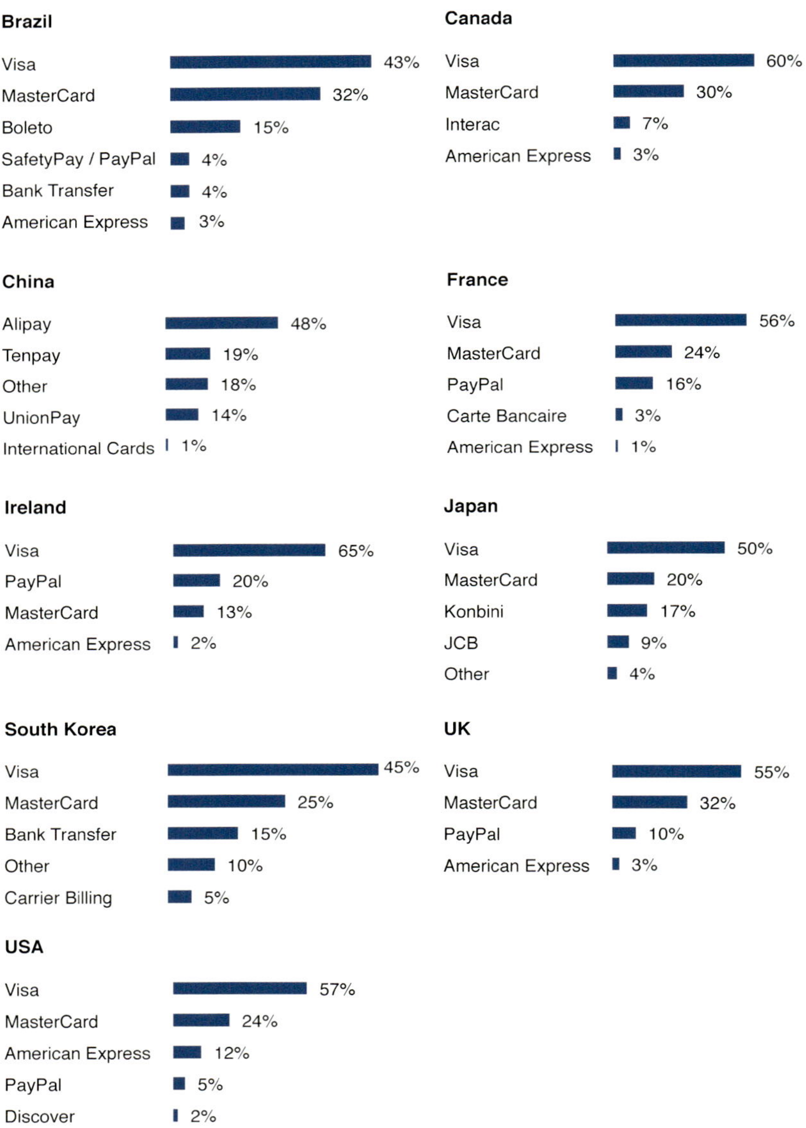

Fig. 2.22: International preferences for methods of payment

Source: https://www.adyen.com/dam/documentation/paymentmethods/global-ecommerce-payments-guide-2015.pdf (as of March 2016)

In what follows, we will take a closer look at customer and seller requirements of payment systems, highlighting the payment options around which they coalesce – and where payment habits and preferences vary considerably between countries. We then move on to examine the most popular methods of payment both from a consumer perspective and as viewed from the point of view of an online shop.

Customer requirements

The central issue for many customers is the **ability to recall a payment**, especially if they are making a first-time purchase: nevertheless, this need finds various forms of expressions worldwide based on local preferences. In the US and UK markets, for example, consumers are perfectly happy to use their credit cards: many card companies offer extensive chargeback, cancellation and insurance services – in case of fraud or faulty goods, there are generally statutory requirements for them to withhold payment or even refund consumers – and, what is more, generous terms of billing give customers ample time between paying and receiving goods. In markets with less favourable statutory and billing conditions, or just lower rates of credit card use overall, consumers may prefer a range of other payment options, from open invoicing (i.e. paying on receipt of goods), popular in a range of countries from Mexico to Germany and Sweden to direct debits (which can be cancelled in much of Europe) and internet-based payment services such as PayPal or, in China, Alipay.

In some markets – and some product segments – an additional issue is **anonymity**: German consumers, for example, have privacy concerns almost unknown in markets such as the US, and these frequently extend to e-commerce payments – even for harmless items such as socks. In many other territories, the need for anonymity is limited to racier fashion segments and other products which consumers may want to purchase with as little connection to their personal data as possible.

Common requirements

Where customers' and shop operators' requirements of payment options meet is in **technical security and reliability**: if payment details are intercepted, customers may suffer considerable inconvenience as their cards and accounts are blocked; sellers, meanwhile, may later lose payments. In data processing, too, neither customers nor sellers benefit from erroneous payments which may result in unpleasant surprises at a later date.

Yet both parties also share an interest in **speed** and **low transaction costs**:

Buyers want to be able to make a purchase without needing to read complicated instruction; sellers want to get their money as quickly as possible; and neither wants to pay too much for the service.

Americans are, for instance, often surprised to find that, outside of the US, many countries' restaurateurs, store owners, and online shop operators will not accept American Express: compared to VISA and Mastercard, however, Amex charges far higher fees to both parties, which keeps customers from using this option and, by extension, robs sellers of any remaining incentive to offer the expensive payment method. It's a vicious circle for Amex which shows just how important it is for a payment method to offer both buyers and sellers a **broad field of application** and **high rates of acceptance**.

This leads on to another must: **universal usability**. Customers do not want a wallet bulging with 10 various plastic cards when, in theory, one debit card and one credit card really should be enough. Increasingly, customers also expect this universality to apply between countries: cross-border shopping is one of the most rapidly growing areas of e-commerce, but growth is slowed if customers find their preferred means of payment are limited to specific territories. Sellers especially need to offer internationally valid forms of payment and, if looking to grow in certain markets, ought to consider adding local methods to their mix.

Another area where consumer and business interests align is **traceability and records**. Both the buyer and the seller like to receive documentation; the latter must, by law, keep records of sales for their accounts. Receipts with the time of the payment, the amount paid, the party paying and the party receiving money – whether printed or electronic – are a must. In two or three-step payment processes, further documentation once payment has been completed is also in the interests of both parties.

Business requirements

Sellers have some requirements, however, which are actually quite contrary to those of buyers. While some customers want a high level of anonymity, shop operators generally want **information about their customers**, both for simple bookkeeping purposes and, of course, with a view to building up comprehensive customer profiles.

The point at which business and consumer requirements are most at odds, however, is the possibility of recalling a payment. For e-commerce businesses, a **guaranteed payment** is the only desirable goal; anything else is compromise. Ideally, payment is drawn immediately – or pledged by a certain date – and cannot be rescinded *post facto*. Yet this ideal is rarely achieved because customers, of course, want the precise opposite: the customer's preference is for a bill with months left until the due date and, perhaps, a generous line of credit to boot. For retailers, the danger of this kind of bill going unpaid – as well as of cancelled direct debits or card payments – is not to be underestimated, especially in view of the paper-thin margins many are running on.

Payment options in e-commerce

This tug-of-war between sellers, who want money now rather than never, and customers, who would rather wait until they've got the product before kissing the cash goodbye, often leads to a discrepancy between the methods businesses offer and the methods customers want to use. In Germany, for example, the methods most commonly offered by e-commerce retailers are various forms of prepayment: customers, on the other hand, repeatedly state in surveys than an open invoice – i.e. delayed payment – is their preferred method of making an online purchase[24]. Direct debit is customers' second preference, but not one of the three most beloved of sellers: the SOFORT online banking transfer solution, however, despite far lower customer acceptance rates, is in the top three preferred methods for retailers. Only PayPal is in both consumers' and businesses' three preferred methods.

24 www.ecckoeln.de, access through www.docplayer.org (as of March 2015)

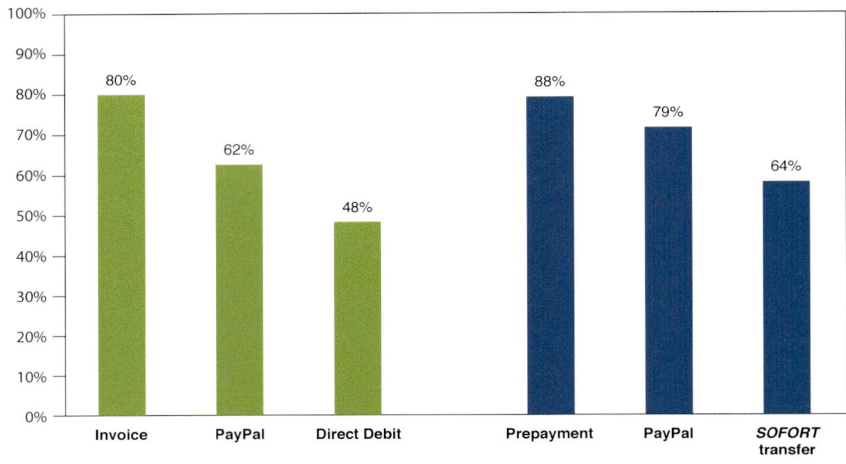

Fig. 2.23: Businesses' and consumers' preferred methods of payment in the German market

Source: our graphic, with reference to www.ecckoeln.de/Downloads/Themen/Payment/PaymentimE-CommerceDerInternetzahlungsverkehrausSichtderHndlerundderVerbraucherIZ2013.pdf (as in March 2015)

This mismatch between the methods of payment into which German businesses are trying to force their customers and the methods customers actually prefer to use may well act as a brake on growth in the market. Certainly, countries in which e-commerce takes a higher share of retail show better alignments between consumer and business preferences: in the USA and the UK, credit and debit cards are extremely popular with consumers and business alike, accounting for 95 and 90% of payments in the two countries respectively; this is both owing to consumer habits predating e-commerce and to widely implemented improvements in card security, which make the method the safest both for buyers and sellers.

Nevertheless, neither Germany nor Sweden are underdeveloped e-commerce markets and run on very high rates of invoicing for payment at a later date, despite sellers' understandable unwillingness to offer this method. It therefore stands to reason that business from outside these two markets looking to enter it would do well to offer open invoicing if they can afford to take the slightly increased risk of non-payment. Another phenomenon characteristic for these two markets – and several others in Europe such as France, the Netherlands, and Poland – are a broader range of popular payment methods featuring country-specific systems: there is SOFORT bank transfer in Germany and similar systems such as the Dutch iDEAL and France's Carte Bancaire interbank systems. China is an even more exotic payment prospect: international credit card brands such as VISA and Mastercard have an extremely low level of penetration while the Alipay escrow system – the market's most popular form of payment – fulfils the role of PayPal in Western e-commerce. Then there is Tenpay, a hybrid internet transfer/credit card/prepaid solution, as well as the UnionPay banking transfer network.

All of which means that, in the foreseeable future, a broad range of payment options are set to co-exist globally, and that e-commerce companies looking to grow internationally will have to take account of local preferences to reach their full potential there. In the following, we will take a brief look at the most important forms of payment and the advantages and disadvantages inherent to them.

An overview of the most common forms of payment

PayPal is a universal payment platform which can be accessed by users worldwide. An e-mail address is used to identify users, and there is no fundamental difference between buyers and sellers: each has an account linked either to a bank account or a credit card. The buyer uses PayPal as a payment option, sending PayPal the funds either by direct debit, credit card, or transfer, and PayPal sends the money to the seller's account. This process offers customers a range of advantages: as payments are made to the seller by PayPal, not the customer, there is a degree of anonymity and data privacy; PayPal also offers some buyer protection, meaning that funds can be recalled if an item does not arrive or is not as advertised. Sellers, too, benefit from a certain level of insurance, and do not have to pay any fees until they actually receive money (currently below 2% plus a fixed per-transaction price). **AliPay** is a similar platform specialising on the Chinese market: as an escrow service which only disburses funds to sellers once buyers have approved goods on receipt, its level of customer protection is extremely high, due primarily to gaps in Chinese consumer legislation; this, in turn, explains its popularity in China.

While internet payment platforms are present to a varying degree in almost all markets, open invoicing is a primarily a feature of wealthy northern European economies: German, Dutch, and Scandinavian consumers are particularly fond of this method of payment by which they receive a bill with the goods; they then pay the invoice, generally by bank transfer (standard terms of payment are a fortnight or 28 days). Customers only need to specify their billing address until they actually remit funds; only if they want to delay payment or pay in instalments do they need to provide sellers with more information for creditworthiness checks. Businesses are not fond of this payment method as they have to go to the trouble of producing and, not infrequently, following up on invoices; many therefore outsource the process to payment service providers who interface with webshops (**PayOne, Easybill, Billomat**) and factoring companies, who buy in the debt and chase non-payers. Despite attempts in some quarters to pass on the cost of this to customers, competitive shops tend still to offer this method free of surcharge.

Credit and debit cards, too, require payment service providers called acquirers: once these have been integrated into a shop system, however, payments made by **Visa**, **Mastercard** and other cards are generally cheap and simple for sellers. Some commission is charged by the acquirer for processing the payment, and many business have therefore started passing on the charges to consumers – especially in English-speaking countries with a habit of paying by credit card and few other widespread payment options; this has, in turn, attracted the attention of consumer watchdogs and lawmakers. Generally, charges are higher for credit than for debit cards – debit card payments generally being free in markets such as the UK and France.

Credit cards remain king.

Nevertheless, credit cards remain king in many of these markets, despite both increasing charges to consumers and decreasing levels of protection for them – especially since the introduction of new checks such as 3D Secure, which have reversed the burden of proof for fraudulent use onto the consumer. At the same time, security checks add a layer of complexity to credit card payments which can hamper conversion, as not all consumers can always remember their passwords. Nevertheless, 3D Secure actually increases conversion in the UK market, reassuring consumers that maximum safety standards are being upheld. In northern and eastern European countries, however, the extra security checks frequently increase aborted purchases and credit card use is generally lower overall; banks are less free in dealing out unsecured credit to consumers, and many businesses, too, do not have company credit cards. As such, e-commerce businesses working in Europe must place more emphasis on other payment methods than in the English-speaking world.

In the Eurozone overall, and Germany and the Netherlands in particular, direct debit (in the form of SEPA) is one of the most popular non-credit, non-card methods of payment in e-commerce. Although customers have little by way of anonymity – they have to disclose their bank account details on purchase – they can reverse the debit for up to eight weeks after payment. This reassures customers that they can recall funds if the purchase goes wrong and unsettles retailers, who know that the money which has appeared in their accounts may disappear again at any time over the coming 56 days. On average, one in twenty payments is actually recalled, which poses a risk for the selling party; the low costs of the method and the ease with which it can be processed by payment service providers do little to make e-commerce businesses any happier about offering it.

This perhaps explains the fondness of European retailers for online bank transfer solutions: like a direct debit, this is a bank-to-bank transfer, yet by getting customers to actively wire the funds, businesses eliminate the risk as banks will not reverse this kind of transaction. As with credit card payments, sellers use acquirers to direct consumers from the webshop to their online banking interfaces, where they then make the transfer; the retailer receives immediate notification of payment. Given the considerable potential for abuse, most European countries have their own authorised system of e-commerce online bank transfers: Germany uses **SOFORT** and **Giropay**, while in the Netherlands, **iDEAL** is the system of choice; in Poland, online banking is by far the most popular method of payment. As with credit and debit card payments, customers who do not have their card numbers and passwords to hand have to break off the transaction. In markets which lack the necessary electronic and banking infrastructure for this kind of online system, prepaid cards and e-wallets have become popular methods of payment – particularly in economies without widespread credit card take-up (Russia, Turkey, many developing economies).

Prepaid cards and e-wallets have become popular methods of payment.

In Russia, e-wallets have become particularly widespread: Qiwi and Yandex have approaching half of the market share in e-commerce payments. Prepaid cards also occupy niches in rich economies, offering as they do a high degree of anonymity for customers concerned about privacy and an option for customers without access to bank accounts or who cannot get credit: their increasing popularity in Spain and several other southern European economies may be read as a symptom of the recent economic crisis. Nevertheless, offline prepaid cards especially do not offer particularly good value for money: by converting cash into a credit balance, customers are then bound to spend it, and some providers deduct money from the balance monthly; sellers, too, can face eyewatering fees of 5% or more (sometimes up to a whopping 35%) per payment and must make an investment to integrate the systems into their shops. This limits their appeal to retailers in specific geographic markets with high demand for this payment method – and to those dealing in product ranges where sales success is predicated on customer anonymity during the purchasing process.

Quite the opposite in terms of anonymity are the new mobile payment systems which look set to spread rapidly in the very near future. Currently, the two biggest competing systems are **Apple Pay** and **Google Wallet**, sent by their eponymous proprietors to try and stake out as much of this new territory as possible. Mobile payment systems share many features with existing internet payment platforms and e-wallets – they are linked, like PayPal, to bank accounts or credit cards and carry out payments to retailers on behalf of their customers – yet combine this with smartphone and contactless card technology to potentially create a system as suited to payment in the online as in the offline world. In bricks-and-mortars payment situations, for example, a smartphone running ApplePay or Google Wallet uses a near-field communication (NFC) chip to link to the till; the user enters a pin on the display and authorises the payment. ApplePay can, however, also be used in entirely online situations: i.e. to make in-app purchases or to buy other apps and content in the Apple Store; Google Wallet can be used in the same way for Google Play purchases. Based on its predecessor Google Checkout, Google Wallet has also been integrated into a range of online shops as an external payment provider. This can and should be construed as an attack on PayPal, and now that battle has been joined, another power turns out to have already deployed an army in the field: Amazon, which is trying to hook up as many shops as possible to **Amazon Payments**. In this battle for coverage, all of the three online giants are providing payment services at dumping rates of commission: Apple's current charge is a few cents on $100 USD. Then again, there is no such thing as a free lunch, and the Big Three are taking their value in the form of the huge amount of payment data this area of business offers and the depth of integration they are achieving into the customer experience. Based on previous form, it is not overly adventurous to predict that the tech giants will use low fees to buy themselves dominant market presence and, once enough other businesses have become dependent on their services, jack up the prices.

Hands and bushes, or: risk management for retailers

Both in terms of potential developments in the future and with a view to today's customer preferences, it is incredibly unwise for online shop operators to become too dependent on single forms of payment. On the internet, retailers must offer the forms of payment their customers demand. While the first instinct of those who are unused to open invoicing, retractable direct debit payments, or payment in instalments may well be to say "A bird in the hand is worth two in the bush" and stick to other methods (credit cards, bank transfers), there is no reason why online retailers can't lay their hands on all three birds: offering one form of payment does not prevent anyone from offering others.

Especially when expanding into European markets with strong, if unfamiliar payment preferences, avoiding what may appear to be risky options such as open invoicing and direct debit is actually a risk in and of itself.

> *Not offering customers their favourite payment options is likely to hem growth and prevent retailers from realising the full potential of the market.*

In Germany in 2014, for example, around one quarter of turnover in the biggest 1,000 online shops was received through open invoices (that ranks ahead of PayPal, which had 20%[25]); retailers experience a higher percentage of purchasing on invoice than many C2C sellers or digital companies as customers in Germany like to use open invoicing for fashion, furniture, and other bigger-ticket material goods, reserving PayPal and credit cards – the other two top online retail payment options – for digital goods and services.

There are a range of financial and socio-cultural reasons behind the limitations to card use compared to many English-speaking countries, from low credit limits (a miserly €500 monthly is perfectly normal even for Germans with a good credit rating) through to a generalised fear of buying on the never-never, and this means that US or UK companies entering the German market are best off going with the flow rather than trying to swim against the current. Despite the risks that – even in a country with such low levels of crime and debt and high levels of interpersonal trust as Germany – open invoicing inherently creates, studies show that, overall, it leads to a clear uptick in turnover for online shops with introduce it: on average, offering customers the option of paying on receipt ups sales by 17.9%; offering

25 EHI Retail Institute (2014), *Online-Payment-Studie*

store credit and payment by instalments adds another 14%[26]. The same study revealed that introducing PayPal and Amazon Payments also increases turnover by more than 20%, meaning that no one option is a trump card, but that each has its strengths. Retailers are well advised to play these kings, queens, and jacks according to their product mix, average basket values, and the market they are in: anyone offering big-ticket items in Germany or Sweden, for example, would be well advised to offer finance deals. Not that the risks can – or should – be ignored.

To manage the potential losses, it is helpful to quantify them.

One method of doing this is to ask other retailers[27]: on average, for instance, German online shop operators lose around 1% of direct debits; while approximately 5% of all direct debits using SEPA are reversed, this includes figures for continuing obligations such as rental or tax payments, both of which are retracted far more frequently. Meanwhile, open invoicing leads to average losses of 1.4%; the real dark horse would appear to be purchases on credit plans, where around 2% of turnover never materialises. Credit card payments and PayPal are very safe indeed (0.5 and 0.25 rates of default respectively), while bank transfers and other methods of pre-payment are, of course, safe as houses. These figures change markedly, however, in a markets such as the US, the UK, and France, where statutory consumer protection allows customers to cancel credit payments far more easily, leading to a higher propensity to chargeback first and ask questions later (a particularly widespread phenomenon in the United States).

Whatever the method in the dock, any payment lost by an online shop is an annoyance, especially – given the high set-up costs and often narrow margins – in the early trading phase. What is more, it is precisely when shops are just starting up which are most often the victims of defaults: while in a tiny minority, there are rogue consumers out there who keep an eye out for young, inexperienced outfits and push their luck with them as far as they can. For many in this thankfully small group, fraudulent shopping is almost a game in which they test the limits to find chinks in the armour: what happens if I reverse the charge on my credit card or recall the direct debit after having received the goods? Is there a follow-up on whether the goods were actually damaged or not as advertised? If so, how professional is the returns department? Can I simply claim to have sent the goods back

26 www.ecckoeln.de (as in March 2015)
27 EHI Retail Institute (2012), *Online-Payment-Studie*

and get a refund, all the while holding onto the product in question? Once they have tricks that work, these consumers will spread the word, alert and on the lookout for threshold order sizes which might set alarm bells ringing: they are, truly, the worst nightmare of every online shop.

For new outfits without a generous line of credit or a lot of venture capital finance behind them, it is always better to get one credit check too many than one too few: while credit bureaus charge fees for the service, it is surprising how many of these mavericks are known to them – as are, of course, those with no malicious intent but equally little ability in managing their financial affairs. This doesn't mean that shops need to categorically turn away customers with a poor credit rating, but it might well be advisable to limit them to prepayment methods, for instance, or pass on any bills sent to them for payment-on-delivery purchases straight onto a factoring firm. Young shops would also do well to keep an internal league table of payers, decreasing the amount of external service provision needed for risk management over time and allowing them to gain experience with their own customers.

In fact, as shops gain in experience and grow their customer base, this kind of internal book-keeping can be a commercial advantage: well-kept customer histories can be just as informative as expensive credit checks.

Assuming, for example, that a loyal customer who generally goes through checkout with a high cart value and rarely returns any products decides to switch from paying by, say, debit card and take advantage of a newly introduced open invoicing option: even if a credit check sets off red lights and sirens, it may well be worth considering allowing them to use this method: there is a risk that the bill won't get paid, but there is also the risk of snubbing a valuable, long-term customer by not showing them trust.

The costs of payment methods

Here at the very latest is where a professional qualification in business studies can have its uses: besides actual loss of payment, what does each method actually cost? While shop operators get bills from payment service providers and acquirers which vary with their turnover and its precise breakdown into individual payments, this is by no means the bottom-line figure for transaction costs. Open invoices, direct debits, and finance not only cause costs for credit checks, but also carry internal costs to cover potential default which cannot be calculated to a high degree of exactitude; yet from a business point of view, even prepayment methods such as bank transfer before delivery create indirect costs, e.g. bookkeeping costs to identify incoming transfers and assign them to the right orders. Other invisible costs are incurred with prepayment processes as goods remains in the warehouse taking up space until payment arrives and is assigned to the right item; if the payment then doesn't materialise, but the goods had been removed from sale, then opportunity costs for further sales are also incurred.

These non-cash costs are systematically underestimated by those who focus on the risk of non-payment or on the costs billed by payment service providers; yet there is empirical evidence which shows that even payment methods with minimal service provider involvement still create high levels of costs[28]. Looking at the matter from a total cost perspective, requesting that customers make a bank transfer prior to dispatch – i.e. a method which causes no direct cash cost to the seller and has a default risk of 0% – still entails costs of 3.52% on average; meanwhile, using an integrated bank transfer system such as SOFORT only eats away 1.87% of the sale, including the fee paid to the service provider. And all of these calculations are prior to trying to put a price on a lack in customer acceptance of certain payment methods (see above).

Nevertheless, even if figures are to be taken with a pinch of salt, it remains well worth examining payment systems with regard to their costs and, consequently, their role for profit margins. Another important reason to examine payment options closely is the role they play in customers' decisions to return products: customers who have yet to pay when their goods arrive have one less psychological barrier to filling out the returns slip. It stands to reason that the most egregious returns (those stained tuxedos stinking of cigar smoke with tickets to the opera in the inside pocket...) are risked by customers who have yet to part with the money and therefore do not have to make a good case for it to be refunded (see next chapter, 2.6 Logistics). Despite this, however, a range of studies has shown that more than half of all online shop operators do not take active measures to steer use of the payment options they offer.

It is not that they are lacking the possibility to do so.

28 www.ibi.de (abgerufen März 2015)

Retailers can, of course, actively channel customers away from certain riskier payment options such as invoicing or direct debit by simply not offering them.

Yet there is, as discussed above, an advantage to offering a wide range of payment methods so that customers do not immediately abort their purchases because their favourite is missing. A gentler way of passively directing customers can be to add fees to those methods which offer less security or, even better, to offer discounts to customers who buy on low-cost, low-risk payment options; free shipping for users of specific payment methods is one way of doing this. This is perfectly legitimate: not all payment methods are entirely equal, and there will always be a *primus inter pares* in every shop which, depending on market segment and territory, gives the retailer more bang from each buck. Trying to channel customers into more profitable payment options is an obvious business reaction to this.

In this regard, indeed, e-commerce check-outs are similar to supermarkets': if customers see that not enough tills are manned, they won't even bother to get in the queue. For a supermarket, the obvious response is to open up another one: but the hourly wage the cashier receives, the speed at which he or she works, and the flexibility with which he or she reacts to last-minute purchases and can spot incongruous sum total prices is worth keeping an eye on in comparison to performance on other tills.

2.6 Logistics

Introduction

As virtual as e-commerce is, the point at which it succeeds or fails is frequently a very physical one: logistics. However sleek and easy-to-use an online shop may be, any non-digital goods which customers order need to be delivered to them fast and without hitches to avoid complaints, returns, and reputational damage. Not all shops face precisely the same challenge, of course: primarily, train companies and airlines sell tickets which can just as easily be sent electronically as by post (with the pleasant side effect that costs for paper and printing are borne by the customer); one step further in this direction is e-ticketing in which travel documents are made available on a mobile device immediately following payment – and can be verified by conductors or airport personnel on the smartphone or pad. These documents need never exist outside of the digital sphere and are, as such, similar to music downloads and video streaming services which can offer real-time digital delivery. In these segments, there is now no break in medium between payment and product; but until *Star Trek*-style holograms have become everyday features, there is no way around a transfer into the physical world for, say, a furniture retailer, who has to move several hundred pounds of wood and metal to customers' homes on a daily basis.

This means that anyone offering physical products in e-commerce needs to spend a lot of planning time and thought on how best to surmount the physical distance between their customers and their stock (or outsource this part of proceedings wholesale to a third-party service provider). This in turn means making sure that processes in the following three areas, usually grouped together as "fulfilment", are fit for purpose:

1. **Commissioning** – also known as "picking and packing", taking goods ordered from their storage location in the warehouse and packaging them ready for dispatch
2. **Shipping** – dispatching and delivering orders to customers
3. **Returns** – receiving and processing goods which has been returned

Malfunctions in just one of these three areas are a serious matter. Errors in commissioning can lead to customers receiving the wrong articles and having to return these or wait for the item they actually purchased to arrive. If these wrongly packed items are sent back to a returns department in difficulty, then the chaos turns into farce. Yet while first-class handling of returned goods is an important service issue, shipping is the most difficult area of the three to get right: commissioning and returns are both process sets which an online shop can design and improve itself; shipping, however, is almost entirely in the hands of the parcel delivery companies. And these couriers are groaning under the sheer weight of packages as e-commerce expands.

This opens up a divide between multichannel retailers and online pure-plays (see 2.4.3 Distribution): the former can use their own network of branches and existing in-house logistics structures to offer customers the option of picking up online purchases in their stores, which not only saves shipping costs but also hands back control to customers about when and where to get their goods. The British Argos chain, for example, an old hat when it comes to multichannelling (it began by blending catalogue and in-store sales techniques) is now making additions to its existing network of shops in shopping centres and high street locations, opening up collection points in London's busy rail stations. The city's commuters can pick up products they order by midday a few hours later on their way home. In Germany, bricks-and-mortar electronics retailer Saturn is also setting up collection points (albeit in its own stores only for the time being).[29] In London, meanwhile, Amazon – never one to be outdone – is also opening its own network of collection points: essentially outdoor boxes to which customers can have their orders delivered; in other cities, too, Amazon looks set to open networks of more or less public collection points. While Amazon certainly has no intention of opening expensive, fully functioning stores (see 2.4 Distribution), it is willing to experiment with this kind of low-cost solution.

After all, one of Amazon's tenets is not to skimp on any investment that will allow it to get products to customers as quickly and flexibly as possible: the global giant realised early on that, in internet shopping, logistics are actually even more important than price leadership or product mix – for two reasons.

Firstly, customers are only willing to order goods online which they could also get in bricks-and-mortar stores if their orders arrive accurately, rapidly, and relatively inexpensively – and if they are able to return them without too much difficulty if necessary.

29 www.internetworld.de (abgerufen März 2015)

If this logistical challenge is mastered, however, then customers become click-happy and will start ordering all sorts of things online they would previously have gone to shops for.

It saves time, after all: rather than spending those precious hours after a long day at work or a hard-earned free Saturday looking for a book, a game, and a DVD in three dedicated stores, busy professionals can simply order all three from Amazon in their lunch-hour at work and look forward to finding them in their letterbox by Friday afternoon: that's more family time on Friday night and a nice, long lie-in on Saturday. That is, in a nutshell, the key to how clicks are killing bricks – but only as long as the logistics are sorted.

Secondly, customers soon realise that Amazon sells at prices which are frequently cheaper than those of in-store retailers – even after shipping costs are included. Amazon's low-low prices are, however, only possible because of its success in organising its logistics activities: the Giant is simply so good at storing, commissioning, and shipping its wares that its costs are a fraction of what heritage retailers have been working with, despite (indeed, partially due to) the speed and reliability it offers in processing orders.

Case study: Amazon

Amazon's special approach to logistics starts with the location of its warehouses – or, in the argot it helped to shape, "fulfilment centres" – which are generally set up in economically depressed, more sparsely settled regions (yet only those offering good connections to urban conurbations). The thinking behind this is simple: there is plenty of space available at cheap rates; local authorities and their planning committees are receptive; there is plenty of willing labour. These geographical and economic factors allow Amazon to build mega-warehouses of over 100,00 yards square and run them with around 1,000 directly employed staff, using a reserve of around 2,000 seasonal workers to cover peaks in demand (especially in the run-up to Christmas).

This pool of labour is cheap, and technology is used to squeeze the maximum possible amount of efficiency out of it: pickers pulling down products from the shelves are given fly-by-wire directions from a central computer showing them the shortest route to the next product based on their current location in the warehouse. This is entirely necessary because Amazon has almost completely randomised storage, moving away from set locations for particular product categories: after all, the computer knows where it all is – and where the workers all are. Why take the time and trouble to produce – and then stick to – a set warehousing structure? Pickers are constantly monitored using their scanners and have to reach their next item within the time calculated by the computer. Process optimisation is a relentless hunt for potential improvements, carried out by managers schooled in lean principles: by way of example, the barcode scanners pickers carry would often need to be recharged during shifts, leading to bottlenecks. One manager realised this and optimised processes so that no scanner is ever handed out at the beginning of a shift with less than full charge.

With this system trimmed to nothing except efficiency, Amazon is perfectly capable of offering customers products at the same price as in-store retailers – often cheaper – although it also needs to locate these products in its warehouses, package and often pay postage on them, and then hand them on to couriers. Yet precisely in this area, the Giant shaves so much off its costs that it can afford to offer discounts. This, in turn, leads to more growth, which in turn means that Amazon can do things like offer free shipping from a certain order value upwards. Turnover, both overall and per order, grows; and the higher the amount of capacity used in a fulfilment centre, the more efficient it is – and the more money is saved to make the Amazon offering even more attractive. It's a virtuous circle.

As such, Amazon sets the standards in logistics against which all other e-commerce companies measure themselves – and to which they must aspire.

Shipping

Fulfilment and logistics service providers

While the Amazon system sets standards, it sets standards so high that most companies will have trouble reaching them, even on a small scale. The sheer level of sustained investment needed is prohibitive, and Amazon is already so far off down the track that it is almost out of sight. In Europe, Amazon fulfilment centres, for example, are often sited directly next to a large DHL distribution warehouse, meaning that they lorries barely get out of first gear before picking up their loads; Amazon is also way ahead of everyone on using high-performance robots to speed up its already speedy processes even more (see below). Indeed, Amazon has stolen such a march on retailers that it has capacity spare to sell back to other companies in e-commerce: both merchants and makers with online shops can use Amazon's fulfilment infrastructure to get their goods to customers, sending products to Amazon for short-term storage until sale, at which point Amazon packages and dispatches. Around 15% of Amazon's annual turnover is, in fact, earned in commission and logistics fees charged to other retailers and product manufacturers[30].

Those using Amazon as a service provider can choose between two levels of integration. Retailers and manufacturers acting as sellers on the Amazon Marketplace can use the whole range of fulfilment services: this means that Amazon not only packages products sold to its usual standards (i.e. customers can even choose gift-wrapping), but also offers delivery at the same service level as orders placed with Amazon directly. What is more, sellers and customers both enjoy the considerable benefits of Amazon's full service package: sellers have real-time access to inventory levels at Amazon warehouses, while buyers can use the Amazon interface to change orders before dispatch and track their packages once they have left the warehouse. If any problems arise during shipping or after unpacking, then Amazon customer service will offer a range of help options and, if necessary, handle returns. In this role as **full-service fulfilment provider**, Amazon charges the seller commission per item it picks and packs, as well as a lump-sum fee for each order it processes; weight supplements are levied for heavier items. On the other hand, Amazon pays shipping costs – either getting customers to shell out or, in many cases, taking the hit itself. For sellers, this is no bargain-basement option, and only really worthwhile for products with a sufficient margin in the sales price.

The second, looser model Amazon offers is on products which are not sold on the Amazon Marketplace: both online shop operators and sellers on other marketplaces such as Ebay may also use Amazon as a **fulfilment provider**, but with certain limits as opposed to the full-service package: in this model, Amazon takes care of packaging, shipping, and returns. Sellers pay pick-&-pack fees per item, a weight supplement, and shipping costs. The reason for Amazon's far less generous offering here is understandable: in Amazon's logic, sellers listing on the marketplace are helping the company to extend the range of products available on its online shop, which in turn attracts more customers and also increases leverage over the seller in line with the proportion of its sales happening on Amazon. This is a key element in Amazon's sales strategy: total dominance (see 2.4 Distribution). Even so, even those who opt for "fulfilment light" to handle orders through their own online shop

30 www.wiwo.de (as of March 2015)

are still automatically sharing sales data with the company: Amazon learns which products are selling well and may well consider adding them to its own product mix.

With this dual role as a fulfilment partner and a competing retailer, Amazon is markedly different from other service providers.

It has an unhealthy interest in sales statistics and is not especially customer-friendly to those using its – admittedly world-beating – services. Once goods are with Amazon, it's worry-free, but Amazon won't come and pick them up: it is the responsibility of retailers and manufacturers to inform the Giant about how much of which product they want to send and then await detailed instructions on how to get the goods to them, how they should be packed, and how they should be labelled. The seller has to organise and pay for the shipment to the fulfilment centre, the core of the Amazon service. The Giant's strength is in this core – this is where it stores goods, processes orders, and handles returns faster and better than anyone else – but transport is not its strongpoint and so it leaves parcel couriers such as DHL and Hermes to take the strain.

So, provided that they have another warehousing solution, online shops can, of course, skip the Amazon step and simply use parcel delivery companies as **logistics service partners**. Here, manufacturers and retailers package orders ready for dispatch to customers themselves, and the logistics company simply picks up the parcels, distributing them to the customers through their sorting centres. Nevertheless, some of these service partners are extending their range of services into areas such as commissioning and returns: DHL, especially, is looking to offer an Amazon-style package, having set up Allyouneed.de in Germany (and expanded into neighbouring Poland), an online marketplace which also offers full-service fulfilment to retailers listing there. Goods are stored in Staufenberg, near the geographical centre of Germany, where they are commissioned and then dispatched by DHL; Hamburg-based rival Hermes has also started offering fulfilment solutions for online shops, but has not gone so far as to open its own online marketplace. That this part of the retail value chain is booming has not escaped the notice of other companies, either, even those which have no previous history in logistics: Ebay now has a network of 27 fulfilment centres across North America and Europe operating under the Enterprise brand.

Sellers who take care of fulfilment activities such as commissioning in house, however, rely on logistics providers primarily as parcels services who simply pick up, ship, and return packages. There is a far broader range of companies offering this key service, and in order to find out which of them best suit their needs, manufacturers and retailers need to ask themselves a catalogue of questions:[31]

- Do the services offered suit the needs of the seller (e.g. if the seller sells internationally, does the provider also deliver abroad?)
- Which prices and conditions apply to which volume of orders?
- At what time precisely are packages picked up at the warehouse? And when are they delivered?
- Which interfaces – such as online order tracking – does the provider offer to sellers and buyers?
- Can particularities be accommodated if necessary (e.g. outsized or bulky items; refrigeration in food home-shopping)?

An online shop for surfboards shipping two or three a week on average will have requirements quite different from, say, an online shop selling up-to-the-minute fashion trends with hundreds of parcels leaving the warehouse every week. Nevertheless, in terms of factors such as price, parcel dimension limits, and delivery times, there is often very little between the various service providers.

The market is, quite simply, highly competitive and, with prices at rock bottom, many of the logistics service providers are looking to gain visibility by offering special services both to sellers and buyers. For business clients sending more than 300 parcels annually, for example, DHL will generally be willing to offer a specific time for daily or weekly pick-up, allowing companies to structure their processes. And for German consumers who order a lot online but aren't usually at home during the day to accept deliveries, DHL offers Packstations, for example, automated self-service booths often found outside post offices, supermarkets, or other high-frequency locations; customers can pick up their parcels when it suits them best – and may also use the Packstation to send off returns. Similar networks have been set up by several other companies in other European countries (many, like DHL, owned by formerly state-run postal services) and Australia.

Rather than constructing self-service boxes, another approach is to use existing infrastructure: Hermes, for example, runs the ParcelShop network across Europe, cooperating with newsagents, tobacconists, kiosks (and sometimes slightly more

31 www.estrategy-magazin.de (as in March 2015)

idiosyncratic small-time retailers) who accept deliveries for neighbourhood customers who are not at home. Meanwhile, most parcels services now offer delivery to offices and other workplaces (a dream come true for the cash-rich/time-poor segment of intensive e-commerce users) and are working to improve their premium services, which allow specific time-slots to be reserved for deliveries or returns if the customer is willing to pay higher delivery charges.

As with the various methods of payment (see 2.5.2), online shop operators should consider offering their customers several types of delivery, and several different parcel delivery services, all the while making sure that their own business interests are not completely forgotten. In e-commerce transactions, both sellers and buyers have an interest in keeping costs minimal while obtaining the best result in terms of pick-up/delivery times; both also have service requirements (easy parcel tracking is a shared need, for example) and are better off with comprehensive transport insurance. Then again, there are points at which the interests of a company selling and person buying are not aligned: while DHL may not offer sellers a particularly good deal in terms of price and conditions, many German buyers who are also Packstation users have little incentive to use any other service.

What is more, they may have had a bad experience with one of the competitors: in the UK, for example, a 2014 consumer satisfaction survey[32] rated Yodel and Hermes as the worst parcel services (customer quote: "Hermes put my parcel in the recycling box... on recycling day"), yet both had record years in terms of parcels handled – in no small part thanks to charm offensives towards retailers. What is impossible to measure, of course, is how many customers are now avoiding Yodel and Hermes like the plague and only buying with shops which offer shipping using DHL and DPD (who came out of the survey smelling of roses).

The best way to avoid suffering from this form of unknown is, wherever possible, to offer a mix of partners for customers to choose.

Any shop not using Amazon or one of the few other full-service fulfilment partners retains sovereignty when it comes to selecting parcel delivery options.

Commissioning and returns are two areas of the logistics link in the chain where online shop operators are not necessarily dependent on other organisations: anyone who has enough space for the stock they need to store can develop and im-

32 www.moneysavingexpert.com (as of March 2016)

plement reliable processes for picking and packing, regardless of scale. Yet when it comes to shipping, online pure players are, in contrast to multichannel retailers with a network of stores, almost entirely dependent on parcel services to get their wares to customers. And this is – given the rapid increase in parcel volume and changing work patterns – a potential brake on growth in e-commerce.

Innovation: When the postman doesn't even ring once

The current system of various vans battling it out for road space to deliver packages days late to customers who aren't even at home to take them is creaking under the weight of e-commerce orders. In order to make sure that customers are not, for example, avoiding placing more urgent orders due to uncertainty about speedy or convenient delivery, e-commerce companies and parcels services will need to work hard on innovative delivery models.

In Germany, for example, DHL is trialling parcel boxes, a kind of private Packstation booth erected in a front garden that only DHL drivers and the owner can open. While this model has potential in small-town Europe and many larger cities in Britain or the American West, in tightly-packed, gardenless urban conurbations such as New York and many European cities – not to mention the megacities of Asia – other solutions will be needed. The established parcels services have no choice: margins are so low that their only option is growth, yet only a different, leaner type of growth will allow them operate profitably. Online shops, too, will need to implement innovative models to make sure that growth continues; otherwise, consumers may still prefer to use good old-fashioned bricks-and-mortar stores for a variety of time-critical purchases rather than paying for expensive express delivery or taking a risk.

Beyond the major players, start-ups are coming up with slews of new ideas for these kind of multi-storey environments, including mini-safes chained to apartment doors which accept deliveries from a range of parcels services (Lockbox in Germany) or, more radically, tech-based solutions such as Shutl in London or Tiramizoo in Munich, which use algorithms, Uber-style, to hook up online shop customers, products, and couriers within a set radius to allow for delivery within hours. The stated aim is to offer same-day-delivery at the same price as standard shipping service by an established parcels company and, given the extent to which demand, supply, and infrastructure is concentrated on urban areas, this ought to become a reality before the decade is out.

Amazon, as in so many other areas, is already half-way there. In the USA, Super Prime service allows customers in several large metropolitan areas to get their orders delivered within two hours any time up to midnight; in Europe, too, Prime customers can use the Evening Express (available in 14 German conurbations, for example) for a range of products: orders placed from the office in the morning are available by the time hard-pressed professionals are leaving their desks. These changes in logistics possibilities are already leading to strong increases is the amount of food and drink ordered online, and the battle lines are being drawn between supermarkets, food delivery services, and Amazon. In the UK, for example, underdog groceries chain Morrisons opened fire in early 2016 by agreeing to start supplying customers through Amazon; other chains will now have to figure out their response. The future world of same-day delivery looks set to cause another e-commerce avalanche in the near future of the kind which has already swept over the media, electronic entertainment, and fashion segments.

Returns

The slogan Zalando would rather forget

New solutions for delivering parcels to customers also entail new solutions for picking them back up: returning items ordered from online shops is as much a part of everyday e-commerce as picking, packing, and shipping. Nowhere more so that in Germany, the country at the top of the European returning leagues. Examining the German experience shows how rates of returns result from the interplay between statutory rights and consumer habit: in the post-war consumer boom years, German lawmakers gave home-shoppers extended rights of return and exchange while German companies started to offer open invoicing (see 2.5.2). Mail-order pioneer Werner Otto led the way, giving consumers the opportunity to buy now, pay later in the 1950s as a way of upping sales; with credit cards not yet widespread, the only other payment option was to send money before delivery and, as Otto rightly recognised, this deterred many customers from catalogue shopping. By taking the risk that customers would not pay, Otto revolutionised German consumer society as customers realised that they could order and return goods without any money changing hands.

The logical consequence of this was what UK retailers call "overbuying" if unsure, known in German as a "selection order" (*Auswahlbestellung*) by which customers order in the same piece in a variety of colours or sizes, fully intending to keep and pay for only the one that suits or fits. While in other countries the continued dominance of prepayment or, in the 1980s, the advance of credit card and bank transfer payments limited this phenomenon, in Germany, ordering on invoice remained standard: although most other territories also offer consumers extensive rights of return and exchange when they have not been able to inspect the product physically, the fact that customers here have had, more often than not, to part with their money before delivery and then go to the trouble of getting a refund, has led to a more cautious approach to ordering. In eastern European countries, where a less developed transport infrastructure could – and sometimes still can – delay parcels for weeks, many consumers prefer to sell on products they do not like on receipt to friends and relatives.

The acquired consumer habit of ordering things to try out at home is a major issue for e-commerce is Germany.

Customers don't see the problem: after all, if I can touch and try on a pair of trousers in a shop, why shouldn't I be able to do so at home? What is more, led by the major players in the early years, e-commerce has done little to tackle this attitude: both domestic and international e-commerce pioneers quickly understood that growth is faster if returns policies are expressly generous. Zalando, for example, which fuelled its rapid expansion with clever advertising, became known with a two-part rhyming slogan: "*Schrei vor Glück, oder schick's zurück!*" – literally: "Scream with joy, or return it." The fact that the second half of this slogan disappeared not long after launch, however, leaving the truncated "*Schrei vor Glück!*" indicates that Zalando is no longer all that that keen on the idea of consumers sending back everything that doesn't elicit cries of joy...

Who would be? While Germany may be a particularly exasperating case, online retailers everywhere are battling with return rates of up to 70%, depending on the product segment. Fashion and shoes are the worst: these are the products which are regularly ordered in multiple sizes and colours and, to add insult to injury, also the products which consumers are most likely to buy on a whim and – taking a look at the bill and their overflowing wardrobes a few days later – send back (German, that language with a word for everything, calls this phenomenon *Kaufreue*: "buy-regret"). On the bottom end of the scale are books, CDs, DVDs, furniture, and wine. Yet whatever the segment, each and every return is a hit to profitability and is therefore one return too many: the item needs to be sent back (parcel services will bill the seller), processed through goods-in and examined (which costs staff time), and then – if possible – freshened up/repackaged and made ready for sale again (more staff time). If the article can no longer be sold, then it gets written off as a total loss; even if it can be returned to sale after transport, unpacking, and repacking, it is now taking up space in the stock room again.

Then again, fashion returns, for all their alarming frequency, can actually turn out to be less costly than far less frequent furniture returns: t-shirts which have been briefly tried on can be given a new label, refolded and packed, and then sold again the next day. Almost 100% of clothing returned is fit for resale[33]. Furniture, however, must usually be put together before customers realise their mistake, and this generally means a total write-off for the retailer as, after being dismantled and transported back, flat-pack shelving is generally not fit for much more than a bonfire. According to the University of Bamberg, on average throughout all segments, each return in the German market costs around €15.

The same study also assumes that around 20% of returns are fraudulent, although of course the word "fraudulent" is, in its actual legal definition, mostly inaccurate: consumer legislation tends to offer cooling-off periods regardless of why the product in question was purchased, and these rights tend to be even stronger in business done away from normal commercial premises – i.e. e-commerce sales; moreover, neither the various US consumer refund laws nor the EU Consumer Rights Directive on which member states must base their legal rights of return define conditions under which goods may not be returned. Actual return fraud is genuinely criminal activity (returning stolen goods, for example, or returning lower value goods for a cash refund). Then again, it is entirely correct to speak of "return abuse" or, in the fashion segment, "wardrobing" to describe the morally questionable manner in which some consumers make use of their rights, especially when goods are returned after clearly having been used – and often abused – to the full extent of their purpose. Ball gowns come back with red wine stains, tuxedos with torn of ticket stubs from a performance of *Swan Lake* the week previous; in early September, outdoor manufacturers and retailers will often get unwelcome returns in the form of mountain bikes or climbing equipment that appear to have been "hired out" for a holiday somewhere rather dusty; and in October, anyone selling authentic Bavarian lederhosen had better get ready for some nasty, sticky surprises as the festivities in Munich and elsewhere draw to a close. Meanwhile, retailers of high-end crockery and cutlery are steeling themselves for the post-Thanksgiving and after-Christmas returns – stuck-on, crusty turkey remains and all...

33 www.zeit.de (as in March 2015)

These war stories are the open secrets of the industry; you won't find anyone, maker or merchant, talking about them on the record, though. Firstly, because most consumers are upstanding, honest, and simply aware of their rights; secondly, because no one running an online shop wants to give the impression that they mistrust their customers; thirdly – and crucially – because:

Although returns may drive costs up, they also drive growth.

They make customers feel more comfortable ordering (see 2.5 Orders & sales), increase trust in the company, and can actually lead to higher sales per order: a customer may, for example, have been planning to keep only one of the three t-shirts ordered to try on, but turn out to be quite fond of two. The inconvenient truth is: without returns, growth drops; with returns, profit falls.

What is more, even changes to consumer law are not enough to make a dent in the high numbers of returns. The new EU Directive, for instance, which came into force in 2014, has set higher barriers to returns: theoretically, customers can no longer get refunds on goods ordered without stating why they are returning them and must pay for shipping back to the seller unless they were not informed of their rights on purchase. Manufacturers and retailers have mainly chosen, however, to continue offering returns periods longer than the statutory requirements and still enclose prepaid return slips and envelopes with every order: this is now entirely discretionary, but none want to give up on generous returns policies as incentives to buy. The gap between what online shops could do and what they are doing will remain as long as the major players set ultra-customer-friendly standards: the first shop to put its head above the parapet will be the one that draws all the fire.

Reasons for returns – and how to avoid them

What some of the major players are doing, however, is working against returns behind the scenes, without any of the damaging media attention which might come from a public change to terms and conditions. The motivation is simple: after years of explosive growth, even giants such as Amazon and Zalando are having to get more profitable to keep investors on board. Lowering the rates of returns is relatively simple way to up the companies' own returns – on investment.

The first step to tackling returns is understanding why the four out of five which are not questionable actually happen. There are four principle reasons why customers return goods they bought online.[34]

- **Customer issues:** These are not simply behavioural issues such as overbuying or try-on/out-at-home orders, but also customer errors such as misreading the description or being overly optimistic about dimensions or sizes. Some orders may have already been superfluous the moment they were placed, as a couple might work out one evening at the dinner table when they realise they had both thought it was their responsibility to get this or that.
- **Product issues:** Items which are defective are, of course, the first to be returned; sometimes, however, there is no genuine defect, but the product is disappointment as compared to its product description and imaging on line: clothes sizing and the colour of fabrics, casing on electronic devices, and furniture are particularly susceptible to gaps between expectations and reality for technological reasons: a lack of good photos – or misleading images – in the product description as well as customers' varying colour settings on monitors and mobile devices. It is often difficult to say precisely where this product issue stops and customer error, over-optimism, or misjudgement begins.
- **Fulfilment issues:** Faulty commissioning can lead to the wrong article being sent to the wrong customer; poor packaging, meanwhile, causes more frequent transport damage – and the shipping process can in some cases ruin even the best-packed of orders (this is a risk which can never be completely eliminated). Then there are schoolboy errors such as wrongly-entered address information, and parcel delivery operatives may have trouble finding even correct addresses, both of which lead to automatic returns to sender.
- **Availability issues:** If, after an order has been placed, an item turns out to be unavailable, the order is cancelled before anything is sent out at all. Delayed delivery can often lead to returns as, if the customer needed the product in question by a certain date, they will have gone out and got it in store and will return the late-comer; some customers will even order the same product from two or more online shops, just to be on the safe side, and return every order that arrives after the winner – who, in this case, takes all.

Action can be taken against each and every one of these issues without changing a thing about existing returns policies – and without getting consumer watchdogs'

34 Source: with reference to Thieme (2013), *Versandhandelsmanagement*, p. 318ff.

or lawmakers' riles up. The first step is to find out which of the issues are particularly frequent causes, and a simple way to do this is to actually ask customers: the German OTTO online shop sends numbered lists out with its returns slips, allowing customers quickly and easily select their reason for sending the item back: there are reasons such as "41: Too long", "43: Too short", and "44: Colour/pattern not as displayed" or fulfilment issues such as "51: Delivery delayed" and "52: Wrong product delivered/Wrong product ordered".

As such, a large number of "40s" would give OTTO cause to rework its sizing tables and take a closer look at its product presentation. Sometimes, the solution is staring companies right in the face: Zalando slashed the high rate of returns on handbags overnight by changing the way they are shown to include photos with models, rather than simply in front of a white background; this gave buyers a far clearer idea of their actual size in relation to the human body. What is more, the potential of customer reviews should not be underestimated: when written from the perspective of a customer who has already viewed the product, read the text, and then received the genuine article, reviews can help customers reach better decisions in the decision phase. This kind of **communications action** is a logical, painless approach which adds value for customers (see 2.2 Product presentation).

Meanwhile, a high number of "50s" at OTTO would mean that there was something awry in logistics, which would in turn call for **fulfilment action**: parcels services would need to be observed and processes in the warehouse optimised (taking a cue from Amazon; see above). Packaging, too, might need to be rethought. Sometimes, **availability action** may be required to stop products not being delivered or arriving too late.

If a large number of non-functional articles are returned or if customer communication reveals recurring discrepancies between the quality expected and the actual look-and-feel of the product, then **product action** may be required: either quality control needs to be taken up a notch, or the product/manufacturer/supplier in question delisted.

Customer issues can best be tackled by taking **customer-focussed action**, starting in the ordering process. Shop systems can be taught rules with which to recognise overbuying – e.g. multiple sizes of the same shoe, one jacket in three colours – and display an appeal to the customer to reconsider ordering all three (reminding them of the environmental cost of shipping can be effective in many cases); coming at the issue from another angle, shops may choose to offer customers discounts on future purchases for not returning goods – also a shrewd customer loyalty move. A more sensitive area is directly addressing customers who return at an above average rate: this could be camouflaged as a "customer satisfaction survey" with questions aiming to get to the heart of the issue; potential stages of escalation start with personal e-mail contact from a customer service representative (see 2.7) asking whether an order was as expected and climb through into warnings that continued excessive returns could lead to an account being blocked.

The most delicate issue is when to implement hard-and-fast measures, such as actually blocking accounts; these should be retained in the armoury for the most incorrigible and irascible returners – or those who are overly-bold in sending back goods they have clearly used to their full satisfaction. Estimates vary, but as many of 2% of customers in western countries have had their accounts shut down at some point.

A less controversial – and very effective – way of deterring unthinking returners is to steer them away from enabling means of payment: the casual nature of open invoicing or the ease with which especially US customers can use chargeback to cancel payment makes it more tempting to over-order – or to give into feelings of guilt and send products back. Channelling disruptive customers towards bank transfers or other means of prepayment changes none of their legal rights to return products and get refunds, but acts as a psychological barrier and may get them some to see sense when ordering.

Another "quiet" way of sieving out consistent returners is to make sure they don't get any more marketing e-mails. No-one hears the click of their e-mail address being removed from a mailing list.

Technology picks up where humans fail

In the long term, there is no option but to reduce rates of return and to make logistics infrastructure more efficient and more effective if there is to be any hope of increasing margins in e-commerce. In order to get to this point, the major players – Amazon at the head of the pack – are investing unheard of amounts of money in reducing the biggest risk factor in the whole business: human involvement.

This includes using technology to improve product presentation. In the near future, customers buying clothes will be given full-body avatars on which they can "try on" clothes digitally in a range of combinations, sizes, and lights. The first augmented reality applications are already in use in home furnishings, allowing customers to measure up and then "view" their rooms as they would look with various new piece of furniture in it on their smartphones (see 2.2 Product presentation). These kinds of technological solutions will eliminate human error in measuring dimensions and counteract wishful thinking with regard to room – or body – size.

Then again, there is only a certain extent to which online retailers and manufacturers with webshops can act as guides and they must, in the final analysis, allow customers to place unsuitable orders if they really want to. In the area of fulfilment, however, humans have, for many e-commerce businesses, become little more than an annoyance – and a costly one. Humans make mistakes commissioning orders, for example, especially under pressure; what is more, humans also dislike carrying out repetitive tasks in a stressful environment, meaning that they tend to look for other jobs or get ill.

In order to continue optimising processes, warehouses are increasingly becoming the territory of robots. Amazon, for instance, uses Kiva bots to tirelessly shift hundreds of pounds of product still on shelving units down predefined highways on a chess-board pattern layout. Linked with the central computer – which directs storage in a randomised way and uses the robots to respond in an agile manner – this results in a system which is best run without people, or, as Amazon calls it, a "Human Exclusion Zone". Fulfilment centres worked entirely with robots and using people for packing only can be four times as productive as typical warehouses: orders are processed live and a generally ready for dispatch within 15 minutes; this in turn is an important prerequisite for same-day delivery (see above). It is only a matter of time until robots can handle packaging, too, and another quantum leap in terms of time-to-dispatch will have been made – and human workers will be locked out of logistics sites for good.

Then it's on to transport. Anyone who still thinks all the Amazon parcels drones stories are part of a clever PR hoax is missing the point entirely: the latest model is already able to steer around other flying objects. DHL, too, is testing fully operational air drones for medicine shipments between the German mainland and the North Sea island of Juist[35]. While the near future may not see *Star Trek* holograms replacing our bookshelves and sofas just yet, it certainly will have semi-autonomous robots flying our parcels home – or at least carrying them up the stairs so that the delivery guys can have a break.

35 www.focus.de (as in March 2015)

2.7 Customer service

Introduction

Claims that nobody wants to buy stuff on the internet are as old as e-commerce itself: "You don't know who you're dealing with on the web", goes the argument, "and you can't see and touch the product, or try it out/on. And if it goes wrong, then there's no shop to take the defective product back to and no-one to clear up the issue with!" As specious as these claims are – and as often as they have been disproven – they are not entirely devoid of meaning, else clicks would by rights have completely replaced bricks by now. What good e-commerce retail concepts show, however, is that none of the hurdles in customer relationships on the internet is too high to be cleared.

Over the years, webshops have continually improved their "display windows": high-resolution images of products from all conceivable angles have made viewing products online easy; comparing them to existing products at home – or reading comments from other customers (see 2.2.3) – allows consumers to make informed choices at a distance. In fact, webshops also offer considerable advantages: the virtual high street is longer than any physical shopping precinct ever can be, and consumers can get from one end to the other and back in seconds; each shop on the way, meanwhile, offers product ranges which dwarf even those of the largest specialist in-store retailers (see 2.1 Procurement). Provided that the product search engine offers a sufficient level of performance, it is easy to pick the right needle out of the haystack – and if it does happen to be the wrong needle, it can easily be sent back (see 2.6.2). In all of these areas, e-commerce can compete with larger chain stores and specialist retailers.

Nevertheless, e-commerce is lacking something: there is no smiling sales assistant with a knack for making a shopping experience so personal and so pleasant that the customer remembers them weeks later; there is no experienced salesperson who has honed the almost superhuman capability to see what people are looking for as they walk into the shop. As precise as recommendation engines can be, precision may sometimes be utterly inaccurate – and tech-driven solutions are (as yet) incapable of reading customers' facial expressions and correcting recommendations based on reactions. What is more, online shops have real difficulty building up customer loyalty and trust in the way that skilled staff of decades' standing or proud shop owners can.

Yet difficulties are there to be overcome. Online shops don't have stylish interiors and sales staff with winning smiles – but they do have a range of other options at their disposal. Clean, simple, trustworthy design principles, especially in the check-out areas (see 2.5) can secure customer confidence, while targeted marketing and communication with existing customers (see 2.3 & 2.4, Marketing and Distribution respectively) can build relationships. Last, but not at all least, makers and merchants running online shops must set the highest standards they can and communicate these standards to prospective customers.

Customer service in e-commerce must be better than customer service in stores – not just by way of overcoming the handicap of anonymity, but also as a genuinely convincing unique sales proposition.

Just like logistics, customer service is therefore a priority area which should receive investment ahead of marketing: reliable service must be assured so that customers overcome any last doubts about ordering for the first time, and if there are problems (which there always will be), customer service must deal with them with such speed and efficiency that customers don't only come back, but also tell others about their experience.

Who, after all, hasn't already heard one of these dinner party stories about how a set of speakers or a new TV ordered on Amazon turned out to be faulty? The acquaintance in question contacts Amazon and is called up by an extremely friendly, competent service operative who, following a short conversation, authorises the shipping of a replacement and closes the call with a friendly apology. The next day, recounts the astounded acquaintance, a fully functional replacement device is delivered – before the old one has even been put back in its box for the journey to the Big Technical Junkyard in the Sky. What your acquaintance (and everyone else sat around the table) has learned is that the retailer can help you if your product doesn't work – and you don't even need to change out of your nightclothes. In fact, buying online can be quite a lot easier than buying in store: it took less time to locate, buy, and return the product; the first customer care operative you spoke to knew exactly what your problem was and didn't need to "go find the boss"; and the replacement product wasn't sold out, but in your living room a day later.

The goal of every online shop must be to get this kind of dinner party story or water-cooler anecdote: setting sights any lower neither helps to win over conservative, risk-averse customers nor to keep up with the competition among savvy online frequent-buyers. New shops are chasing the Amazons of this world, who have been online for years and have set the customer service bar so very high. The ways, however, in which an online shop clears the obstacles, will vary according to its characteristics:

- Is it a **manufacturer/brand online shop** or an **online retailer/reseller shop**?
- Which **types of goods** are being sold? How much **service**, **consultation**, and **maintenance** do they require? What **price segment** are they in and do any **manufacturer guarantees** apply?
- How high is **turnover**? What kind of systems (full-time customer care team, a purpose-built call-centre) are appropriate to the size of the shop and can be financed?
- What are the **expectations** of customers in terms of contactability and conditions?

These factors are the meat and bones of frequent customer service questions: which problems are likely to occur most often? What can/must be promised to customers? What can be financed from the sales the shop generates? The answers to these questions may vary strongly between, say, a large-scale fashion retailer and a quality tools manufacturer selling directly on the internet, or between an antique bookstore and a furniture-maker running online shops.

Then again, all of the service channels available can be used by any online shop: there a very low cost barriers to all forms of customer communications. The question is therefore more about which channels to use and how to weight them. In the following, we examine the various channels before moving on to look at whole customer service concepts from a strategic point of view.

Channels

Telephone hotline

In many territories – all EU countries, for example – retailers must provide customers with a clearly marked contact telephone number; there are also frequently statutory limits on the maximum costs of calls made by customers to hotlines post-purchase; even where there are no such limits (America and Australia, for example), business are advised to offer toll-free numbers if for no other reason than as a competitive advantage.

A telephone number is a telephone number: whether it leads to a single, beat-up phone with a cord and earpiece in someone's garden shed (which is now doubling up as a stockroom) or a full-service call centre is a different matter. Sole-traders selling on the internet would at least be advised to get a second line switched on before putting a number out there; larger shops will, of course, need to take a far more professional approach.

Whether a telephone number is communicated or not is not just a matter of legal requirements, but is also about the customer service concept at play. Amazon, for example, purposefully conceals its telephone numbers because its concept is about channelling service issues prior to calls with customers: before a service operative can be reached by phone, customers have to contact Amazon in writing, explain their problem, and request a call back. This way of working has some considerable advantages: the company dictates the number of calls which are made by answering any queries or resolving any issues it can by e-mail first. This means that the calls which are made are of higher quality: customers who are rung up rather than ring themselves don't have to spend a frustrating half an hour listening to a Verdi loop while on hold; the calls are also tighter because the operator already knows what the basics of the matter are (see the explanation of Self-Service below).

Then again, as a wealth of frustrated internet forum entries documents, this approach – as effective as it may be – is not to everyone's taste. Other retailers make a service selling point out of the ease with which they can be contacted by phone, using automated menus to better channel calls: operatives answering phones will already know roughly what the problem is and, in larger call-centres, calls can be directed to the right specific teams.

For smaller-scale operations, there can be no discussion about whether to provide a telephone number or not. Firstly, two-man retail operations or specialist manufacturers don't generally tend to have the legal resources of a tech giant and so do not want to get involved in nasty arguments with regulators and consumer rights organisations. Secondly, customers will not give smaller shops the same benefit of the doubt as they do a brand as well-known as Amazon; for while some customers who like to do their business on the phone may be ruffled by Amazon's concept, they don't have a problem buying stuff there because, well, millions of others already have – and didn't have any major complaints. An unestablished or smaller webshop simply has to provide a telephone number as a way of reassuring customers that it is legitimate: those digits have a greater effect than all the Trusted Shop badges in the world.

As a matter of fact, however, online customers generally prefer to write e-mails anyway: professionals in open-plan offices aren't always in the position to blatantly make a 15-minute call about a personal consumer issue while their colleagues and bosses are within ear-shot; they can, however, use a quarter of an hour of downtime typing an e-mail about it and still look nicely busy. What is more, once they leave the office, they're not in much of a mood to call either: talking into a mobile phone over the roar of street traffic after a hard day's graft at the coalface of capitalism is not most people's idea of a relaxing start to the evening.

What customers want in terms of service is the possibility of calling, not the necessity of doing so.

When they do call, however, good service on the telephone is an absolute dealbreaker: whether the focus of the customer care approach is to clear everything up online or not, the telephone is the part of e-commerce where customer and company come closest on a human level. If the human representing the online shop is not friendly and cooperative, customers will be put off. There is, however, nothing wrong with saying: "Would you mind writing us an e-mail about that and attaching a picture? Here's our service address..." It's not what is said, but how it is said, that is key.

Written electronic communication

Electronic communication in written form is one of the key elements of e-commerce customer service. Customers who have made a purchase in-store will go back to that store if there is an issue and deal with things face-to-face; in online shopping, written form is equally as natural since the actual purchase occurred in text, not speech, too.

Service **e-mail** addresses are often put at the bottom of an order confirmation so that customers can click on them and compose an e-mail directly. Other shop operators place the address prominently on their websites, too. All else failing, the service address must be listed in the Contact Us section – unless, of course, you're Amazon, in which case you break all the rules and simply offer a dialogue box solution, but only to customers who are logged in. Following several complaints, Amazon has set up e-mail addresses in countries which require it by law to do so – the German Telemedia Act stipulates that a compliant *Impressum* ("imprint", i.e. legal notice) must include an e-mail address, but don't expect impressum@ amazon.de to deal with any product issues you've been having. You'll also have noticed that Amazon's order confirmation e-mails don't include much by way of contact details either but, as ever in this area, what works for Amazon is unlikely to work for most others.

Contact forms are, however, popular with many shop operators because they offer customers a pre-defined structure which makes sure that as much information as possible is given. Many fields can be asterisked so that customers don't forget to share important data – their names, address, telephone number, a customer number in some cases – or indeed offer enough information to sort the issue into the right department: often, a range of reasons for contacting the company is show, or order numbers are requested. This preventative step can avoid redundant e-mails further down the line and make sure that customer care agents have what they need to start working on the issue.

Sometimes, very elementary e-mail and contact form best practice – as simple as it may appear – is not followed, even by large, professional operations:

- Wherever possible, customer service e-mail addresses should sound like customer service e-mail addresses: customercare@insertshopnamehere.com, for example; separate e-mail addresses can also be used for various parts of the e-commerce process where issues may occur: orders@insertshopnamehere. com, returns@insertshopnamehere.com, etc. Even if, in smaller shops, these e-mails may all reach the same team (or even person), having separate addresses can help channel and sort e-mails.
- Automatic receipt confirmations help to cut down on follow-up e-mails or calls. Some more demanding customers expect a response to a (purportedly) urgent issue within half an hour and will send another e-mail or make a call if they hear nothing. This not only eats up time and resources, but can lead to embarrassing mix-ups if an e-mail issue was solved by the customer following up with a call, but another customer service operator starts work on the original e-mail an hour later.
- Confirmation should also be sent once a customer has filled out and transmitted a Contact Us form because the customer cannot see the e-mail in their sent

items. This kind of confirmation has the same role as the good old "I'll be right with you..." in a bricks context: the customer feels like they have been acknowledged and is happier to wait for a response.

- Online shops dealing with greater numbers of service issues generally use a ticketing system, and the number of the ticket raised must also be communicated in confirmation e-mails; this allows customers to proffer the number whenever calling or e-mailing about the issue down the line.
- It is a good idea to build up a stock of standardised answers or building blocks which can be used for recurring issues; this both speeds up the rate at which staff can respond and lowers the potential for mistakes and omissions in answers; this, in turn, leads to fewer queries and saves staff time.

Another way of avoiding unnecessary e-mails is to use **chat** solutions: i.e. live exchanges of written messages in a small browser screen. Many companies offer this as a service option – primarily for trickier cases in which service operatives require a lot of information from customers to resolve the issue. The advantage of chat solutions is that customers can copy ticket numbers and other long alphanumeric codes out of e-mails and into the chat box, or send staff screenshots, photos, or other documentation: attachments can't be done by phone and can often lead to long e-mail trails. Chats also allow agents to use standard phrases and answers, which guarantees a level of professional service in exactly the right tone that can be far harder for staff to achieve on the phone without considerable training; pre-set text also hits the right note if a member of staff is having a bad day (something many find more difficult to disguise on the phone), or indeed a bad year (i.e. if they're just bad).

Chat solutions, however, can only be implemented using special software, making them more complex to offer than telephone numbers, e-mail addresses, and contact dialogue boxes. Not all shop software ships with them, but it can be well worth the effort sourcing and integrating chat capability to offer a high-performance, speedy customer service solution – one which can suit both customers and customer care staff.

In early 2016, Facebook introduced "bots" on its Messenger chat tool, which are supposed to raise customer service to a new level by means of artificial intelligence and machine learning. Customers may interact with these bots and retrieve information on their last order, request bookings, and other services. While first experiences were a bit dull these tools may soon help to speed up consumer interactions without staffing additional service representatives.

Social media

A lot of social networks also offer chat functions, and these can be used both by customers when signed in and, of course, by online shops who have accounts. Indeed, consumers who spend a lot of time online and have profiles on social networks such as **Facebook** and **Twitter** have by and large come to expect that companies they deal with will also have a presence in these networks – and are generally much happier to see customer service contact options there than advertising (see 2.3 Marketing). Messaging on Facebook or DMing on Twitter can therefore be just as effective in some customer segments as a fully-fledged chat solution, especially given that these networks offer the infrastructure free of charge and are broadly accepted by customers.

Nevertheless, caution is advised. Most users will ask service-related questions in publically visible posts, which in turns draws retailers and manufacturers out of areas under their own control and into the public sphere: this means that the potential social media offers is proportional to the danger is creates. Just as customers can be contacted directly and publically, they can also reply directly and publically – and do so, often detailing their issues for all the world to see and sharing their opinions in a forthright manner. The act of tapping on keys has always led some consumers to forget their manners – complaints to catalogues written on typewriters were often trenchant in stylistic terms, to say the least – but social media has the effect of amplifying the dissonance between what customers would be prepared to say down a telephone line and what they are prepared to write. What is more, once they are outside of the chat and messaging areas of social networks, consumers are publishing shareable content; the group mentality is, after all, the defining feature of social networks.

So one disappointed customer lambasting a company will quickly attract a crowd of other assorted malcontents.

This situation becomes more dangerous the longer a company refuses to enter into the interactive spirit of social media, and silence or – worse, perhaps – patently canned, pre-written responses will only add fuel to the fire; or, to say it in the social media lingo, further whip up the "shitstorm".

Case Study: Deutsche Bahn

Companies with social media presences will often have criticism publically heaped on them for the smallest of errors – even if the presence is actually only there to offer customer service and not to intrude on users with annoying advertising.

An interesting example of how companies deal with this is Deutsche Bahn, the trains company born out of the state run rail operator when the railway was privatised in Germany in the mid-1990s. It still runs a sizeable portion of services, the network infrastructure, and remains the "default rail company" – especially when passengers are, once again, facing hefty delays (the proverbial German efficiency does not extend to the country's rail network).

Nevertheless, part of Deutsche Bahn that does work very well indeed is live Twitter help channel, which is manned around the clock and offers up-to-the-second information. Anyone tweeting @DB_Bahn about current conditions on the network can generally expect an informative, friendly answer within minutes: it's a great service, especially for passengers on trains which are delayed, who frequently find out that they will be late at their destinations before the conductor does. Nevertheless, this helpful, professional service channel attracts more than its fair share of needlessly passive-aggressive, self-righteous comments. After all, tearing railway staff a new one is an accepted discipline in one of Germany's national sports: complaining.

Deutsche Bahn isn't ruffled, though: it also tweets at @DB_Info, where it posts planned service status reports, ticket offers, and other corporate information, passing on all customer service queries to @DB_Bahn. This split between advertising and information on the one account and service on the other means that the latter acts a kind of lightning rod for all of the questions, complaints, and insults, picking them up and directing them away from the corporate image side of the company's Twitter presence. What is more, the 20 or so skilled professionals manning the service account often manage to reengage with angry users, grinding those who have forgotten their Ps & Qs down with constant politeness. The strength of the channel is that customers get information if something goes wrong – and get it in public. This makes @DB_Bahn into a successful hybrid of service, customer relationship management, and advertising.

Yet even online shops who do not have the resources of a globally active former state transport monopolist can make social media work for them. As competent handling of service queries out in the open where everyone can see it sends a strong signal about the company ethos, there is no categorical need to split informational and service-orientated activities into multiple accounts. What is important, however, is to give training to staff running social media accounts – or at least make them aware of the issues which can arise. There is a balance to be struck between entering into the spirit of the networks – communicating on first-name terms with customers, avoiding obviously standardised or canned answers where possible – and becoming imprudent or flippant. Crucially, it is utterly unproductive to engage with those looking for conflict: it is never a good look to, as a company, be caught in a public spat with a customer, regardless of the facts of the case. It should be standard practice to get another pair of eyes on every tweet or Facebook post before it hits the ether.

And then there is the golden rule
so obvious that even social media professionals
of many years standing keep forgetting it:
it is pointless trying to cover up any mistakes that are made.

A telephone call with an unpleasant customer which gets out of hand can be aborted by "accidentally" hanging up: the customer will probably mouth off about it, but would have to prove that his or her version of events were true and that he or she had not contributed to the escalation. A badly-phrased response on Facebook, however, has been put into the public domain in writing and will be shared within seconds: screenshots make it easy to prove that alterations have been made to texts; users see these changes and are merciless with companies who try to silently whitewash away mistakes.

It is also worth remembering that social media can be a real minefield with respect to the lack of clarity as regards the personal and professional spheres: the informal tone and the general trend towards transparency can make staff who also have their own personal accounts more liable to post things that are ill-advised from a professional standpoint. It is very easy for conflicts of interest to arise for employees who curate a company account, have their own social media presences, and also spend a lot of time at social media conferences and barcamps: some get carried away by the cosy chattiness of it all and forget which bit is which – and where "insights into the company" stop and "breach of confidentiality" starts. This means that all online shop operators need to compile clear rules for social media use at work – whether in a personal or professional capacity – and remind employees of the terms of their contracts.

Beyond customer service specifically, company presentation on social media is a highly complex affair; nevertheless, it cannot be ignored, especially in e-commerce, because it won't go away. Companies who do not keep up accounts on Facebook, Twitter, and other popular networks can just as easily be drawn into the fray – and will find that they have no means of steering the conversation. In the worst cases, spoof accounts are the only "company representation" on these important networks with millions of users; a company with no understanding of social media would not even realise it is being pilloried by satirical impersonators. To return to Deutsche Bahn: some of the more excoriating criticism of the rail operator is to be found, incongruously enough, on the popular German recipe site chefkoch.de. Why? Because the company can't do anything like delete posts or shut down threads; all it can do is try to steer discussion. A company without digitally savvy employees wouldn't even find out that this kind of secluded parallel forum had opened up.

Self-service and contact centres

Self-service

The complete opposite of the risks of social media are customer service concepts such as self-service. In this model, as much interaction with customers as possible is initiated by the company: the overarching aim is for customers to have a little reason to write as possible – and even less reason to call. By providing as much information on the website in texts as clearly and comprehensibly phrased as possible, companies can enable customers to find the answer to the vast majority of issues themselves. If the problem is more complex, then the next step is for customers to send a written query using a contact form, allowing a service agent to get an overview of the situation before contacting the customer using their preferred channel.

If this shift from a push to a pull model works, companies can expect to unlock considerable advantages in terms of efficiency and quality.

Amazon is a shining example here: the Help area of its website offers a clearly-structured overview of a full range of contents and processes, meaning that many customer questions are dealt with by the customers themselves.

The online returns management centre, for example, allows customers to initiate and administer a return completely independently: an automated processes even lets them print out their own returns slip with the parcels carrier of their choice. Anyone not feeling like reading through the instructions can take the easy route and watch the two-minute returns-for-dummies style video tutorial, featuring helpful screenshots and all the details explained. Staff time expenditure at Amazon: 0 hours. Costs for paper to print returns slips? $0.

With return rates reaching up to 70% in some product segments and eating away at profits every time (see 2.6 Logistics), Amazon will do everything it can to keep the expense of processing them to a minimum.

Another classically time-consuming aspect of e-commerce service are the customers who like to check their order status. Amazon counteracts this by offering so much information in its Track Packages or View Orders area that anyone still wanting to contact the company really does need help. One page helps customers calculate the normal delivery timeframe and shows them where to find estimated delivery dates for each of their specific orders: the days when customers would call at their wits' end three whole hours after having ordered their 50-inch full-HD flatscreen wondering what had happened to it are well and truly past. If a delivery actually is delayed, Amazon's help page simply refers customers to the tracking options offered by the parcels services and lists their contact numbers (the only ones on the website, as it happens).

This whole concept, of course, does not work if customers simply ring up without having informed themselves first. The help pages are extensive, dense, and have layer after layer: many a customer would love nothing more than to reach for the phone and dial a number – if one were shown. Given, however, that Amazon really does not hand out its telephone number, customers have no choice but to start reading up. Anything not covered in official Amazon texts is often to be found in the forums, which are also displayed to customers in the Help navigation bar. Users can ask questions of the company – or other customers – in the forum; answers are on public display and if particular issues resurface often enough, Amazon forum moderators can use this as a basis to add standard text, using the problem-solving experience listed in the forum to enrich the new page and make sure that it answers as many recurring user issues as possible.

If an issue is identified which does require company action, the customer is directed to the contact form: the order and product concerned must be entered and the request given a topic; users also select their preferred method of contact (telephone, e-mail, chat). Only when they actually click Send does an Amazon operative start to consume labour hours. These hours, however, are efficient since a range of preliminary steps have already been taken care of:

- **Verification:** customers are logged in when they fill out the Contact Us dialogue box and enter their e-mail and telephone contact details, so there is no need to identify the customer using personal questions.
- **Problem-finding:** the issue has already been identified, so the customer care operative can start resolving from the first minute onwards.
- **Solutions:** the operative can access solution options from the Amazon system before calling; this system has stored millions of similar cases, and can distinguish between average and top customers, for instance – the latter get particularly generous treatment if they do have any issues, for example by not being asked to return a faulty item and simply getting a refund (if, for example, the value of the product in question is so low that returning it would be disproportionately costly).

This process generates customer care experiences with a real "Wow!" factor that get customers talking. *Post facto*, many forget the long search for information they had to undertake and remember instead the ultra-fast call-back from an incredibly friendly, switched-on customer care agent who immediately suggested a sensible solution to the issue. Customers are unlikely to realise just how work they did themselves, and the call was convincing enough in tone – when they are the ones making the calls, not being called up, call-centre operatives can be far more relaxed – that they won't be contacting a consumer rights watchdog anytime soon about the lack of a telephone number

Contact centres

Another strength of Amazon's customer service is the multichannel approach: customers can speak to somebody from Amazon by phone in the morning and use chat software to continue in the evening – whichever is currently more convenient – and assume that whoever they are talking or writing to is fully aware of the precise facts of the matter. Any company selling through a range of channels must be ready to do so in customer service, too, because consumers are getting less and less patient with organisations who try to limit them to the channel in which they bought or first made contact with customer service (see 2.4 Distribution). Customers are also increasingly intolerant of having to explain something on the phone about which they have already written an e-mail because the operative at the other end doesn't have access to the e-mail correspondence.

For customer service across all channels, there is therefore no way around bundling all communications into a customer interaction centre (CIC), also referred to as a contact centre.

This is where telephone hotlines, live chat support software, and e-mails are handled and entire customer files are available to all service operatives in every channel either using customer identification numbers or names and addresses.

This allows staff to take a call and use previous e-mails and photos or other attachments to resolve issues. What is more, everyone dealing with customers is better informed about them if their entire communication with the company is available in one file: what kind of tone does this guy use on Facebook? Are there any particularly sore points to be taken account of in his case?

This is one area where smaller-scale operations actually have an advantage in that all channels automatically blend if the customer department is composed of one or two members of staff. Larger multichannellers, meanwhile, have to make major investments to integrate various data sets and systems into a centralised contact centre; yet there is no choice in the matter in the long term if the company in question does not want to become the subject of derogatory dinner party anecdotes which have quite the opposite effect of those traded about Amazon's customer service.

The last – and first – link in the value chain

Customer service may be the last link in the e-commerce value chain, but it is a matter of overarching priority. It is, for instance, of crucial importance to the preceding link, logistics: good customer service prevents premature returns by keeping customers informed about where their orders are, stopping them from panic-buying an identical item from the competition. What is more, sleek customer service operations recognise when returning a defective product is needlessly costly and prevent disproportionate outlay.

In processing payment, too, customer service is indispensable as a trust-building measure: a clearly visible telephone number or contact details help nervous customers take the leap and place an order, while well documented interaction with existing customer offers material for interesting deductions regarding payment options: a customer who returns frequently and is always calling about something will eventually start to cost the company more than he or she contributes – it might be time to switch this one onto prepayment and see if he or she takes the hint... What should not be underestimated is the role good customer service plays in marketing: customer care so thorough that people talk about it is word-of-mouth advertising of the same value as an expensive media campaign.

Customer service is also a good source of information for the beginning of the value chain. Working with those who buy their products can help shops identify items which need to be presented differently: if customers continually complain about a specific article not meeting their expectations, then this is a hard-and-fast indication that the product text should be focussing on something different – or that photos for the product in question need to be reshot. One customer may be wrong, but several thousand can't be. And if enough of them complain about the quality of a given product, or if it breaks quickly after purchase, then this is a matter for the very first link in the value chain: procurement. This kind of product needs to be taken out of the mix, and this too is part of the customer-orientated procurement process (see 2.1 Procurement) which all online shops should be aiming to implement.

3 Case Studies

After the internet is before the internet

Despite the numerous claims to the contrary, the challenges posed by e-commerce are not fundamentally different from those in traditional retail environments. As such, they too can be examined using the widespread 'five forces' analysis – something which didn't escape the notice of the model's creator, Michael E. Porter, who was noticeably quick to recognise and, in an essay published all the way back in 2001, summarise the true challenge posed by the internet.[1]

> *Does the Internet render established rules about strategy obsolete? To the contrary, it makes them more vital than ever. Why? The Internet weakens industries' profitability, as rivals compete on price alone. And it no longer provides proprietary advantages, as virtually all companies now use the Web.*
>
> *The Internet is no more than a tool—albeit a powerful one—that can support or damage your firm's strategic positioning. The key to using it most effectively? Integrate Internet initiatives into your company's overall strategy and operations so that they 1) complement, rather than cannibalize, your established competitive approaches and 2) create systemic advantages that your competitors can't copy. Integrating Internet initiatives enhances your company's ability to develop unique products, proprietary content, distinctive processes, and strong personal service—all the things that create true value, and that have always defined competitive advantage.*

Given the early stage at which this was written, the foresight of this idea that the internet, rather than disabling the rules of commerce, actually enables them to a new and far fuller degree, is astonishing. The fact that Porter published this in 2001 and that almost all of what he wrote stands true to this day, in 2016, makes it required reading for anyone holding this book in their hands. In detail, this is

1 M.E. Porter, Strategy & Internet, Harvard Business Review 03/2001

how e-commerce models can be transposed onto his widely accepted 'five forces' structure.

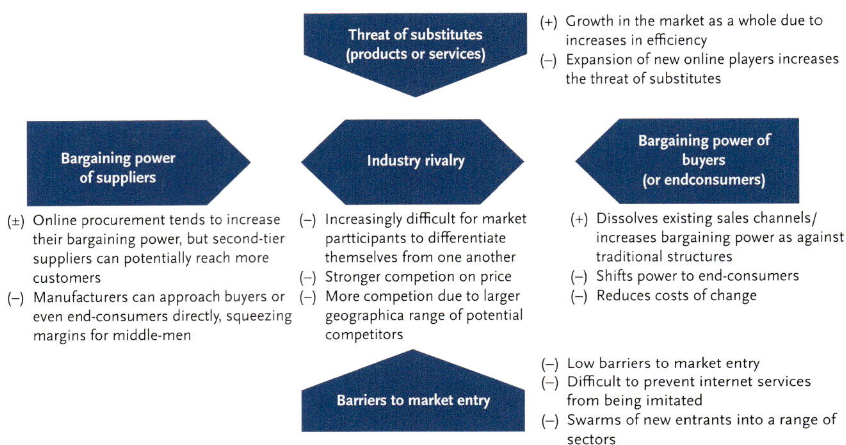

Threat of substitutes (products or services)
(+) Growth in the market as a whole due to increases in efficiency
(–) Expansion of new online players increases the threat of substitutes
Bargaining power of suppliers
Industry rivalry
Bargaining power of buyers (or endconsumers)
(±) Online procurement tends to increase their bargaining power, but second-tier suppliers can potentially reach more customers
(–) Manufacturers can approach buyers or even end-consumers directly, squeezing margins for middle-men
(–) Increasingly difficult for market partticipants to differentiate themselves from one another
(–) Stronger competion on price
(–) More competion due to larger geographica range of potential competitors
(+) Dissolves existing sales channels/ increases bargaining power as against traditional structures
(–) Shifts power to end-consumers
(–) Reduces costs of change
Barriers to market entry
(–) Low barriers to market entry
(–) Difficult to prevent internet services from being imitated
(–) Swarms of new entrants into a range of sectors

Fig. 3.1: Competition effects using the Porter model
Source: M.E. Porter, Strategy & Internet, Harvard Business Review 03/2001

The ways in which each of the individual opportunities and risks work are easy to understand, and across the market as a whole, people are increasingly coming round to the idea that the principal effect of the internet is that of a catalyst: good ideas and solid models become successful more quickly than they used to as. By the same token, average or downright poor ones fail faster, too. In our view, it is this aspect – a turbo-charged competitive environment – which is the genuine novelty and the central challenge in e-commerce.

So in this chapter, we will be looking in more detail at 50 case studies of some of the the biggest, most innovative, or otherwise notable e-commerce companies around the world, describing their business models and examining the strengths and weaknesses in an effort to see who is best suited to deal with the increasingly relentless competition unleashed by e-commerce. We then offer a strategic outlook for the coming years, examining developments which will be of particular importance to each model.

In terms of **selection criteria**, we looked both at metrics (such as sales, growth, gross merchandise volume) and the degree of innovation of a range of companies, but also at significance in the market environment. This meant viewing market reports, trawling through databases, and using our own knowledge of the industry to shortlist exciting business models. Our aim has been to present an overview encompassing dominant market participants such as Amazon and Tmall, successful specialist shops like Zooplus and Zappos, large offline retailers with online ambitions like Walmart and Home Depot and new concepts such as AboutYou and Warby Parker which may not yet be doing the numbers, but are nonetheless worth mentioning in this context. As well as future prospects, we have by way of contrast also included some companies struggling such as Sears and Gilt.

Each case study begins with an introductory table of basic information such as launch year and indicators of the size of the company – not that figures such as turnover and staff numbers should be read as part of an effort to rank the companies examined here, the aim being instead to give the reader a rough idea of the shape and size of the company. The business models featured are then displayed as a canvas and their position on the market mapped onto a matrix, allowing us to examine them from a commercial point of view.

Business model canvas

First published by Alexander Osterwalder In 2010[2], a business model canvas[3] is a tool used to show business models in a standardised, at-a-glance way; it has now become the standard both in academic theory and business practice, and is used not only to record and depict existing business models, but also to sketch concepts for new ones.

The business model canvas is composed of four main categories:

1. **Infrastructure** is made up of the key partnerships, resources, and activities of a business which produce a particularly strong contribution to value creation.
2. **Offering** consists in the value propositions describing what the business offers its customers: what is the customer requirement or problem, and how is it dealt with?
3. **Customers** is subdivided into the customer segments served by the business model, the type of customer relationships it focusses on, and which channels it uses to communicate and sell.
4. **Finances** list the costs in the business model against the revenue streams, showing if and how the company can operate profitably.

2 Alexander Osterwalder, Business Model Generation, John Wiley and Sons, 2010
3 www.businessmodelgeneration.com (as of March 2015)

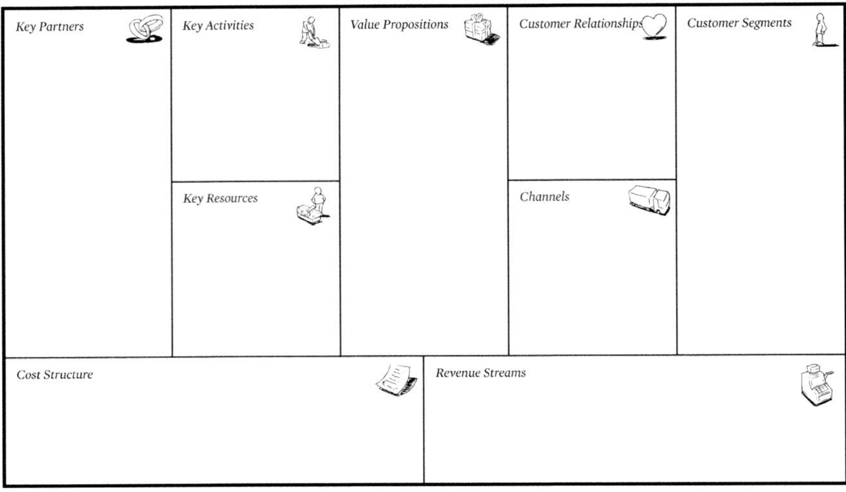

Fig. 3.2: Business model canvas

Source: Alexander Osterwalder (2010), Business Model Generation

The aim of this model is to create a common language to visualise, evaluate, and modify business models. Its method is to use a simple visualisation technique which describes processes within companies and makes it easy to challenge them. While it certainly does not replace more detailed business plans, it is of great value in examining the positioning of a company and is often used during start-up conferences to probe new ideas for weaknesses or contradictions.[4] When applied to businesses already active in the market whose premises are often not re-examined closely, this model can, for all its simplicity, lead to a real gain in insight.

4 www.startupweekend.org (as of January 2015)

Positioning matrix

Most companies attempt to position their business model using specific unique selling propositions (USPs); USPs are intended to differentiate the company from its competitors and give customers a reason to purchase its goods or services. Typical USPs include a level of service above and beyond that of competitors, a product range not available from other providers, or especially competitive pricing. Each business model gives different weight to different selling propositions, and by plotting this weighting on a matrix, the overall positioning of a company can be made clear. Figure 3.3 shows how this kind of matrix looks for commerce models.[5]

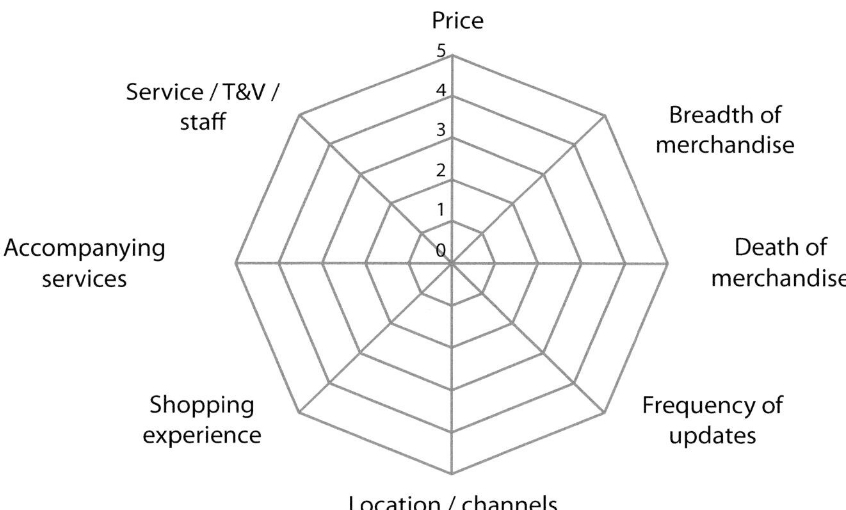

Fig. 3.3: Market positioning matrix

Source: with reference to Finne & Sivonen (2009), The Retail Value Chain

Various commerce models can then be plotted onto this matrix by looking at which of its points they focus on and to what extent; the result is the overall market position of the company. In this example, we map Amazon against H&M to show how, in the fashion segment, companies can be differentiated in their sales channels, the frequency with which they update their product range, and the breadth of this range.

5 with reference to Finne & Sivonen (2009), The Retail Value Chain

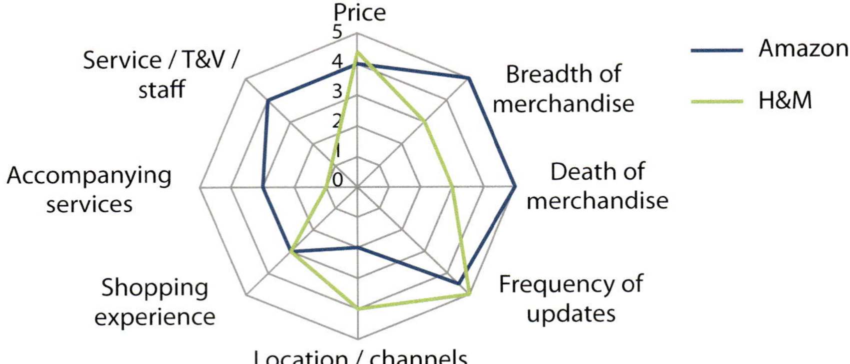

Fig. 3.4: Market positioning matrix, Amazon vs. H&M
Source: our graphic

This matrix allows us to both recognise any genuine USPs and gain an impression of the strength of a market position at a glance. Simply put, the greater the area the business model can stake out on this matrix by pushing out on each of the various competitive issues, the stronger its overall position on the market.

Strategic considerations

It is worth taking note of two key effects regarding strategic positioning in online retail, which become particularly clear on this market positioning matrix. The first issue is the increasing **competitive pressure** in e-commerce: for several years now, there have been waves of new start-ups, often equipped with considerable amounts of investment capital, who make a dash for the lead in various areas, pushing product range sizes, service offerings, or low prices to new extremes as their USPs. They have every reason to bolt for leadership on price, availability, and product range, too, as study after study has shown that these are the factors on which customer interest is focussed in online shopping[6]; 'soft factors' such as emotional connection or linking channel may support growth but have not yet proven to be enough to support a stable business model alone.

This trend is likely to see continued growth for Amazon, for example, which has set up its business model to cover these three key factors. It is worth remembering this whenever the increasingly popular click and collect strategy[7] is rolled out by yet

6 www.ecckoeln.de (abgerufen Januar 2015)
7 www.bcgperspectives.com (abgerufen Januar 2015)

another legacy retailer as a competitive advantage; connecting online and offline channels usually has nothing more than a superficial effect on the basic criteria of price, availability, and product range.

Unfortunately for these multichannel hopes for salvation, the speed of technological change is piling on even more competitive pressure in the 'hard factors', and the axes on the positioning matrix are being pushed further and further out. There was once a time when delivery from most online shops cost a few dollars, pounds, or euros across the field: then big players such as Amazon and Zalando started to slash their delivery charges, and in the five years between 2008 and 2013, a range of other shops were forced to match them – often, delivery charges reached zero and have stayed there since. Now, with Amazon Prime having proven so popular, it is becoming a huge customer satisfaction downer for serious competitors on the same product segments to even ask for extra fees to get a product to customers within 24 hours: after all, for $99, £79, or €49 annually, Prime customers can get *all* of their deliveries dispatched as express deliveries – and in several urban areas in the US and Europe, Amazon can now offer same-day-delivery on some products as part of the package. Just to ramp up the pressure, Amazon Super Prime is offering customers two-hour-delivery in many major US metro areas: in Germany, Amazon has even announced a 90-minute deadline for some postcodes by the end of 2016. Classic business strategy processes assume a well-defined playing field, making them singularly unable to handle this kind of constant shift as the goal posts are moved again and again in each dimension of competition. The acceleration enabled by the internet and driven as fast as possible by its agile native companies has turned that level playing field into a very bumpy ride.

The second strategic effect – **transparency** – acts as an amplifier for this competitive pressure, influencing not only the positions of players in the market but also the way customers perceive these positions. The transparency provided by the internet means that consumers today notice changes in positioning much faster than in a traditional retail environment: the next online shop is only ever one click away, and powerful intermediaries such as Google Shopping and price comparison engines allow users to compare service offerings and prices between competing shops in an instant. The results of this comparison are easier to communicate too, thanks to online consumer portals and social media. This means that the public spots a strong position far more rapidly than it used to, which in turn reduces the effectiveness of loyalty programmes and makes it difficult to use lock-in effects to tie customers to companies in the long term.

Companies with strong positions get noticed quickly in e-commerce – and so too do companies whose position weakens: new players can rise to the top overnight and then be banished into oblivion with equal speed if they do not innovate rapidly enough to stay ahead of, or at least keep up with, competitors. It is those companies which do manage to adapt and innovate consistently enough to keep their place at the head of the pack which are particularly successful now: yet the shifting sands of competition on the internet may yet upset any of the businesses in these case studies – or, in some cases, have already done so. Online Shop A, currently a leader on, say, speed of delivery, may find itself having been overtaken at any moment, meaning that its USP – speedy delivery – has now been lost to Shop B or, if Shops C & D also get ahead, relegated to a simple matter of expected basic service. In other words, companies which are not themselves pushing the limits of the various competitive issues ever further will, sooner rather than later, find themselves struggling to keep up with those who do manage to.

What would once, in a less competitive pre-internet environment, have looked like pointless over-exertion, has become part and parcel of being on the market. Any slippage vis-à-vis competitors is immediately plain for all customers to see. This is why Peter Thiel, one of the original investors behind Facebook, has argued that successful internet companies have no other choice than to aim for a monopoly position if they want to successfully conquer markets.[8] Depending on your definition of monopoly, Google already has one in search engines and Amazon may well have one in online retail. Whatever the moral and economic arguments about such a concentration of market power may be, this kind of competitive advantage does seem to be becoming increasingly common and is being discussed by popular media across the Western world.[9]

> *Something about the internet clearly favours such mushrooming quasi-monopolies. But rather than being a regrettable by-product of internet commerce and in need of strict oversight, might they instead be an integral part of what makes it so prone to rapid growth and life-improving innovation—not a bug, as the phrase has it, but a feature? Peter Thiel, one of the founders of PayPal (now the market leader in online and mobile payments), and an early investor in Facebook, argues that monopolies add "entirely new categories of abundance to the world". If he is right, then treating monopolies in the digital realm just like their bricks-and-mortar—or 'oil-well-and-pipeline'—predecessors would be very bad for innovation and growth.*

8 www.wsj.com (as of January 2015)
9 www.economist.com (as of January 2015)

3.1 About You – A retailer re-invents e-commerce

Key facts

Name: ABOUT YOU GmbH
Headquarters: Hamburg, Germany
Total staff: 250 (Collins)
Global turnover 2015: n. a.
Founded in: 2014
Origins: Online pure player

About You is the flagship store of the Collins Group, one of Europe's fast-growing e-commerce projects. As part of the overarching Otto structure, About You runs online fashion shops in Germany, Austria, and Switzerland,[1] focussing strongly on offering user experience, inspiration, and personalisation. It's a formula that seems to have taken fast, and About You looks able to break clearly into nine-figure sales in 2016.[2] Two particularly innovative approaches are striking at Collins: personalised shopping experience and open commerce. At About You, the focus on personalisation starts in the name, which responds to customers who log in by including their first name: "AboutJoe". Moreover, customers have the opportunity to save their preferences (style, size, colours, etc.) and then get customised recommendations and use intelligent product filters. The About You app world is predicated on open commerce, allowing external developers to integrate applications into the shop and take a share of sales generated there. Currently, About You offers customers more than 50 inspiring apps – and growing.[3] With 50% of staff working in IT, the tech-driven approach of the Collins Group is clear.[4]

Positioning

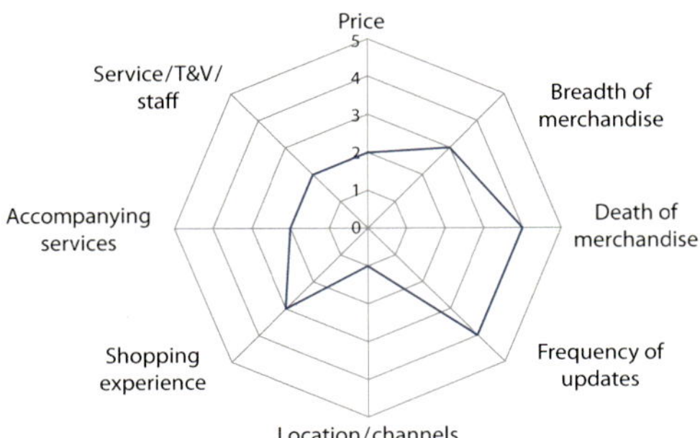

1 www.handelsblatt.com (as of March 2016)
2 www.internetworld.de (as of March 2016)
3 www.internetworld.de (as of March 2016)
4 t3n.de/magazine (as of March 2016)

About You concentrates on its shopping experience as the factor on which it positions itself most clearly against competitors. Its shop is not only state of the art, but also offers an emotional, inspiring environment. A constant slew of content makes sure it retains relevance while user-generated personalisation supports the shopping experience. Customers reactions show that this is popular, with one in four having already inputted their preferences in their profile.

Business model canvas				
Key partners Investor and parent company Otto Group, app-developers, fashion blogger and other content producers	**Key activities** Technology, CRM, marketing, product and developer sourcing **Key resources** Platform, network, online expertise	**Value proposition** Personalised online shop, inspirational shopping experience	**Customer relationships** Self-service shopping, strongly personalised online shop **Channels** Online, mobile, stores (affiliate Edited)	**Customer segments** Young, fashion-conscious demographics, 80% female*
Cost structure structure Platform, staff, marketing		**Revenue streams** streams Direct revenue from transactions (app developers also get a share)		

* http://etailment.de/thema/player/Tarek-Mueller-About-You-Wir-haben-ein-ueberraschendes-Potenzial-der-Apps-entdeckt-2726 (as of March 2016)

Authors' evaluation and assessment of perspectives

We are delighted that About You has essentially gone ahead and set up a new category in e-commerce. This ecosystem approach aims to include external developers and other companies by offering access to products and customer groups; as such, About You has essentially transposed the Apple AppStore concept for digital products into the world of physical e-commerce retail. What is more, with its good reserves of paid-up capital, About You will be able to continue to work in an innovative way, testing new concepts and even proprietary brands. As it is the first platform acting as an e-commerce system from its inception, About You's development – and lessons learned from its mistakes – are of value not just to e-commerce retailers in Germany, but worldwide. Without a doubt, this is one of the most exciting start-ups of recent years.

3.2 Ali Express – The Golden Gate to Western Consumers

Key facts

Name: AliExpress.com
Headquarters: Hong Kong, China
Total staff: n. a. (Alibaba: 36,465)
Global turnover 2015: n. a.
Founded in: 2010
Origins: Online pure player

Ali Express is part of the Chinese Alibaba Group and one of the online giant's platforms aimed at international customers.[5] This B2C marketplace brings together the offerings of more than 10,000 Chinese manufacturers and exporters, earning a 5% commission on sales. On Singles' Day 2015, Ali Express handled over 21 million orders placed by customers in 220 countries, among which Russia, the USA, and Brazil represented the largest markets.[6] In Russia, for example, the website is already generating twice as much traffic as Ozon.ru, the "Russian Amazon",[7] with around 22 million monthly users;[8] this makes Ali Express the biggest e-commerce website on the market.[9] A key element of Ali Express' success is its ability to build up trust by offering protection against non-delivery and generous customer service; this works as a counterweight against concerns consumers might have buying from the often unknown Chinese manufacturers selling on the platform.[10]

Positioning

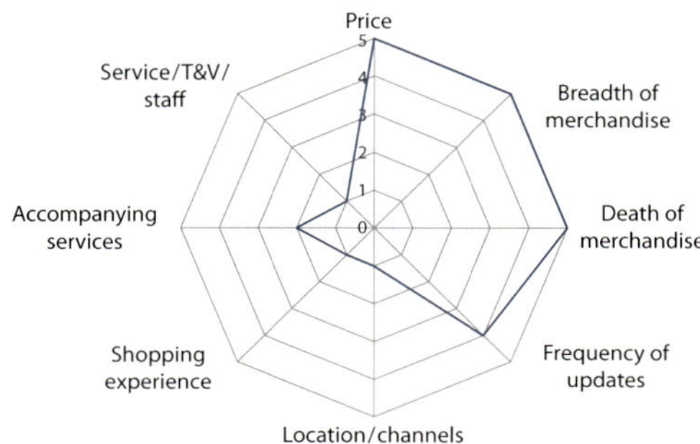

5 www.chinainternetwatch.com (as of March 2016)
6 evigo.com (as of March 2016)
7 www.internetretailer.com (as of March 2016)
8 www.bloomberg.com (as of March 2016)
9 www.internetretailer.com (as of March 2016)
10 www.chinacheckup.com (as of March 2016)

Price and product range are the two main points on which Ali Express positions itself for its international customers. As purchases are made directly from Chinese manufacturers, cutting out high-margin middlemen in the distribution chain, the prices it can offer are very low in comparison to competitors; with around 100 million products listed in over 30 categories, meanwhile,[11] its product range is as broad as it is deep. Thus far, however, the company has made little effort to differentiate on either shopping experience or service.

Business model canvas				
Key partners 10,000 Chinese manufacturers and exporters, logistics, Alibaba	**Key activities** Sourcing, platform, customer care **Key resources** Network of manufacturers	**Value proposition** Order an extremely large range of products direct from Chinese manufacturers	**Customer relationships** Self-service **Channels** Online, mobile	**Customer segments** Mass market, price-sensitive customers
Cost structure Sourcing, platform, logistics, trader quality assurance		**Revenue streams** Traders pay 5% commission on all sales and also for marketing services		

Authors' evaluation and assessment of perspectives

Ali Express offers a foretaste of the Alibaba Group's potential in B2C e-commerce: the provider has already made it possible for customers to order products straight off of the production line in China and have them delivered to Europe or America in 3-7 days without paying delivery charges. By integrating closely with manufacturers and cutting out a whole series of links in the distribution chain, Ali Express is able to undercut Amazon by anything between 10% and 40% in no small number of product categories. The momentum generated both by Ali Express and the various copycat approaches sure to follow soon will be one of the key trends going into 2017. Not convinced? Just try ordering something on Ali Express, banggoods.com, or a similar site and you'll see just how much these providers stand to change the markets in advanced Western economies.

11 www.internetretailer.com (as of March 2016)

3.3 Alibaba Group – An Amazon-killer or a paper tiger?

Key facts

Name: Alibaba Group Holding Ltd
Headquarters: Hangzhou, China
Total staff: 36,465[12]
Global turnover 2015/16[13] : ¥101.1bn (US$15.7bn)[14]
Founded in: 1999
Origins: Online pure player

The Alibaba Group is the largest Chinese online retailer with international activities, reaching over 400 million active users. The company went public in 2014 with what was, at that time, the biggest initial public offering in the world with a total value of $21.727bn . The manifold subsidiaries of this monolith have dominant positions in China and are making ever greater inroads into international retail. Alibaba runs a total of six marketplaces, three domestic and three cross-border operators: on Tmall Global, Chinese consumers buy foreign goods while on Ali Express, foreign consumers get access to Chinese products; Alibaba.com offers wholesale of Chinese goods to customers outside the country. It also has a proliferation of companies in other areas such as cloud computing, mobile internet services, and finances. As such, the Group should be understood as a self-supporting ecosystem which controls many areas of the most important e-commerce customer cycles from customer journey through ordering to logistics.

Measured on gross goods sold, the Group-level result on Chinese retail marketplaces[15] alone is, at US$115bn as of the fourth quarter of 2015, already scraping at the heels of Amazon's annual GMV (estimated at $160bn).[16] At the same time, the Group's actual turnover of $15.7bn is, when compared to Amazon's $107bn, puny. The discrepancy is primarily a function of Alibaba's far lower transaction fees which, depending on the marketplace, vary between 2% and 5%; the Group's business model is far more dependent on fees charged on additional services in areas such as marketing, financial services, and logistics.

Strategically, the Group has five focal points: 1. imports to China; 2. expanding into rural areas, 3. increasing market share in these Chinese first-tier cities of Beijing, Shanghai, Guangzhou, and Shenzhen; 4. cloud computing; and 5. mobile. In the first quarter of the year 2016, more than 70% of gross sales on Alibaba's China retail marketplaces took place on mobile devices.[17]

Besides its 126 offices in China, the Group has another 29 locations worldwide: its presence in California, London, and Bombay underscores its ambitions for global online retail, as do the 17 strategic investments it made in 2015 – of which eight were internation-

12 www.businesswire.com (as of March 2016)
13 Fiscal year ends March 31st, 2016
14 www.statista.com/statistics/225614/net-revenue-of-alibaba/ (as of March 2016)
15 Per company definition,"China retail marketplaces" are Taobao Marketplace, Tmall and Juhuasuan.
16 www.marketwatch.com (as of March 2016)
17 www.alibabagroup.com (as of March 2016)

al.[18] These stakes include investments in Amazon's competitor Jet.com and in Snapdeal, the "Indian Alibaba", while the Group's efforts to sell in European and American markets are increasingly being understood as a threat by domestic businesses as a direct sales channel to Western consumers would enable Chinese manufacturers to cut out the middlemen in these economies.[19] On the other hand, Alibaba offers Western producers a channel for an initial entry into the Chinese market, principally in the form of brand shops; this option is mostly used by larger brands from the European and American markets, and even Amazon has its own flagship store here.[20]

Positioning

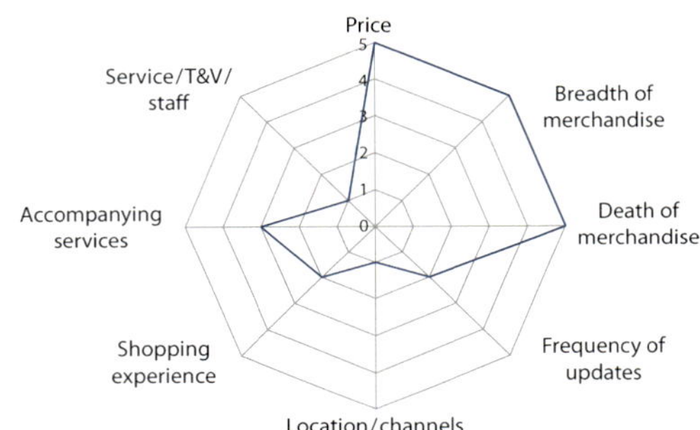

E-Commerce		Services	Other
tmall.com *B2C marketplace*	Ali Express *Global B2C marketplace*	Ant Financial *Financial Services*	aliyun.com *Cloud computing*
juhuasuan.com *Group buying marketplace*	Taobao.com *C2C marketplace*	Cainiao *Logistics information*	
Alibaba.com *Global wholesale marketplace*	1688.com *China wholesale marketplace*	Alimama.com *Online marketing platform* **and many more**	

Authors' evaluation and assessment of perspectives

In the course of producing this book, we have read an awful lot about Alibaba and spoken to people about it time and time again. The result is that, even after all this research and all these talks, we still cannot understand how stock market analysts can have any basis for their valuations. Alibaba is not a retailer, but rather an extremely heterogeneous collection of business divisions and – while the company is now so dominant in China that state intervention is needed to give its competitors a chance – abroad, the holding company is investing in what appears to us to be an extremely unfocussed fashion. We remain deeply unsure as to whether the company's rag-bag of assets and business models will ever work, but as long as the company is making money and investing it abroad, it will continue to have an effect on various markets.

18 www.techinasia.com (as of March 2016)
19 digitalkaufmann.de (as of March 2016)
20 www.reuters.com (as of March 2016)

3.4 Amazon – Every retailer's worst nightmare

Key facts

Name: Amazon.com, Inc.
Headquarters: Seattle, USA
Total staff: 245,200
Global turnover 2015: US$107bn[21]
Founded in: 1994
Origins: Online pure player

Amazon is far more than just a general-stockist online department store with more than 300 million active customers[22] – and has been for some time. It has branched out into everything from express shipping (Prime) and streaming, into owned-logistics, and hosting and cloud computing (Amazon Web Services). Its marketplace hitches its own merchandise to that of third parties, allowing other companies and private persons to sell products both used and new; as well as extending its product range exponentially, the marketplace also feeds Amazon with data which it uses to optimise its own product mix and pricing. Prime, meanwhile, now reaches 46% of US homes[23] and offers a membership package with premium shipping and digital on-demand products such as music, videos, and books; these extras have led to a level of customer loyalty the likes of which e-commerce has never seen and a vastly increased rate of repeat business. Then there are Amazon's ambitions in last-mile delivery: besides its logistics network with around 290 warehouses,[24] it already runs Amazon Flex (individuals make deliveries in their spare time) and Amazon Fresh, specialised in food delivery, in America. Recently, Amazon passed the one-billion mark in turnover on its B2B marketplace,[25] hit sales of seven billion in Amazon Web Services,[26] and got fashionistas talking with its new own-brand clothing.

Positioning

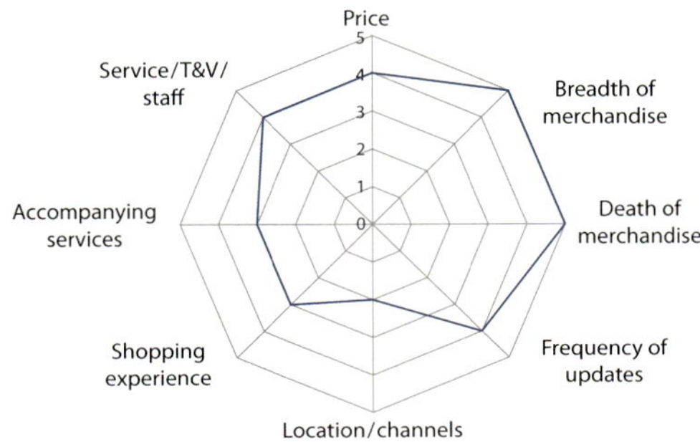

21 phx.corporate-ir.net (as of March 2016)
22 www.statista.com (as of March 2016)
23 www.usatoday.com (as of March 2016)
24 www.mwpvl.com (as of March 2016)
25 www.cnet.com (as of March 2016)
26 phx.corporate-ir.net (as of March 2016)

Amazon's main USP is its range of merchandise (both in breadth and depth) and the prices it offers. The lowest prices on the platform are generally to be had on the marketplace, however, where sellers generally undercut Amazon's own prices on average in 2014.[27] While its navigation and other elements of its shop are pronouncedly user friendly, as a whole, the Amazon shopping experience is rather flat and unemotional.

Business model canvas

Key partners	Key activities	Value proposition	Customer relationships	Customer segments
Manufacturers and brands, logistics companies, publishers, marketplace sellers	Logistics, compiling product mix, CRM, IT / analytics	Huge selection of products at bargain prices, excellent customer service and high availability	Customer-centred, Self-service	Online-shoppers; price-sensitive customers looking for fast delivery and good service
	Key resources		**Channels**	
	Data, software		Online and mobile	

Cost structure	Revenue streams
1. Sales costs 74%	1. Direct takings from its own retail activities
2. Technology 9%	2. Commission from its marketplace
3. Fulfilment 8%	3. B2B income (e. g. for hosting, fulfilment, web enabling)
4. Marketing 4%	

Authors' evaluation and assessment of perspectives

The speed at which Amazon is developing is, quite simply, phenomenal. No other company of this size is changing the retail landscape faster and more lastingly than Amazon. Provided that shareholders continue to support Amazon' growth strategy (more sales, low profits), Amazon will continue to trigger avalanches in all of the markets in which it is present. The company has now reached the critical mass necessary to mobilise its customer base for attacks on new segments, too, as in the case of Amazon Instant Video. What is more, the company still has the potential to cut costs in its already tight supply chain (see "robots"), which will free up yet more resources to invest in the drive for growth. This includes test-and-learn innovations such as Amazon Dash and Echo with the aim of getting even closer to customers whenever they have a requirement in everyday life than is already the case. In our view, the really exciting period in Amazon's development has only just begun. As its boss Jeff Bezos famously said: It's still Day One.

27 www.shopanbieter.de (as of March 2016)

3.5 Amorelie – A recipe for niche domination(?)

Key facts

Name: Sonoma Internet GmbH
Headquarters: Berlin, Deutschland
Total staff: 75
Global turnover 2015: €21m (US$22.9m)
Founded in: 2013
Origins: Online pure player

Two years after Amorelie was set up, in April 2015 the Munich media company ProSieben Sat1 acquired a 75% stake in this online shop for adult products.[28] Amorelie sells sex toys, lingerie, and associated accessories in five European countries, applying an innovative concept by marketing to young women, couples, and first-time buyers[29] to shift erotic products from a taboo niche into the mainstream. Marketing itself as the "online sex shop for normal people",[30] it reaches its target groups using positive branding and upbeat communication focussing on product quality, explanatory online content, and attention-grabbing PR initiatives. As such, Amorelie shows how high-quality content and publicity can be used to win over a hesitant target group; it also runs a TV programme, *The Amorelie Love Lounge*, on a the German channel for young women, Sixx. Thanks not least to the ProSieben Sat1 group involvement and a consequent ramp-up in television campaigns, Amorelie sales hit €13.25m in the first nine months of 2015.[31]

Positioning

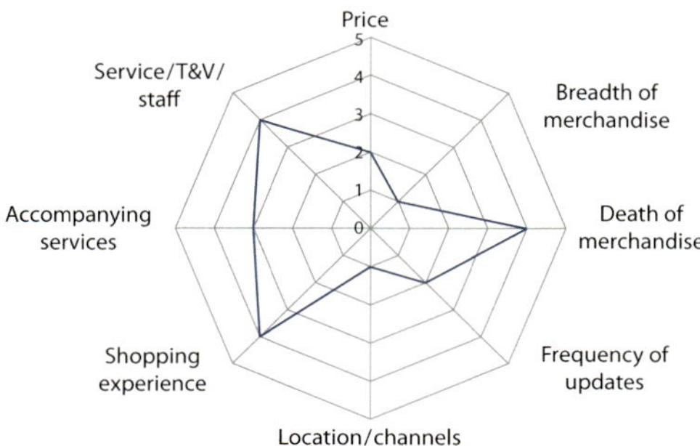

28 www.prosiebensat1.com (as of March 2016)
29 www.amorelie.de (as of March 2016)
30 t3n.de (as of March 2016)
31 excitingcommerce.de (as of March 2016)

Amorelie emphasises stylish online shopping and user experience. Its user-friendly, discreet design is used to support this approach, as is a high level of customer information and prolific online content; customer service is also good, encompassing options such as hotlines, e-mail, and live-chat. The main drive of the concept is to build trust fast – especially with new customers – thus positioning itself against traditional purveyors of erotic products.

Business model canvas				
Key partners brands, media partners, content networks	**Key activities** Sourcing, marketing, PR **Key resources** Brand relationship, PR team	**Value proposition** Erotic products for newbies, service and advice, discretion	**Customer relationships** Relationship building by offering advice (principally indirectly using online content) **Channels** Online, offline showrooms (testing)	**Customer segments** Target group: young, female internet users, couples, newbies
Cost structure Personal, marketing, sourcing		**Revenue streams** Transaction-dependent direct sales turnover		

Authors' evaluation and assessment of perspectives

The sex toy industry in Germany was focused on the two big retailers Beate Uhse and Orion. Those two big retailers dominated the market for decades and most online competitors focused on the same customer segment. Amorelie successfully managed to expand the market to new Customer segments, because of its approach to sell the products as life style accessories instead of just selling the next dildo 2.0. The business is driven by very good PR work and the strategic partnership with the media company ProSiebenSat1. Nonetheless the success of Fifty Shades of Grey came at the right time for Amorelie. It helped the business to grow at an impressive level. Today Amorelie is not just a retailing company anymore. It can be seen as a marketplace for lifestyle sex toys with the power to create new products and brands. We expect that Amorelie will fundamentally threaten traditional retailers like Orion in the next decade, because it is much easier for Amorelie to expand its business in the "sex toy industry" niche than the other way around.

3.6 AO.com – Is white goods a niche ripe for a champion?

Key facts

Name: AO World plc
Headquarters: Bolton, England
Total staff: 1,450
Global turnover 2015: £476.7m (US$706.6m)
Founded in: 2000
Origins: Online pure player

Appliances Online is an online pure player from Britain selling white goods (home appliances) and generating almost half a billion pounds' turnover (around US$706.6m) in 2015. Active in the UK since 2000, AO expanded into Germany in 2014, the Netherlands in 2016, and is planning to enter other new markets in the near future.[32] As a consequence of its growth, AO is now starting to compete against the "big boys" like Amazon, Otto, and MediaSaturn; nevertheless, it expects to turn over 60 million Euros in Germany despite the strong competition[33] and is aiming for 18.5% growth in its home market in the same period.[34] The listed company's strategy is to win over customers with low prices and high service levels, and has built up its own fleet of delivery vehicles in the UK and Germany;[35] the concept behind this is to offer a consistently convincing service on the "last mile", installing new appliances and picking up old ones. In the UK market, AO has recently expanded its product range into consumer electronics.[36] Currently, its expensive European expansion is being funded by its profitable UK business.[37]

Positioning

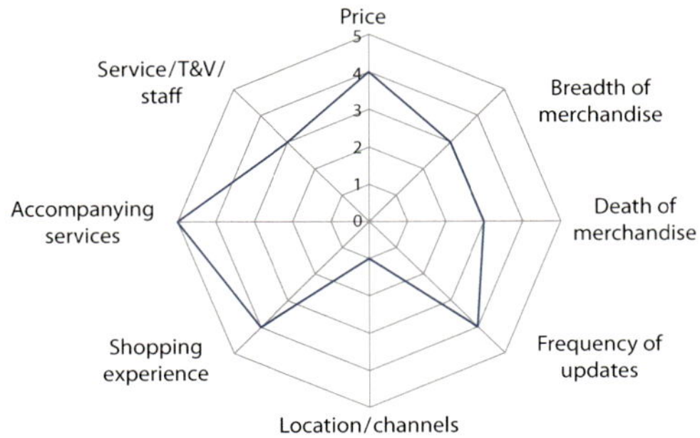

32 ao.com (as of March 2016)
33 excitingcommerce.de (as of March 2016)
34 www.insidermedia.com (as of March 2016)
35 neuhandeln.de (as of March 2016)
36 neuhandeln.de (as of March 2016)
37 www.insidermedia.com (as of March 2016)

AO's real USP is its delivery service – not that it comes for free in all cases (appliance disposal costs extra like it does with Amazon or Otto). What is more, AO uses its low price guarantee to headline bargain deals which, once compared to Amazon with all added costs, are not always the cheapest. In comparison to competitors, its product range is far narrower, too; but its user experience is tailored to the product segment and runs smoothly.

Business model canvas				
Key partners Manufacturers and brands, advertising platforms	**Key activities** Marketing, sourcing, distribution **Key resources** Distribution, sourcing	**Value proposition** Home appliances at a good price; fast, reliable delivery	**Customer relationships** Self-service **Channels** Online	**Customer segments** Mass market
Cost structure Logistics and warehousing, stock, marketing, IT		**Revenue streams** 1. AO website sales 2. Third-party website sales 3. Third-party logistics services		

Authors' evaluation and assessment of perspectives

From the authors point of view, e-commerce retailing business will eventually be successful when they are dominating the market in terms of: Price, Assortment, Availability. AO.com actually managed this for the UK plus added the service perspective to the value chain. In 2014, after the ao.com IPO, analysts doubted that this can be a scalable business model outside of the UK and is only successful in UK because it was one of the first e-commerce businesses with that Value proposition. After 12 months in Germany AO.com is still around and fast growing, giving incumbents like Mediamarkt a lot to think of. We think it is a remarkable success and the profits in the future will be based solely on service revenues.

3.7 Apple – A textbook case of brand manufacturer direct sales

Key facts

Name: Apple Inc.
Headquarters: Cupertino, USA
Total staff: 115,000[38]
Global turnover 2015: US$233.7bn[39]
Founded in: 1976
Origins: Hardware manufacturer, software maker

Besides being the world's most valuable brands,[40] Apple is also, according to Internet Retailer, the second-largest online retailer in the USA – despite the fact that online revenue made up only 11.3% of its total sales in 2014.[41] Active in over 119 countries,[42] Apple can balance out the flattening of growth in North American and Europe with strong expansion in Asia,[43] China above all, where its sales are increasing by 70% annually.[44] Its brand is valued at an astonishing $145.3bn and its return on sales is, at 31%,[45] is unparalleled, thanks primarily to the fact that Apple has, more than almost any other manufacturer, been able to use lock-in effects to keep customers from switching to devices from other makers: Apple products synch with one another at the swipe of a finger, but there are genuine software barriers towards other operating systems. In e-commerce terms, the new AppleTV and the ApplePay system are of particular interest: since September 2014, users of Apple Pay have been able to use fingerprint authentication on their smartphones to pay in countless shopping apps and over two million retail stores; the new TV, meanwhile, also allows users to shop in apps.

Positioning

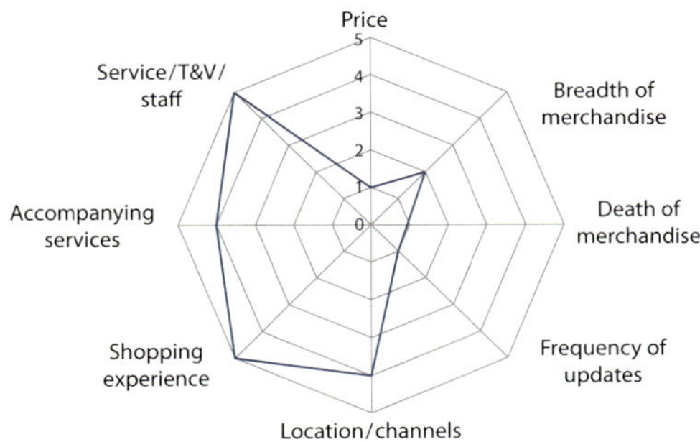

38 www.bloomberg.com (as of March 2016)
39 de.statista.com (as of March 2016)
40 www.forbes.com (as of March 2016)
41 www.internetretailer.com (as of March 2016)
42 www.apple.com (as of March 2016)
43 www.fool.de (as of March 2016)
44 images.apple.com (as of March 2016)
45 www.wikinvest.com (as of March 2016)

In the minds of its customers, Apple has achieved a very strong brand status while positioning itself in the premium price segment. The corporation makes a great deal of its support and service (e. g. the Genius Bars in its stores), and of the shopping experience, enabled by design excellence and fantastic product presentation. The real core of Apple's positioning, however, is the product and its intuitive user-friendliness.

Business model canvas				
Key partners Mobile network operators, record companies and publishers, suppliers, app developers	**Key activities** Design, software-development, HR **Key resources** Brand, patents	**Value proposition** Brand, user-friendliness, service	**Customer relationships** Self-service online, personal offline **Channels** Online, mobile, stores, third-party providers	**Customer segments** Mass market
Cost structure Staff, suppliers, sales and marketing		**Revenue streams** 1. Hardware sales 2. Content sales (apps, music, films, books) 3. Commission on music and film streaming services		

Authors' evaluation and assessment of perspectives

In our case studies, Apple represents a genuine exception. It is not a retailer by any usual definition of the term, but a manufacturer. Nonetheless, with its powerful platforms such as the iOS Store and iTunes, it is up there with the best of retailers when it comes to breaking into new product segments, especially in digital content (music, videos, and online games). By spreading iOS, the company has reached a position of strength.

There are no indications that Apple will relent in the coming years. It has a mountain of cash at its disposal which will allow it to continue its own stream of innovations and to buy up companies in new fields of growth. To what it extent it will penetrate further into retail and e-commerce is, however, impossible to predict.

3.8 Asos – Britain's favourite fashion shop and its international ambitions

Key facts

Name: ASOS Plc
Headquarters: London, UK
Total staff: 2,038[46]
Global turnover 2015: £1.2bn (US$1.8bn)
Founded in: 2000
Origins: Online pure player

Asos is an acronym for "as seen on screen" and was set up with the mission of providing customers outfits they saw on their favourite celebrities at affordable prices. Today, the company runs one of the largest online shops in the fast-fashion and beauty segments, offering over 80,000 products and 850 brands,[47] including some own-brands which are already generating 50% of turnover in the UK.[48] As such, Asos is a textbook example of how an e-commerce start-up can find an organic path[49] to profitability, with a return on sales stable at around 4% for several years now. Asos is concentrating increasingly on internationalisation, offering country-shops in nine languages[50] and shipping to 240 countries; it now generates more than half of its turnover outside of the UK.[51] In addition to its main business, Asos also runs a marketplace which allows external shops to sell straight to Asos customers.[52] The company has openly communicated its medium-term sales target of £2.5bn, a goal it is looking to achieve with product innovation and a strong focus of the French, German, and US markets.[53] The Chinese market, too, is a priority; Asos' strategy here is mobile first.

Positioning

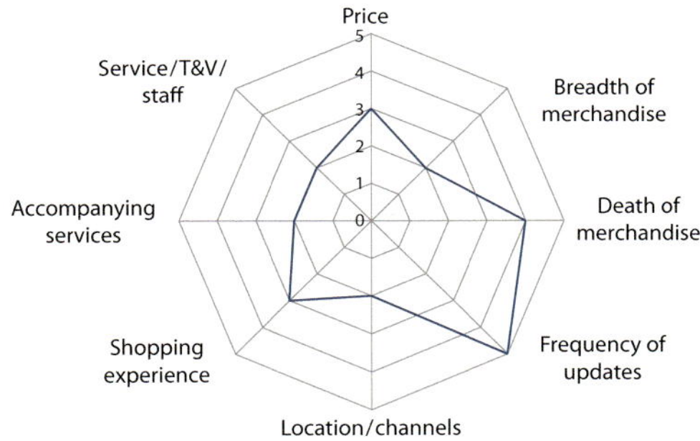

46 www.asosplc.com (as of March 2016)
47 www.kassenzone.de (as of March 2016)
48 uk.reuters.com (as of March 2016)
49 www.bloomberg.com (as of March 2016)
50 www.businessoffashion.com (as of March 2016)
51 news.markets (as of March 2016)
52 www.asosplc.com (as of March 2016)
53 www.businessoffashion.com (as of March 2016)

Asos' principle positioning tool is its trend-driven product range; celebrities' outfits are a part of the marketing strategy, whether in the Asos magazine, on social media, or when popular personalities are given Asos goods to wear. Besides this, despite Asos' claims that its product range is fundamentally different, its positioning is similar to that of Zalando.[54]

Business model canvas

Key partners	Key activities	Value proposition	Customer relationships	Customer segments
Brand manufacturers, parcels services, celebrities	Creating and updating product range, marketing, dispatch, technology	Latest trends (fast fashion) at a good price	Self-service, content marketing drives customer loyalty (e. g. Asos' own fashion magazine	Youth (16-35 years old), fashion conscious
	Key resources		**Channels**	
	Image as fashion experts		Online, Mobile	

Cost structure	Revenue streams
Distribution & logistics, marketing, platform	Transaction-dependent direct sales turnover, commissions (20%) on Asos marketplace

Authors' evaluation and assessment of perspectives

As a listed company, Asos is one to watch in e-commerce at the moment. Consumer reactions are positive and both the overall margin Asos takes and its own-brand verticality make for strong profitability. As such, Asos' model has become a blueprint for several retailers in Europe; what is more, generating a turnover of over one billion pounds one a such a small capital investment is a trailblazing achievement. Nevertheless, the extent to which this structure can be expanded further abroad is questionable given the rash of new competitors who are flooding into precisely those market segments in which Asos is active. Cross-border comes with a range of other challenges for the company, too, especially in terms of a coherent pricing image: especially with brand goods, simply converting the pounds sterling tag into Euros often produces prices which are uncompetitive. The company is aiming to implement localised pricing to resolve this issue,[55] but only time will tell whether Asos can hold its market position in Germany or France, for example. The recent model of Asos seems to be limited.

54 www.onlinehaendler-news.de (as of March 2016)
55 www.asosplc.com (as of March 2016)

3.9 Blue Apron – Food subscription for lazy hobby chefs

Key facts

Name: Blue Apron, Inc.
Headquarters: New York City, USA
Total staff: 2600
Global turnover 2015: US$300m (estimate)[56]
Founded in: 2012
Origins: Online pure player

In just three years, the New York meal-kit start-up Blue Apron has made it to a valuation of two billions dollars – i. e. it has become a unicorn faster than almost any other e-commerce project in the US. For a weekly fee of $60, the company delivers ingredients bundled with recipes into kits for three meals, which customers then prepare at home; in 2015, Blue Apron was already shipping five million meals every month – an impressive ten-fold increase on the 500,000 monthly it was selling one year previous.[57] This growth hasn't come cheap, yet in a recent round of finance, the start-up took $135m, besting its European competitor HelloFresh, which raised $126m.[58] In terms of traffic, too, Blue Apron is ahead of its competitors in North America, HelloFresh and Plated.[59] In 2015, the company launched its app and has since been focussing on quality content and additional information for its recipes;[60] by offering a wine matched to its meals, Blue Apron has also extended its product portfolio.[61]

Positioning

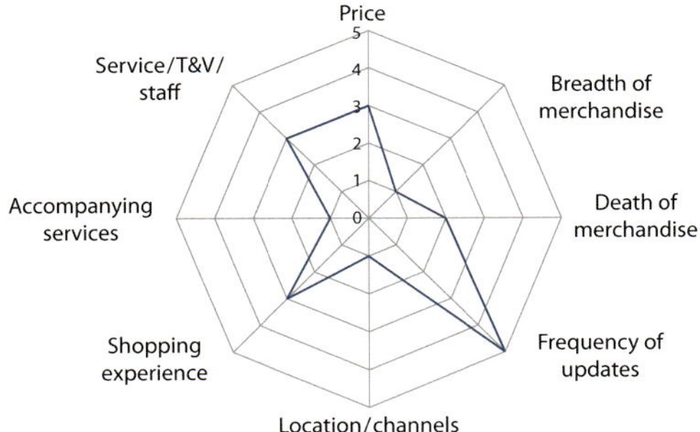

56 www.forbes.com (as of March 2016)
57 www.forbes.com (as of March 2016)
58 www.fastcompany.com (as of March 2016)
59 www.businessinsider.com (as of March 2016)
60 www.mobilestrategies360.com (as of March 2016)
61 www.fastcompany.com (as of March 2016)

The New York start-up uses slightly lower prices[62] and very high-quality product presentation and recipes to position itself against the competition.[63] Nevertheless, its prices are not particularly low when compared to standard food retail or Amazon Fresh, the difference being measured against its competitors Hello Fresh and Plated. It also refreshes its offering regularly, using frequent recipe updates to stake out its position; this should sustain the business model in the long term as long as the menus remain inventive enough.

Business model canvas

Key partners	Key activities	Value proposition	Customer relationships	Customer segments
Supplier, local farmers, logistics	Sourcing, content, marketing	Recipes developed by experts and all the ingredients needed as a subscription	Self-service	Hobby chefs, couples and families
	Key resources		**Channels**	
	Subscribers, partnerships		Online, mobile	
Cost structure			**Revenue streams**	
Marketing, sourcing, content, technology			Transaction-dependent direct sales turnover	

Authors' evaluation and assessment of perspectives

We would not dispute that there are more than enough potential customers in major cities who are genuinely keen on this kind of service – and that rural regions will probably harbour a few new subscribers too as, in the coming years, existing store networks begin to shrink away. Nevertheless, we remain unconvinced that the company can continue to acquire customers at its present rate and are sceptical about its valuation. To our minds, the business model looks very much like an attempt to build up a delivery network in parallel to Uber which will, in the future, be used by third parties to offer their products. This would make it into a classic race to invest. If we're wrong on this, then Blue Apron will remain a niche company with no claim to the kind of valuation it is currently trading on. What is more, it remains to be seen whether the business model can actually survive on its own merits if other, bigger players start to offer it as simply another of their many services (cf. Amazon Fresh).

62 www.blueapron.com (as of March 2016)
63 www.businessinsider.com (as of March 2016)

3.10 Blue Nile – THE online destination for high-end jewellery

Key facts

Name: Blue Nile, Inc.
Headquarters: Seattle, USA
Total staff: 301[64]
Global turnover 2015: US$480.1m[65]
Founded in: 1999
Origins: Online pure player

Blue Nile is the world's largest online diamonds and jewellery store and focusses primarily on engagement and wedding rings,[66] dispatching an average of 300 to 400 rings daily in the first three and up to 1000 rings in the last quarter of the year.[67] Its turnover of $480 million breaks down into an average order value of $2000 – or $7000 for engagement rings. On the stock market since 2004, this pure-play sells in 45 countries and accepts 23 currencies,[68] making a net profit of $11m and an EBIDTA of $25m. In 2015, its growth was stagnant, with an increase of only 1.4% in turnover and a 4.8% year-on-year decline in sales in the final quarter; as such, the company missed its goals for the year,[69] citing lower prices for diamonds and unfavourable exchange rates. Indeed, 2015 saw the company break its own record for the volume of engagement rings it shipped.[70] The company has put out pessimistic predictions for continued 0% growth in 2016.[71]

Positioning

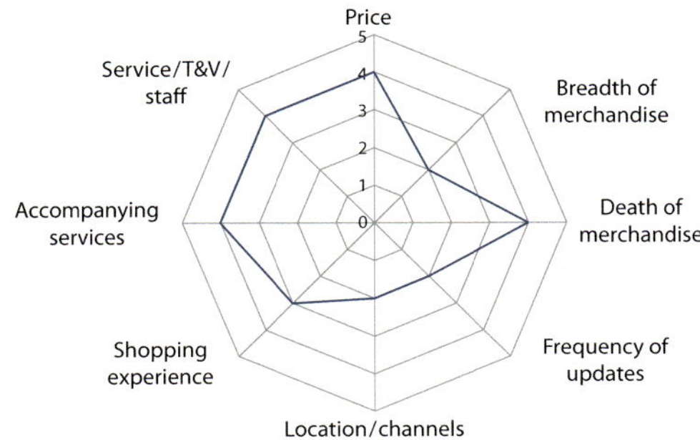

64 www.stockpup.com (as of March 2016)
65 investor.bluenile.com (as of March 2016)
66 www.bluenile.com (as of March 2016)
67 www.internetretailer.com (as of March 2016)
68 www.bluenile.com (as of March 2016)
69 investor.bluenile.com (as of March 2016)
70 investor.bluenile.com (as of March 2016)
71 www.fool.com (as of March 2016)

In the high-end jewellery and gemstone segment, Blue Nile's positioning is built on its comparatively low prices, which it keeps competitive by cutting out many of the middlemen in the traditional jewellery value chain. Its shopping experience and customer service propositions such as shopping advisors and financing deals also contribute to its market position. Local partners offer prospective buyers the opportunity to try on jewellery before purchase, and since 2015, the company has been extending its channels by opening up its own showrooms[72] and entering into cooperation with Nordstrom in North America.[73]

Business model canvas				
Key partners Suppliers, local partners, goldsmiths, and service providers	**Key activities** Sourcing, content und education, marketing **Key resources** Brand image, sourcing processes, diamond procurement partnerships	**Value proposition** High-end jewellery – especially engagement rings – at a good price	**Customer relationships** Self-service, customer care in showrooms **Channels** Online, mobile, showrooms, Nordstrom cooperation	**Customer segments** Price and quality-sensitive customers, couples engaged to be married
Cost structure Inventory, quality management, marketing		**Revenue streams** Transaction-dependent direct sales turnover		

Authors' evaluation and assessment of perspectives

BN is showing all the classic symptoms of an old-style category leader as it ages: while it dominates it niche and generates a tidy profit in so doing, it is – in our view – impossible for an e-commerce business model to endure if it is not growing at market pace at the very least. If things continue as they are, Blue Nile is likely to fall victim to younger challengers with innovative concepts offering jewellery which is in higher demand, of higher quality, or in some other way superior. In fact, this is a question of when, not if. What is more, the bricks-and-mortar infrastructure Blue Nile has built up over the last decade is, in an ever more digital world, no longer a key asset as custom-made rings can now be tried on and experienced without jewellery shops.

72 www.internetretailer.com (as of March 2016)

73 www.internetretailer.com (as of March 2016)

3.11 Bonobos – The online fashion brand the world wasn't ready for

Key facts

Name: Bonobos, Inc.
Headquarters: New York, USA
Total staff: 320
Global turnover 2015: n. a.
Founded in: 2007
Origins: Online pure player

Set up in 2007, Bonobos is an online men's fashion brand focussing on brand trousers and also featuring an extended range of shoes, suits, tops, and accessories. On launch, Bonobos got people talking with its new-style retail concept in which, as well as selling in a browser-based shop and through a mobile app, it also opened 21 "guide stores" in the US in which particularly service-orientated customers could try on items and talk to salespeople. Customers book an hour-long consultation, receiving a chilled beer on arrival and then personalised fashion advice; purchases get sent straight home to them – items cannot be taken with. Besides this, 120 Nordstrom stores also stock Bonobos brand articles. In 2015, Bonobos is reputed to have cleared the $100-million turnover mark and made a profit.[74] Currently, the chain is only present in the USA after initial international sales were nixed shortly after starting. Its AYR spin-off brand offering the same concept to women become independent in March 2016 and is no longer part of the company.

Positioning

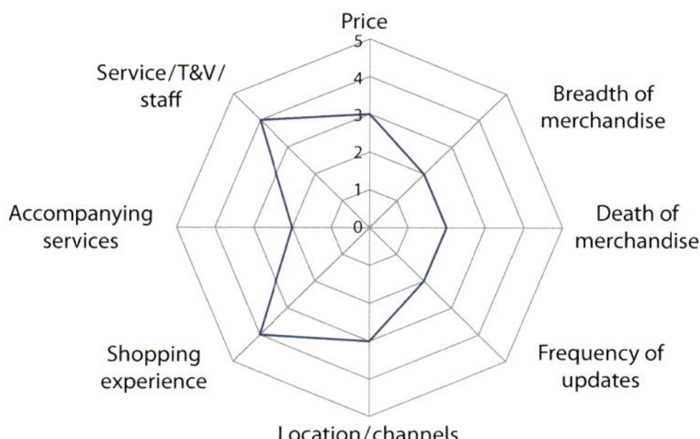

Bonobos' mission statement is to offer the best shopping experience possible to men both on and off the internet. Known for its service staff – called "Ninjas" in Bonobos-speak – it focusses on personalisation and comfort. Its structure as a two-channel concept focussing

74 www.businessinsider.com (as of March 2016)

both on online shops and its guide stores gives Bonobos a particularly unique brand identity. In terms of price, Bonobos is mid-market.

Business model canvas				
Key partners Nordstrom (investor in Bonobos since 2012)	**Key activities** Branding, product development **Key resources** Brand image	**Value proposition** High-end men's fashion with excellent service	**Customer relationships** Strong service focus **Channels** Online, offline, mobile	**Customer segments** Male customers, 25-40, annual income in excess of $100,000
Cost structure Sourcing, retail structures, marketing		**Revenue streams** Transaction-dependent direct sales turnover		

Authors' evaluation and assessment of perspectives

Bonobos has us beat. Measured against the amount of capital invested in the company (more than $100m paid up), turnover and growth figures are, frankly, disappointing – and expansion into other markets, target groups, and product areas has failed, depriving investors of precisely their reason for paying such a high price for a share of the company. That's why we think it best to split the valuation: for existing customers and in the company's current niche, Bonobos is a successful model; for investors, it is a promise broken.

3.12 Casper – Masters of the art of direct sales

Key facts

Name: Casper Sleep, Inc.
Headquarters: New York, USA
Total staff: 100
Global turnover 2015: n. a.
Founded in: 2014
Origins: Online pure player

Casper Sleep is the producer of the hip Casper Mattress, a product which the company sells exclusively through its online store. Just one year after launch, Casper had already booked over $100 million in sales in 2015 using nothing more than this single direct sales channel. In its first month of trading in 2014, it had already passed the million mark,[75] investing in a successful marketing campaign and offering a strongly design-orientated, fashionable product. Starting as a one-product company, Casper Sleep has now started to produce pillows and bedclothes. Its success is not just down to its high-end product design optimised for logistics processes, but also to its marketing strategy: the mattress is heavily compressed prior to shipping, allowing it to be delivered with little logistics outlay; customers then opens the mattress in their home and watch as it expands; yet the product does not compromise on quality. Casper has been adept at using marketing and social media to promote this sales argument, with YouTube offering hundreds of "unboxing videos". The company also has two showrooms in New York and Los Angeles.[76]

Positioning

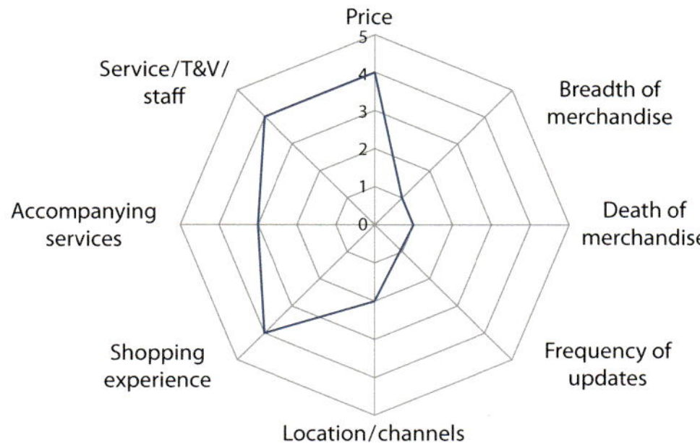

75 www.huffingtonpost.com (as of March 2016)
76 casper.com (as of March 2016)

Casper's primary USPs lie in its shopping experience, its service levels, and the prices it offers. With tags ranging from $500 to $950, Casper is near the bottom end of the price spectrum in the mattress segment and does not charge for delivery. With only three products and no depth of merchandise, Casper's positioning is crystal clear, summed up in the marketing message of "one mattress fits all". Its service offering includes a generous trial period and a hassle-free returns policy.

Business model canvas

Key partners	Key activities	Value proposition	Customer relationships	Customer segments
Suppliers, investors	Marketing, product development	Quality mattress design at a good price – and with a comfortable shopping experience	Self-service, customer care in showroom	Quality-focussed customers
	Key resources		**Channels**	
	Branding, processes		Online, showroom	
Cost structure			**Revenue streams**	
Marketing, content, logistics			Transaction-dependent direct sales turnover	

Authors' evaluation and assessment of perspectives

Casper has successfully transferred what was, until recently, an almost wholly analogue business onto the internet. The Casper marketing concept has been a success, customers recommend the company giving it word-of-mouth upwind, and worldwide, imitators have sprung up. The mattress industry has been disrupted and yet the newcomer has low rates of return, no-hassle logistics, and a high profit margin, so it's hats off to Casper all round – for now. In the long term, we see several hazards. Competitors may – indeed, almost certainly will – replicate the model, drawing Casper into an online marketing battle in a segment in which repeat-business frequency is so low as to be almost non-existent in the first three years, i. e. a segment providing little prospect for profit. As such, we will be interested to see whether Casper moves into increased vertical integration or finds another way of expanding its business model to put it on a more stable footing in the medium term.

3.13 Conrad – Why "multichannel" is not enough of a USP

Key facts

Name: Conrad Electronic SE
Headquarters: Hirschau, Germany
Total staff: 3,900[77]
Global turnover 2014: €998.7m (US$1.21bn)[78]
Founded in: 1923
Origins: Mail order since 1939, in-store since 1951[79]

Conrad is a family business in the electronics, DIY, and hobby segment; besides its B2C activities, the company has, since 2013, been placing increased emphasis on building up a B2B customer base.[80] It has 37 stores in Europe and an ailing catalogue arm which has led it to move into e-commerce, stressing its multichannel credentials and building up a strong reputation in its ability to link channels both at a customer-facing and a business process level.[81] The stores feature internet terminals, for example, and the online shop advertises local offers; customers can click-and-collect or have items in stock at nearby stores home-delivered within two hours.[82] In addition to this, its new logistics facility can pack and ship up to 100,000 deliveries daily to up to 150 countries.[83] Its 2013 acquisition of Get-it-Quick GmbH, an insolvent operator of two online shops Getgoods.de and HOH.de, proved to be a misstep with no prospect of profit, and Conrad shut down both of these sites at the end of 2015.[84]

Positioning

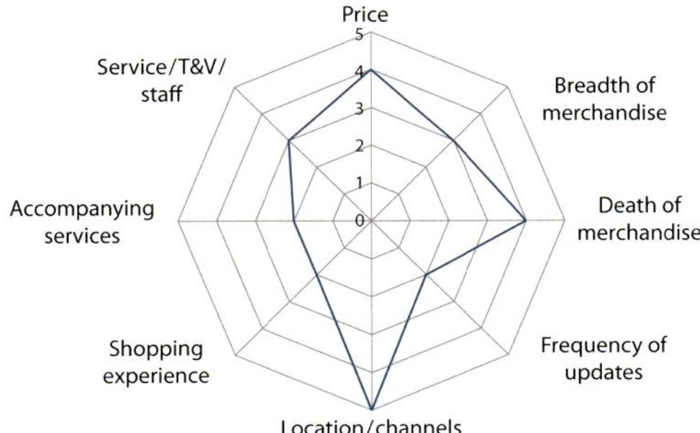

77 www.conrad.com (as of March 2016)
78 neuhandeln.de (as of March 2016)
79 www.conrad.de (as of March 2016)
80 www.elektroniknet.de (as of March 2016)
81 www.channelpartner.de (as of March 2016)
82 www.conrad.de (as of March 2016)
83 www.logistra.de (as of March 2016)
84 neuhandeln.de (as of March 2016)

In comparison to its competitors, Conrad defines itself principally by its multichannel activities and by low prices.[85] Currently, its multichannel competence is a positive, but if the competition starts to catch up quickly, it remains to be seen how Conrad will manage to secure its position going forward and actually generate genuine added value for customers from its integrated structures.

Business model canvas				
Key partners Logistics companies, brand manufacturers	**Key activities** Compiling product mix, technology **Key resources** State-of-the-art logistics, stable finances	**Value proposition** Tools and electronics at an attractive price; comfortable multichannel customer experience	**Customer relationships** Self-service, in-store customer care **Channels** Online, offline, catalogue	**Customer segments** Mass market
Cost structure Turnover costs, store staff, IT/technology		**Revenue streams** Transaction-dependent direct sales turnover		

Authors' evaluation and assessment of perspectives

In recent years, Conrad has developed into a textbook multichannel operator. Its classic stationary positioning has been reconfigured with an online strategy and its service focus considerably strengthened. Now barely a consultant's presentation about the potential of multichannel and omnichannel goes by without some reference to it and yet, to our mind, the decisive criteria for future success in the e-commerce age remain untouched by Conrad's development. USPs such as service quality and merchandise available on site are increasingly irrelevant for many target groups: only older customers or those who place a real premium on trying before they buy will be persuaded. In this respect, Conrad has optimised its business model for a shrinking market; there is, however, no long-term future in this model.

85 www.cognitivepricing.com (as of March 2016)

3.14 Delivery Hero – Europe's most aggressive unicorn

Key facts

Name: Delivery Hero Holding GmbH
Headquarters: Berlin, Germany
Total staff: 3000
Global turnover 2015: €198m (US$216.3m)
Founded in: 2011
Origins: Online pure player

One of the world's biggest food delivery companies, Delivery Hero is currently working with over 200,000 restaurants[86] in 34 countries – in 29 of which it claims to be the market leader.[87] The company is organised as a holding which runs a variety of delivery services: in Germany, for example, it has Lieferheld, Pizza.de, and Foodora. With €1.6 billion gross turnover in 2015, Delivery Hero moved tangibly on its KPIs and looks to be staying on the growth path in 2016. Valued at €3.1 billion[88] processed 14 million orders in January 2016, a year-on-year increase of more than 100%[89]. Its marketing spend, however, is high too, and in the German market, this unicorn is still knee-deep in the red. Over the course of three rounds of funding in 2015, it nevertheless took in €586 million[90] and is said by many sources to be considering an IPO[91] to match that of its two largest competitors, GrubHub and Just Eat.[92]

Positioning

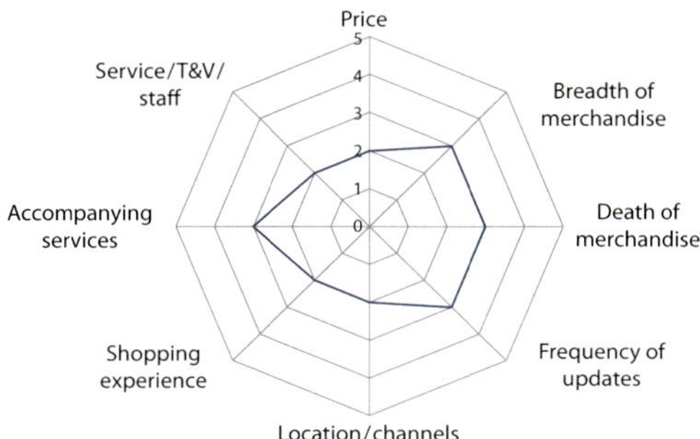

Delivery Hero's USP is the depth and width of its offering. It offers a particularly large range of restaurants and meals, running operations in 34 countries and counting 200,000

86 www.deliveryhero.com (as of March 2016)
87 www.welt.de (as of March 2016)
88 www.deliveryhero.com (as of March 2016)
89 www.gruenderszene.de (as of March 2016)
90 www.welt.de (as of March 2016)
91 www.internetworld.de (as of March 2016)
92 www.welt.de (as of March 2016)

participating restaurants; it has desktop and mobile channels.

<table>
<tr><th colspan="5">Business model canvas</th></tr>
<tr><td rowspan="2">Key partners
Restaurants, over 4,700 suppliers, chain restaurants, ad networks</td><td>Key activities
Expanding partner-ships, technology</td><td rowspan="2">Value proposition
Order food and drinks from a wide variety of restau-rants and take-away places – easy-to-use</td><td>Customer relationships
Self-service</td><td rowspan="2">Customer segments
Mass market</td></tr>
<tr><td>Key resources
Brand portfolio, market knowledge, momentum</td><td>Channels
Online, mobile</td></tr>
<tr><td colspan="2">Cost structure
Marketing, expansion, delivery service</td><td colspan="3">Revenue streams
Commission on marketplace sales (8-15% depending on product category)</td></tr>
</table>

Authors' evaluation and assessment of perspectives

We are of the opinion that Delivery Hero's' business model will only work if it can become the sole platform in the relevant markets. What we don't understand why the company is driving internationalisation so hard because, as we see it, there is little-to-no synergy to be had: the costs of establishing in each new market remain the same. The real risk to Delivery Hero, however, comes in the form of other large applications such as Uber, who could also offer a similar service within their business model. So there are plenty of question marks over Delivery Hero when it comes to evaluating the business model: nevertheless, we can well imagine it managing to dominate this market and then using that position to totally reinvent the food business.

3.15 Ebay – Twilight of an E-Commerce Legend

Key facts

Name: eBay Inc.
Headquarters: San Jose, USA
Total staff: 36.500
Global turnover 2015: US$8.6bn[93]
Founded in: 1995
Origins: Online pure player

Together with Amazon, internet auction house Ebay has been a driving force behind e-commerce over the last 20 years. Its position today is nevertheless weak: it is trailing Amazon and even contracted for the first time ever last year, recording $200m less in sales than in 2014 – although taking a profit of $6.8m.[94] Ever since it was founded, Ebay has been on a trajectory from a C2C auctioneer through to a standard marketplace; currently, it still maintains both models. From 2014 onwards, sellers on Ebay don't have to take care of processing purchases themselves, but can also use the professional "Valet" service.[95] Overall, Ebay is in a phase of consolidation: in 2015, it sold off both Ebay Enterprise, Magento, and, most notably, Paypal; the latter has often been a driver of turnover growth at Ebay. In order to withstand Amazon's aggressive attacks, in 2015, Ebay introduced Ebay Plus, a subscription service similar to Prime with no-cost express dispatch and a range of promotions on offer. The company's stated aim is to maintain and expand its 157 million active customers and 25 million sellers.[96]

Positioning

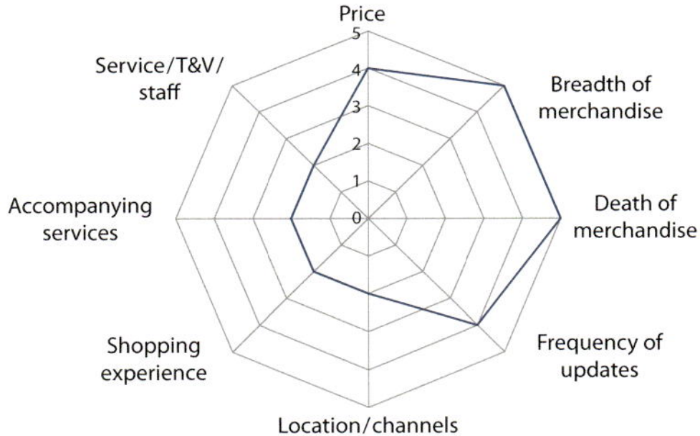

93 investors.ebayinc.com (as of March 2016)
94 Primarly as a result of the weak Euro
95 www.ebay.com (as of March 2016)
96 presse.ebay.de (as of March 2016)

As an auction platform and marketplace, Ebay's primary USP is its range of merchandise – i. e. both in terms of breadth and depth, although depth is the more important of the two with the C2C model allowing collectors to locate rare items and implementing the long-tail principle. Ebay also relies on price as a positioning factor, while service and shopping experience carry less weight; as sellers send goods and offer customer service, the company itself cannot control transactions and after-sales to the same extent as other platforms.

Business model canvas				
Key partners Manufacturers and brands, marketplace sellers	**Key activities** Marketing, brand relationship, technology **Key resources** Data, software	**Value proposition** Huge selection, good prices, and access to millions of customers for items used and new	**Customer relationships** Self-service **Channels** Online, mobile	**Customer segments** Customers for and sellers of used and new goods
Cost structure 1. Sales & marketing 2. General & administrative 3. Product development		**Revenue streams** 1. Sales fee 2. Marketing services		

Authors' evaluation and assessment of perspectives

We personally are big Ebay fans. There is no comparable marketplace playing the same role in moving superfluous items from one consumer to the next: this is the model which made Ebay big and there is still no-one capable of challenging Ebay in this area. In comparison, however, to this core strength, every other strategic measure taken – especially in Germany – to try and push B2C trade and grow larger was simply part of a rather poor Amazon interpretation. This woolly strategy and a lack of genuine innovation has led Ebay to lose its relevance in a range of markets today, and its future prospects are anything but rosy. While we hope that Ebay doesn't turn into the next AOL/Yahoo, we don't really believe it can turn things around, either.

3.16 Etsy – Hand-made, long-tail, gold mine

Key facts

Name: Etsy, Inc.
Headquarters: New York, USA
Total staff: 819
Global turnover 2015: US$273m[97]
Founded in: 2005
Origins: Online pure player

Etsy is a worldwide marketplace bringing together buyers and sellers of handmade, vintage, and arts-and-crafts products; it focusses particularly on hobbyist makers and small businesspeople, who sell through Etsy as an easy-to-use sales channel and can build up their brand on the platform. Most of the products sold are made by the sellers personally, meaning that they can frequently be personalised on buyer request.[98] As a marketplace, Etsy offers around 35 million products listed by 1.6 million sellers;[99] around half of the company's turnover comes from seller services such as pattern – a package allowing sellers to turn their Etsy shops in to a user-defined website. Etsy's principal competition comes from Ebay and Amazon, the latter of which, just recently, launched Amazon Handmade to strengthen its efforts in this segment.[100] Etsy itself is moving in the other direction, having successively loosened its definition of "handmade", which has led to mass-market produce from China being listed on the platform; many sellers now see Amazon as a good supporting channel.[101] Last year, Etsy Manufacturing, a platform connecting manufacturers and people who want to produce handmade items, began its beta phase.

Positioning

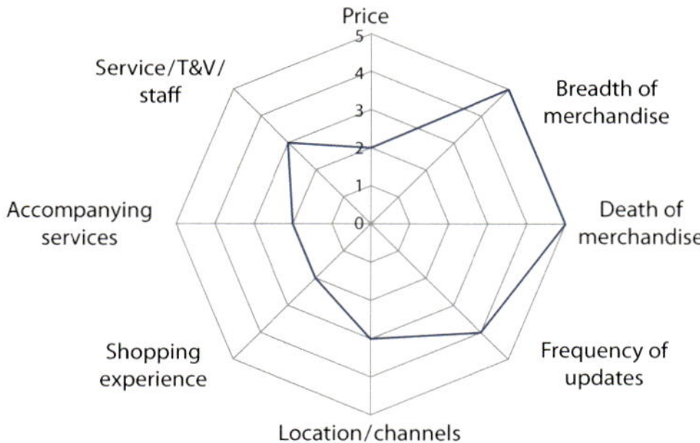

97 investors.ebayinc.com (as of March 2016)
98 Primarly as a result of the weak Euro
99 investors.ebayinc.com (as of March 2016)
100 www.ebay.com (as of March 2016)
101 presse.ebay.de (as of March 2016)

As the largest marketplace for handmade products and with a huge selection of unique pieces, Etsy is positioned above all on the breadth and depth of its merchandise. For its sellers – small businesses and arts-and-crafts enthusiasts – Etsy defines itself by ease of use, making it easy to list products with little-to-no technological skills, all the while offering customers a pleasant shopping experience and good customer service.

Business model canvas				
Key partners Small-time makers and merchants, creatives/artists	**Key activities** Seller services **Key resources** Manufactures, community, platform	**Value proposition** A marketplace for people interested in unique/hand-made products	**Customer relationships** Self-service **Channels** Online. mobile	**Customer segments** Buyers and sellers of unique products (small companies and artists)
Cost structure – Marketing – Product development		**Revenue streams** – Commission from listings and transactions – Seller services		

Authors' evaluation and assessment of perspectives

When we get asked if there are business models which won't be affected by Amazon, we often think of Etsy. The marketplace's spiel is that it offers the right environment for home-made arts and crafts products and that this is innovative enough – and not something Amazon can replicate. In recent years, however, Etsy has tried to take this business model in new directions and, in so doing, moved away from the core of its community. Unfortunately for Etsy, however, the strategic options it went for have turned out to be dead ends while new platforms and technologies make inroads into its original customer base: there are more and more increasingly simple shop solutions out there allowing people to sell their own products. As such, Etsy is a prime example of how business models which are successful today may fail tomorrow.

3.17 Fahrrad.de – Niche winner looking to expand Europe-wide

Key facts

Name: internetstores GmbH
Headquarters: Stuttgart, Germany
Total staff: 350
Global turnover 2015: €140m (US$153m)[102]
Founded in: 2003
Origins: Online pure player

fahrrad.de is the largest online shop in the internetstores portfolio, which includes another three bike shops and two outdoor equipment providers in the European market. Along with a range of around 600 brands and 40,000 products, founder René Köhler and his team have also development high-end mountain bikes and racers for their own brand Votec.[103] The shop, its customer service, and the start-up success have won fahrrad.de plenty of prizes[104] and sales, too: the sustained growth in turnover[105] has helped internetstores to more than 25% growth in the first half of 2015[106] and annual sales of €140 million;[107] EBITDA was upped by 190% year on year to €10 million.[108] After financing its own growth for a long period of time,[109] the company is looking to continue internationalising to keep growth going,[110] with shops for Denmark, Finland, and Sweden being the latest launches.[111]

Positioning

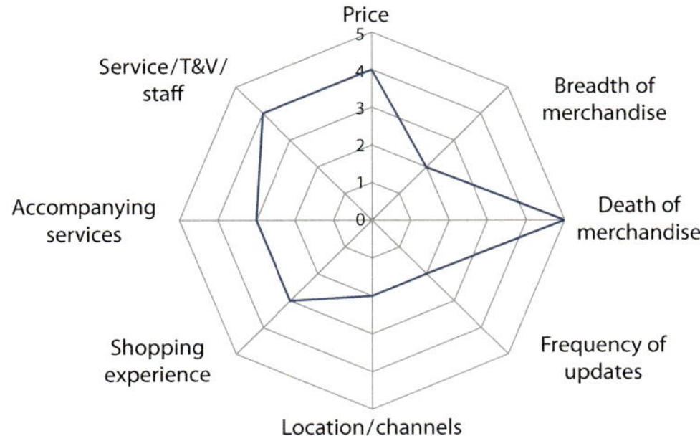

102 excitingcommerce.de (as of March 2016)
103 www.internetstores.de (as of March 2016)
104 www.internetstores.de (as of March 2016)
105 de.statista.com (as of March 2016)
106 www.internetstores.de (as of March 2016)
107 excitingcommerce.de (as of March 2016)
108 www.internetstores.de (as of March 2016)
109 www.deutschergruenderpreis.de (as of March 2016)
110 www.internetstores.de (as of March 2016)
111 www.internetstores.de (as of March 2016)

As the largest online shop specialising in bicycles, fahrrad.de positions itself above all on price and depth of merchandise. A range of added services such as telephone customer care and generous delivery conditions also help internetstores' online shops to keep a clear profile against competitors. fahrrad.de also distinguishes itself with logistics and shipping, using its slim-line structures to offer same-day delivery for orders placed by 4pm on weekdays.

Business model canvas				
Key partners Investors, brands, sales partners	**Key activities** Sourcing, CRM, logistics **Key resources** Online expertise, logistics	**Value proposition** Big selection of brand bikes at good prices	**Customer relationships** Self-service **Channels** Online, mobile	**Customer segments** Mass market, internet users
Cost structure Staffing, logistics, platform		**Revenue streams** Transaction-dependent direct sales turnover		

Authors' evaluation and assessment of perspectives

fahrrad.de is one of the very few online pure-plays who have managed to take on a category leader role and reliably generate profit while so doing. This is all the more extraordinary in view of the fact that bicycles are low-frequency items and existing customers are therefore of limited value inasmuch as they will probably need to be reacquired by the time they need their next pair of wheels. This will make it interesting to see how fahrrad.de intends to grow in future, especially in view of its aversion to the competition on price which will soon be forced in this segment by Amazon and Ebay. The company's strong orientation to customer care and service will be one to watch here, and the annual reports for the coming years will make interesting reading for e-commerce buffs.

3.18 Gilt – How a flash seller became a flash sale

Key facts

Name: Gilt Groupe, Inc.
Headquarters: New York, USA
Total staff: 1000+
Global turnover 2014: US$650m[112]
Founded in: 2007
Origins: Online pure player

Gilt is a US-based flash sale retailer originally offering fashion items and now home furnishings, activity packages, and – most recently – travel deals. As one of the first shopping clubs to start up in the fashion segment in the North American market at a time when the popularity of the flash-sale approach was growing rapidly,[113] its turnover rocketed from a cold start in its early years as it expanded into segment after segment (e. g. Gilt Taste, Park & Bond, Jetsetter). In the space of just four years, this investors' darling reached a valuation of one billion dollars – a valuation of which only one quarter remained when it was acquired by the Canadian Hudson Bay retail holding in January 2016.[114] The first issues became apparent back in 2012 as the company tried to shrink back to profit by making staffing cuts and terminating some of its vertical operations;[115] many of Gilt's competitors such as Zulily, RueLala, and Hautelook have come to face similar difficulties since then. In buying Gilt, Hudson Bay's primary aim is to absorb the fêted retailer's e-commerce knowledge in customer service and experience; it is particularly keen on Gilt's mobile strategy smarts.

Positioning

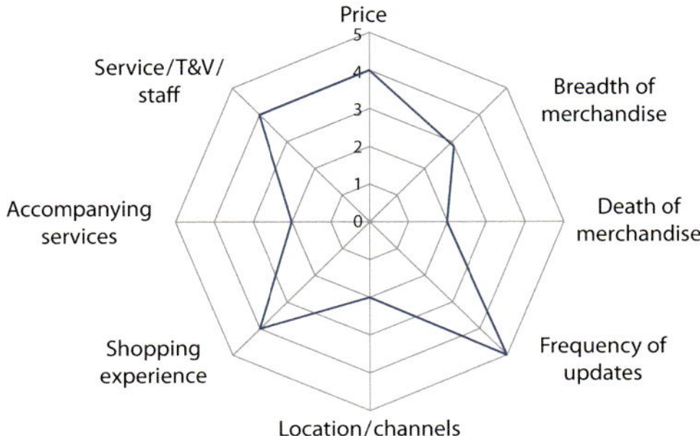

112 www.recode.net (as of March 2016)
113 www.orckestra.com (as of March 2016)
114 www.forbes.com (as of March 2016)
115 www.businessinsider.com (as of March 2016)

As a flash-sale model, the Gilt Groupe's primary positioning takes place on price: the shopping club offers strongly-discounted luxury fashion and design articles for a limited period. As well as the price, the high frequency of merchandise updates entailed by the model is also a USP; in the German market alone, the club pumps out upwards of 200 new deals every week. Gilt also remains known as a leader in providing a customer-friendly shopping experience.

Business model canvas				
Key partners Brand manufacturers, Hudson Bay (owner)	**Key activities** Sourcing, relationship management with brands **Key resources** Technology, customer and partner relationships	**Value proposition** High-end brand goods at greatly discounted prices; stylish selection of products and broad range of deals frequently updated	**Customer relationships** Self-service **Channels** Online, mobile	**Customer segments** Brand-conscious but price-sensitive millennials, bargain hunters
Cost structure Marketing, sales costs, staffing		**Revenue streams** Transaction-dependent direct sales turnover		

Authors' evaluation and assessment of perspectives

We're going to keep things short – but not sweet – here. Gilt is a perfect example of the central issues we've been talking about in this book. Here's how the story goes:

1) Company starts out with a clear USP and grows fast.
2) Company faces strong competition which kills margins.
3) Company realises that, regardless of the model, online shoppers are fundamentally disloyal and that the day-to-day business of e-commerce is tough.

Company folds.

3.19 Grainger – A.k.a The last hurdle for Amazon in B2B

Key facts

Name: W. W. Grainger, Inc.
Headquarters: Lake Forest, USA
Total staff: 23,600[116]
Global turnover 2015: US$9.4bn[117]
Founded in: 1927
Origins: In-store retailer

As North America's largest industrial supply company,[118] Grainger has 1.4 million business customers in the USA and over 2 million worldwide. Its range includes tools, general supplies, and a range of materials for maintenance, repairs, and production equipment; it is present in North America, where it has 320 stores, as well as in Europe, Asia, and Latin America. It currently generates around 40% of its turnover online and is posting strong e-commerce growth;[119] overall, however, this traditionally high-performing outfit has been battling against sinking overall sales. In 2015, turnover grew by 0% while profitability dropped; in 2016, the company is therefore planning to close 55 stores and drive growth online and in Europe,[120] where it has acquired the British company Cromwell with the aim of bring both in-store and online growth back on track with two-digit increases.[121]

Positioning

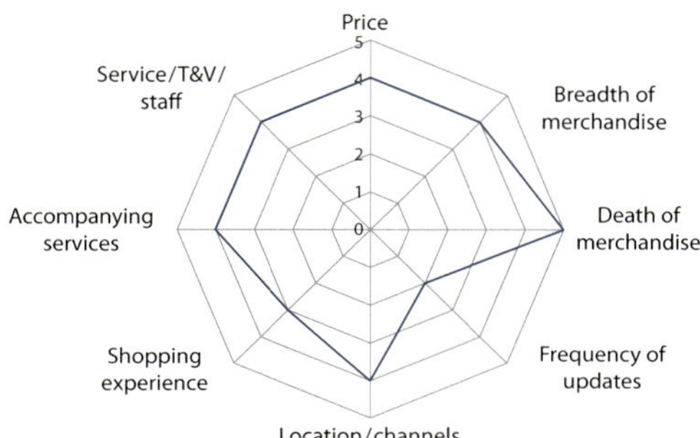

Grainger is second to none in its ability to position itself in the B2B landscape using outstanding service and a clear value-add for business clients. The depth of its merchandise

116 phx.corporate-ir.net (as of March 2016)
117 www.inddist.com (as of March 2016)
118 phx.corporate-ir.net (as of March 2016)
119 www.internetretailer.com (as of March 2016)
120 www.inddist.com (as of March 2016)
121 www.internetretailer.com (as of March 2016)

is its principle sales argument, as are competitive prices. This heritage company sells both online and offline and delivers to 160 countries.

<table>
<tr><th colspan="5">Business model canvas</th></tr>
<tr><td rowspan="2">Key partners
Manufacturers, industry associations, construction companies</td><td>Key activities
Sourcing, relationship management</td><td rowspan="2">Value proposition
Huge selection of industrial supplies at good prices with a service concept tailored to B2B customers</td><td>Customer relationships
Focus on in-store/ telephone care, online self-service</td><td rowspan="2">Customer segments
B2B customers (manufacturers, construction companies, government)</td></tr>
<tr><td>Key resources
Infrastructure, customer base</td><td>Channels
Online, in-store, mobile, telephone ordering</td></tr>
<tr><td colspan="2">Cost structure
Sales costs, infrastructure</td><td colspan="3">Revenue streams
Transaction-dependent direct sales turnover</td></tr>
</table>

Authors' evaluation and assessment of perspectives

If you take classic e-commerce consultancy dogma at its word, in recent years, Grainger has barely put a foot wrong: it's developed new services, modernised its structures, and made efforts to compete with Amazon and the like on price, taking on a pioneering role in the B2B market. Yet none of this seems to be sufficient to stop Amazon catching up at an alarming rate. Turns out that customers are just as keen on Amazon in a B2B context as they are in B2C situations. Grainger doesn't have a concept for the future.

3.20 Harry's – New York start-up insources value creation

Key facts

Name: HF Global, Inc.
Headquarters: New York, USA
Total staff: 615[122]
Global turnover 2015: n. a.
Founded in: 2013
Origins: Online pure player

Since setting up in 2013, Harry's aim has been to take a bite out of the market for wet shaving products. Traditionally a market strongly dominated by Procter & Gamble's Gillette brand (over 70% market share in the USA.[123] 2011 saw the first disruptive online outfit set up in the market in the shape of Dollar Shave Club (DSC), which made a name for itself with its razor-blade subscription service and a lot of social media buzz. Harry's hit the market in 2013 with a similar concept but two genuinely unique twists: firstly, it ran a successful targeted influencer marketing campaign as more effective and lower-cost growth strategy than its competitors'; secondly, in 2015 it took the bold step of spending over $100 million of its total $287 million of paid-up capital on a razor-blade factory in Germany.[124] This has given it control over the quality of its products and more independence from price competition. DSC, on the other hand, offer some brand shavers which are available for less elsewhere. According to Harry's own estimates, it has a customer retention rate of 60%.[125]

Positioning

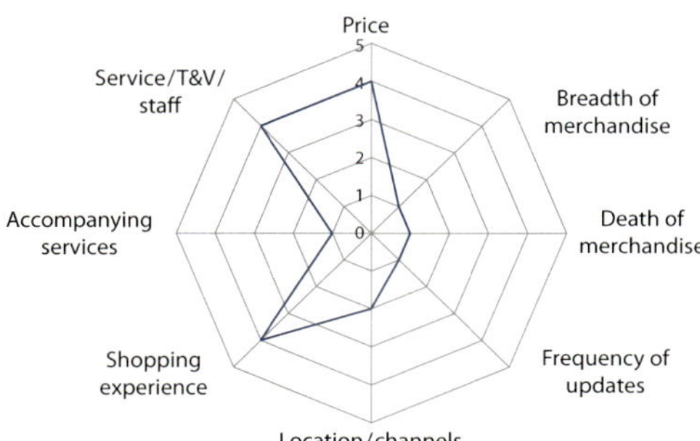

The main thrust of Harry's positioning is price which, at $2 per blade, is far below the $4 charged by its competitor Gillette. Harry's also provides a high-end shopping experience and gets very good service evaluations; the depth and breadth of its mer-

122 www.businessinsider.de (as of March 2016)
123 www.forbes.com (as of March 2016)
124 www.businessinsider.de (as of March 2016)
125 www.businessinsider.de (as of March 2016)

chandise are minimal, with only two different types of razor, one kind of blade, shaving foam, gel, and a handful of accessories.

<table>
<tr><th colspan="5">Business model canvas</th></tr>
<tr><td rowspan="2">Key partners
Investors, advertising, networks</td><td>Key activities
Marketing, product design</td><td rowspan="2">Value proposition
Quality razor blades and accessories at a good price and as a subscription model</td><td>Customer relationships
Self-service</td><td rowspan="2">Customer segments
Price-conscious male customers</td></tr>
<tr><td>Key resources
In-house production, brand awareness, customer base</td><td>Channels
Online, mobile</td></tr>
<tr><td colspan="2">Cost structure
Marketing, manufacturing, technology</td><td colspan="3">Revenue streams
Transaction-dependent direct sales turnover</td></tr>
</table>

Authors' evaluation and assessment of perspectives

While Harry's has probably not produced the definitive manual on how to reshape the landscape of retail, it has found a way to anchor a new brand in a market so long dominated by an oligopoly. To our minds, the subscription service is actually quite a small step: the real story is in how it wins customers with a good product, excellent marketing, and strong service. With its own brand, Harry's could conceivably even sell its products on Amazon (which offers subscriptions too).

3.21 HelloFresh – IPO or not, it's the foodbox start-up that continues to grow

Key facts

Name: HelloFresh AG
Headquarters: Berlin, Germany
Total staff: 800[126]
Global turnover 2015: €305m (US$333m)
Founded in: 2011
Origins: Online pure player

HelloFresh offers a subscription service of recipes and the ingredients to cook them for up to five meals a week. Whether it's garnering valuations of 2.6 billion Euros, reporting growth of 380%, or delaying its IPO, the hype around it is strong – and currently concentrated primarily on the Berlin start-up scene. Even in the Rocket Internet stable, there are few companies who have this kind of pizazz; not that the growth comes cheap, as HelloFresh has invested considerable sums in both customer acquisition and extending its logistics network, concentrating ever more on the US market as it goes;[127] with or without its (indefinitely postponed) IPO, a new injection of venture capital will be enough to keep its momentum going.[128] Its current customer base of half a million subscribers is located in the German-speaking countries, the Netherlands, Belgium, UK, USA, and Australia[129] and, according to HelloFresh's own calculations, each new customer becomes profitable after seven months.[130] Besides its aggressive marketing, HelloFresh is strongly positioned in terms of technology and more data-driven than almost any other e-commerce start-up currently in operation.[131]

Positioning

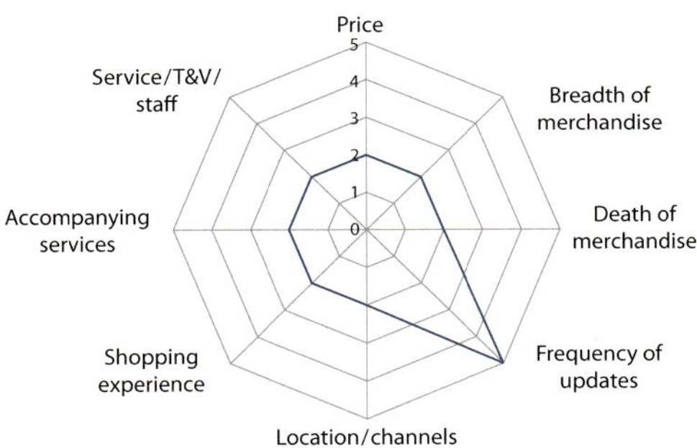

126 www.welt.de (as of March 2016)
127 excitingcommerce.de (as of March 2016)
128 excitingcommerce.de (as of March 2016)
129 www.hellofreshgroup.com (as of March 2016)
130 excitingcommerce.de (as of March 2016)
131 excitingcommerce.de (as of March 2016)

A particular positioning strength for HelloFresh is frequency of updates, with more than 5000 recipes and ingredient boxes already having been delivered to customers; by the same token, both the depth and breadth of its merchandise are seriously limited, with customers being able to choose between "Classic", veggie, and fruit boxes only. In price terms, HelloFresh is mid-market when compared with its American competitors Blue Apron and Plated.

<table>
<tr><th colspan="5">Business model canvas</th></tr>
<tr><td rowspan="2">Key partners
Advertiser networks, investors, opinion leaders (cooperation with Jamie Oliver)</td><td>Key activities
Sourcing, marketing, logistics</td><td rowspan="2">Value proposition
A continuous slew of new recipes and all the ingredients you need to cook them</td><td>Customer relationships
Self-service</td><td rowspan="2">Customer segments
Couples, families, households who like to cook</td></tr>
<tr><td>Key resources
Customer base</td><td>Channels
Online, mobile</td></tr>
<tr><td colspan="2">Cost structure
Marketing, sourcing, technology</td><td colspan="3">Revenue streams
Transaction-dependent direct sales turnover</td></tr>
</table>

Authors' evaluation and assessment of perspectives

HelloFresh is a very exciting start-up which – Amazon aside – is probably the one with the best chances of revolutionising the food segment. While its growth to date has been expensive, it's worth betting that its pre-defined recipes are probably only the beginning...

3.22 Home Depot – Buying bricks and mortar online

Key facts

Name: Home Depot, Inc.
Headquarters: Atlanta, USA
Total staff: 385,000
Global turnover 2015: US$88.5bn
Founded in: 1978
Origins: In-store retailer

Home Depot is the largest DIY and home improvement retailer in the United States, Canada, and Mexico,[132] and grew its turnover on the internet by around one billion dollars in 2015, hitting $4.7 billion in online sales, just shy of 6% of overall sales.[133] At 26%, its internet growth outstripped that of Amazon's for the second time in a row[134] and it garnered an Internet Retailer Excellence Award in recognition of its success in expanding into e-commerce. Home Depot has come to see online shopping as its most important growth area and, since 2012, has invested more than $300 million in technology and logistics; the company terms its overriding strategy "interconnected retail", a programme in which its 2200 store locations are used as warehouses for e-commerce; its aim is to have retrofitted all locations with fulfilment centre capability by late 2016[135] and to organically grow from $82 billion in turnover to $100 billion by 2018 without adding even one more store.[136]

Positioning

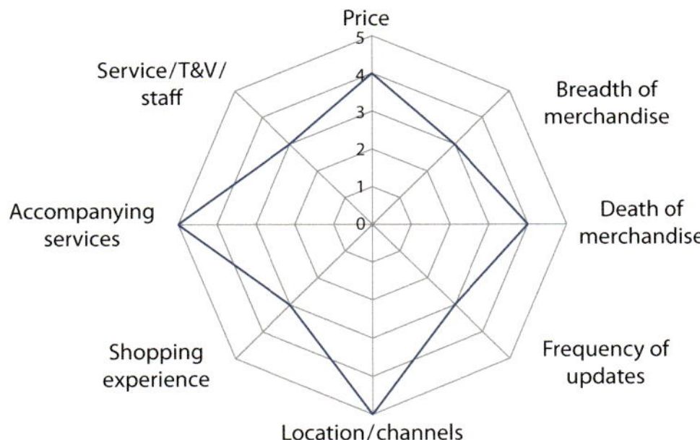

With its gigantic depth of merchandise and very cheap prices, Home Depot is also investing more heavily than almost any other heritage retailer in multichannel link-ups between its 2200 stores, its online shop, and its mobile application (the latter of which is already

132 ir.homedepot.com (as of March 2016)
133 www.internetretailer.com (as of March 2016)
134 www.internetretailer.com (as of March 2016)
135 www.internetretailer.com (as of March 2016)
136 www.bloomberg.com (as of March 2016)

booking 50% of its online traffic). Home Depot also has a strong footing in customer service, offering customers local workmen or tool rental and a range of B2B services.

Business model canvas				
Key partners Local contractors and service providers, brands and manufacturers	**Key activities** Marketing, sourcing, service **Key resources** Brand image, customer base	**Value proposition** Large selection of hardware, tools and construction supplies for hobbyists and local contractors	**Customer relationships** Service-oriented, self-service online **Channels** Online, offline, mobile	**Customer segments** Mass market, especially home improvement and DIY enthusiasts
Cost structure Infrastructure, marketing, sourcing, technology		**Revenue streams** Transaction-dependent direct sales turnover		

Authors' evaluation and assessment of perspectives

Rather than reheating the old eulogies to Nordstrom et al. as shining examples of digitisation, conference speakers could do us all a favour and take a look at Home Depot for a change. Its concepts make sense and, thus far, its channel integration has worked well, even allowing it to optimise its merchandise across its various outlets. What is more, its product segment is more difficult to sell on the internet than many other ranges which Amazon has come to dominate. So while Home Depot has a long and expensive slog ahead of it, it also has good chances of success.

3.23 Home24 – The online David to Ikea's Goliath

Key facts

Name: Home24 AG
Headquarters: Berlin, Germany
Total staff: 1200[137]
Global turnover 2015: €317m (US$346.3m)
Founded in: 2009
Origins: Online pure player

Rocket Internet's answer to selling furniture and home furnishings online is Home24, active in Germany and seven other markets. In 2015, Home24 overtook Ikea on the internet by a tangible margin, posting €317 million in sales – or almost twice its turnover in 2014. With a product range of 180,000 items from 800 manufacturers, Home24 works with both buy-in and own-brand ranges – the latter of which grew by seven new brands in the course of 2015.[138] The company's strategy is rampant growth. It has opened one of the Continent's largest fulfilment centres in Lower Saxony,[139] Germany and acquired Fashion For Home GmbH,[140] a high-end designer furnishings shop[141] which will strengthen its position Europe-wide.[142] This Berlin start-up places a strong emphasis on technology, with 120 of its 700 staff in IT, developing the innovative smartphone and tablet apps through which it is already making 40% of its sales.[143]

Positioning

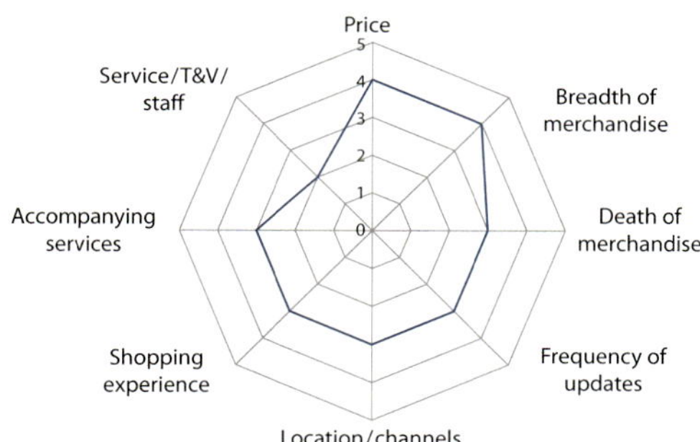

137 cdn.home24.net (as of March 2016)
138 www.rocketinternet.com (as of March 2016)
139 www.berlinerzeitung.de (as of March 2016)
140 cdn.home24.net (as of March 2016)
141 cdn.home24.net (as of March 2016)
142 cdn.home24.net (as of March 2016)
143 excitingcommerce.de (as of March 2016)

Home24 distances itself from competitors in the home furnishings segment with the depth of its merchandise: it boasts that no other German online shop has even half as many items listed as it does under home24.de.[144] An exciting development to watch in future is that Home24, having more than tripled its logistics capacity over the last 18 months, will soon be able to position itself strongly in dispatch and delivery.[145]

Business model canvas				
Key partners Suppliers and brands, production partners in Asia, affiliates, logistics	**Key activities** Marketing, platform, CRM **Key resources** Sourcing relationships, platform	**Value proposition** Large selection and good prices available in a user-friendly online shop; free delivery to and through front door	**Customer relationships** Self-service **Channels** Online, mobile	**Customer segments** Mass market, advertising in aimed above all at young fathers*
Cost structure Marketing, logistics, sourcing			**Revenue streams** Transaction-dependent direct sales turnover	

* http://meedia.de/2014/11/03/vier-jahre-im-moebelmarkt-verschollen-wie-sich-home24-ueber-ikea-lustig-macht/

Authors' evaluation and assessment of perspectives

In 2016, we expect Home24 to have had a much greater effect on the market than it has over the two years previous. The German market for furniture online is growing much more slowly than previously assumed, and process issues in furniture product – a heavily make-to-order area – can't be simply be circumvented using the usual e-commerce box of tricks. The key will lie in optimising production, and this is not something that can be done in a matter of months. In our view, Home24's business model will start to become genuinely exciting when it finds an investor ready to put up the kind of sum needed to keep a sufficiently large proportion of the product mix in stock; but getting to this stage will mean surmounting a range of logistics problems in furniture production. Home24 might well be the market participant which drives this change. We are also keen observers of Home24's auxiliary activities such as its own-brand mattress Smood (as inspired by US pioneers Tuft&Needle and Casper.com).

144 www.kinnevik.se (as of March 2016)
145 www.berlinerzeitung.de (as of March 2016)

3.24 Ikea – An e-commerce late bloomer trapped in multichannel hell?

Key facts

Name: Ikea Group
Headquarters: Leiden, Netherlands
Total staff: 155,000[146]
Global turnover 2015: €31.9bn[147] (US$34.9)
Founded in: 1943
Origins: In-store retailer

With 328 stores,[148] Ikea is the world's largest corporate group in the home and furniture segment. Online, Ikea broke the one-billion-barrier for worldwide sales in 2015, reporting 1.9 billion visitors to its online shops,[149] active in 13 of the overall 28 countries in which the group has operations; further online openings are planned. Ikea is aiming for a total of €50 billion in annual sales by 2020, and it sees internet shopping as a way of helping it reach this goal.[150] A new website, flanked by smartphone and tablet apps, and improved logistics[151] are slated to help it reach €5 billion in five-to-six years.[152] It is planning to set up pick-up points for online orders,[153] but will keep the range available online limited, not selling its entire product palette on the internet.[154] Growing middle classes in India and China will increase sales potential in Asia, and Ikea is reacting by planning 10 new stores in India over the coming decade with an investment of two billion dollars.[155] Europe is set to remain the strongest sales market, however, with 67% of all sales on the continent and Germany, with 14% of overall turnover, its largest single market.[156]

Positioning

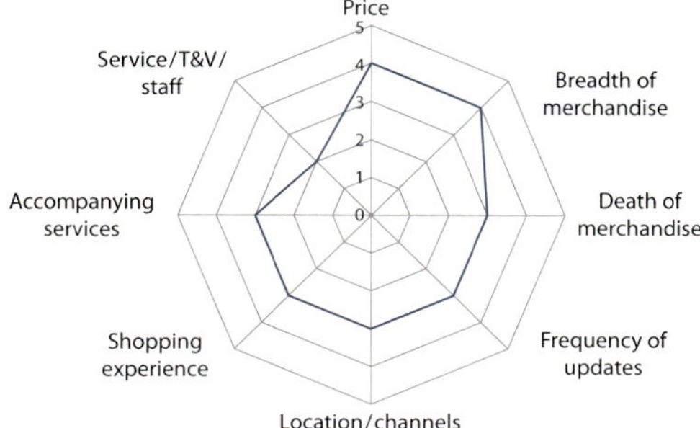

146 www.ikea.com (as of March 2016)
147 www.ikea.com (as of March 2016)
148 www.ikea.com (as of March 2016)
149 www.ikea.com (as of March 2016)
150 www.bloomberg.com (as of March 2016)
151 www.applianceretailer.com (as of March 2016)
152 ecommercenews.eu (as of March 2016)
153 www.onlinehaendlernews.de (as of March 2016)
154 www.stern.de (as of March 2016)
155 fortune.com (as of March 2016)
156 www.ikea.com (as of March 2016)

Ikea's main strengths against competitors are price and the breadth of its merchandise. It uses scaling effects in production and savings in service – e. g. self-service pick-up and flat-pack home assembly – to keep prices low. To date, it has been notable for its strongly offline positioning: combined with online-supported services, the new city-centre location concept, however, could be the first step towards multichannel.

<table>
<tr><th colspan="5">Business model canvas</th></tr>
<tr><td rowspan="2">Key partners
Suppliers, distribution partners,</td><td>Key activities
Production, marketing</td><td rowspan="2">Value proposition
Furniture and home items for easy everyday use at low prices</td><td>Customer relationships
Self-service (extending to self-assembly of furniture)</td><td rowspan="2">Customer segments
Mass market, above all young, price-sensitive customers</td></tr>
<tr><td>Key resources
Brand, customers, existing logistics structures</td><td>Channels
Offline, online, catalogue</td></tr>
<tr><td colspan="3">Cost structure
Store network, logistics and production, marketing</td><td colspan="2">Revenue streams
Transaction-dependent direct sales turnover</td></tr>
</table>

Authors' evaluation and assessment of perspectives

Outsiders have little chance of genuinely understanding what Ikea's online strategy is: as such, the position and intentions of this monolith remain a very popular subject of speculation for e-commerce buffs. Ikea's web shops are, all things told, not online-shops, but still try to sell things on the internet – doing so without directing users, without prioritising important information over irrelevant material, and with little or incomprehensible visual guidance.[157] The group seems to have no detailed web excellence, and yet seems to be doing everything right, as everyone realises when they remember that Ikea earns the highest margin on small take-away items sold in-store: Ikea simply cannot afford to let its customers avoid coming into the shop and making impulse buys, and an optimised online shop would, of course, allow them to do precisely that. Ikea is therefore under no pressure to try and implement a genuinely good online shop until there is serious competition from an internet challenger. For now, the site it has is just about functional enough for customers to order a Billy or a Pax, and that's all that matters.

157 cx-commerce.de (as of March 2016)

3.25 JD.com – A foot in the door to the Middle Kingdom

Key facts

Name: JD.com Inc
Headquarters: Beijing, China
Total staff: 105,963[158]
Global turnover 2015: ¥181.3bn (US$28bn)[159]
Founded in: 2004
Origins: Online pure player

With 155 million active customer accounts, JD.com is China's second-largest online retailer,[160] beaten only by the Alibaba Group.[161] Yet in terms of its ¥181 billion (US$28bn) of sales, it is clearly ahead of its competitor, which only generated ¥76 billion ($12bn) of turnover. The gross volume of goods sold in 2015 was ¥462.7 billion (US$71.4bn), representing 78% growth; overall sales increased by 58%.[162] The JD.com business model is a relatively simple Amazon-style marketplace concept mixed with owned product inventory; by buying in merchandise, JD.com guarantees its customers quality. Just like Tmall, JD runs a domestic and a cross-border marketplace, the latter of which is open to foreign retailers. What is more, besides it proprietary network of 213 warehouses and 5,367 delivery and pick-up points, it offers its own country-wide delivery network;[163] JD can even sell same-day delivery in 134 areas. In this way, this e-commerce monolith has control of much of the value chain, from purchasing through to shopping and delivery; it has also made its delivery network available to corporate partners, making it a popular channel for many companies from outside of China (e. g. Tom Tailor). Last year, 61.4% of all sales in JD were made on mobile devices; much of this has been made possible by cooperation with Tencent's WeChat[164] service which, with 650 million monthly users and 200 potential customers,[165] is JD's most important driver of growth.[166]

Positioning

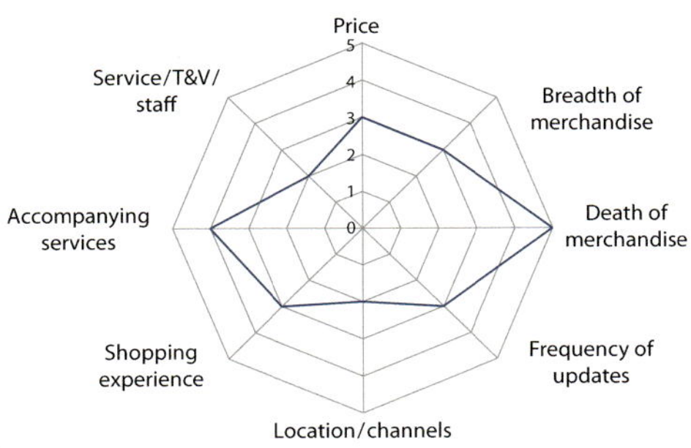

158 globenewswire.com (as of March 2016)
159 According to EUR-USD rates on 31/12/2015 (1,0859)
160 JD is China's second largest online retailer as measured by GMV, but the largest as measured by revenue.
161 The Alibaba Group figures also contain those of Alibaba.com, Tmall, Taobao, Alipay and Juhuasuan
162 ir.jd.com (as of March 2016)
163 ir.jd.com (as of March 2016)
164 See chapter 1.2 for more on cooperation between JA and Tencent
165 Applies to customers who have entered their credit card details on WeChat and already used other paid services
166 venturebeat.com (as of March 2016)

JD.com positions itself first and foremost as close to customer needs as possible: quality assurance and guaranteed authenticity of products from abroad are of particular importance to customers. The depth of the merchandise offered, too, with over 40 million products across a comparatively narrow range of product categories, is notable: JD started life as an electronics and home appliances retailer and has added other areas since. Another strong point in JD's position is the convenient same-day delivery and immediate returns it offers, proprietary, as is its payment system (Tenpay/JD pay); its cooperation with China's biggest and best-loved chat service WeChat is also a strength.[167]

Business model canvas

Key partners	Key activities	Value proposition	Customer relationships	Customer segments
Manufacturers and brands, WeChat (Tencent), market-place retailers	Logistics, quality guarantees, compiling product mix	Huge selection of branded goods from at home and abroad available to order safely and hassle-free	Self-service with direct customer contact on delivery (enabling immediate returns)	China's growing middle class; manufacturers at home and abroad.
	Key resources		**Channels**	
	Data, logistics software		Online und Mobil	

Cost structure	Revenue streams
1. Traffic acquisition 2. Direct sales	1. Direct takings from merchandise 2. Commission from trading platform

Authors' evaluation and assessment of perspectives

In the West, Amazon has already all but won the race of the marketplaces. In China, however, we can make out clear indications that – in contrast to most other economies – there could be room for more than one winner in the long term. This makes the competition between JD and Tmall of particular interest. What we cannot make any predication about is the extent to which cooperation with Wechat will be sufficient to generate customer loyalty to JD.com in the long term.

167 www.china-briefing.com (as of March 2016)

3.26 Jet.com – A real Amazon contender or just a black hole for venture capital?

Key facts

Name: Jet.com, Inc.
Headquarters: Hoboken, USA
Total staff: n. a.
Global turnover 2015: US$1bn[168], **9 months from launch**
Founded in: 2014
Origins: Online pure player

Jet.com started out in summer 2015 as a highly ambitious online marketplace aiming to challenge Amazon both for customers and sellers by offering competitive prices, dynamic "smart cart" offers, and better conditions for merchants. Launching with a 50-dollar membership for customers similar to the Costco concept, the platform quickly dropped these fees and is now concentrating above all on its "smart cart" functionality which offers customers real-time bulk discounts and sends product suggestions aimed at reducing the overall price of the shopping cart. Jet does this by scanning all sellers and all conditions offered and customers don't actually see who the seller is until they place their order. Jet claims that this approach can lead to savings primarily on delivery costs as products are ordered from sellers nearer to customers wherever possible. The company states that it has brought 3.6 million customers, 1,600 merchants, and over 10 million products onto the platform since launch,[169] but this has only been possible with an extremely high marketing spend funded by around $800 million of venture capital.[170]

Positioning

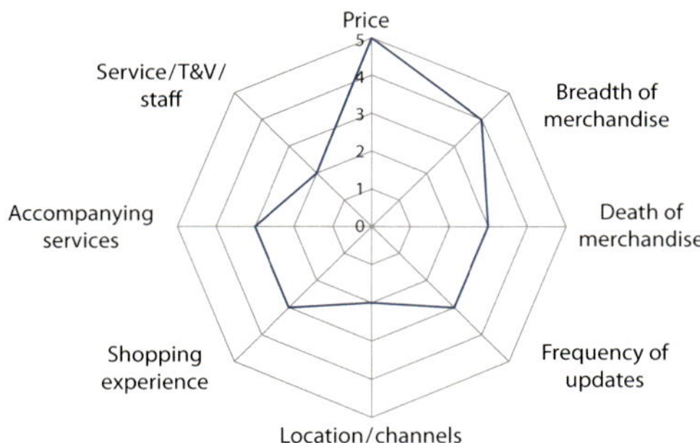

168 www.newsslash.com (as of March 2016)
169 www.internetretailer.com (as of March 2016)
170 www.investors.com (as of March 2016)

Jet is all about price. Its dynamic real-time price finder, developed with a sizeable investment in proprietary technology, is currently unique and aims to help customers save money wherever possible in a gamified way. As a competitor to Amazon, Jet it is aiming to get big in terms of breadth and depth of merchandise – and fast. It is still failing to genuinely challenge Amazon here, however, listing 10 million products to Amazon's 500 million.

Business model canvas

Key partners	**Key activities**	**Value proposition**	**Customer relationships**	**Customer segments**
Manufacturers and brands, logistics companies, advertising networks	IT/analytics, sourcing, marketing **Key resources** Dynamic pricing engine	Transparent shopping for bargain-hunters	Self-service **Channels** Online	Price-sensitive customers

Cost structure	**Revenue streams**
– Sales costs – Technology – Marketing	Commission on marketplace sales (8-15% depending on product category)

Authors' evaluation and assessment of perspectives

Jet.com's sales argument is that products are sold at the lowest possible price. This promise is, in turn, predicated on squeezing as high a margin as possible out of the system, and this means that it doesn't make sense for manufacturers or retailers to supply Jet.com or use its marketplace to sell. Customers, on the other hand, have every reason to buy on Jet.com for as long as its enormous funding reserves are being used to subsidise the offer. This is not, however, genuine customer loyalty. While Jet.com may certainly have raised an impressive amount of cash, this sum will in no way be sufficient to pose any serious challenge to Amazon et al. and we can therefore do little except shake our heads at the Jet.com "strategy".

3.27 JustFab: The next Zara – or the next "Fab" bust?

Key facts

Name: JustFab Inc.
Headquarters: El Segundo, USA
Total staff: 2,000[171]
Global turnover 2015: US$504m[172]
Founded in: 2010
Origins: Online pure player

JustFab is a fashion shopping club based on a monthly subscription model which sells the FabKids, ShoeDazzle, Fabletics, JustFab and FL2 fast-fashion ranges. These ranges cover clothing, shoes, jewellery, and handbags, and include own-brand items.[173] The 35 million members get a monthly lookbook with personalised fashion ideas and, for an extra VIP membership fee of $39.95 monthly, can buy each item in the book for a flat rate (also $39.95); since setting up in 2010, Justfab has managed to get 4 million VIP members in 10 countries. Thanks to the high levels of customer loyalty, the business model is considered extremely lucrative, with 80% of turnover generated from existing customer[174] and the monthly pre-payment of almost $40, which motivates customers to buy regularly. Accordingly, investors have thus far pumped over $300m into the business, currently valued at over a billion dollars. JustFab is aiming for $675m in sales in 2016, with marketing spend slated at over $100m.[175] Nevertheless, it's not all beer and skittles: many customers are not aware of the monthly payment when they sign up and have difficulty terminating their contracts, leading to thousands of complaints and a range of law-suits being filed against the company; consumers protection organisations regularly criticise it for misleading customers.[176]

Positioning

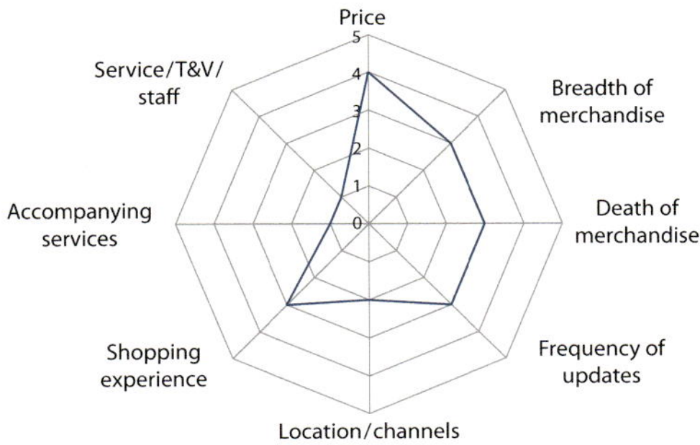

171 vator.tv (as of March 2016)
172 www.buzzfeed.com (as of March 2016)
173 www.presseportal.de (as of March 2016)
174 corp.justfab.com (as of March 2016)
175 www.buzzfeed.com (as of March 2016)
176 www.internetretailer.com (as of March 2016)

JustFab's positioning is based on low prices for high-end fashion brands, especially for VIP customers; also, the frequency with which it updates its range is another USP for JustFab, with customers receiving new, personalised catalogues every month. The depth and breadth of the merchandise are limited, but in autumn 2015, JustFab added 5000 items from its own-brand collection, extending its product mix considerably. Service is a recurring bugbear, with criticism that it is especially difficult to access when customers want to cancel their subscriptions.

<table>
<tr><th colspan="5">Business model canvas</th></tr>
<tr><td rowspan="2">Key partners
Brands, retailers, ad networks</td><td>Key activities
Sourcing, marketing</td><td rowspan="2">Value proposition
High-end fashion brands at a low price in a monthly package</td><td>Customer relationships
Self-service</td><td rowspan="2">Customer segments
Fashion fan, price-sensitive women 26-40 – recently extending to sporting men (FL2)</td></tr>
<tr><td>Key resources
Customer base, brand relationships</td><td>Channels
Online, mobile</td></tr>
<tr><td colspan="2">Cost structure
Marketing, sales costs</td><td colspan="3">Revenue streams
Direct revenue from transactions</td></tr>
</table>

Authors' evaluation and assessment of perspectives

We don't have any trouble at all understanding Justfab's business model: the underlying idea is to set up a sort of improved H&M online. What we don't get is why they've chosen to go for growth with the dark arts of online marketing – spam newsletters, subscription tricks, etc.. This decision is likely to have a very negative effect on customer loyalty and will do their plans no favours.

3.28 Limango – Exciting e-commerce, made in Germany

Key facts

Name: Limango GmbH
Headquarters: Munich, Germany
Total staff: 240[177]
Global turnover 2015: €129m[178] (US$140.9)
Founded in: 2007
Origins: Online pure player

Limango is a shopping community for women and young families with around 4,000 flash sales annually featuring 1,500 brands[179] from the fashion, home, and living segment along with travel and leisure. As well as flash sales, the shopping club also launched the Limango Outlet concept a few years back offering reduced brand goods in an online shop.[180] Limango is a 100%-owned subsidiary of MyToys GmbH which wants to start using synergy effects with the toys pure-play and start addressing their joint target group more efficiently and concertedly.[181] Today, the Limango shopping community has six million members[182] and is active in Germany, Austria, Poland, and the Netherlands; it is currently planning to expand into other European countries[183] and wants to strengthen its market position in Poland and the Netherlands[184] while also broadening its product range. Its home and living category is currently undergoing expansion and, by the end of 2016, it will be offering non-perishable food and drink.[185] With repeat business making up 80% of turnover, Limango is an exciting business model with very good KPIs.

Positioning

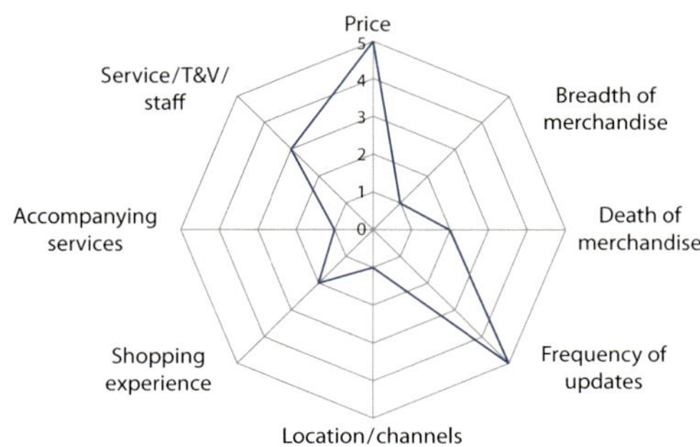

177 www.ottogroup.com (as of March 2016)
178 www.kassenzone.de (as of March 2016)
179 www.ottogroup.com (as of March 2016)
180 www.limango.de, www.ottogroup.com (as of March 2016)
181 www.internetworld.de (as of March 2016)
182 a3.cdn.limango-media.de (as of March 2016)
183 www.ottogroup.com (as of March 2016)
184 www.internetworld.de (as of March 2016)
185 www.internetworld.de (as of March 2016)

Like Vente Privée,[186] Limango positions itself by tying together low prices and a high rate of updates to its merchandise, whose breadth it is continuously extending. In 2015 alone, it increased the number of sales it held by 66%,[187] discounting branded goods by up to 70%. The Limango outlet, too, offers strong price reductions in an online-shop, while the core flash-sales site is constantly being updated, running around 60 sales every week for between one and four days each.

<table>
<tr><th colspan="10">Business model canvas</th></tr>
<tr>
<td colspan="2" rowspan="2">Key partners
1000 brands,*
MyToys and Otto Group (Limango is a wholly-owned subsidiary)</td>
<td colspan="2">Key activities
Sourcing and relationship management with brands, customer communication</td>
<td colspan="2" rowspan="2">Value proposition
Branded products reduced by up to 70%, opportunities to browse and discover new products and brands for mothers and families</td>
<td colspan="2">Customer relationships
Self-service, sale-specific e-mail communication</td>
<td colspan="2" rowspan="2">Customer segments
Mothers and families</td>
</tr>
<tr>
<td colspan="2">Key resources
Brand relationships, members/ regulars</td>
<td colspan="2">Channels
Online, mobile</td>
</tr>
<tr>
<td colspan="5">Cost structure
Sourcing, staffing, CRM</td>
<td colspan="5">Revenue streams
Transaction-dependent direct sales turnover</td>
</tr>
</table>

* http://www.onetoone.de/Limango-geht-nach-Polen-und-in-die-Niederlande-20188.html

Authors' evaluation and assessment of perspectives

When Limango launched in 2007, the whole shopping club concept was brand new and far more hyped than it is now. In the intervening years, the company has gone hybrid, positioning itself somewhere between shopping club and brand outlet – meaning that it too must, like other online shops, invest heavily to acquire customers. Meanwhile, its potential margins are slim inasmuch as the brand promise of a heavy discount only works if the company refrains from taking too large a cut. There is an overall stagnation in the shopping club segment – in which Limango has become one of the strongest competitors in Germany. If it continues to optimise, there is no reason it can't continue to work successfully in the German children's and women's fashion segments; but we have difficulty discerning to what extent there is any great potential for growth left.

186 Cf. Vente Privée company profile
187 www.ottogroup.com (as of March 2016)

3.29 Media-Saturn – Has the electronics giant woken from its slumber?

Key facts

Name: Media-Saturn Holding GmbH
Headquarters: Ingolstadt, Germany
Total staff: 65.000
Global turnover2014/15: €21.7bn (US$23.7bn)
Founded in: 1979
Origins: In-store retailer

With the MediaMarkt, Saturn, and Redcoon brands, Media-Saturn is the largest specialist electronics retailer in Europe. While Media Markt and Saturn originally had a tough time starting in e-commerce, the group as a whole is now, with €1.8bn in internet sales, not doing too badly at all nowadays. Then again, e-commerce was only responsible for around 8% of total turnover (€21.7bn) in 2014/15, although it is, at 20% annually, growing far faster than the overall rate of 3.6%;[188] the fly in the ointment is that subsidiary Redcoon is shedding sales at a rate of more than 10%.[189] By Investing heavily in logistics and shipping – e. g. to offer same-day delivery across Germany – Media-Saturn is looking to seize the initiative from Amazon,[190] and has defined its strategy as becoming a partner to its customers who are looking for orientation in an increasingly complex digital world; it is therefore increasing its investment in service, too, which was already bringing in €1bn in turnover in 2015, by buying RTS-Services[191] and expanding its proprietary streaming offering JUKE.[192]

Positioning

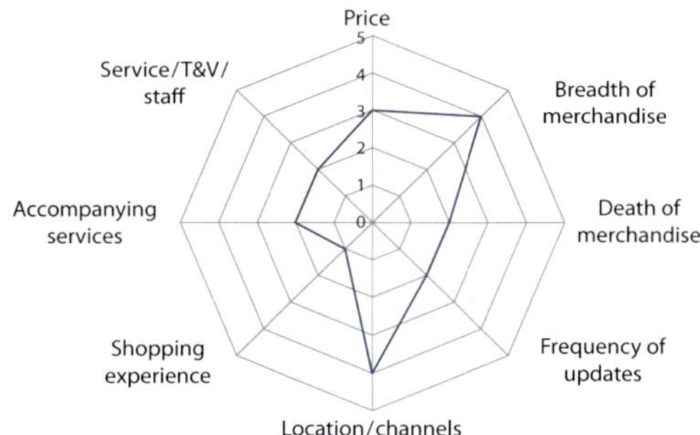

188 www.metrogroup.de (as of March 2016)
189 www.channelpartner.de (as of March 2016)
190 www.heise.de (as of March 2016)
191 www.metrogroup.de (as of March 2016)
192 www.metrogroup.de (as of March 2016)

Media-Saturn defines itself by low prices, a broad range of products, and its multichannel approach. In the e-commerce age, however, it is becoming increasingly difficult for the chain to effectively distinguish itself from its competitors. The much-talked-about multichannel click-and-collect in-store service is used by 40% of all online customers.[193]

Business model canvas				
Key partners Electronics manufacturers, advertising platforms, investors	**Key activities** Marketing, sourcing, pricing **Key resources** Brand, brand identity	**Value proposition** Broad offering and attractive prices (compared to other high-street retailers)	**Customer relationships** Customer care in store, self-service online **Channels** In-store, online, mobile	**Customer segments** Mass market
Cost structure Stores (rentals, staffing, inventory), marketing		**Revenue streams** Transaction-dependent direct sales turnover		

Authors' evaluation and assessment of perspectives

We see the Media-Saturn group as an interesting example of what the internet does to existing competitive markets. What has become clearer and clearer is that this group's business model was really a product of the 80s and 90s and cannot be upheld in the age of the internet. While the consumer perception of them as being cheap and their (expensively rented) city-centre locations offering a wide range of products are strengths, this is not enough to hold out against Amazon and others. Old tricks such as using cheap offers to get customers in through the door and then upsell them expensive accessories are wearing increasingly thin in this age of price transparency, too, and in recent years, the group has not been able to define any new USPs or to use its store space to generate acceptable profit. While targets to make 8% of sales online are, as far as we can see, not particularly unrealistic, we strongly expect these sales to be cross-financed from other areas of the business. In summary, we simply do not see how a stable business model can be implemented here: press releases in which Media-Saturn claims to see its future as "customer's daily assistant in a digitised world" don't exactly fill us with confidence, either.

193 www.channelpartner.de (as of March 2016)

3.30 Nordstrom – The Great Omnichannel Hope?

Key facts

Name: Nordstrom, Inc.
Headquarters: Seattle, USA
Total staff: 67,000
Global turnover 2015: US$14.1bn[194]
Founded in: 1901
Origins: In-store retailer

The roots of fashion retailer Nordstrom lie in Seattle in the early years of the last century. What started as a single shoe shop has since grown to become one of the largest multichannel retail chains in the USA. Selling in the high-end segment, Nordstrom recorded a turnover of $14.1bn in 2015; many of its 323 stores are operated under the Nordstrom Rack outlet brand, whose sales grew by 10%, while the regular Nordstrom locations actually lost 1% turnover year-on-year. As of 2015, online sales made up 20% of overall turnover, posting growth broadly in line with the market average of 15.[195] Among the traditional American retailers, Nordstrom has been one of the boldest in its multichannel approach, investing heavily in its growing online presence and publically setting a target of 30% of overall sales[196] while acquiring stakes and making investments in online pure-plays to prepare itself of the future. Nordstrom has, for instance, bought up shopping club Hautelook[197] and the curated Trunkclub, entering into partnerships with Etsy, Warby Parker, Bonobos, and several others.[198] Since this expansion, however, Nordstrom has been struggling to keep profitability up, and margins remain strongest in its stores;[199] at the same time, its growth is coming from the less profitable channels such as Nordstrom Rack, for which the chain is planning to open 199 new stores by 2020,[200] and e-commerce.

Positioning

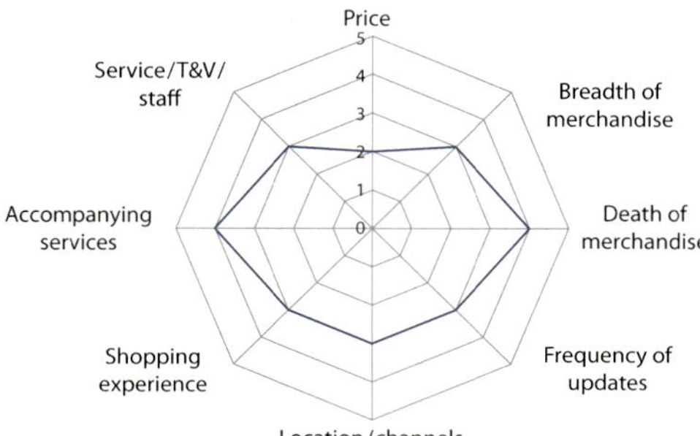

194 investor.nordstrom.com (as of March 2016)
195 investor.nordstrom.com (as of March 2016)
196 www.internetretailer.com (as of March 2016)
197 www.trunkclub.com (as of March 2016)
198 www.cbinsights.com (as of March 2016)
199 www.internetretailer.com (as of March 2016)
200 www.businessinsider.de (as of March 2016)

Nordstrom concentrates on providing high-end brands and seasonal merchandise; at the same time, the depth of the range and the interchangeability of its sales channels are also part of its positioning. Following heavy investment in 2015, the chain's omnichannel activities are being increasingly orientated towards mobile commerce;[201] the lavishly-furnished stores are, more often than not, anchor locations in popular malls and form a key part of the shopping experience, flanked by Nordstrom's focus on customer service, e. g. introducing mobile point-of-sales devices allowing customers to pay any passing member of staff rather than having to queue at the check-out.[202]

Business model canvas				
Key partners Manufacturers and brands, technology providers, mall operators, investors	Sourcing, M&A, technology **Key resources** Brand image, prime store locations	**Value proposition** High-end, curated fashion range with lots of choice	**Customer relationships** Personal (in-store), Self-service (online) **Channels** Online, offline, mobile	**Customer segments** Broad segment/ mass market; higher price category
Cost structure Rents, technology development, staffing		**Revenue streams** Transaction-dependent direct sales turnover		

Authors' evaluation and assessment of perspectives

Nordstrom makes no bones about its conviction that it will be sufficient to build up market share and then, at a later date, earn money online with it. The coming quarterly reports will show to what extent this assumption holds up – and our view is that future reports will reveal it to be flawed. Nordstrom has in no way shown that an old-school retailer can be transformed. All it has shown, in fact, is that the investment strategy it has been pursuing since the mid-2000s has a top-line effect –and little else going for it. In today's market, the sums required to invest in the kind of business which would come into question for Nordstrom are far higher. By the same token, however, Nordstrom shines in comparison to other retailers: if it does manage to continue its investment activities, then it will eventually end up as a solid financial holding company. In order to continue, however, it will have to give up on its avowed multichannel goals. Currently, however, it remains deeply attached to its bricks-and-mortar stores. We will be interested to see which direction it heads in.

201 www.internetretailer.com (as of March 2016)
202 www.businessinsider.de (as of March 2016)

3.31 Otto – From mail order company to retail holding

Key facts

Name: Otto GmbH & Co. KG
Headquarters: Hamburg, Germany
Total staff: 4,350[203]
Global turnover2014/15: €2.6bn[204] (US$2.8bn)
Founded in: 1949
Origins: Mail order company

This traditional mail order company was set up over 60 years ago with a catalogue as its sales channel; since then, online shopping has changed Otto – and the competition. Its old mail-order rivals Quelle and Neckermann went bust, helping Otto into new customers while underlining just how difficult it is to move sales from catalogues to the internet. Its new competitors are Amazon, Zalando, and Wayfair, who use efficient processes, low prices, sales-orientated online strategies, huge product ranges, and technical skills to attack Otto in every segment in which it is present. Otto is responding, though, having launched its own new webshop in 2013 with a modern system architecture with a view to responding to innovations in the market as they come. Nevertheless, the retailer's ability to remain competitive going forward remains a topic of often heated discussion: its below-market-rate growth in recent years fuels debate. At group level, Otto made €6.6bn online in 2015/2016 (of an overall turnover of $12.57bn)[205] and, with its 123 component companies, is the second-largest online retailers worldwide;[206] the group includes MyToys, which posted sales of over €500 in its most recent financial year.[207]

Positioning

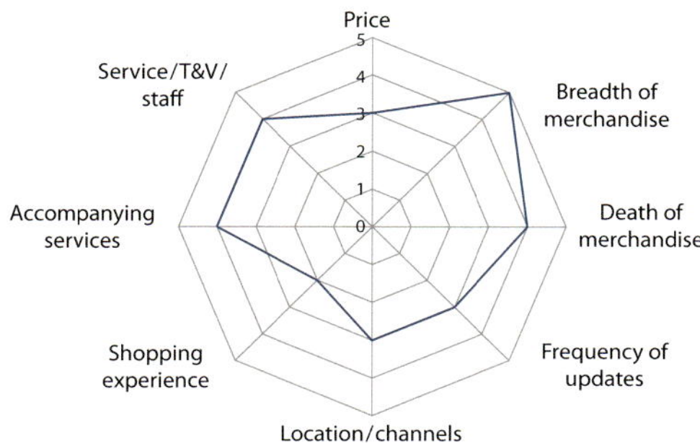

203 www.otto.de (as of March 2016)
204 www.otto.de (as of March 2016)
205 www.wiwo.de (as of March 2016)
206 www.ottogroup.com (as of March 2016)
207 www.ottogroup.com (as of March 2016)

Otto is positioned as a general store with a full breadth and depth of merchandise; it manages to extend in depth above all by including third-party retailers in its online shop. It also tries to make USPs of its service offering, which includes payment in instalments or delayed payment (up to 100 days).[208] In terms of price, Otto is mid-market.

Business model canvas				
Key partners Brands and manufactures, parcels services	**Key activities** Compiling product mix, CRM, SEM **Key resources** Customer base	**Value proposition** Large selection of products, additional services such as credit and delayed payment	**Customer relationships** Self-service **Channels** Catalogue, online, mobile	**Customer segments** Very broad segments/mass market
Cost structure Inventory, sales costs, staffing		**Revenue streams** Transaction-dependent direct sales turnover, commission from marketplace		

Authors' evaluation and assessment of perspectives

As the last man standing of the old German mail order triumvirate, Otto now has, in fact, little to do with catalogues as an independent sales channel, having switched to online sales. Its structures, however, remain reminiscent of the catalogue years, so expect to see some far-reaching internal transformations and modifications to the business model. Its customer base and e-commerce experience are nonetheless indicators that it can expect several more good years in retail, but competitors such as Zalando, Asos, et al. have now reached a level which will mean that Otto will have think about emulating their verticalisation. Nevertheless, fashion remains quite a diverse market in e-commerce – probably because it not (yet) bought with the same hard-nosed, value-for-money attitude as other product ranges. This is Otto's opportunity.

208 www.otto.de (as of March 2016)

3.32 Overstock – The outlet concept goes online

Key facts

Name: Overstock.com, Inc
Headquarters: Salt Lake City, USA
Total staff: 1,500
Global turnover 2015: US$1.7bn[209]
Founded in: 1999
Origins: Online pure player

Set up In 1999, Overstock.com took the proven factory outlet concept onto the internet and grew to a turnover of $80m annually without any outside capital until going public in 2002.[210] In its early years, this pure-play got the stock it needed for its "online closing-down sale" from other e-commerce start-ups which really were closing down in the Dot-com bust, buying up their inventory for a nickel and a dime. Today, Overstock – or O.co for short – is a comprehensive stockist of furniture, carpets, bedclothes, electronics, clothing, and jewellery,[211] with over one million articles listed and 180 countries to which it delivers.[212] It was selling home furnishings on the net long before competitors Amazon and Wayfair, and still makes around 18% of its turnover with them today.[213] In 2015, it increased sales by 11% to $1.7bn, making a profit of $2.4m;[214] since early 2014, it has been accepting payment in Bitcoins, which currently account of 0.1% of turnover.[215] With subsidiary Worldstock Fair Trade, it set up a marketplace for handmade products from across the world which is also a form of development programme for poorer countries.[216]

Positioning

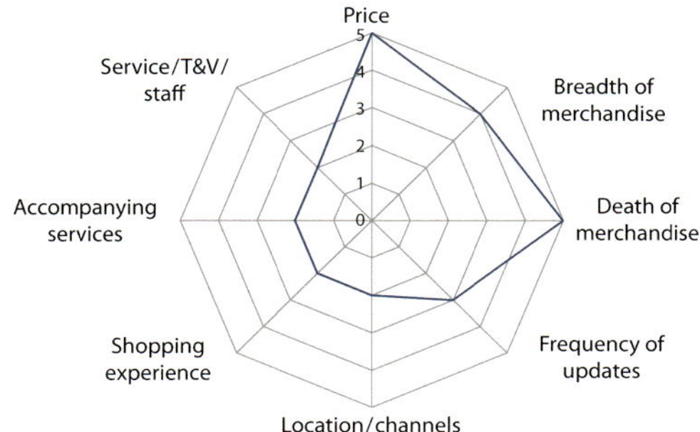

209 www.overstock.com (as of March 2016)
210 www.overstock.com (as of March 2016)
211 www.overstock.com (as of March 2016)
212 help.overstock.com (as of March 2016)
213 www.furnituretoday.com (as of March 2016)
214 www.internetretailer.com (as of March 2016)
215 www.wired.com (as of March 2016)
216 www.overstock.com (as of March 2016)

Overstock's positioning is focussed on low prices and depth of merchandise. List prices are heavily discounted, and today still, some of the merchandise is booty from insolvencies of e-commerce start-ups gone bust. It also plays on the breadth of its product range and was one of the first online retailers to allow Bitcoins as a method of payment.

Business model canvas				
Key partners Brand, ad networks, shareholders	**Key activities** Sourcing cheap outlet merchandise **Key resources** Relationships to brands and retailers	**Value proposition** Wide range of outlet merchandise at discount prices available online	**Customer relationships** Self-service **Channels** Online, mobile	**Customer segments** Mass market
Cost structure Sales costs, marketing, technology		**Revenue streams** Direct revenue from transactions		

Authors' evaluation and assessment of perspectives

This is a solid online business model from the early days of e-commerce which, if it continues to even grow moderately, will keep going well into the future. There's little to get excited about or go into detail on here, though.

3.33 Rakuten – Dreams of becoming the world's biggest internet service provider

Key facts

Name: Rakuten, Inc.
Headquarters: Tokyo, Japan
Total staff: 11,723[217]
Global turnover 2015: JP¥713bn (US$6.3bn)[218]
Founded in: 1997
Origins: Online pure player

With a market share of 35% in its home market, Rakuten is Japan's largest e-commerce company. Worldwide, Rakuten has 100 million customers[219] in 28 countries[220]and lists over 60,000 traders large and small across its various marketplaces.[221] Inasmuch as Rakuten limits itself to providing the technology solution and does not itself have any retail activities, Rakuten is similar to Ebay; like Amazon, however, it runs as a marketplace and, like Etsy, runs on small merchants selling from customised storefronts.[222] The Japanese platform has extended this personalised shop approach[223] with a broad service portfolio, creating trader loyalty and giving it an advantage against its aggressive competitor Amazon;[224] when it comes to actually competing with Amazon worldwide, however, Rakuten has not been able to reach its ambitious goals.[225] Its expansion into new segments has, however, helped the company to up turnover by 19% to $6.3bn in the 2015 fiscal year, costing it 38% of its profits, however, which sunk to $393m. In the course of 2016, Rakuten intends to optimise its performance by closing some of its marketplaces in south-east Asia.[226]

Positioning

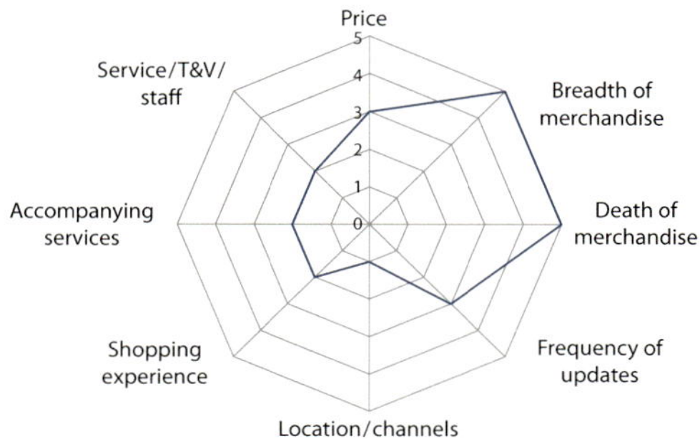

217 global.rakuten.com (as of March 2016)
218 techcrunch.com (as of March 2016)
219 newsroom.rakuten.de (as of March 2016)
220 newsroom.rakuten.de (as of March 2016)
221 newsroom.rakuten.de (as of March 2016)
222 www.kassenzone.de (as of March 2016)
223 excitingcommerce.de (as of March 2016)
224 techcrunch.com (as of March 2016)
225 excitingcommerce.de (as of March 2016)
226 techcrunch.com (as of March 2016)

As a marketplace, Rakuten concentrates on the breadth and depth of its merchandise: worldwide, it lists over 100 million products with over 60,000 specialist retailers.[227] By allowing its merchants to customise the look-and-feel of their storefronts, Rakuten also manages to emotionalise the shopping experience to a greater extent than many e-commerce portals.

Business model canvas				
Key partners Excellent relationships with its marketplace traders	**Key activities** Acquiring merchants, platform, CRM **Key resources** Trader network, customer base	**Value proposition** Traders: good relationship with advice and support. Customers: more personal online shopping experience with small-scale sellers	**Customer relationships** Self-service, with some customer care (dependent on trader) **Channels** Online, mobile	**Customer segments** Mass market
Cost structure Sourcing, platform, staffing		**Revenue streams** 1. Fixed fees for storefront 2. Commission*		

* https://www.internetretailer.com/2013/05/17/rakuten-kicks-its-fifth-european-e-marketplace

Authors' evaluation and assessment of perspectives

Incredibly successful in Japan and decidedly happy to experiment internationally with an agile growth strategy, Rakuten is an interesting case – but one which is hard to judge. Marketplaces everywhere such as Hitmeister and Yatego in Germany, and indeed Rakuten, are under a lot of pressure from Amazon and Ebay and have been unable to claw back market share in recent years. The Rakuten service model for traders based on a light shop structure and cross-border commerce has been losing so much ground to the Big Two that it is looking increasingly difficult to establish operations in new countries with bought-in technology: in our view, Rakuten is far too fixed on trying to transplant its successful Japanese structure onto other markets, such as Germany, where it is no longer an exciting newcomer. We are not expecting Rakuten to trigger any real growth or innovation in 2016 and 2017.

227 www.global.rakuten.com (as of March 2016)

3.34 Staples – Last-chance saloon for this stationer

Key facts

Name: Staples, Inc.
Headquarters: Framingham, USA
Total staff: 85,000
Global turnover 2015: US$21.1bn
Founded in: 1986
Origins: In-store retailer

Staples is one of the world's largest office stationers and, at online sales of 44%, it has moved a relatively high proportion of its business onto the internet when compared to many an in-store retailer. This switch is being increasingly reflected in the corporate strategy, with all efforts being orientated towards the net while stores are closed;[228] a new online shop system has been implemented as internal solution, too.[229] With Staples International, the company has a far-reaching network of stores in 37 countries on five continents,[230] yet this cannot insulate it from its new competitors, Amazon – in the form of Amazon Business – and its overall turnover has been declining for years now. With a view to expanding its product range by a noticeable margin and keeping its prices half-way competitive, in December 2014 Staples set up its own online marketplace in North America under the name Staples Exchange which, similarly to Amazon Marketplace, is intended to link external retailers into the company's infrastructure.[231] In addition, its plans to acquire competitor Office Depot is intended to allow for an increase in its product range and service offering in the future.[232]

Positioning

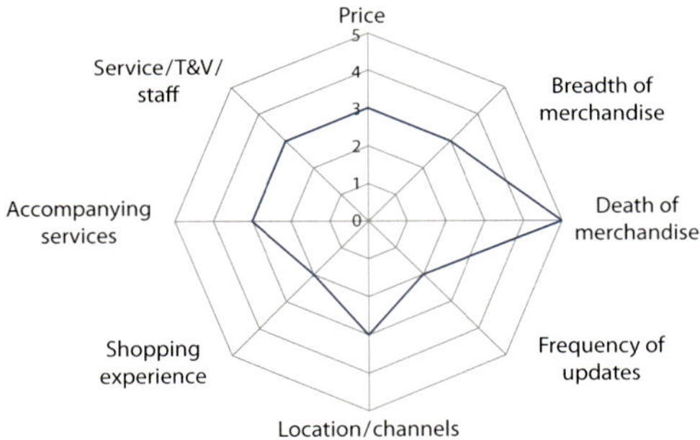

228 investor.staples.com (as of March 2016)
229 www.computerweekly.com (as of March 2016)
230 www.staplesadvantage.de (as of March 2016)
231 www.pymnts.com (as of March 2016)
232 investor.staples.com (as of March 2016)

Staples is increasingly having difficulties finding an effective position on the market. Until now, its principal USP was its geographical closeness to business customers as a specialist retailer; yet online trading has eroded the importance of this positioning, and Staples' best option now is to distinguish itself from competitors with the depth of the merchandise it stocks.

Business model canvas				
Key partners Suppliers, market-place traders	**Key activities** Compiling product range, CRM **Key resources** Brand, customer base	**Value proposition** Specialised merchandise, depth of merchandise, local penetration thanks to stores	**Customer relationships** No focus on personal customer care **Channels** Stores, online, catalogue, mobile	**Customer segments** 80% B2B 20% B2C
Cost structure Staples has been making efforts for some years now to reduce store costs markedly and increase efficiency.*		**Revenue streams** 1. Direct takings from product sales 2. Commission from marketplace		

* http://investor.staples.com/phoenix.zhtml?c=96244&p=irol-reportsannual

Authors' evaluation and assessment of perspectives

For our money, Staples is a classic victim of Amazon's hunger for growth. Its product range is easy to sell and the B2B Customer relationships on which Staples is currently basing its success are set to become increasingly fragile. On top of that, Staples' model is facing a strategic challenge inasmuch as modern offices simply require much less paper and are increasingly switching to digital solutions, meaning that Apple and Samsung are now competitors. This challenge needs a response – and tweaking service propositions is not one.

3.35 Stitch Fix – Is a personal style advisor the next stage in e-commerce evolution?

Key facts

Name: Stitch Fix, Inc.
Headquarters: San Francisco, USA
Total staff: 4,400 (incl. stylists)[233]
Global turnover 2015: approx. US$200m[234]
Founded in: 2011
Origins: Online pure player

Stich Fix is a curated shopping pure-play selling women's fashion. Customers start by filling out a short questionnaire regarding their taste and style and are then assigned a personal stylist; new customers then receive a selection of five pieces of clothing, of which they may keep as many as they want and receive the $20 service charge off the price. The complete process, from matching stylists and customers to generating product recommendations is supported by a range of algorithms, making the entire business model strongly data-driven – and very successful. Around 60 data scientists now support the more than 2800 stylists in advising their customers, optimising the process as they go.[235] Customers may choose between a surprise from their fashion "fix", as corporate jargon has them, or express a specific desire for the next selection of five pieces. Although the services has, thus far, only been available for women, a launch for men looks to be planned for the end of the year (the beta version has been up and running since 2016). As well as buy-ins, Stitch Fix also has its own brands such as 41 Hawthorn, Market & Spruce which are also sold in other shops.[236] That the company – kitted out with over $45m of venture capital[237] – is growing steadily is clear from the fact that it is planning a new sales centre with space for up to 500 staff.[238]

Positioning

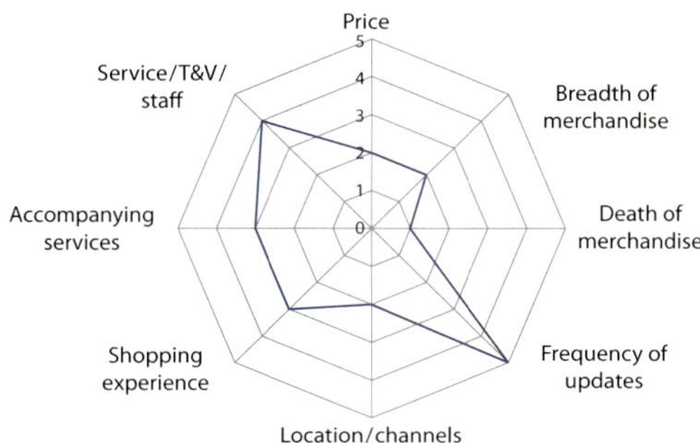

233 www.computerworld.com (as of March 2016)
234 www.recode.net (as of March 2016)
235 www.computerworld.com (as of March 2016)
236 modernmrsdarcy.com (as of March 2016)
237 www.mystatesman.com (as of March 2016)
238 www.mcall.com (as of March 2016)

The Stitch Fix proposition is primarily defined by service: the goal is to advise customers as personally and as stylishly as possible and, in so doing, to up the chances that the items dispatched will be bought. The personal touch and the ability to send stylists specific questions and wishes online strengthen this position. Price-wise, Stitch Fix is mid-market to high-end, but customers can influence this too.

<table>
<tr><th colspan="5">Business model canvas</th></tr>
<tr><td rowspan="2">Key partners
Brand manufacturers, stylists</td><td>Key activities
Curation, sourcing</td><td rowspan="2">Value proposition
Curated shopping for all fashion tastes, tailored to customers and delivered to their doors</td><td>Customer relationships
Personal customer care administered by stylists</td><td rowspan="2">Customer segments
Women who either do not have time to shop or do not enjoy/have difficulties with shopping</td></tr>
<tr><td>Key resources
Algorithms, 2800 stylists</td><td>Channels
Online, mobile</td></tr>
<tr><td colspan="2">Cost structure
Staff, sourcing, technology</td><td colspan="3">Revenue streams
Styling fees, transaction-dependent direct sales turnover</td></tr>
</table>

Authors' evaluation and assessment of perspectives

We are of the opinion that this business model has a small, but very stable market – and one which actually has customer loyalty. It will be interesting to see what happens when this kind of curated shopping provider tries to scale up using its technology and, in so doing, opens up its data to third parties. We think there is a lot more to come in this area.

3.36 Tmall – World Champion of Gross Goods Volume

Key facts

Name: Zhejiang Taobao Mall Network Co., Ltd.
Headquarters: Hangzhou, China
Total staff: n. a.
Global turnover 2015: n. a. (Alibaba 2015/16: ¥101.1bn (US$15.7bn)[239]
Founded in: 2008
Origins: Online pure player

A subsidiary of the Alibaba Group, when it comes to the gross volume of goods sold, Tmall.com is China's biggest B2C online marketplace for brands and retailers, The marketplace is split into Tmall for domestic businesses and Tmall Global for sellers from outside of China; while Chinese companies process orders themselves or pay third-party suppliers to handle them, foreign retailers are offered access to a logistics network run by the Tmall partner company Cainiao. Foreign brands and retailers such as Amazon and Procter & Gamble run their own virtual shops on Tmall, offering more than 140,000 brands; international sellers are attracted by the possibilities for targeted advertising campaigns, the gigantic sales potential, and the comparatively uncomplicated access to Chinese consumers. Tmall's business model relies on transaction fees of up to 5% on the sale generated by retailers, most of which flows through Alipay; sellers also pay annual service charges. The depth of the well of sales potential becomes clear on the annual Singles' Day: in 2015, the Alibaba Group[240] generated a total of 14.4 billion dollars of turnover in 24 hours on this online shopping promotional day, now the biggest in the world, of which it is the principal promoter.[241]

Positioning

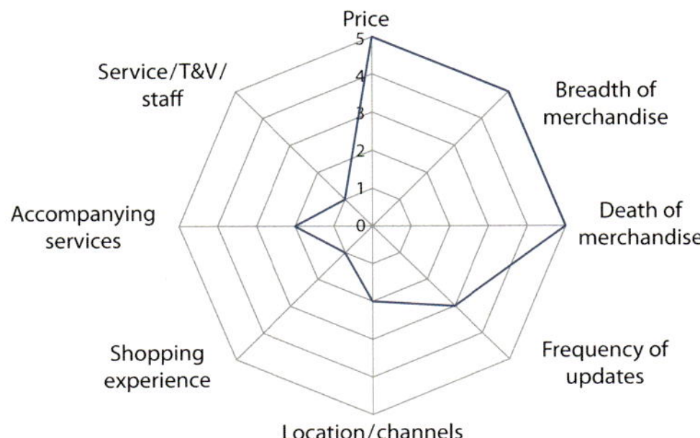

239 www.statista.com (as of March 2016)
240 We can assume that Tmall has booked most of these sales for itself
241 www.chinadaily.com (as of March 2016)

Tmall positions itself with its huge selection of branded goods offered both by domestic and international manufacturers and retailers. It is the biggest marketplace for foreign goods in China and the sheer breadth of its merchandise is what really distinguishes it from its competitor, JD. On the other hand, neither the shopping experience nor the service it offers are particular USPs. For sellers, the platform's attractiveness comes primarily from its high user numbers.

Business model canvas

Key partners	Key activities	Value proposition	Customer relationships	Customer segments
Manufacturers and brands, market-place traders, Alibaba ecosystem	Marketing commu-nication, Singles Day	Huge selection of branded products	Self-service for end consumers, logistics for foreign sellers	China's growing middle class, do-mestic and foreign sellers.
	Key resources Data		**Channels** Online und Mobil	

Cost structure	Revenue streams
1. Traffic acquisition 2. Website operation	1. Commission from marketplace 2. Online marketing services (pay-4-performance marketing , display marketing) 3. Commission on transactions

Authors' evaluation and assessment of perspectives

As detailed in our evaluation of JD.com, we see potential for more than one winner in China. In terms of this book, we see the Alibaba Group's strategy in its home market – focus on price, merchandise, and availability – as the most convincing. In our estimation, Tmall is likely to come out of the clash with JD.com as the winner.

3.37 Vente Privée – The mother of all flash sales

Key facts

Name: Vente-privee.com SA
Headquarters: La Plaine Saint-Denis, France
Total staff: 2,500[242]
Global turnover 2015: €2bn[243] (US$2.2bn)
Founded in: 2001
Origins: Online pure player

Launching in 2001 as the first flash-sales platform and triggering a worldwide wave of copycats in the process (from Gilt in the USA to brands4friends in Germany), the Vente Privée concept is based on crossing the exclusivity of a "members only" club with strong price reductions on premium products, limiting the timeframe of the offers to a maximum of five days to create a sense of urgency. As such, the shopping club is a good environment for many high-end brands, which can use Vente Privée to shift overstocks into a closed community, thus avoiding price erosion in the market as a whole. With over 30 million members today[244] in eight countries and a range of product categories beyond fashion (electronics, jewellery, travel), Vente Privée has expanded significantly; nevertheless, it's attempt at cracking the USA[245] was unsuccessful and the company withdrew after three years in 2014.[246] In Europe, it is growing at a two-digit rate, hiring almost 800 new people in 2015 in order to help it keep pace with sales increases.[247] It was still, however, making around 70% of its turnover in France.[248]

Positioning

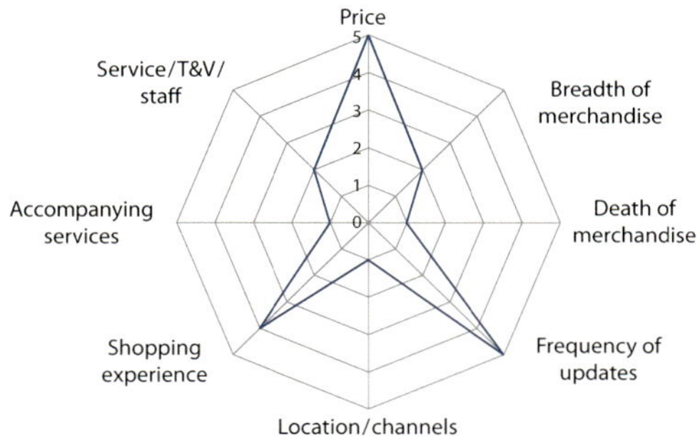

242 pressroom.venteprivee.com (as of March 2016)
243 de.fashionmag.com (as of March 2016)
244 pressroom.venteprivee.com (as of March 2016)
245 www.businessinsider.com (as of March 2016)
246 fortune.com (as of March 2016)
247 de.fashionmag.com (as of March 2016)
248 www.textilwirtschaft.de (as of March 2016)

The key Vente Privée USPs are price and frequency of updates to merchandise; it's a very clever combination as the cut-price products are only available for a short period of time, creating a strong buy-impulse and often provoking spontaneous orders for products they may never have otherwise bought.

Business model canvas				
Key partners 2,500 brands	**Key activities** Sourcing, platform, logistics	**Value proposition** 30-70% reductions on list price; emotional, exclusive shopping	**Customer relationships** Self-service, sale-specific e-mail communication	**Customer segments** Brand and price-sensitive customers (high proportion of members are women)
	Key resources Infrastructure, members (=subscribers)		**Channels** Online, mobile	
Cost structure Platform, logistics, sourcing, CRM		**Revenue streams** Transaction-dependent direct sales turnover – low-risk as merchandise is often only bought from retailers after orders have been placed.		

Authors' evaluation and assessment of perspectives

One of the pack of hot new shopping club start-ups in 2007 and 2008, Vente Privée made full use of the great advantage of this business model: the ability to build up functioning customer relationship management. Club members get e-mails and don't need to be continually won back over with other, expensive marketing tools. The model has worldwide potential – e. g. Gilt Groupe or Limago, which, all things told, are substantially based on the Vente Privée idea. Vente Privée itself, however, despite being one of the first to apply the shopping club model, has not had much success internationalising the concept and is actually withdrawing from several markets; it generates over 80% of its turnover in its domestic market, France – where it has, however, reached a level which now allows it to experiment. This is an exciting situation in which Vente Privée has become an exclusive channel for several manufacturers who now use it to test new brands and products. While we don't expect Vente Privée to have a great effect on markets abroad in the coming year, we do expect to see it driving intriguing innovations in France, even if it has lost some of its initial élan and wasted a lot of energy thus far in a dead-end international expansion.

3.38 Vipshop – China's stock-market listed, profitable Fab.com

Key facts
Name: Vipshop Holdings Limited
Headquarters: Guangzhou, China
Total staff: 16,920[249]
Global turnover 2015: ¥40.2bn (US$6.2bn)[250]
Founded in: 2008
Origins: Online pure player

Describing itself as China's third-largest online retailer, Vipshop has specialised in selling a range of cut-price branded goods (including clothes, furniture, and beauty products). Its business model is based on flash sales of a limited number of reduced branded products for a limited time.[251] Similarly to outlet models, its product range is generally surplus inventory, much of it (in fashion) from the previous season.[252] In 2013, it became China's first profitable e-commerce company and was, thanks to a year-on-year growth rate of 72%, able to push its results to US$1.53bn – that's a yield on sales of 5.2%. Another impressive figure is the proportion of mobile sales, which was at 82% in 2015: JD and Alibaba stack up at 60%[253] and 50% respectively.[254] The stock-market listed company continues to turn heads with its speedy growth, taking at €30-million stake in France's Showroomprivee online shopping club during 2015.[255]

Positioning

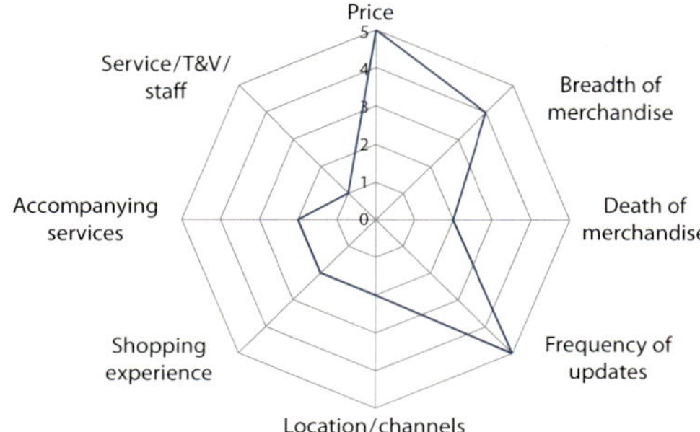

With its flash-sale model, Vipshop positions itself quite clearly as a low-price provider of branded goods over a broad selection of merchandise categories ranging from fashion

249 www.macroaxis.com (as of March 2016)
250 ir.vip.com (as of March 2016)
251 www.reuters.com (as of March 2016)
252 www.bloomberg.com (as of March 2016)
253 ir.jd.com (as of March 2016)
254 ar.alibabagroup.com (as of March 2016)
255 excitingcommerce.de (as of March 2016)

and accessories to cosmetics, furnishings, and lifestyle products. The flash-sale approach is also present in the daily discount offers, which nevertheless limit the depth of the merchandise available. Members do not have to pay fees.

Business model canvas				
Key partners Brand manufacturers	**Key activities** Sourcing, flash sales, curation **Key resources** Merchandising expertise, members	**Value proposition** Cut-price branded products, emotional and exclusive shopping experience	**Customer relationships** Self-service, sales-driven communication **Channels** Online, mobile, outlet stores	**Customer segments** Brand and price-sensitive customers
Cost structure Fulfilment, marketing, CRM, sourcing		**Revenue streams** Transaction-dependent direct sales turnover		

Authors' evaluation and assessment of perspectives

In the world of European shopping clubs, Vente Privée is by far the most successful: yet its success remains limited to the French market, in which it dominates its core shopping club segment as a quasi-monopolist. All things told, Vipshops may well have a similar position in China and this ought to lead to a tangible increase in profitability in the future. What we cannot say with any certainty, however, is what is driving the company to acquire shares in so many shopping clubs outside of China given the lack of cross-border scaling potential in this segment. All things said, however, the business model here is a very promising one.

3.39 Walmart – Too big to fail? No such thing in e-commerce

Key facts

Name: Wal-Mart Stores, Inc.
Headquarters: Betonville, USA
Total staff: 2.2m
Global turnover 2015/16[256]: US$485.7bn
Founded in: 1962
Origins: In-store retailer

The Walton Family success story begins in 1962 with the first ever Walmart shop,[257] paving the way for what has grown into the largest retail company in the USA[258] today with more than 11,000 stores in 27 countries and 260 million customers every week. As well as the Walmart brand, it also owns other retail chains such as Sam's Club and ASDA in the UK.[259] In 2015, its growth, however, was just 2%, with sales up to $486bn,[260] 28% of which was generated outside of the USA.[261] Sales on Walmart.com, launched in 2007, grew by 12% in the same time frame by 12% to $13.7bn – far below market growth rates and only 3% of Walmart's total turnover.[262] With intensified investments in technology and research and development to the tune of $1.1bn, Walmart wants to drive its online activities more strongly in the future,[263] and will be closing hundreds of markets – including many Walmart Express stores – in order to take better account of changes in consumer behaviour.[264] It is currently in the initial stages of testing a scheme to open up its own platform to third-party retailers.[265]

Positioning

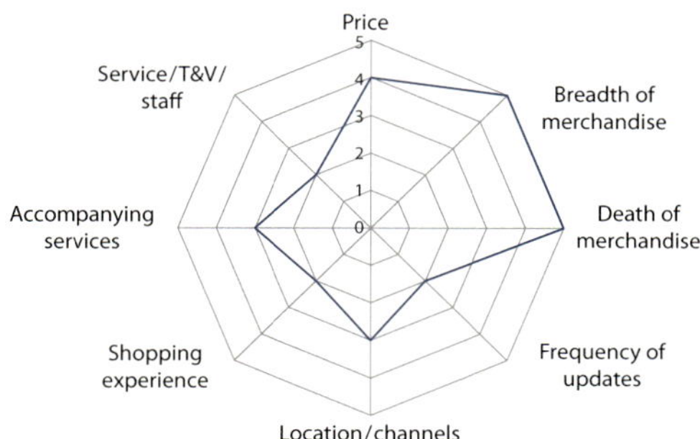

256 Financial year ends on 31/01/2016
257 corporate.walmart.com (as of March 2016)
258 www.internetretailer.com (as of March 2016)
259 corporate.walmart.com (as of March 2016)
260 s2.q4cdn.com (as of March 2016)
261 corporate.walmart.com (as of March 2016)
262 www.internetretailer.com (as of March 2016)
263 www.internetretailer.com (as of March 2016)
264 fortune.com (as of March 2016)
265 www.internetretailer.com (as of March 2016)

Walmart is an unquestioned expert in low-price positioning, known for its aggressive discounting and undercutting tactics directed against other in-store retailers – and online shops such as Amazon. It also uses the breadth and depth of its merchandise as a sales argument, while shopping experience and service are far less important to the USA's largest retailer.

Business model canvas				
Key partners Brands, suppliers, shareholders	**Key activities** Sourcing, development, marketing **Key resources** Distribution network of over 150 warehouses	**Value proposition** Huge selection of products across a full range of categories at attractive prices	**Customer relationships** Self-service **Channels** Stores, online, mobile	**Customer segments** Mass market
Cost structure Sales costs, technology, logistics, and infrastructure, marketing		**Revenue streams** Direct revenue from transactions (takings from marketplace recently added)		

Authors' evaluation and assessment of perspectives

Walmart is caught in the Amazon trap: it has no recognisable strategy, its online activities look flailing, and it's growing at below the market rate; it doesn't have any clever concepts for what to do with all of its store space and how it could be used to make it successful online. It is, in short, an truly pitiful example of how a company starting out with the best possible position (plenty of assets and large budgets) is managing to not find a way into the digital world. We hope to see genuinely innovative ideas in 2016 and 2017.

3.40 Wanelo – Can a social network disrupt the fashion sector?

Key facts

Name: Wanelo
Headquarters: San Francisco, USA
Total staff: n. a.
Global turnover 2015: n. a.
Founded in: 2012
Origins: Online pure player

Wanelo launched in 2012 as a social network about fashion and design inspiration, growing fast to reach 12 million active users – principally female millennials, who share products, compile product lists, follow each other, and interact with their favourite brands on the network. Since then, the company has developed from a Pinterest-style collect-and-share platform to a fashion online marketplace with 550,000 stores,[266] compiling its range from over 30 million products from other websites in a particularly user-friendly, target-group orientated way without holding any of its own inventory. At first, orders we handled entirely by the sellers linked – i. e. to buy the product they had discovered on the platform, users were sent directly to the shop from which it came, meaning that Wanelo generated turnover using the affiliate model. Since late 2014, however, product supplies by over 200 fashion brands can also be bought on the network itself; in 2015, it also integrated Shopify, making the platform easier to use for smaller merchants looking to sell directly on it.[267]

Positioning

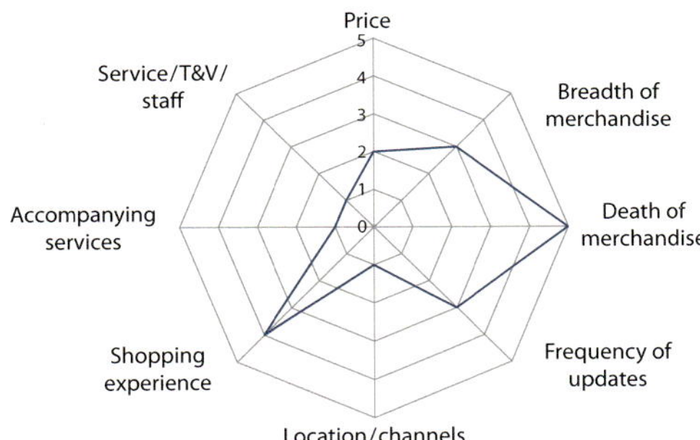

Standing for "want, need, love", Wanelo positions itself on the variety of products it lists and on its shopping experience. Its product range is broad and very, very deep, compiling

266 wanelo.com (as of March 2016)
267 blog.wanelo.com (as of March 2016)

over 30 million products from 550,000 different shops. The simple, attractive design aimed at young, digital smartphone users is the company's key focus, making for a positive shopping experience.

Business model canvas				
Key partners Fashion brands, manufacturers, Etsy sellers in the fashion segment, investors	**Key activities** Marketing **Key resources** Customer base, technology, brand relationships	**Value proposition** Attractive online shopping experience in Pinterest-style environment	**Customer relationships** Self-service **Channels** 10% online, 90% mobile*	**Customer segments** Female millennials, fashion enthusiasts
Cost structure Technology, marketing		**Revenue streams** Affiliate takings		

* https://wanelo.com/about/shopify

Authors' evaluation and assessment of perspectives

In a number of ways, Wanelo is of interest. Its business model comes from a time when Pinterest, Instagram, et al. were all very much in the early stages and Wanelo could provide a valuable extra layer on top of these platforms, and was also able, in our view, to scale it. Now that Instagram and Pinterest have evolved so much further, though, it's very hard to see what the point is – and we think customers will have difficulty recognising any use for it, too.

3.41 Warby Parker – THE model for successful direct sales

Key facts

Name: JAND, Inc.
Headquarters: New York, USA
Total staff: 500
Global turnover 2015: n. a.
Founded in: 2009
Origins: Online pure player

Warby Parker designs, makes, and sells prescription glasses and sunglasses at lower prices than traditional manufacturers. With the high margins it promises and the strong domination of one company – Luxottica – glasses are a particularly enticing market for new online concepts, with the vertically-integrated Warby Parker concept making itself a name with fashionable, affordable models, a comfortable virtual fitting with real-life articles sent to try on as a follow-up, and an uncomplicated returns process.[268] Currently, Warby Parker is only active on the Canadian and American markets,[269] operating 27 in-store locations since April 2013 in addition to its online shop,[270] and has also recently entered into a partnership with Nordstrom with the aim of increasing its reach and brand awareness.[271] Valued at $1.2bn, the company has thus far taken $115m from 21 investors over five rounds of financing.[272]

Positioning

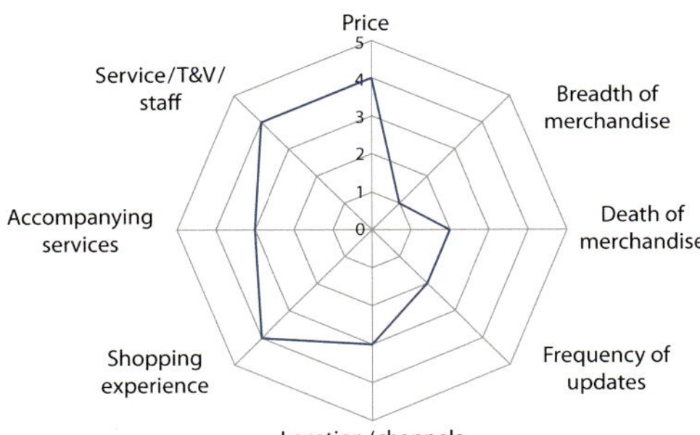

Warby Parker's key sales argument is low prices and high quality, reached by cutting out the middleman by selling is glasses frames directly to customers. It also trades on a highly

268 techcrunch.com (as of March 2016)
269 ca.warbyparker.com (as of March 2016)
270 ca.warbyparker.com (as of March 2016)
271 fashionista.com (as of March 2016)
272 www.warbyparker.com (as of March 2016)

positive shopping experience and on best-in-class service, offering virtual fittings and a selection of five models sent to try on at home.

Business model canvas

Key partners	Key activities	Value proposition	Customer relationships	Customer segments
Suppliers, investors, influencers	Product design, marketing	Hip glasses and sunglasses at low prices and in high quality	Self-service online, service-focussed offline	Price-sensitive glasses wearers
	Key resources Brand image, customer base		**Channels** Online, showrooms	
Cost structure Marketing, staffing, technology		**Revenue streams** Direct revenue from transactions		

Authors' evaluation and assessment of perspectives

Another darling of e-commerce conference presentations, Warby Parker is held up as a poster child for digitisation. And indeed, Warby Parker has been deft in building up a strong brand online and has demonstrated a lot of business acumen, even expanding successfully into brick-and-mortars. Nevertheless, it shouldn't be forgotten that Warby Parker also got the right market: until recently, opticians in the US earned a fortune off of the backs of their customers – it was an open invitation for e-commerce disruption and we're sat, popcorn and sodas in hand, watching the spectacle.

3.42 Wayfair – Or: Proof that furniture can be sold online

Key facts

Name: Wayfair, Inc.
Headquarters: Boston, USA
Total staff: 3.250
Global turnover 2015: US$2.3bn[273]
Founded in: 2002
Origins: Online pure player

Listed on the stock exchange since autumn 2014, Wayfair is a US online pure-play in furniture and home furnishings. Wayfair's story begins with two entrepreneurs who, in 2002, set up a fleet of vertically-integrated online shops in the segment approaching 270 in number and primarily operating on a competitive search optimisation strategy: barstools.com or everymirror.com are two examples.[274] In 2008, the duo switched and decided to set up one central shop in order to increase customer loyalty and reduce acquisition costs. The result, Wayfair, now brings together more than 10 million products which are dispatched using a network of 7,000 drop-shipping sellers.[275] As well as product sales in the shop, Wayfair also earns money auctioning off advertising space on its platform and by selling products through other retailers' web shops.[276] In 2015, it grew turnover by a whopping 71%,[277] and yet it continues to operate below break-even as its marketing costs remain very high. Following the 2015 end of its Australian business, Wayfair is active in five markets: USA, Canada, UK, Germany, and Austria.[278]

Positioning

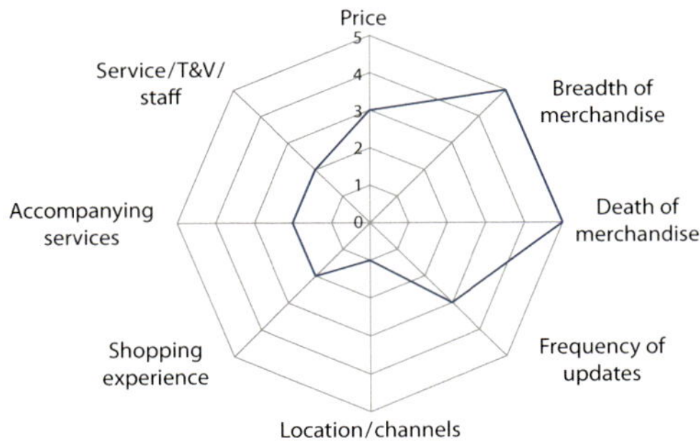

273 s2.q4cdn.com (as of March 2016)
274 www.businessinsider.com (as of March 2016)
275 www.forbes.com (as of March 2016)
276 www.internetretailer.com (as of March 2016)
277 excitingcommerce.de (as of March 2016)
278 investor.wayfair.com (as of March 2016)

Wayfair's key position is the selection of merchandise it offers. In terms of both the breadth and depth of its product mix it is, with 10 million listed items, streets ahead of the competition. This online pure player stocks over 3,400 different cushion and pillow cases, 12,000 table lamps, and 3,700 dining tables. Its state-of-the-art online shop also offers a shopping experience with a comparatively high degree of emotion.

Business model canvas				
Key partners Retailers and manufacturers, distribution and sales partners	**Key activities** Logistics, CRM, sourcing, platform **Key resources** Product mix, customers, brand	**Value proposition** Inspiring, easy online furniture shopping experience with lots of product choice.	**Customer relationships** Self-service **Channels** Online, mobile	**Customer segments** Core target-group: women, 30-65
Cost structure Marketing, technology, staffing		**Revenue streams** Transaction-dependent direct sales turnover		

Authors' evaluation and assessment of perspectives

Wayfair did not decide to look for finance from outside investors until a later point in its growth story and has now gone on a drive for further growth which shows little sign of turning into profit any time soon. Essentially, Wayfair is betting on an e-commerce breakthrough in home & living – and there are good reasons to enter into that wager. Nevertheless, harnessing this switch to online shopping successfully and getting long-term customer loyalty will depend on excellent performance, and we think that Wayfair's drop-shipping model is going to make it difficult to provide this excellence. Until the company has owned warehousing space of any notable amount, it will be hemmed in by this obstacle.

3.43 Williams-Sonoma – Is this what true omnichannel looks like?

Key facts

Name: Williams-Sonoma, Inc.
Headquarters: San Francisco, USA
Total staff: 28,100
Global turnover 2015: US$5bn[279]
Founded in: 1956
Origins: In-store retailer

Williams-Sonoma is specialised in the high-end furniture and home furnishings segment, operating both its eponymous retail brand and seven other merchandising chains such as Pottery Barn, Mark and Graham, and West Elm under its group structure. Founded in 1956, the company sells in a store network of over 620 locations in four countries,[280] over the internet (worldwide), and using mail order;[281] its catalogue is nevertheless less a channel and more a central plank in its advertising and content marketing strategy. Thanks to high levels of investment in e-commerce, the group is already booking more than half of its $5bn turnover on the internet,[282] making it into something of a poster-boy for multichannel strategists. Despite this, however, Williams-Sonoma posted 6.4% growth in online shopping for 2015, well below the market rate of 15%, a set-back the company attributes to increased competition in the furniture and home furnishings segment, which is seeing a rise in new-concept entrants and shifts to online on the part of existing in-store retailers.[283]

Positioning

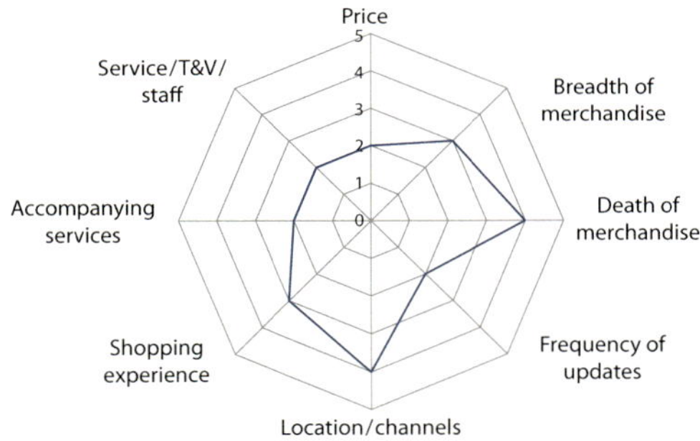

279 ir.williams-sonomainc.com (as of March 2016)
280 ir.williams-sonomainc.com (as of March 2016)
281 multichannelmerchant.com (as of March 2016)
282 www.internetretailer.com (as of March 2016)
283 www.internetretailer.com (as of March 2016)

Principally, Williams-Sonoma uses the breadth of its merchandise and diversity of its sales channels to position itself against the competition. In a market environment which is currently experiencing a sustained increase in competition – above all on the internet – Williams-Sonoma's high proportion of own-brand sales (85-90%[284]) and its strong identity are the aces up its sleeve; its proprietary approach makes its merchandise less interchangeable while its focus on quality and branding place it in a comparatively high-price category.

Business model canvas

Key partners		Value proposition		Customer segments
Key partners Suppliers, brands, advertisers	**Key activities** Sourcing, CRM, marketing **Key resources** Strong brand, real estate in prime locations	**Value proposition** Furniture, home furnishings, and kitchens with a design approach	**Customer relationships** Personal (in-store), Self-service (online) **Channels** Online, offline, catalogue, mobile	**Customer segments** Design-conscious customers who value high-quality products
Cost structure Personal, inventory, operations, marketing			**Revenue streams** Transaction-dependent direct sales turnover	

Authors' evaluation and assessment of perspectives

While there is no shortage of press reports about how WS is integrating sales channels to an ever higher degree, we have yet to understand what is actually going on here. At first glance, WS looks like a classic retail outfit which has recognised the potential in the new market and is growing with it. This is, however, mainly a function of vertical integration (e.g. its 90% own-brand share in furniture) and no panacea for struggling department stores. What is more, WS is now lacking new platforms posting strong growth, and is lucky in that formerly hyped online models such as OneKingsLane are currently in the publicity doldrums. This puts it out of immediate danger from online attackers, but doesn't make it into an example to be imitated by those in search of an e-commerce strategy. The lesson WS does provide is in how to extend the scope and reach of its brand and monetarise it well using the internet. Yet WS's enduring love of catalogues speaks volumes about its true nature.

284 multichannelmerchant.com (as of March 2016)

3.44 Windeln.de – When expansion stops being driven – and starts driving

Key facts

Name: Windeln.de GmbH
Headquarters: Munich, Germany
Total staff: over 400[285]
Global turnover 2015: €178.6m[286] (US$195.1m)
Founded in: 2010
Origins: Online pure player

With around 55,000 items and 800 brands, Windeln.de is Germany's largest online shop for baby products. This pure-play has a huge selection of consumables such as nappies (from where it gets its name: the German is Windeln) and one-off products such as prams and buggies, clothing, and toys. While it now has over one million active customers in its online shop,[287] the company recognises that recurring non-durables such as nappies is a low-margin segment and is concentrating on cross-selling activities with a view to maximising shopping basket sizes and profit.[288] Following impressive rates of growth in 2014 (100% year on year), Windeln.de and its shareholders – it's been on the stock exchange since May 2015 – have had to make do with 30% in 2015 and, for 2016, the company has already scaled back its whole-year growth forecast from 50% to 30% again. The reason behind this is, more than anything, the stagnating China business caused by changes to import rules in April 2016, which led uncertainty among Chinese consumers.[289] Windeln.de currently has operational activates in 10 countries.

Positioning

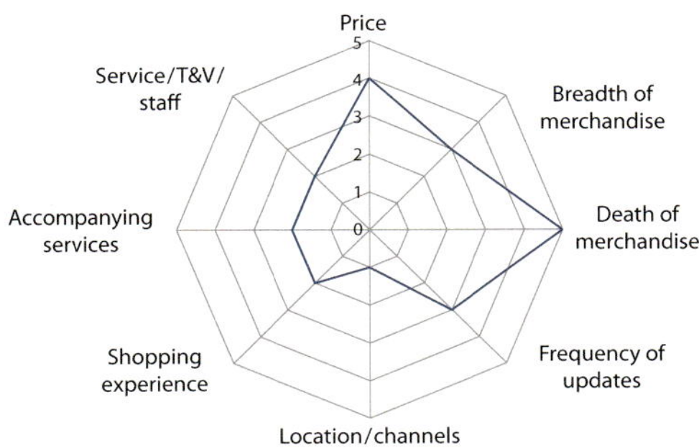

285 corporate.windeln.de (as of March 2016)
286 corporate.windeln.de (as of March 2016)
287 www.finanznachrichten.de (as of March 2016)
288 neuhandeln.de (as of March 2016)
289 www.internetworld.de (as of March 2016)

Similarly to Amazon, Windeln.de is positioned on price and offering: its shop has the broadest, deepest selection of baby products in Germany, while its attractive prices are achieved by shipping large packs of non-durables, keeping prices per individual item low. In terms of service and shopping experience, Windeln.de is solidly middle-of-the-road and not particularly distinguishable from its competitors.

<table>
<tr><th colspan="5">Business model canvas</th></tr>
<tr><td rowspan="2">Key partners
Brands and manufacturers, parcels services, affiliates</td><td>Key activities
Sourcing, platform, analytics, CRM</td><td rowspan="2">Value proposition
Ordering baby products such as nappies from home at a good price.</td><td>Customer relationships
Self-service</td><td rowspan="2">Customer segments
Mothers, pregnant women, and young families</td></tr>
<tr><td>Key resources
Brand, online expertise, logistics network</td><td>Channels
Online, mobile</td></tr>
<tr><td colspan="2">Cost structure
Platform, staffing, marketing</td><td colspan="3">Revenue streams
Transaction-dependent direct sales turnover</td></tr>
</table>

Authors' evaluation and assessment of perspectives

When we need an exemplary pure-play, we are always happy to cite Windeln.de as an unqualified success. It has very high levels of operational capability, as proven by the favourable developments of its main KPIs, and two major problems: its dependency on the Chinese market and its current growth doldrums. The question we are asking ourselves is whether its niche is too niche: the bottom line is that there may be no reason for customers to continue ordering their baby and toddler products on Windeln.de when Amazon has got them, too. What is more, the name ("nappies.de") prevents them from expanding too far into segments for older children; as such, they are facing the same issue as other German pure players with overly-defined names: notebooksbilliger.de ("cheapernotebooks.de") and buch.de ("book.de"). It will be interesting to see the effect of Amazon's own-brand strategy, Amazon Elements, on this part of the market in 2016 and beyond.

3.45 Wish – Mobile junkshop aiming to become the next Walmart

Key facts

Name: ContextLogic, Inc.
Headquarters: San Francisco, USA
Total staff: 900[290]
Global turnover 2015: n. a.
Founded in: 2011
Origins: Mobile-first online pure player

Wish is a mobile marketplace application focussing on fashion, cosmetics, and accessories allowing (usually no-name) Chinese retailers to sell directly to end-consumers worldwide; products in the store are sold at a substantial mark-down and Wish takes care of all marketing. This mobile-led marketplace started life in 2011 as a wish list application based on product feeds from other online shops; working on the affiliate model, Wish then sent customers on to the respective retailers.[291] Today, however, purchases are made directly on Wish.com and manufactures/retailers dispatch the products, leading to average delivery times of two to three weeks. The shopping app with a strong design resemblance to Pinterest describes itself as being very tech-driven, with proprietary algorithms said to position products in the catalogue, individually price them per customer, and optimise marketing measures in social networks automatically;[292] advertising spend on Facebook alone is said to be $100m annually.[293] According to its own reporting, Wish has hundreds of millions of customers who already buy goods to a low billions value[294] and earns around 12-15% commission.[295] There is no small amount of controversy in view of the fact that the majority of the products on the app are counterfeit or arrive damaged.

Positioning

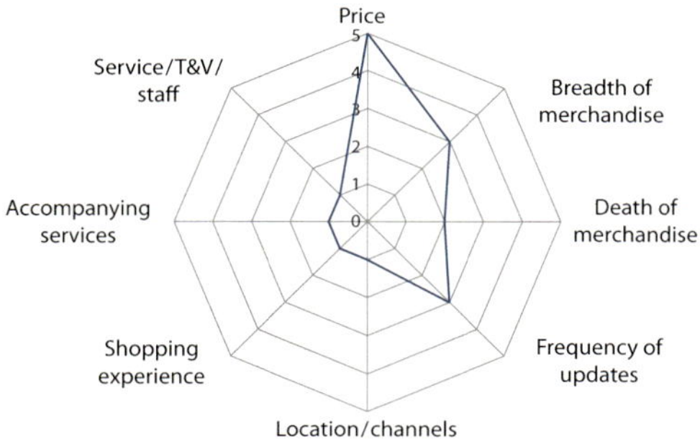

290 www.recode.net (as of March 2016)
291 www.recode.net (as of March 2016)
292 www.bloomberg.com (as of March 2016)
293 www.recode.net (as of March 2016)
294 techcrunch.com (as of March 2016)
295 www.recode.net (as of March 2016)

Wish's USP is quite clearly limited almost entirely to price. Almost all articles are available for under $25 and some clothing retails at $2-$5. As such, Wish's approach is similar to Primark, which focuses on a very young, primarily female target group. Complementary service and shopping experiences are rudimentary, and often, goods reaches customers weeks later damaged or in the wrong size. Wish is continually expanding the breadth of its product mix.

Business model canvas				
Key partners Manufacturers (mainly Chinese)	**Key activities** Marketing, algorithms and recommendation engines **Key resources** Mobile application, algorithms	**Value proposition** Extremely cheap products direct from maker/merchant	**Customer relationships** Self-service **Channels** Mobile, online	**Customer segments** Young, primarily female, and highly price-sensitive customers with little interest in either brand or quality
Cost structure Technology, marketing		**Revenue streams** Commission of 15% on all sales		

Authors' evaluation and assessment of perspectives

Wish has a business model which we find, simply put, astounding. Although there is no shortage of product reviews exposing serious quality issues, Wish manages to use the sales price to – so it seems – banish any last remaining thread of rationality from the personal purchasing process. Or, to put it more kindly: the price is the only thing that counts. Whether this model can be scaled up is another question, of course, but this kind of direct transaction with Chinese manufacturers is, if you ask us, just the beginning. It won't take long for Amazon et al. to start offering similar propositions and this will overcome consumers' inhibitions about buying from far afield. As such, it's an impressive model.

3.46 Xiaomi – China's hardware and technology powerhouse

Key facts

Name: Xiaomi Inc.
Headquarters: Beijing, China
Total staff: 8000
Global turnover 2015: US$20.5bn (estimate)[296]
Founded in: 2010
Origins: Hardware/software manufacturer

Xiaomi is Asia's biggest manufacturer of smart devices and is expanding increasingly into the internet of things with the aim of positioning its smartphones as the central device from which others will be steered.[297] To achieve this aim, Xiaomi is attempting to get the young Chinese consumers – who are the principal customers for its smartphones – to kit out their first apartments or houses with its proprietary digital devices from the get-go; the ecosystem based around its smartphones has its own Android section with a matching app-store. Xiaomi only sells through its own-brand channels – primarily its online shop and a limited number of stationary stores. In 2015, it sold around 70 million phones globally[298] in its domestic market, China, as well as in India, Brazil, and other developing and emerging economies.[299] In view of its rapid economic growth, India is a particular focus for the company, which generates the lion's share of its estimated $20.5-billion sales turnover with smartphones, tablets, and wearables.[300]

Positioning

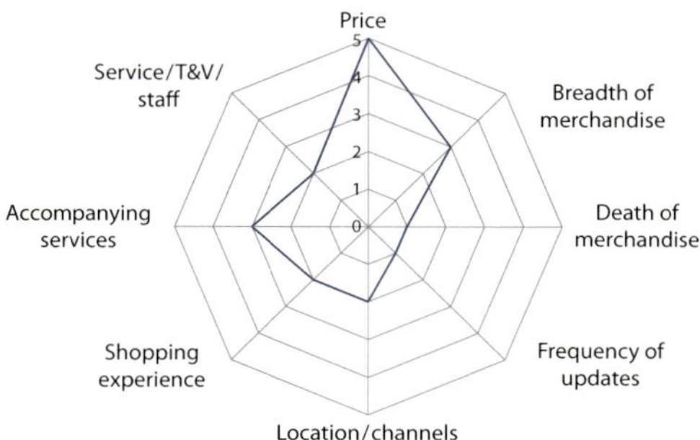

Xiaomi's position is defined principally by low prices for high-quality smartphones and other devices such as its own-brand fitness tracker. Retailing at between $100 and $300

296 www.forbes.com (as of March 2016)
297 stratechery.com (as of March 2016)
298 fortune.com (as of March 2016)
299 www.businessinsider.de (as of March 2016)
300 www.forbes.com (as of March 2016)

(USD), its phones run its own Android operating system with an app store and internet payment and gaming services, thus extending the breadth of its product range. Its channel positioning is very clearly that of online direct sales.

<table>
<tr><th colspan="10">Business model canvas</th></tr>
<tr><td colspan="2" rowspan="2">Key partners
Foxconn, manufacturers and brands</td><td colspan="2">Key activities
Manufacturing, software development</td><td colspan="2" rowspan="2">Value proposition
High quality and high usability for a low price</td><td colspan="2">Customer relationships
Fan culture, self-service, some limited in-store operations</td><td colspan="2" rowspan="2">Customer segments
Young Chinese consumers (connected spenders)</td></tr>
<tr><td colspan="2">Key resources
Brand, data, software (Android Fork), app store</td><td colspan="2">Channels
Online, offline (collection/accessories only)</td></tr>
<tr><td colspan="5">Cost structure
Research & development, production</td><td colspan="5">Revenue streams
Takings from hardware, software, and services</td></tr>
</table>

Authors' evaluation and assessment of perspectives

At first glance, Xiaomi looks like a potentially powerful gatekeeper in a world thus far dominated by Alibaba, Amazon, et al.; if nothing else, its leading valuation among non-listed companies always manages to draw attention to Xiaomi. Nevertheless, what we feel is lacking is a genuine lock-in effect: China's growth story is nearing a turn, domestic competitors Huawei and OnePlus are growing faster, and the devices themselves are simply not innovative enough to stake out the kind of independent ecosystem that Apple has managed to set up since 2007. At the same time, we share investors' confidence that the company will continue to be able to offer new services on the basis of the platform it has now: this means additional business.

3.47 Zalando – Internet retailer or technology company?

Key facts
Name: Zalando SE
Headquarters: Berlin, Germany
Total staff: 9,987[301]
Global turnover 2015: €3bn (US$3.3bn)
Founded in: 2008
Origins: Online pure player

Until recently, Zalando was "just" a German fashion retailer with impressive sales figures, 1,500 brand cooperations, and one of the most successful IPOs of European e-commerce history. Now, however, Zalando is selling itself as an altogether more ambitious project with the aim of establishing an eco-system around the entire e-commerce value chain. Zalando wants to become a diverse fashion platform on which brands have their own tailored shops, getting relevant data and access to advertising services. Zalando also wants to enable same-day delivery as part of its Fulfilment by Zalando initiative[302] while apps such as Fleek and Movmnt generate independent concepts in the mobile segment offering services such as direct delivery from manufacturers to consumers[303]. Despite the intensive technology investments these plans require, the company managed to build on 2014 – the year in which it first came out of the red in EBIT terms – and reach a result of €107.5m in 2015 with a margin on 3.6%. Outside of the German-speaking countries, Zalando is also present in another 13 European markets, posting sales growth to €1.2bn with a total turnover of just under €3bn.[304]

Positioning

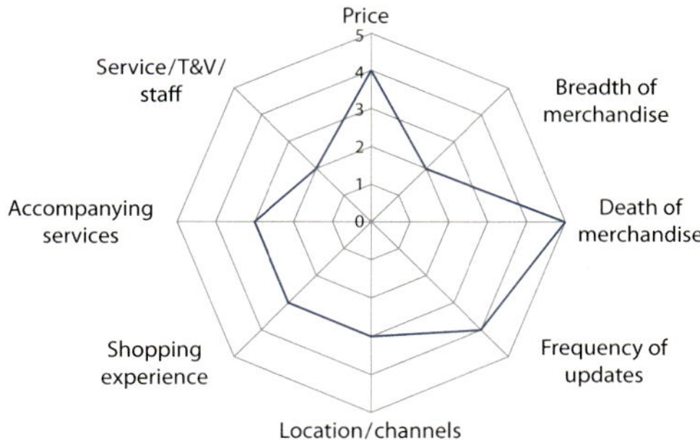

301 corporate.zalando.de (as of March 2016)
302 excitingcommerce.de (as of March 2016)
303 The strategy behind the Movmnt app
304 excitingcommerce.de (as of March 2016)

Zalando spent many years making massive investments in marketing and creating a strong retail brand; it positioned itself primarily on the depth of its merchandise in shoes and clothing, as well as its additional services (free delivery and returns, 100 days' right of return, curated shopping) and, not infrequently, better prices than competitors such as Otto.

Business model canvas

Key partners	Key activities	Value proposition	Customer relationships	Customer segments
1,500 brand manufacturers, affiliates, logistics, investors	Analytics, CRM, updating merchandise	Big selection, easy ordering/returns, good prices	Self-service	Mass market (mainly women)
	Key resources		**Channels**	
	Data, internal experts		Online, mobile	

Cost structure	Revenue streams
Marketing, technology, service (incl. logistics with 50% rate of returns)	Transaction-dependent direct sales turnover; in the future, seller services and commission on marketplace

Authors' evaluation and assessment of perspectives

We're surprised by Zalando. After its very strong start in 2009 and 2010, a lot of time has since been invested in professionalising the company and it has, today, reached a scale that makes it one of Germany's, indeed Europe's, top e-commerce companies. It's initial public offering put a lot of money into its coffers, and we're sure that Zalando will know just what to do with it to make its structures even more efficient and, above all, to cut even more costs. We are therefore of the opinion that the stock market's expectations *vis-à-vis* profitability are entirely feasible. What we will be interested to see, however, is if the company returns to old form with its expensive advertising activities (throttled in the run-up to the IPO); if so, then we'd have another chance to observe the "Zalando Effect" of 2009-2011. Its curated shopping subsidiary, launched in 2014, is another one to watch, and we will be interested to see whether Zalando manages to anchor relevant – i. e. turnover-relevant – innovations in a market dominated by quarterly reports. Zalando's transformation to a technology company began in 2013, and thus far, very few others are making such consistent efforts to build up real tech-led structures, as shown by the company's acquisition of platform outfits such as Tradebyte in early 2016. In other words: keep up the good work, Zalando!

3.48 Zappos – Amazon dreams of shoes and fashion

Key facts

Name: Zappos.com , Inc.
Headquarters: Las Vegas, USA
Total staff: 1,600[305]
Global turnover 2015: n. a.
Founded in: 1999
Origins: Online pure player

Zappos is one of the world's largest online shoe sellers, listing over 59,000 footwear articles[306] as well as fashion, jewellery, bags, and accessories. Founded in 1999, the company was quick to take on in-store concepts for customers – and successful in drawing turnover away from them, pushing e-commerce forward with considerable energy into difficult, then hotly-disputed product category terrain. Zappos has to this day enjoyed particular success with its corporate culture, based on a strong service focus and effective social media and PR – and used to distinguish itself from its competitors. Its holocracy structure remains unique in a company of its size,[307] and one third of all staff are in service, guaranteeing continuing customer contact. In 2009, Zappos was bought by Amazon for $1.2 billion,[308] turning over around $2 billion annually according to expert estimates.[309] After shutting down sales in Canada, Zappos today is present on the US market only.[310]

Positioning

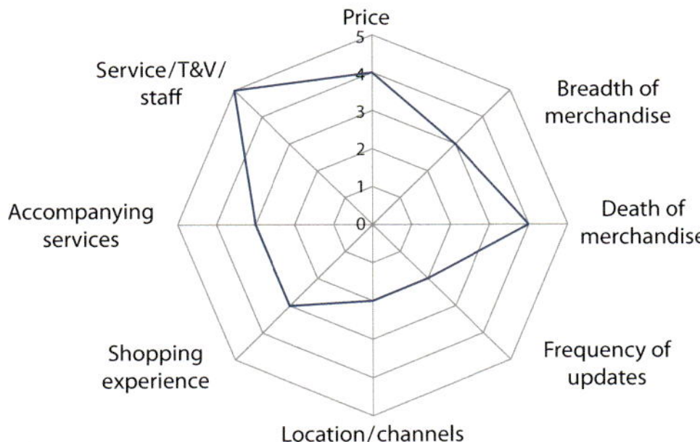

Zappos has focussed strongly on customer service, making itself a name with exceptional strategies such as giving call-centre service staff as much time per customer as they think

305 www.businessinsider.de (as of March 2016)
306 www.zappos.com (as of March 2016)
307 www.forbes.com (as of March 2016)
308 www.zappos.com (as of March 2016)
309 www.forbes.com (as of March 2016)
310 www.zappos.com (as of March 2016)

necessary: it gained media attention with hour-long calls, for example,[311] demonstrating its customer-friendliness. It also positions itself on breadth and depth of merchandise and on competitive pricing.

Business model canvas

Key partners	Key activities	Value proposition	Customer relationships	Customer segments
Amazon, brands, ad networks	Sourcing, marketing, service	Very large selection of shoes and fashion products online at a good price and with fantastic service	Self-service with excellent customer service	Mass market
	Key resources		**Channels**	
	Amazon, customer relationships, brand		Online, mobile	
Cost structure			**Revenue streams**	
Sales costs, marketing, technology			Direct revenue from transactions	

Authors' evaluation and assessment of perspectives

It is a matter of great sadness to us that the Amazon take-over has utterly extinguished the energy that Zappos was bringing to the market. It was once a very promising technical and social experiment – and is now a boring run-of-the-mill online shop with no discernible strategy.

311 www.zappos.com (as of March 2016)

3.49 Zooplus – Successful niche shop with potential for growth

Key facts

Name: zooplus AG
Headquarters: Munich, Germany
Total staff: 267[312]
Global turnover 2015: €742m[313] (US$810.6m)
Founded in: 1999
Origins: Online pure player

For years now, this retailer of pet products has been posting strong sales growth,[314] expanding in the 2015 financial year by an impressive 30% on an overall turnover of€742m.[315] With its range of 8,000 products, zooplus is active in over 30 European countries and, given the €25bn value placed on the animal companion market, there seems little reason to expect an end to growth anytime soon.[316] One driver seems to be the company's effective customer retention processes[317] on regular orders of recurring requirements. In a way similar to Amazon, zooplus passes on savings from internal streamlining and economies of scale to its customers, allowing it to pull away from the competition;[318] this strategy seems to be having the desired effect, too, as zooplus is very frequently rated very highly in customer satisfaction surveys.[319]

Positioning

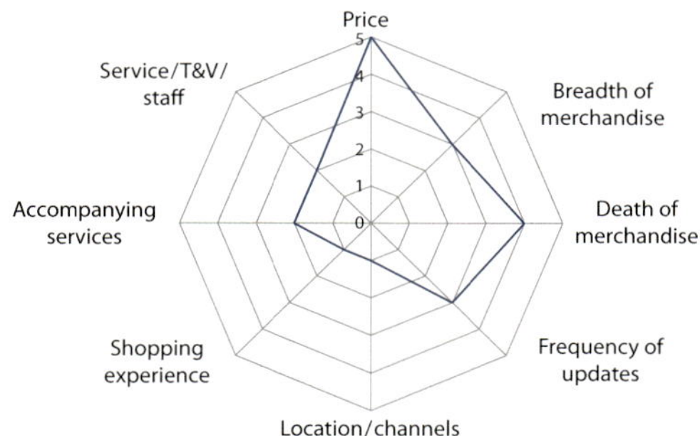

312 investors.zooplus.com (as of March 2016)
313 investors.zooplus.com (as of March 2016)
314 de.statista.com (as of March 2016)
315 investors.zooplus.com (as of March 2016)
316 investors.zooplus.com (as of March 2016)
317 www.internetretailer.com (as of March 2016)
318 www.finanzen.net (as of March 2016)
319 www.haufe.de (as of March 2016)

zooplus' strategy is based on attractive prices and depth of merchandise. The more it grows, the lower the prices it can offer its customers – and its drive for growth has been successful thus far. It is the largest specialist animal companion retailer in Europe, offering 8,000 products, and invests in content marketing, with a corporate blog and popular forum for pet owners.

Business model canvas

Key partners	Key activities	Value proposition	Customer relationships	Customer segments
Manufacturers, online advertising platforms	Logistics, CRM, platform	Selection, price, service	Self-service	Pet owners
	Key resources		**Channels**	
	Brand, online competence		Online, mobile	
Cost structure		**Revenue streams**		
Logistics, IT, staffing*		Transaction-dependent direct sales turnover		

* http://investors.zooplus.com/downloads/IR-Presentation_November2014.pdf

Authors' evaluation and assessment of perspectives

Simply put, zooplus is one of the most impressive pure-plays yet. The idea of selling pet food and accessories online – and the business model behind it – was first had in 1999, i. e. around the time that many of today's biggest online pure players were set up or expanded rapidly. In our view, zooplus' aggressive price positioning is a concern as, with Amazon entering this segment in the future, trying to win on price will become increasingly difficult. On the other hand, however, we think that the size of zooplus and its relatively simple shareholder structure will not only allow it to shake up the segment in 2016 and beyond, but also to drive consolidation with competitors who are likely to be very receptive to strategic tie-ups.

3.50 Zulily (QVC) – Another flash-sale flash in the pan

Key facts

Name: zulily, Inc.
Headquarters: Seattle, USA
Total staff: 3000
Global turnover 2015: US$1.4bn
Founded in: 2010
Origins: Online pure player

Zulily is a flash sale retailer aimed primarily at young mothers and offering a family-orientated product range spread across clothes, shoes, home furnishings, and toys.[320] It runs offers for up to 72 hours and only buys in from suppliers and dispatches products to its customers in more than 100 countries once orders have been placed.[321] For a long time, this particularity has allowed Zulily to produce very good offers at a very profitable rate; by the same token, this M. O. entails long delivery times of 14 to 18 days.[322] As competition hots up, Zulily has realised that this represents a serious brake on growth as customers don't return and not enough new ones can be acquired at an acceptable cost. As a result, the Seattle pure-player is now setting up its own logistics infrastructure and will be stocking inventory with a view to slashing delivery times. Its 72% growth in 2014 gave way to 17% in 2015; listed on the stock exchange since 2013, Zulily was acquired by tele-shopping company QVC in October 2015 for $2.4 billion.[323]

Positioning

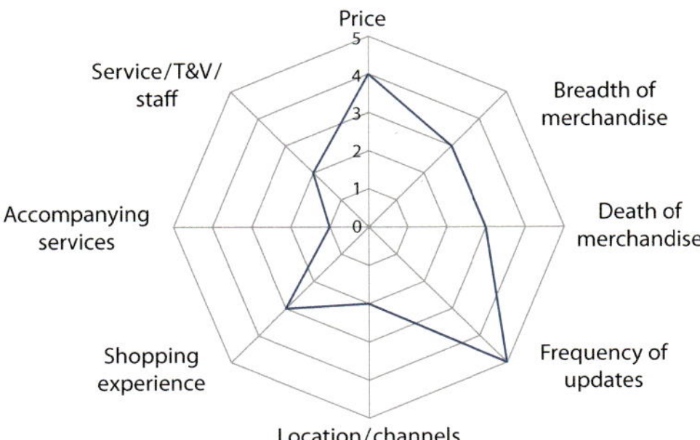

As a flash sales model, Zulily's primary USP is low prices and frequent updates to merchandise. It has new offers daily and they are only available for a maximum of 72 hours, cre-

320 mcdn.zulilyinc.com (as of March 2016)
321 www.zulily.com (as of March 2016)
322 www.wsj.com (as of March 2016)
323 excitingcommerce.de (as of March 2016)

ating a sense of urgency and functioning as an excellent conversion driver. The shopping experience is predicated on curiosity, but service is deficient, with a no-returns policy; only damaged goods can be reported for a replacement.

Business model canvas

Key partners	Key activities	Value proposition	Customer relationships	Customer segments
Brands, manufacturers, advertiser networks, QVC	Sourcing, CRM	Constant stream of new offers for young mothers at a strong discount	Self-service	Young mothers, families
	Key resources Customer base		**Channels** Online, mobile	
Cost structure Marketing, technology, infrastructure expansion		**Revenue streams** Direct revenue from transactions		

Authors' evaluation and assessment of perspectives

Rather than going into detail on shopping clubs again (see our evaluations of other players in this segment), we'll cut to the quick: Zulily is a looser in this niche because it has never found a way to create organic customer loyalty. Too bad!

4 Strategy in E-Commerce

There's a saying that periodically does the rounds among military strategists: "Armies are always preparing to fight the last war." It's a malaise of which history has no shortage of examples. At the beginning of the First World War, for example, the French assumed that, as in the Franco-Prussian War four decades previous, daring moves to outflank the enemy would still be the key to victory – and ignored the fact that the machine gun had been invented, sending thousands of their troops over the top and into the line of fire (famously, in bright red trousers). When these offensives failed, the generals' answer was simply to up the number of soldiers, not to question the strategy.

Similarly, in the interwar period, French forces had indeed learned one belated lesson from the Great War – that strong fortifications and big guns were of more use than infantry – but overlooked another development from the final months of that conflict: motorised armoured forces, i.e. tanks. The result was poured into concrete in the shape of the mighty forts of the Maginot Line, the best of their kind ever built and impossible to take in a full frontal assault. Yet tanks can move; fortresses cannot. And so the battles of 1940 happened elsewhere and many of their gigantic guns never even fired a shot.

The lesson of this is that the advantage is often with the attacker because the defender is generally preparing for a re-run of previous encounters and is investing resources accordingly – even when indications about the coming conflict run to the contrary. That's why the American navy was still building battleships at the outbreak of the Second World War (the Japanese, of course, had specialised in aircraft carriers) and why military spending worldwide on all kinds of hardware from tanks to nuclear missiles still dwarfs the sums spent on cyber defence today, despite clear evidence that the vulnerabilities future attackers will exploit are more electronic than metallic. As early as the 1990s, the first strategy think-tanks were already positing scenarios in which enemy powers use media disinformation and irregular forces to destabilise regions and countries without actually declaring "war" or sending in the tanks, yet convincing answers to this new mode of conflict remain notorious by their absence.

In other words, the strategic situation changes much faster than military planners' ways of thinking, and so the attacker has the initial advantage – especially if it doesn't look and act like previous aggressors.

It doesn't take much imagination (although perhaps a momentarily misplaced sense of proportion) to transfer this lesson to our own, far less deadly area of human endeavour. In Chapter 1, we told the story of how e-commerce rose out of nowhere to shake up the whole retail market and challenge existing business models – and showed how difficult it has been for established players to get a grasp on what is happening – before we, in Chapter 2, examined in detail how e-commerce changes (and, in some cases, revolutionises) the day-to-day work of people in retail organisations. In Chapter 3, we looked at the ways in which the e-commerce environment affects various companies specifically and made forecasts about market participants based on current developments.

What these case studies show as much as anything is that, although the attackers often have the element of surprise on their side, there remains a difference between simple shock tactics and genuine strategic superiority. Some challengers launch a lightning offensive out of left field which catches established businesses off guard and leaves them quaking in their boots – only to beat a hasty retreat when it turns out that they can't hold the ground they've taken. New shopping club/couponing entrants such as vente-privée.com and Groupon, for example, were briefly seen as all-conquering menaces to retail – and have now been cut back down to size or, as in the case of Fab.com., disappeared more or less entirely.

Yet while established retailers may be able to withstand this kind of temporary onslaught, hunkering down during the initial bombardment and then emerging once the smoke has cleared, other newcomers on the battlefield are far more dangerous. Instead of awe-inspiring displays of strength and lightning attacks, they are concentrating on changing the rules of engagement and the topography of the theatre itself to the point where the war will have been won without anyone realising it. In this chapter, we take a closer look at how the real challengers in the age of e-commerce are quite literally redrawing the map of retail – and, as they do so, of other sectors too.

Regardless of whether you are in the embattled B2C commerce sector or observing the clashes from an area of comparative safety:

Once you've finished reading, you'll realise why what is happening in e-commerce is of importance to how much of the economy as a whole will come to work in the coming decades.

If you, at any point, catch yourself thinking that this all sounds a bit outlandish and that Amazon, for all its current size and wealth, is unlikely to go for and topple an insurance giant or a major bank in the near future, then just remember two things: on Amazon's twentieth birthday, Jeff Bezos went on record as saying that, as far as he was concerned, "today is still Day One for the internet" (note that he said "internet" and not just "e-commerce"); Bezos also originally toyed with the idea of calling Amazon "relentless.com".

There's no reason to become demoralised, however: forewarned, as the military strategists say, is forearmed. The problem, as these same strategists will tell you, is that those doing the actual fighting don't always hear the warnings. French statesman Georges Clemenceau, looking back on World War One, put it more succinctly: "War is too serious a matter to entrust to military men". In the coming years, for many businesses, this pithy morsel will translate as: "Tech is too important to be left to the IT department".

Continued success – survival, even – for companies in many areas in the coming years will depend on stepping back from the tactics of day-to-day clashes and having a high-level strategic rethink. It's just as well to make sure you're not fighting the last war, because this is very much the next one.

4.1 The GAFA Economy

Google is a search engine, Apple makes phones, Facebook runs a social network, and Amazon sells stuff to people – right? Yes, but even with a correct answer, the wrong question remains the wrong question. For while these may be the things that the four companies in their present form started life doing, they are neither the only things they do nor, more importantly, the key things they do.

We could now spend several pages listing all of the various activities in which each of these four concerns are involved; an exhaustive account of Amazon alone would make a mini-chapter. Yet the crucial element of their approach is actually fundamental enough to be phrased in five words: they control access to consumers. The problem in understanding Google, Apple, Facebook, and Amazon – "GAFA" – and in responding to them correctly is that they are still viewed primarily as service providers, manufacturers, and retailers, rather than as the brokers they have in reality become.

	Google	Apple	Facebook	Amazon
TELECOM & IT	Fiber	Apple Sim	WhatsApp	Cloud Drive
HEALTH	Calico	HealthKit	Move	Marketplace
RETAIL	Shopping Express	iBeacon	Facebook "Buy" Button	Grocery Delivery
ENERGY & UTILITIES	Smart Home	Solar Power	Internet.org Project	Fulfillment by Amazon
MEDIA & ENTERTAINMENT	Play	iTunes Radio	Oculus	Gamers Video Platform
FINANICALS	Wallet	Apple Pay	Friend-to-Friend Payment	Payments API
MOBILITY, TRAVEL & LEISURE	Car	CarPlay	Messenger + Uber Integration	Media App for Connected Cars

Fig. 4.1: Various industry activities of Google, Apple, Facebook and Amazon
Source: http://zurumnewsdigest.blogspot.de/2015/07/disruptive-innovation-gafanomics-and.html

The attempt to grasp GAFA business models and their effects on the economy splits commentators into two diametrically opposed camps: while one group focusses on classic business theory – above all profit, and GAFA's seeming disregard for it – the other declares the old rules dead and sees GAFA in a never-ending spiral of growth in which puny margins are nothing but a diversion. Trying to synthesise between these two extremes is like trying to get a square peg into a round hole and is, inasmuch, the Business Studies equivalent of the never-ending dispute between Keynesian and Classical economists. The latter fundamentally believe in Say's Law (that supply automatically generates demand) and therefore in laissez-faire management of the economy; the former see the role of the state in regulating markets to manage supply and demand.

Although their conclusions are utterly opposed, Classical and Keynesian economists by no means disagree on everything; quite to the contrary, both share a joint of understanding of many of the cause-and-effect mechanisms at work in the economy. Yet their models are nevertheless built on completely opposing premises and churn out quite contradictory recommendations; as such, there can never be an understanding between them. Decisions taken by regulatory institutions, especially central banks, can never be both Classical and Keynesian – and this becomes as clear as day in times of economic crisis.

Similarly, when business specialists discuss Amazon's sky-high growth and low-low profits, it becomes impossible to ignore the gaping fault-line running between "traditionalists" and "evangelists".

One analyst's lack of earnings is another's investment in the future; by extension, one commentator will see Amazon as a form of glorified pyramid scheme while another has it pegged as, all things told, the only stock worth keeping hold of. Just as we are in no position to end two hundred years of economic disagreement with a synthesis of Keynes and Hayek that suits everyone, it is not for us to say who is right about GAFA: perhaps the whole house of cards will come crashing down one day when everyone realises that these conglomerates are hopeless in investment terms; by the same token, perhaps these companies will keep increasing their rate of growth to the point where every other investment opportunity has been consigned to the garbage heap of business history? Who knows? What we can say with certainty, however, is that this debate between profits-naysayers and growth-advocates will continue – and continue unresolved – because there are two fundamentally different ways of viewing the world of business at play here.

When is a business a platform?

What can really help us to understand GAFA better is move away from this polarised dispute and look at them outside of the usual business frameworks. What if, for example, we experiment with viewing GAFA as economic institutions rather than market participants? Online marketing expert Florian Heinemann (see interview in Chapter 5) has, for example, compared "GAFAnomics" to the financial markets: in finance a small number of banks worldwide controls a central value – money – which, in the "GAFAnomy", is access to consumers. Assuming this equation holds for a moment, the clever thing to do as a business is to find a niche within this system which builds on its structures and exploit it rather than trying to compete with it: i.e. being Goldman Sachs rather than, say, the Argentinian government. Viewing e-commerce from the GAFAnomics perspective explains why companies which offer curated shopping or WhatsApp buys may be onto something whereas those trying to compete with GAFA on their own terms are being ground down.

Phrasing this change of perspective by referring to GAFA as platforms makes it sound much less like a fascinating but laxly-moderated university economics seminar and more like genuine professional discussion; but essentially, this GAFA-as-institutions equation is what people mean when they say:

"Amazon is a platform, not a business".

Platforms, after all, make money, but not on the same terms as those who use them (look at the companies who run stock markets). Talking about platforms also frees up discussion from the kind of apocalyptic pall which tends to fall over discussions of GAFA as untouchable monopolies intent on running all other business out of the market and enslaving us all: Yahoo and Ebay, after all, are platforms – platforms which were incredibly powerful at the turn of the Millennium – and within a few years, Uber, Alibaba, and even Zalando may have joined the ranks of GAFA (even displacing one of its current initials in the process).

None of this will be of much comfort to business models in the line of fire, of course: in fact, it robs them of all hope, because even if one or more of the GAFA companies disappears tomorrow, structural changes in favour of platforms mean that others will rise to take their place. This is the key change in the internet economy between the Dot-Com years and now: in the 2000s, many new companies were, for all the hype around them, somewhat conservative, focussing on making improvements against competitors and relying on their product, not a sales team, to take them forward; today's wave of companies coming out of Silicon Valley is radical and on a mission to stake out as much ground as possible, as fast as possible in new areas, regardless of whether their product is genuinely market-ready – in some cases, indeed, regardless of their product. Instead of trying to improve on the competition, they are looking to remove the competition as early as possible. They see themselves as being in a sprint, not a marathon; they know that the GAFA economy only needs a certain number of platforms. From Uber's point of view, UGAFA might work, but too many letters spoil the alphabet soup, so there's certainly no room for an "L for Lyft". Concurrently, WhatsApp is looking to add a W to GAFA, and Viber knows that there can be no place for its V in the acronym, too. That Google has restructured as Alphabet shows that it has understood this perfectly: if there should one day be no place for a G anymore, the newly-formed conglomerate will simply fire off other letters standing for other platforms in its portfolio until another one sticks.

GAFA: a dog-eat-dog world

In each sector, the winner takes all – but it's not always the early bird which catches the worm, rather the one which is most aggressive in staking out the territory on which it can look for it. This is where the hunger in young tech start-ups comes from, where the side-lining of profit and the willingness to expand first and think later are anchored. It can currently be observed in Europe in the food delivery sector, for example: the idea of delivering food from restaurants to people's homes is nothing new – ask New Yorkers – but hadn't really caught on in cities such as London, Paris, and Berlin. Yet as rental prices shoot up, kitchen sizes go down, and working hours increase across the continent, there is no reason it shouldn't: an entire flock of young tech-birds such as Foodora, Lieferando, and Deliveroo has now caught the scent of a worm and is pecking at the ground for it – knowing that, in all likelihood, only one of them will be around to eat it in a few years' time. What this battle will mean for restaurants' margins, for supermarkets, food manufacturers, and, most of all, for existing providers of take-away food remains unclear, but they are all equally unlikely to come out of the mêlée completely unscathed.

So how should restaurateurs, supermarket bosses, and food producers – or indeed stakeholders in many other sectors such as banking and insurance or the automotive industry – be preparing for GAFAnomics? Clearly, there is no easy answer; there's not even a difficult one. There are, however, three perspectives from which existing positions need to be examined:

1) Does our business model make sense in a GAFA world?

2) When does risk management become a risk in itself?

3) Can we find a niche in the GAFA structure?

The answers to these questions will look different depending on where the company asking them stands in the value chain. A farmer's business model always makes fundamental sense because people need to eat food and someone needs to grow it; producers of high-end ready-meals may find themselves in trouble, however, if consumers get used to ordering in expensive restaurant food. There are no hard-and-fast answers, though, because the topography of segments which have not yet had the "GAFA treatment" is still unclear: making cars may, in the long-run, prove less profitable than it has been to date if the most important item in them becomes proprietary software made by Google or Uber. Whatever the industry, companies with business models which start to look shaky need to either try to create platforms themselves (and invest like hungry start-ups to do so) or start buying shares in the emerging champions.

Sound risky? It is. Yet efforts to manage – i.e. minimise – risks in a classic corporate way are actually risks in themselves. Or as Mark Zuckerberg puts it:

> *"In a world that is changing really quickly,*
> *the only strategy that is guaranteed to fail is not taking risks."*

Companies whose answer to GAFAnomics is to set up "innovation task forces" and tell them to come up with "disruptive ideas" while paying them full salaries (and yet limiting their budgets to annexes in the annual statement) are taking no risks at all – and therefore taking the risk of total irrelevance at a later date.

On the surface, smaller auxiliary organisations such as agencies and service providers are in the enviable position of being able to cut ties to sinking ships and sail towards more stable prospects. Many who advise ill-fated projects at big legacy organisations have the gift of an outsiders' perspective and can spot futility and lazy thinking a mile off. Nonetheless, tugs cannot manoeuvre tankers which are underway at high speed and many agencies are forced into projects they have openly criticised because these projects nonetheless remain what the client wants and what the client is willing to pay for: for these companies, GAFA is about having the courage of their convictions – and about choosing the right moment to cut loose so as to avoid the twin perils of going under and being lost at sea.

In the following sections, we will take a closer look at the strategy of various incidents of GAFAnomics, starting with the most advanced: Amazon's effect on retail to date and its potential to revolutionise other sectors, looking at the failure of established retailers to grasp the strategic lesson in time, before we move onto a detailed examination of a retail segment currently in full flux: home furnishings. We will then examine one of the many markets which, in our view, is long due a "GAFAlution", the insurance sector, and close with a detailed look at the weaponry of the e-commerce war, tech, and what it can tell us about the wider problems of strategic procurement in face of the changes about to sweep wide swathes of the economy.

4.2 to amazon [verb, syn.: to buy, to purchase]

It's 11:59pm on 24th December 2015 as, on a porch somewhere on the outskirts of San Antonio, Texas, a courier hands the last Amazon Super Prime delivery of the day over to an anxious customer and in so doing – and quite probably without realising it – writes business history.

For the customer, this delivery guy is about as close to Santa as anyone will ever get.

Granted, his eight reindeer look more like an eight-cylinder truck engine, and he doesn't have much time for milk and cookies (after all, Saint Nic is looking to get back to the depot and finally clock off for the festive season), but he does come bearing gifts in the middle of the night before Christmas.

It has certainly been a long day, both for our suburban Kris Kringle and for his employers. On 24th December 2015, Amazon Super Prime breaks its own record for single-day sales. Super Prime, in case you're wondering, is the comparative of

Prime, the programme introduced ten years ago to offer Amazon customers a kind of full-service package in which, for an annual fee, they pay no further charges for delivery on any of their orders and get them within a few days, guaranteed; Prime customers also get extra perks such as streaming access to Amazon media. Super Prime is the next logical step. At its launch, customers in eight major US cities can get their orders delivered in under two hours: in metropolises such as New York, Chicago, and San Antonio, Amazon now has storage sites which keep thousands of popular products on hand, located within easy reach of millions of consumers. It is a dream come true for stressed-out executives stuck in offices, who would otherwise need to dash out to the shops before they close on Christmas Eve and buy some of the horrifically overpriced last-minute gifts stores typically keep stockpiled for just this eventuality. More to the point, however, it is a dream come true for Amazon, because Super Prime customers now have no reason to ever go back into a shop.

It's one of the oddities of recent linguistic developments that Amazon hasn't yet been turned into a verb. With all the tech-brand neologisms floating around, with all the things we google and tweet and instagram, with all the facebooking and snapchatting that goes on, it seems somehow strange that we haven't started amazoning stuff. We may yet, though: as Super Prime is extended to cover more and more urban areas across the English speaking world, the combination of being able to order on a smartphone and get your product delivered almost immediately to your precise location will need a snappy verbal designation. After all, it happened with Fedex, which was different enough to sending something in the mail to warrant a verb: "I'll fedex it to you" has, like the word "to hoover" in British English, turned a brand name into an action.

It wouldn't be surprising to hear
"I'll superprime it"
used soon for placing an order
and getting near-immediate delivery.

Then again, perhaps Amazon has already gotten itself a verb: to buy. For many of the company's customers, the two have become more or less synonymous: 30% of searches for products on the internet now start in the Amazon search engine; googling is something people do for knowledge, but Amazon is increasingly the first port of call on the search for a specific item. By extension, a substantial proportion of consumers is now no longer even thinking of looking at any other site except Amazon in whole categories of products.

And why should they? Customers want everything wherever they are and a.s.a.p. (see 2.1 Procurement) – and, month by month, Amazon is getting ever closer to being able to offer them just that. On the classic positioning matrix for business models, Amazon is pushing out on each and every axis while other players have difficulty standing out in even one or two points. Price; breadth and depth of, as well as frequency of updates to, product range; shopping experience; accompanying services; customer service, terms and conditions: Amazon has already set standards in each of these areas or at least matched its competitors. Now the last spoke on the matrix, the last bastion of in-store retailers, is set to fall: location. With Super Prime, Amazon is now reachable in two hours. The last redoubt of traditional stationary retail has been taken by the giant from Seattle, which can now dedicate its energies to fortifying this new position and defending it against its competitors in the online retail sector – who, from now on, will need to start offering two-hour delivery or risk irrelevance.

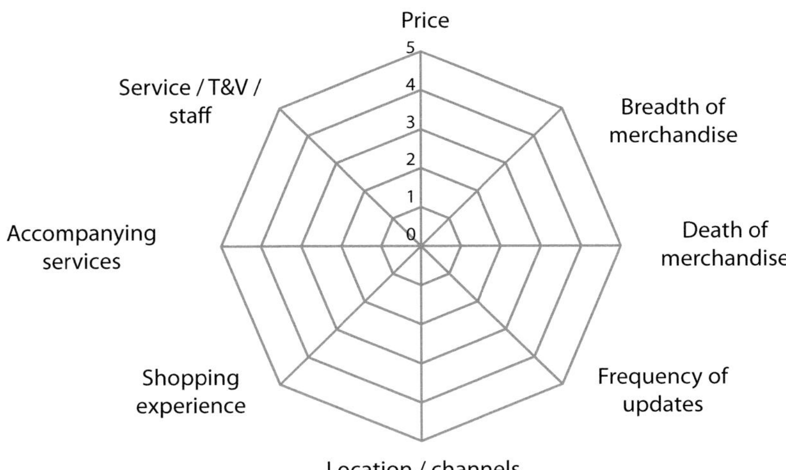

Fig. 4.2: Market positioning matrix
Source: with reference to Finne & Sivonen (2009), The Retail Value Chain

Whether it's the legendary customer service, the reliably effective A9 search, the unparalleled range of products it lists – of all kinds, to all levels of detail, and as soon as they become available on the market – or the increasing number of extras such as streaming services, and – crucially – prices which are never much higher than the competitions' (and often quite a lot lower), Amazon has again and again made other outfits, both merchants and makers, look shabby. If Amazon becomes the first company to really reach the maximum service level feasible in each area of business model positioning, then it will have *de facto* turned the verb "to buy" (from the Old English *bycgean*, in the language in its present form since the 1300s) into a branded word in under 30 years.

In this way, Amazon is both revolutionising the retail market and rebuilding it in its own image as it pushes the limits of the possible ever further.

Amazon is a giant,
but a lean one which carries no dead weight.

It reinvests whatever profit it has in making its processes more efficient, putting itself in a position to offer a lower price at ever more attractive conditions; it then takes the profits this positioning produces and launches itself into the next area. Broadly speaking, after setting up in 1994, Amazon reinvested the money it made from selling books into music; it then took profits on CD sales and built up web hosting capacity while expanding into electronics, household goods, and fashion; now that it is earning good money here, it is investing huge sums in the future: fully-automated fulfilment centres close to urban conurbations, streaming services, autonomous delivery drones... What is interesting about this is that the amount of money Amazon is re-investing is now actually growing faster than at any point since the company was founded. Amazon could have been a highly profitable business long ago (and likes to remind doubters of this fact every now and then by pushing profits up for a quarter), but believes that every dollar which could be removed from the company is working harder when left inside it.

This means that Amazon is not just a virtuous circle – it is a whirling tornado which is growing bigger and bigger. Once upon a time, it was only book sellers who were afraid of losing their roofs; then music stores got sucked in. Then came the turn of the home electronics stores. Now it is publishers, record labels, and television channels who are battening down the hatches as Amazon is no longer just selling media content but actually producing its own.

Even agile competitors from the internet economy
are being sucked into the storm.

While it used to be only Netflix which was producing series like *Narcos* for internet streaming consumption, now Amazon is there with *The Man in the High Castle*. When he left the BBC, Jeremy Clarkson, the *Top Gear* presenter everyone just loves to hate, signed with Amazon.

It's not just media products, either, but everyday items such as batteries, coffee cups, and backpacks that Amazon is selling – and now producing – for almost nothing. Soon enough, the conglomerate from Seattle is likely to start taking pops at parts of the manufacturing industry which have thus far been going about their daily business without a care in the world. From the industrial suppliers with which Amazon is now starting to compete, it's only a short step to manufacturers of worldwide importance – carmakers, for example. Essentially, by applying its extreme efficiency to segment after segment and industry after industry, swallowing up more and more of the value chain from sales all the way back down to manufacturing as it goes, Amazon is creating its own ecosystem into which more and more once independent stakeholders are being drawn.

Who is under threat from Amazon – and how?

The prospects are uninviting for everyone – but they are darker for some than for others. The clearest and most present danger is to classic retail business models based on reselling standard consumer products, both in a bricks-and-mortar and a classic home-shopping environment. The simple fact of the matter is that Amazon's sheer size and unbeatably efficient processes now allow it to decide any and every price war in its favour; this in turn means that any business model based on selling products which can also be bought on Amazon, and which consumers buy based largely on price, is staring down the barrel.

> *Whether it's department stores, electronics outlets, or home furnishings chains, all of them are now competing with Amazon.*

The mail order companies were competing with Amazon, too, and look at what happened to them: they couldn't even offer the one remaining advantage of stationary retail concepts, the ability to try before you buy (a sales argument which is wearing thinner by the day).

Nevertheless, Amazon is no less dangerous for other online retailers, whether they are pure-plays like Zalando or legacy companies who made it to the internet in time

(OTTO in Germany, John Lewis in the UK). Amazon is setting the pace here, too, and it's one with which everyone else is having trouble keeping up. Whatever the competitive advantage, Amazon is racing away with it; the fact that any online pure players are still growing is more down to the overall growth in internet shopping as a percentage of retail overall – and Amazon's percentage is growing faster anyway. So while some other online retailers might be able to grab a niche (in the German online fashion segment, OTTO offers socially-conscious shoppers a fairer, friendlier alternative, while Zalando is now offering exclusive own-brand products at a good price), the Giant has already cast its shadow over this theatre of war.

Exclusive retailers are in a better position, as are vertically-integrated chains ...

... who have never done anything except sell their own merchandise through their own structures, retaining comprehensive control over both their products and the sales channels. Anyone who wants to buy H&M clothing, for example, has to go to H&M – either to a store, to their website, or (for that genuine retro feel) to the catalogue. While we're looking at Swedish companies, Ikea, too, produces popular products which are still only available from branded outlets. Chains like this are fine for as long as their brands remain as attractive as they currently are; if consumers at some point stop caring about the name and start to look for similar products elsewhere, they'll end up on Amazon...

The safest in the current environment are manufacturers. Companies who concentrate on making products are generally unconcerned by whether their products get sold in bricks or by clicks; and as long as Amazon is happy with the paper-thin margin it takes, manufacturers don't even need to be worried if the giant retailer sells their products cheap, as all this does is push up sales figures. The manufacturer still decides at what price to sell to retailers, and sells more than ever before with Amazon. Simple, right?

The Faustian Pact between manufacturers and Amazon

Regardless of the prospects of high sales it offers manufacturers – or indeed precisely because of these prospects – Amazon is not benign. The Trojan Horse, the Pied Piper of Hamelin, Hansel and Gretel, or indeed Doctor Faustus: you can choose your cautionary tale and apply it to the way relations between manufacturers and Amazon tend to run their course. First, the Giant is all sweetness and light, buying in product at attractive conditions, providing the Maker with plenty of sales and even undertaking efforts to put buyers his way – only, later, to let slip its mask and start abusing its power. Suddenly, the Maker sees that he is at the mercy of the Giant, and needs to act fast to save his city/get his children back/escape from the oven. In Faustian terms: Amazon offers manufacturers the potential to grow faster and bigger than in their wildest dreams, but the price is nothing less than their soul – i.e. their products.

Yet beyond this allegorical sketch, how does the archetypal Amazon-Manufacturer relationship develop in detail?

The Turnover Temptation

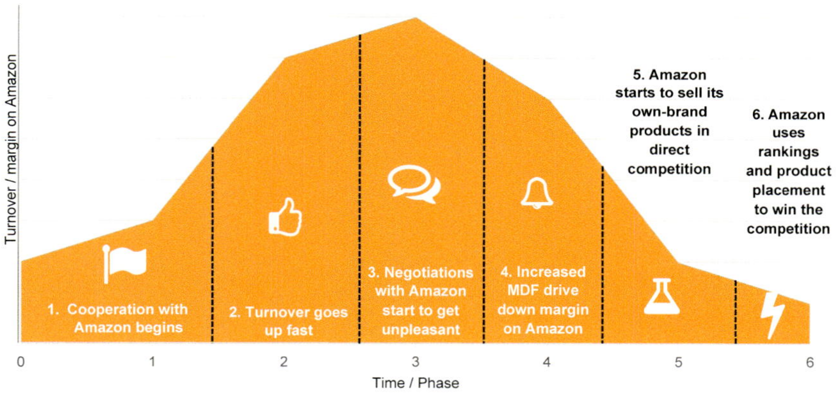

Fig. 4.3: Why everybody needs an Amazon strategy
Source: factor-a GmbH

Manufacturers who start selling on Amazon almost always experience a tangible uptick in turnover – which is hardly surprising given the size of Amazon's sales overall. While the Giant is very guarded about its actual turnover figures and uses highly idiosyncratic accounting techniques to disguise the exact provenance of its sales from competitors (and, in some cases, the taxman), it is not wildly overstating the case to put Amazon's overall share of e-commerce sales at near 50% in most Western markets.

A look at the German case is enough to illustrate the amount of detective work needed to put a number on Amazon, however. The only two methods are multiplying up those turnover figures we do have or comparing them with statistics about courier companies. Using the first method is tricky because Amazon is a hybrid between an online retailer buying in and reselling products and an Ebay-style marketplace operator which provides a fee-paying platform for other retailers to sell their goods. The turnover figures Amazon releases for Germany, however, are only for sales it makes as a retailer and for the commission it takes from third-party retailers using its platform (i.e. not overall turnover on that platform): the two are combined into an overall figure, meaning that we have to work with estimates of what the average rate of commission is (this, of course, varies by category and volume); the issue is further complicated by the fact that we also have to guess which proportion of the turnover is generated on the marketplace.

In terms of commission, experienced observers put the figure at an average of 15 percent, basing it on talking to a range of third-party users of Amazon Marketplace; when it comes to overall sales on the marketplace platform, however, everyone is beat – the only people who know the answer are in Munich or Seattle – and we are forced to work on the very generalised assumption that Amazon generates somewhere between a minimum of 30% and a maximum of 60% of its overall sales turnover on the marketplace, not as a retailer.

As if this weren't complex enough, Amazon doesn't like to publish figures in a timely manner. What will Amazon's growth have been in 2015? We need to apply our guess to previous turnover figures and then factor in the non-commission marketplace takings. Doing so gives us a range of between €15 billion and €30 billion for 2015: assuming 20% growth, an average of 15% commission, and a marketplace share of 40%, our best guess for 2015 is €20 billion overall turnover.

By comparison, the German e-commerce market overall in 2015 is estimated to have been worth around €50 billion, meaning that, in our calculations, Amazon is getting close to a 50% share of it.

We can use a comparison with courier companies' figures to try and verify this claim – although these figures, too, vary quite considerably. Statistics for 2013 put the number of parcels sent in Germany overall at 2.8 to 3 billion and assign somewhere between 400 and 700 million of them to Amazon. Stripping out the 7% C2C and 41% B2B parcels in line with industry figures, that's 52% B2C – and the B2C growth curve is headed up year on year. So assuming for simplicity's sake that B2C parcels were at 60% of all dispatches in 2015 and taking a conservative estimate of three billion parcels overall, that would give us 1.8 billion parcels sent from businesses to consumers. Depending on which source you take, Amazon can be said to have sent between 400 million (22%) and 700 million (28%) of them and, once mail order and teleshopping is accounted for, we are once again at a figure of near 50% for Amazon.

What is more, e-commerce is growing at a faster rate than the retail market overall – and has been for years. In Germany, retail as a whole has been stable at around €300 billion annually for a while now, whereas online sales already made up €20 billion in 2010 and will probably have had a near miss with the €50-billion mark in 2015. Even if growth in e-commerce were to slow somewhat (and there is no grounds to assume it will), it is a pretty safe bet to assume that, by 2020, online shopping in Germany will be worth €100 billion – i.e. around one third of Europe's largest retail market overall.

This third will by and large be bitten right out of sales in established retail channels – and Amazon's bites are going to get ever larger. This is both the nightmarish future which is pushing manufacturers to start looking at alternatives to their existing distribution partnerships with legacy retailers and the shimmering mirage which is drawing them into the embrace of the Giant. It is a promise of noticeable sales growth, and one which is made good on the moment the manufacturers start to list their products and optimise them to even a minimal degree. Just like Doctor Faustus, though, they shouldn't believe that they will get away without keeping up their end of the bargain.

The Conditions Fallacy

At the beginning, though, it is easy to forget that there is no such thing as a free lunch, especially for manufacturers looking to sell to Amazon as a retailer (the Vendor Model). For manufacturers happy to supply directly to it, Amazon does everything it can to look like the perfect sales partner as defined in Business Studies textbooks, buying in respectable amounts of product – its warehouses have plenty of capacity and it sales are high – and paying the listed price without batting an eyelid. If manufacturers give it a 3% fixed rebate, it will even agree to handle all returns, which is a real plus-point for organisations which have yet to build up their own distribution structures and have no experience of customer-facing activities.

Yet, to return to parables:

Amazon is a wolf in sheep's clothing.

Amazon is only so happy to handle returns because this allows it to implement its own extremely high standards of customer service automatically; it expects precisely this level of service from its suppliers, too, however – as manufacturers discover if they have trouble making deliveries on time and as agreed. Amazon operates a zero-tolerance policy towards supply issues, and does so for a very good reason: because Amazon's competitive advantage is, to a large extent, derived from its fulfilment structures – it is process optimisation here which gives it the reserves to be able to offer both suppliers and customers best prices – any disruption to its logistics system, however small, starts to eat into its margins. That is why sales agreements often include punitive fines for late or non-compliant deliveries: examples include a 60 euro cent fee per item delivered to the wrong warehouse, a €20 fine per product not in agreed packaging, and a €500 lump-sum punishment for missing or cancelled deliveries. Breaches of agreements are recorded on the notorious Vendor Score Card and any supplier with poor marks in logistics can expect to be dressed down and asked to accept worse conditions during annual negotiations. Forgive and forget? "Goodwill gestures" are all Greek to Amazon.

What is stopping manufacturers from positioning themselves sustainably

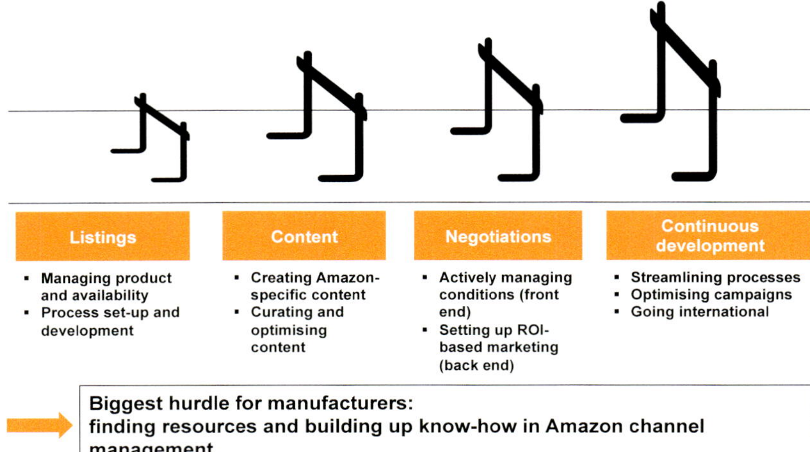
Listings
▪ Managing product and availability
▪ Process set-up and development
Content
▪ Creating Amazon-specific content
▪ Curating and optimising content
Negotiations
▪ Actively managing conditions (front end)
▪ Setting up ROI-based marketing (back end)
Continuous development
▪ Streamlining processes
▪ Optimising campaigns
▪ Going international
Biggest hurdle for manufacturers:
finding resources and building up know-how in Amazon channel management

Fig. 4.4: The 5 Ps of Processes

Source: factor-a GmbH

Even manufacturers who dovetail effortlessly into the Amazon logistics system can quickly find themselves paying a premium to sell on the platform. Amazon does indeed offer a good price for the products it buys in, but claws back some of this by selling additional services at a premium. Larger producers, especially, often lose track of their spend as whole teams are put together to handle the sudden jump in turnover: even premium brands such as WMF (cutlery), 3M (consumer goods), and L'Oréal (cosmetics) take part in the Special Vendor Services programme and actually pay wage costs for the Amazon staff who work on their brands (providing them with training beforehand out of their own budgets, too, of course). Amazon even takes a fee for inputting longer product texts.

Buying in all of these extra services does not mean, however, that the suppliers concerned are buying real partnership; in fact, they don't even get a courteous greeting when they pick up the phone. Amazon's vendor managers usually have about 350 companies on their books, tend to change jobs within the organisation on a regular basis, and so like to use impersonal group e-mails to do things like ask for discounts from manufacturers who are now well-established in the shop and booking high turnover. If you know where to look, you can see the sheepskin falling to the floor.

The Dependency Trap

Now, there is nothing unusual about a retailer, realising that it is now providing a manufacturer with a noticeable proportion of its overall sales, making the most of the situation to try and get a better deal; by the same token, it is in no way abnormal for a manufacturer to be unwilling to hand over some of its margin to the retailer. What shocks many, however, is just how blasé Amazon is about using force to extract its tribute – and just how broad its range of torture implements is.

Amazon likes to start by reminding manufacturers who is who in this game: suppliers who are unwilling to offer a lower price get punished in short order as things like banner adverts for "similar products with better customer ratings" made by other, competing manufacturers start appearing on their product pages. It's easy enough to do the maths and show that the words "better ratings" are inaccurate: a legendary example was when tools manufacturer Metabo's chop-saw product pages were hit with adverts for "similar products" from the Bosch and Makita ranges "with better customer ratings"; as it happened, the "similar" products were in a completely different price category and customers had actually rated them far lower than the Metabo hardware (number of ratings multiplied by rating average).

Amazon doesn't shrink from jabbing at the heart of trademark law, either: the water-filter company Brita caught Amazon manipulating search results when customers entering the brand name "brita" got shown search adverts for the second-rank manufacturer BWT as the top result.

Whether this kind of behaviour is criminal is a matter for researchers into trademark legislation and commercial property law, but not lawyers and judges: after all, who is going to take its most important retail partner to court? (Especially if that partner holds the future of shopping in its hands.)

And who is going to delist their products if Amazon is earning them one in every two bucks (and increasing) that they make on the internet?

With Amazon, manufacturers can very soon end up in a golden cage.

What is more, they hand over the key at the door in the form of data about product sales and end-consumers: when selling to it as vendors, manufacturers let Amazon handle all of the direct customer contact, which in turn gives Amazon huge amounts of data about customer preferences. The next thing to do from Amazon's point of view is to develop its own products with which it can satisfy the customer requirements it now knows about – and having successfully stepped from just-selling to also-producing in so many areas (from selling books to publishing them, from streaming to making TV shows), Amazon has a proven ability to attack even well-established brands. Worse still, Amazon can then favour its own creations in the product search or advertise them on manufacturers' product pages as cheaper alternatives.

This is the nightmare scenario when entering into cooperation with Amazon. Those manufacturers it happens to find themselves growing ever more slowly on Amazon, and yet remaining reliant on the turnover they still generate there. In order to get anywhere close to the growth rates to which they became used on Amazon, they need to make heavy marketing investments against none other than Amazon itself, when can access the same range of marketing tools internally at no cost. Mephistopheles wins and Doctor Faustus laments in his golden cage.

How can manufacturers avoid catastrophe?

Since there is not a manufacturer out there who can give a coherent answer to the question of why Amazon shouldn't – provided that it is able to do so for a reasonable cost and with good prospects of returns – develop own-brands in every segment, and since no-one has a got a convincing remedy to the fact that Amazon controls both customer contact and product presentation on its site, by rights, manufacturers should be steering well clear of Amazon. There may be some manufacturers with brands so strong that they are immune from all forms of imitation – Adidas will always be Adidas and no-one is going to want "Amazodas" jogging bottoms; Prada is Prada, darling, and so there's no point in even thinking about "Amazada" – yet even for brands of this calibre, there is a clear case for preventing the emergence of one all-powerful retailer.

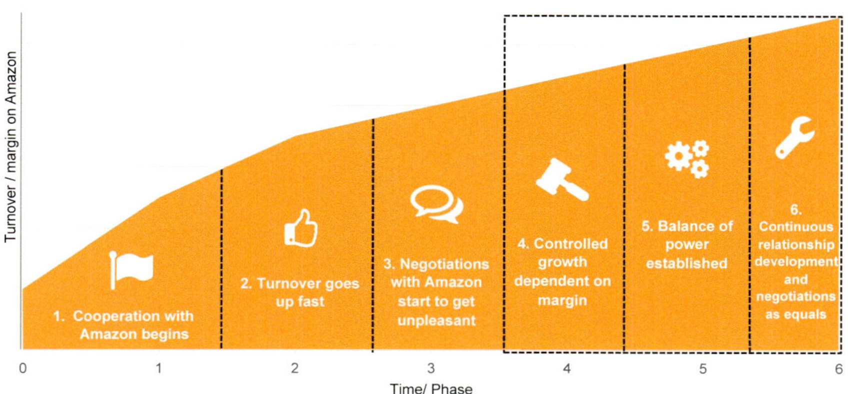

Fig. 4.5: Examples of a Successful Amazon-Strategy
Source: factor-a GmbH

Yet how could this be achieved? As a classic example from game theory shows, it is almost inconceivable if we look at the situation between Amazon and manufacturers as a classic Prisoner's Dilemma.

Two suspects are imprisoned and stand accused of having colluded to commit a crime. They are both being held in solitary confinement and are questioned individually, leaving them to no chance to coordinate their responses. If found guilty, the highest possible sentence for the crime of which they stand accused is six years. If both prisoners decide, independently of one another, to remain silent (cooperation), they will both receive shorter sentences of two years each. If each betrays the other, however, they will both receive longer, but reduced prison terms of four years each because they have helped the authorities (defection). If only one confesses, betraying the other (defection) while the other does not talk (cooperation), then the one who turns gets a symbolic one-year sentence while the other is given the full maximum penalty of six years.

This situation leads to a dilemma which can be shown on a matrix as follows:

	B stays silent	**B betrays**
A stays silent	A: 2 years B: 2 years	A: 6 years B: 1 year
A betrays	A: 1 year B: 6 years	A: 4 years B: 4 years

For each individual prisoner, the most attractive option is to betray the other: assuming that the other party is also intending to betray them, turning will reduce the sentence from six to four years; even if the other party is intending to keep schtum, then betrayal still halves the remaining sentence from two years to one.

From an individual point of view, then, there is no better strategy than betrayal, and this remains so regardless of what the other prisoner decides; it therefore always appears more advantageous to turn. This strategy, chosen independently of the other player, is called the "dominant strategy".

The core of the dilemma is that an individual and a collective analysis produce different recommendations. Both players should actually cooperate to get the best result overall, but they both decide to betray and get the maximum penalty: their joint loss if they both cooperate is four years' jail time; if they both betray one another, they will serve a total of eight years in prison.

When dealing with Amazon, the "Manufacturer's dilemma" looks similar.

Let's say that 1,000 manufacturers are selling their products to Amazon. They are all aware that they are entering into the risk that Amazon will squeeze the price and therefore decrease their overall profitability, and that this risk will be greater the larger Amazon's share of the market, which will give Amazon ever more bargaining power. (We are assuming, for the purposes of the thought experiment, that turnover away from Amazon remains constant.) Given the sheer number of vendors, often supplying Amazon with similar products, there is no realistic way of coordinating action – much like prisoners in solitary confinement. This means that the manufacturers concerned each individually have two options:

- Keep selling to Amazon ("defection")
- Stop selling to Amazon ("cooperation")

Regardless of the high number of manufacturers, we can still carry out the exercise with two parties, A and B, because the decision of only one manufacturer has the same influence on the remaining 999. If only one manufacturer stops selling to Amazon ("cooperates"), the others who are still selling to Amazon ("defect") do better: the one who stops loses the turnover as long as the others keep selling, and those who are still selling can divide up the same turnover among themselves, each getting slightly more.

If, however, all manufacturers were to stop selling to Amazon – i.e. to cooperate – then they would all suffer a drop in turnover – let's put a price-tag on it and call it 10% for the sake of the game. If all of them continue selling to Amazon, however, then they lose, say, 50% of the turnover (and probably a lot more of their margin) because Amazon's market share grows even faster and it is more able than it would otherwise be to replace existing vendors' products with its own or squeeze their margins. If only some of the manufacturers stop selling to Amazon, then the rest are better off because this lost turnover gets shared out among them. The businesses who "cooperate" lose, for the sake of argument, 70% of their turnover because Amazon continues to dominate the market and they are no longer profiting. Those who "defect" and keep selling only lose 5% of their turnover because there is more space for them on Amazon (although they too stand to lose far more in the long run).

As a matrix, this Manufacturer's Dilemma looks as follows:

	B stops selling	B keeps selling
A stops selling	A: –10% B: –10%	A: –70% B: –5%
A keeps selling	A: –5% B: –70%	A: –50% B: –50%

The best possible outcome for all manufacturers is for them all to stop selling to Amazon.

Yet from each individual manufacturer's point of view, continuing to sell to Amazon appears to be the dominant strategy.

That's the theory. Now, in back in the real world, in which everyone is already selling on Amazon and is not about to stop for any reason, there are still some tactical tricks which manufacturers can use with the overall strategic goal in mind of stopping Amazon from becoming an outright monopolist. Larger manufacturers can delist their product ranges and renegotiate with Amazon, driving a harder bargain; meanwhile, smaller producers in a single segment can club together and agree on minimum conditions to bolster their negotiating positions. This would mean that companies who were previously rivals would need to build up trust between one another, but if they could rely on strength in numbers, they would be able to stand up to harsh interrogation in annual negotiations and come out with settlements with which they can all get by well enough. Another possibility is not to become a vendor, but to work with Amazon as a marketplace seller (Seller Model): this means that Amazon doesn't get customer contact and the data that goes with it.

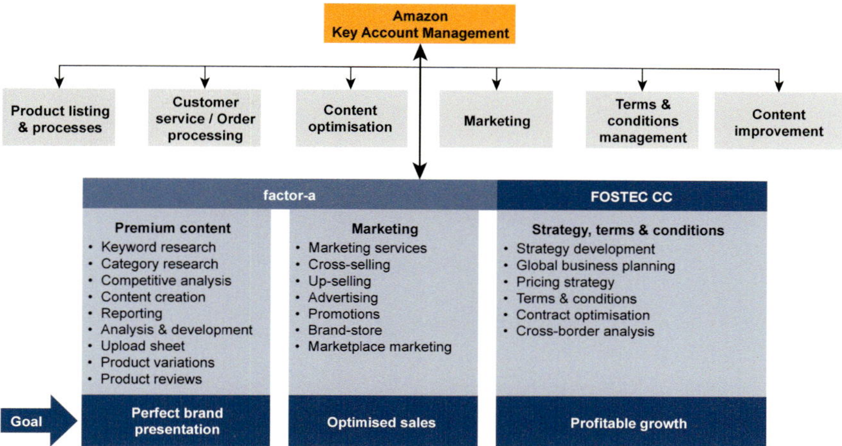

Fig. 4.6: Required functions and resources for Amazon
Source: factor-a GmbH

Need help with your Amazon strategy? **factor-a** will consult on preparing, optimising, and weighting your Amazon operations. Learn about the importance of the 5 Ps – product, price, processes, personnel, and promotion – and improve your decision-making in dealings with the conglomerate.
www.factor-a.de

Fig. 4.7: How the ideal relationship between manufacturers and Amazon develops over time

Source: FOSTEC Commerce Consultants (2016)

Another thing that all manufacturers can do is to concentrate on maintaining and extending their own online presence. Although proprietary online shops can be costly at first – just ask Sony, the latest big brand to close its internet sales operation due to high costs and low takings in autumn 2015 – not running them is a long-term strategic mistake. Anyone investing all of their budget for product presentation and marketing with Amazon is, to speak once again in proverbs, putting all their eggs in one basket (a basket which may turn out to bite). It is far more advisable to maintain a proprietary shop and interweave sales on Amazon with it so that customers get genuine value from switching to buying directly. It's a balancing act, but one which, if carried out successfully, turns Amazon back into what it always has had the potential to be: an incredibly powerful engine for growth. What is more, maintaining proprietary sales channels evens out the power in the relationship, which in turn has a positive effect on margins on sales which still have to happen on Amazon. Success here can turn the golden cage into the golden scales – and allows Doctor Faustus to pull one over on Mephistopheles in the end.

Earlier this year, Hamburg city authorities turned down a planning application from Amazon for a fulfilment centre in the buzzing St. Georg area near the main station. The application will, however, be resubmitted soon. Meanwhile, Amazon is nearing completion of its first inner-city depot near Berlin's Kurfürstendamm thoroughfare. On 24th December 2016, expect the Amazon Super Prime Santas to be taking off for their first last minute gift-giving mission in Germany, Europe's very own land of Christmas magic ...

4.3 Grand designs in home furnishings

From an e-commerce point of view, the home furnishings segment is, strategically speaking, one to watch in the coming years. Thus far, online sales of sofas, tables, and other large items of furniture have been lagging behind those in other areas: in Germany, for example, e-commerce accounts for somewhere between a minimum of three and a maximum of ten percent of furniture sales, depending on which source you use. At the same time, all observers agree that, across the Western world, large out-of-town furniture stores have their most profitable days behind them and that disruption from the internet is long overdue. The only question is when this disruption will come, and from where.

Why, though, have furniture sellers had such a long stay of execution? Why did books, electronics, and fashion chain stores have to put their head on the block so much earlier? Why isn't Amazon muscling into the segment and showing Poco and Bauhaus in Germany, DFS and Dreams in the UK, and Ashley Home Stores et al. in the States who's boss? Where are the hungry Zalando-style pure-plays? And why, oh why, do so many customers still sacrifice a Saturday to schlepp to the stores and schlepp back with unwieldly purchases hanging out of their car boots, swearing and sweating as they go, when there are already hassle-free ways of doing it? Essentially, what e-commerce experts have been asking themselves for a while now is how bricks-and-mortar furniture stores can just keep running in thin air like Wile E. Cayote chasing after Roadrunner, despite the fact that there is technically nothing left under the feet of their business models.

To a considerable degree, the answer to this conundrum is to be found in the nature of the products. The home furnishings business remains very focussed on stationary retail concepts because:

For the moment, it is still more difficult to display a sofa or a bed on the internet – and even more difficult to get it delivered – than it is in the case of books or trousers.

What is more, consumers don't want to customise media and fashion items before buying: anyone who wants a book to suit their thoughts will have to write one themselves, and customers unhappy with the cut of a pair of slacks will either refrain from buying them or have them altered. When they are buying a three-piece suite, however, customers generally want to have more say in the product: there are questions of colour, fabric, and composition (foot-stool, yes or no? Two or three-seater sofa?). Many pieces of furniture never even see the light of day until they have been ordered: custom-made is not compatible with click-and-buy and next-day delivery.

Yet this is by no means the only, or the whole, answer. What is more, these facts are often misunderstood as laws of nature, which leads to a misunderstanding of cause and effect in the segment. Many in home furnishings retail are convinced that customers don't want to buy furniture on the internet: "Who would want to buy a sofa without having sat in it?" Heritage retailers see their justification in furniture's role as a lasting investment, not a seasonal throw-away item: consumers will be spending large sums on something that will be in their home for many years, goes the argument, and won't want to speed-buy on the internet.

This is, however, a classic case of getting the cart before the horse. The continuingly high percentage of offline sales is misunderstood as the cause when it is, in truth, simply the effect of the current market conditions – conditions which could change in the blink of an eye, and will. It's not that consumers avoid shopping for furniture online because they can't imagine buying sofas and tables on the internet; the only reason they haven't yet switched to doing so in their droves is because there are, as yet, no genuinely attractive propositions in the segment with the presence and publicity of Amazon.

The difficulties in presenting furnishings attractively on the internet and the frequent delays in their availability are certainly reasons why it has taken longer for good web-based concepts to emerge in the segment; then there are the dimensions of the products and the difficulties involved in delivering, assembling, and – more than anything – returning them, which continue to present serious issues for those online retailers already active in the market. Importantly, however, none of these arguments rules out success in selling home furnishings on the internet once and for all, and anyone assuming that innovative tech start-ups can't clear these hurdles is working on a false premise – and, to stick with the Wile E. Coyote analogy, running out into the canyon without looking down into the abyss.

There's no need to take our word for it, either, as the figures show. While the home furnishings segment is certainly lagging behind in e-commerce overall, it is growing at an astounding pace:

What is more, most of this is being driven by new online concepts rather than the internet efforts of established players.

In 2013, furniture webshop Home24 was already able to match Ikea Euro for Euro in online sales, racking up a turnover of €90 million in Germany and reaching level pegging with the Swedish giant; in the following year, it added a breath-taking 72.5% to sales, reaching €160 million in the German market alone. Meanwhile, Otto is already way out in front, having broken the billion barrier for home furnishings in 2013 mainly through online sales. Surveys have revealed that only 15% of German consumers would still not be prepared to buy furniture online; according to Bitkom, around a quarter of them already has. A study conducted by the Cologne retail research institute IfH in 2014 revealed a similar readiness and – confusingly enough for dyed-in-the-wool believers in "sofas aren't trousers"-theory – even showed that 60% of respondents could imagine that buying furniture online might, in future, become as unremarkable as shopping for clothes and shoes.

This should be ample proof that the home furnishings segment is in no way an exception which will remain immune from the rules of e-commerce, but simply one of the last bastions of bricks-and-mortar. And, as with every last bastion, whether its defenders surrender early or fight to the last man, their fate is sealed. The war is already lost.

The thing everyone knows about the Road Runner cartoons is that Wile E. Coyote only ever falls out of thin air once he has looked down. Classic chain furniture stores are, however, already in free-fall – and many of them have not yet noticed that there is nothing left under their feet.

Why has it taken so long – and where are Amazon and Ikea?

Besides the dimensions, complexity, and prices of many pieces of furniture – enough to delay, but not lastingly prevent a switch to internet sales – there are other, far more important forces behind the lag in home furnishings. And no, we are not talking about the supposed "long product life-cycle" that is also frequently and misleadingly credited with hampering furniture sales online: as a matter of fact, home furnishings have become short-lived consumer lifestyle products which are being replaced at ever shorter intervals. The mahogany dining table you'd "be able to pass onto your children" went out along with crystal ash trays and carriage clocks at retirement parties: now, post *Changing Rooms*, it's all MDF boarding that lands up in a skip when the room gets redone two years later. No, the real brakes on e-commerce in home furnishings have actually been the structure of the segment and the companies active in it – and no-where more so than in Germany.

Here, as in many other markets, the home furnishings segment has until now been structured by a triangle of manufacturers, buying groups, and retailers.

With the sub-premium market being extremely brand-poor in comparison to other segments (e.g. fashion), manufacturers have always been more dependent on retailers than in other areas; this has made it difficult for the numerous B and C-list furniture brands either to supply newcomers who might threaten existing retailers' business or to sell directly to consumers. So while A-listers such as Vitra, Rolf Benz, and Kartell in Germany or Laura Ashley and David Linley in the UK have been able to launch successful online shops or throw themselves into cooperation with new online retailers, the rest have had no basis on which to build up customer relationships and have thus been concerned with keeping their existing partners sweet – going it alone or playing the field have never been options. What is more, the new online pure players have often overlooked or ignored less prominent manufacturers with weaker brands, and while this state of affairs is now in flux, it will not change overnight.

In comparison to the manufacturers, the various buying groups (group purchasing organisations, or GPOs) – of which around 20 operate in Germany, for example – have far more bargaining power. Yet collective purchasing organisations are coming under serious structural strain and there is no conceivable way of lessening it: turnover and footfall in furniture stores is stagnant to sinking, yet new ideas for competitive online solutions are blocked by the members themselves (who are afraid that it is their business which will be cannibalised) or by legal constraints. What is more, buying groups are often lacking the competence to implement their own solutions, and several German GPOs have already launched and then canned unsuccessful webshops. Not too infrequently, their current sites offer little more than a shopping list function and a directory of bricks-and-mortars stores.

The retailers running the stores listed, meanwhile, have been more concerned with keeping pace with the ruinous expansion of square-footage in the segment: it's a game of chicken on a market which is already saturated and only a select few will come out of it the other end.

Whether the US, the UK, or Germany, there is simply too much sales space for the size of the home furnishings market.

In Germany in 2015, for instance, the combined surface area of furniture stores' retail space reached six million metres square for the first time ever; by 2017, another 500,000 will have been added; at the same time, however, footfall is declining steeply and will never climb back to previous peaks as younger cohorts stay urban for longer and are increasingly turning their backs on personal motorised transportation – i.e. their own cars. In Germany, DIY and furnishing retail groups such as Steinhoff and Höffner have knowingly entered into a brutal war of attrition in which productivity per square foot of retail space is set to decline to unprecedentedly low levels and only the one who can bear the losses the longest has a chance of winning what will be a decidedly Pyrrhic victory. It goes without saying that this kind of war effort leaves little leeway for investment in online infrastructure, and even less for genuine innovation in internet shopping. The status quo is that most of the German Top 10 do have webshops, but that monthly visitor numbers are generally closer to five digits than seven; a few have even been taken back offline in recent months.

After all, building and running a proprietary online shop can't be done on a shoestring (just ask B&Q in Britain how much it paid domain-name flippers for "DIY.com" for starters...) – and it's even pricier when the products in question are furniture (you don't need to ask about this, as managers in the segment never shut up about it). To complicate matters even further, the complexity is increased by multichannel issues such as standardising product texts and images, how to deal with variants and customisation in both offline and online environments, and which special offers to serve in which channels: if home furnishings chains don't manage to fine automated solutions here, high recurrent costs beckon. Then there are country-specific issues, too, such as the German home segment's chronic illness: "discountitis". Anyone who doesn't have a *Keine Werbung* ("No junk mail") sticker on their letterbox (and even many who do) will be familiar with the leaflets from Poco, Bauhaus, Obi and others promising "70% off this Saturday 5th May ONLY!", followed by another mailshot the following week offering "80% off this Saturday 12th May ONLY!". Besides being ruinous in and of itself, the really pernicious effect of this pathological discounting is to push listed prices up so that some margin will be left over after the manifold rounds of premeditated price-slashes; if these numbers are served on webshops, however, they scare customers off and make the sites' pricing so uncompetitive than consumer comparison portals won't even display them when users order results by price. Then there is the fact that, whether in Germany or elsewhere, many furniture stores don't want customers to actually buy using their webshops because someone who acquires a bed at a distance can't be upsold matching linen, a bedside table, and a load of other bits and bobs as easily as they can be in store. That explains the furniture stores' preference for click and collect wherever possible:

The best customer is the one who comes in to pick up their order and then leaves with a high-margin take-away coffee and a load of stuff they didn't really want, too.

If you've ever wondered why Ikea's online shop is so awful, by the way, that is one part of the answer: Ikea has nothing to gain by sending existing in-store customers to its webshop because they can't spend on foodstuffs like coffee and *köttbullar* meatballs while they are at it; then there are all the impulse-buy items like plastic beakers, rugs, and glasses on which Ikea earns a far healthier profit than fully-fitted kitchens or storage units. That is why the furniture giant wants its customers to keep coming into the store to buy the big-ticket items – and why all of those popular last-minute knick-knacks that people pick up just before check-out to make them feel like their three-hour round-trip was worthwhile are not even listed in the webshop.

While Ikea does present most of its furniture range on its site, many items are still not available to actually purchase online. This forces customers to switch media from digital to physical if just one of the items they wanted cannot be bought in the webshop; while fans of the brand will put up with it, Amazon-accustomed agnostics are likely to reach their frustration threshold within minutes.

Even once a customer has decided to try and place an order online, Ikea is by no means ready to roll over and stretch out its paws: delivery charges frequently total more than 10% of the value of the products purchased, and if the customer decides to opt for click and collect, they get hit with a fee for that, too. At five days minimum, delivery times are a joke, and payment options are frequently out of synch with the country in which it is operating: in Germany, for example, Ikea doesn't offer online payment by open invoice, direct debit, or PayPal, meaning that it fails to use any of the three most popular methods of payment (see 2.5.2. Payments).

One mistake like this in an online shop would be careless; two would be foolish – but three "errors" of this order of magnitude are part of a considered approach. The fact of the matter is that Ikea wants to be present on the internet if for no other reason than to make sure that its name is not left open to imitation or parody; customers must, however, be kept from making purchases there to the greatest possible extent so that they keep coming to the stores.

From Ikea's point of view, it all makes sense – and in the short term, the company's business is unlikely to suffer. After all, Ikea is vertically integrated, meaning that its products can only be bought from Ikea and not, as in the case of other manufacturers, from a range of outlets.

In the long term, it remains to be seen whether Ikea can afford to maintain this position.

All the while its brand is so strong that people will ruin their weekends just to get at its products, it's fine; but if customer preferences – or just their habits – change significantly, then Ikea might end up having to revise its approach on the double.

Where would the threat come from, though? While Amazon may well be the culprit behind the death of the Saturday spent in the shopping precinct – as well as the villain of the piece when it comes to endangered past-times such as browsing in a bookstore – Amazon is not showing any immediate signs that it is planning to do away with bricks-and-mortar furniture stores. While there is no shortage of manufacturers and retailers listing their products on Amazon as sellers, the sparse customer ratings are proof that they have yet to land genuine sales hits here. Product presentation is frequently poor, with lots of pictures straight out of catalogues which show the item in a distractingly busy showroom context; many listings lack detailed close-up shots of important parts of the piece in question (beds without pictures of the slats, for example, or cupboards with no inside view). What is oddest is that some of the worst listings are in fact Amazon's own efforts as a vendor: Amazon dropping the ball to this extent is highly unusual and shows that, for whatever reason, it has not prioritised furnishings. Yet.

Who is exploiting the gap?

It is precisely because juggernauts such as Ikea and Amazon are currently bypassing home furnishings online that the market is, measured by turnover, still largely a bricks-and-mortar one; in terms of growth, however, the furniture segment is already in the middle of a transformation towards online shopping (see figures above). After all, the clear gap between the loveless webshops run by a range of established stores, Amazon's unattractiveness in the segment, and the consumer desire to acquire furnishings on the internet has not gone unnoticed. It's the same kind of inviting space that was open in fashion ten years ago and that drew in pure-plays such as Zappos and Zalando, who filled it out with huge amounts of start-up investment until Amazon and others started to get serious and buy up or push back the newcomers respectively.

While the gap is still open, online pure players are trying to fill up as much of it as possible: the idea, as with fashion, is to make the running before everyone realises there is a race on. Yet while history repeats itself, it never repeats itself exactly, and similar initial situations will often play out quite differently all things told. In the Battle for Furnishings, the armies are lining up differently, with two types of pure-plays preparing to duke it out: one the one hand, there are the Zalando-style approaches (one of which is also, like the online fashion retailer, financed by Rocket Internet) aiming to reach critical mass at top speed; on the other, a new curated shopping and shopping club models are trying are trying to establish themselves.

The go-for-growth approach is, of course, reliant on transactional marketing. The US Wayfair brand, for example, is going hard on the classic e-commerce trio of price, product, and availability (although, given the make-to-order nature of many furnishing products, "availability" is a relative in this case); this line of attack is being flanked by a ginormous advertising budget spent freely to acquire customers by any means necessary. This all-out approach has driven marketing costs up by a staggering 50% between 2012 and 2014 – and these sky-high spends will have to sink back down by about a half if Wayfair ever wants to actually earn money. This is a serious issue for the American player: the ruinous TV-commercial carpet-bombing is driving up active customer figures, but the all-important repeat-business curve remains stubbornly flat. This will make it difficult to decouple growth rates from the increasing outlay for advertising in the future.

It's not just Wayfair, but rather a known weakness of bought-in, fast-action growth; like a junkie drying out, the figures collapse when the marketing budget is cut.

The same problem is visible at many of the (pun intended) Rocket-fuelled moonshots – especially Zalando – which just refuses to grow without supplements. Perhaps, however, the Berlin-based start-up accelerator is learning from its mistakes as, with Home24, its headline foray into the furnishings segment, it is pursuing a quite different strategy. Rather than going for growth at any price, it is actually keeping a tight rein on advertising spending, and costs per new customer are lower than at rival Wayfair. Nevertheless, the results are sobering: genuine profitability has yet to set in, an issue which the company has said it wants to tackle by using economies of scale in purchasing, logistics, and marketing. The problem will be that scaling requires huge upfront investment for a delayed pay-off, while the very idea of achieving savings through size in the business may well prove to be illusory in any case: yes, furniture is being bought and changed more frequently than ever before, but not at the same rate as, say, fashion products. T-shirts and scarves get bought several times a year, while the wardrobe that holds them gets swapped every five years; while that is still an advance on the old product lifespan of 20 years, it doesn't make home furnishings into a fast turnover segment in which customers just keep coming back for more. There is little room for marketing savings here, and tried-and-tested e-commerce techniques such as personalised recommendations based on previous purchases don't work because the vast majority of customers simply do not place orders frequently enough for data-sets with genuinely predictive potential to be built up – or to take advantage of any suitable suggestions which are served to them in spite of this. In this segment, big data may well turn out to be a toothless tiger.

What is more, any portal hoping for free Google traffic thanks to lots of product pages and good SEO is in for a disappointment:

New customers need to be bought in, expensively, either on TV or on Google. Facebook traffic, too, is not as cheap as it used to be.

And this is before we've even considered the fact that Amazon is now the preferred search engine for around one third of customers looking for products online (see above, 4.1). Once all of this has been taken into account, it is hard to see how Home24 wants to keep growing and become profitable.

Another thing that is hard to understand is why Rocket Internet persists in valuing Home24 so much higher than its other furniture pure-play, Westwing. This other furniture start-up in the Berlin accelerators stables is following a far more promising shopping club approach which, at least for the time being, seems a far better fit for the home furnishings segment. Westwing gets prospects to register so that they can view offers which are updated daily and available only for a limited time and in limited number; e-mails lead these registered users onto product pages, and editorial content is used to guide them through the fast-rotating product range, invitingly photographed and beautifully presented. Discounts and deal various are offer to turn users into customers, and anyone who gets their friends to sign up is rewarded with a voucher. This makes customer acquisition into a self-sustaining – and, importantly, low-cost – process.

Not that Westwing's M. O. comes cheap: in fact, maintaining this kind of high-end platform is a pricey business. Then again, marketing costs are close to zero, and a look at competitor Wayfair's figures shows just how high these can get. Meanwhile, Westwing's club structure seems to encourage repeat business, shown by the start-up's high numbers of returning customers. Moreover, with its exclusive style, Westwing is building an environment in which brands can be developed (not something that is easy to accomplish in the home furnishings segment) and in which manufacturers can be persuaded to pay for market development.

The strategy appears to be working well: sales are up strongly year-on-year (from €112 million in 2013 to €186 million in 2014) and margins are headed up, not down; as such, Westwing will most likely be one of the first furniture concepts to get out of the red.

Then again, shopping clubs should always be taken with a pinch of salt, as a look at club-approach pioneers in fashion such as vente-privee.com, private-outlet.com, and brands4friends.de suffices to show: their rise and fall between 2007 and 2010 is a cautionary tale if ever there was one, and a stark reminder of the core weakness of the model. After an explosive start, the fashion shopping clubs soon ran into trouble as the number of market participants looking to take their slice of the pie went up rapidly; soon enough, the end-of-line exclusives the first clubs had begun by marketing were becoming scarce, which led to a sudden rise in prices. The pressure was such that some collections were produced as straight-to-club merchandise, which in turn devalued the core brand promise of the clubs – viz. exclusivity and that fuzzy feeling of having got at a real bargain through a secret, "speak-easy"-style backdoor connection. What is more, competition for the members of these clubs heated up; as a result, the customers got choosier and had to be kept active with ever sweeter deals. In short, the whole approach ate itself up in fast-forward mode and many of these much-hyped clubs have now closed or crawled back into the semi-profitable niche from which they came.

Furniture online: unpacking the boxes

Yet history, of course, does not repeat itself entirely, and furniture – as we have seen – is not the same as fashion. What Westwing has done by padding its club model with difficult-to-imitate curated content and by not concentrating on leftovers alone is to create a more stable system in which a sudden wave of copy-cat competitors is unlikely. If there is a path to growth which leads past bought-in traffic, Westwing has found it – and it is probably wide enough to handle a few others, too.

What is also quite likely is that furniture manufacturers will continue to emancipate themselves from existing partners, working with pure-plays and shopping clubs and – for those with strong enough niche or premium brand credentials – opening direct sales channels. While the strong dependency on bricks-and-mortars retailers so characteristic for the home furnishings segment will not disappear overnight, every time another online pure player enters the market, another brick in the wall around the prison yard crumbles. A few years back, the number of online furniture retailers was so low that existing partners were bound to see if one of their suppliers was also selling to internet outfits and could take measures against this. Nowadays, legacy retailers know that their suppliers are also listed on Home24, ikarus, reuter, Connox, et al., but can't measure the impact: neither these partners nor the GPOs can estimate what percentage of their turnover manufacturers are now making in cahoots with the proliferation of intermediaries and internet shops both at home and abroad; this has in and of itself reversed the balance of power.

Lastly, but by no means least importantly, all eyes remain on Amazon and Ikea.

How much longer is Amazon going to ignore the home furnishings segment?

And, crucially, how much longer will Ikea be happy to use its multichannel structure to keep optimising its in-store business while only growing at just-below-market rates on the net? Yes, even with the veritable obstacle course Ikea lays out for customers wanting to buy online, it still made €92 million in Germany in 2013 and upped this to €145 million in 2014: this makes Ikea's online growth into the segment's baseline figure inasmuch as, if Ikea can manage 60% growth annually, everyone else should be able to, too. If Ikea does at some point switch strategies and start lowering the barriers to its webshop because, despite its best efforts, in-store footfall starts to stagnate, this will send out waves which will be felt across the segment – especially by the other bricks-and-mortar outfits.

Once even Ikea has understood that all future growth is to be had online, then the rest of the old-style DIY and home furnishings stores will realise it too – and have their Wile E. Coyote-moment as they suddenly notice the chasm gaping beneath their feet.

4.4 Insurance, or: How I learned to stop worrying and buy everything online

There's no shortage of things which would surprise a time-traveller from the 1990s. "What, you mean we *still* don't have a handle on global warming?" they might ask, or: "So electric cars are only just taking off?" Taking a look at the online environment, they might be surprised that approximately 78% percent of the internet seems to be constituted of cat content of all things. And, while we're on the subject of the internet, they might well be surprised that, from buying books in the mid-90s, people have now graduated to buying large items like sofas online.

After all, even in the 90s, it was easy to imagine that selling books at a distance wouldn't be too much of a problem.

They've always been easy to pack and send – so much so that many jurisdictions had special rates of postage for printed materials enshrined in law – and books are also easy to identify beyond a shadow of a doubt based on simple information such as their title, the author, and the edition; add a (very pixely) image of the cover and our period "surfer of the web" had a very good idea of what he or she was getting. But buying a telephone table or a television cabinet (yes, it's the 90s...) on the internet? Crazy.

It's this kind of environment that led business experts back then to assume that smaller, more select goods would end up being sold on the internet, as well as immaterial goods which don't even need to be stored, commissioned, and dispatched. That's why some of the world's earliest e-commerce applications from the 1980s were made for B2B tourism: transactions between airlines and tour operators didn't require any products to be transported, so why not do things electronically? Later on, flights and travel packages would, along with books and music, become some of the earliest product segments to migrate onto the internet: high-street travel agencies were already feeling the pressure from internet booking engines such as Expedia and airlines' own websites around the turn of the Millennium.

So in 1990s-logic, products which, such as insurance, consist essentially in nothing more than their written incarnation (in the physical world, out of ink on an eminently-postable sheet of A4 paper and, perhaps, an accompanying brochure) looked like very likely candidates for migration. Many observers thought the idea of selling expensive designer clothing and shoes with price-tags in the thousands on the internet was a far less realistic proposition: customers wouldn't even know whether the product was up to their standards – and indeed fitted them – until it got delivered.

Today, we know better. Amazon sells Prada ladies' trousers at a retail value of roughly $500 (an absolute bargain when reduced to $150!) and has Marc Jacobs handbags on sale for well over the $1000 mark. The most expensive bed customers can buy from Amazon retails at well over ten times that. (All of this holds true for prices in pounds and Euros, too.) Insurance policies, however, are scarce on the world's biggest e-commerce site: there are a few which cover damage to technical products ranging between $30 and $100 – and that's it.

Back in 1996, though, people interested in e-commerce would probably have guessed insurance and not beds if you'd asked them on what consumers would be spending five-figures sums on the internet twenty years later. After all, an insurance policy can (only) be described in words, which of course can be distributed in electronic form; all the data an insurer needs from a customer, too, such as age, gender, and address, can be inputted electronically. Given this, is there actually any need for insurers and insurance customers to meet at all? Signatures are legally binding if transmitted by fax, after all (yes, the 90s).

This logic makes even more sense inasmuch as it could also lead to more efficiency in the value chain (i.e. "Sianora suckers!" to brokers with their offices, company cars, and briefcases), which would in turn lead to more attractive prices for consumers. So in view of these advantages, where are the companies looking to use them to entice new customers?

And where are the customers willing to desert the traditional middlemen to save a buck?

To put no too fine a point on it: why does today's world look different to the one people previously imagined?

Insurance is different

Well, for a start, there are indeed good reasons why the vast majority of insurance policies isn't already being sold on the internet as has become the case with a variety of other immaterial goods. The following particularities need to be remembered when looking at the insurance industry.

Types of insurance and regulation

There are various types of insurance which have to be marketed differently, and insurers are working in a tightly regulated field. What is more, demand for insurance is not the same as demand for consumer goods: some policies are so complicated and yet so crucial that customers need professional help to take informed decisions.

Limited potential for savings in new models

Economies of scale are less pronounced in insurance than in other categories of goods. Once a certain amount of premiums has been amassed, most insurers work with marginal costs structures: switching to direct sales on the internet or going for high growth in the number of policies sold does not necessarily lead to headline-grabbing savings; in fact, uncontrolled growth can even become a serious risk factor.

Lack of room for price reductions

Many insurance policies are already too cheap in their current forms.

They will have to become more expensive if anything (e. g. car insurance), regardless of how they are sold and what the fixed costs are. Starting a price war in these segments would be a kamikaze operation.

Pronounced conservatism in the industry

Insurance companies are often highly profitable and are – quite rightly – afraid of e-commerce because it has proved impossible to earn money on the internet (thus far). What is more, they are often congenitally risk-averse and view e-commerce as a minefield on which it is always best to let someone else be the plucky pioneer.

Just as in other areas of the economy, there is no reason why any single one of these conceits will represent a lasting, insurmountable barrier. Yet taken in conjunction, they do offer a convincing explanation of why a range of other goods, both material and immaterial, has been taken onto the internet first. Primarily from the point of view of the providers (but also as seen from the customer end and from the positions of potential challengers), it has simply not been worth trying out new insurance sales models on the internet.

The insurance policies which are already sold in number on the internet are often little more than extensions to products being bought (cancellation insurance for travel, damage/theft insurance for technical devices) or are of the simpler sort (car insurance).

Most insurance policies sold online are little more than product extensions or are of the simpler sort.

A range of other products is only present on the internet in an advert (if at all), and customers then go to a bank, broker, or bureau to become a policyholder.

Insurance as a product

The particularities of several types of insurance and the legal frameworks in which they can be sold generate the complexity that is one of the reasons why you can buy a bed for a five-figure sum on Amazon but still can't get a life insurance policy from them. Although various countries and jurisdictions have different insurance markets, what they all have in common (in developed economies, at least) is a large amount of red tape.

There are two key forms of insurance. One is compulsory insurance prescribed by lawmakers to citizens: in several European countries such as Germany, for example, citizens are required by law to take out health insurance. Other typical mandatory policies are limited to specific activities: car insurance for drivers, for example, or professional insurance in various fields of work or circumstances (the US requires Defence Base Act insurance for workers hired by the government to work abroad, for instance). The other category is non-compulsory insurance: these are policies which consumers may choose, but are under no obligation, to take out to cover various risks; they vary from country to country in popularity, but include big sub-categories of policies to cover products purchased or home contents insurance (in Germany, almost all adults have third-party liability insurance to boot).

In terms of marketing them, these two categories line up with the two key forms of sales: compulsory insurances are **pull**, while non-compulsory policies are **push** products. All things told, there is about as much demand for compulsory policies as lawmakers say there should be, which means that customers generally come to insurers. With non-compulsory products, meanwhile, insurers need to explain their value to customers and thus persuade them to sign up, thereby creating demand.

To analyse the current state of the insurance market and identify the risks and opportunities for insurers in e-commerce, however, we need to nuance this somewhat broad-brush definition. After all, there are plenty of policies which are very sensible but not compulsory (income protection insurance for borrowers taking out a mortgage, for example); yet because customers are aware of their benefits, they will often go to insurers of their own accord, meaning that pull sales are not a one-to-one match to legally mandatory policies. For insurers, this means that they can often only reach customers who have already made the decision to insure a specific risk and convince them of the benefits of their policy when compared to others; by the same token, customers have a choice to make between various providers, but must choose one in the end. After all, they are either required – or feel required – to take out a policy. It is neither necessary nor, in most cases, possible to persuade customers of the benefits of insurance *per se*.

Other policies, however, need to be pushed.

A cancellation insurance policy is by no means necessary for every customer who buys a holiday or a travel ticket.

Customers frequently need the policy explained to them and to be given a specific example of a case in which it would be of value to them before they will even consider the product. The same is true of supplementary health insurance: even in countries with comprehensive health cover like Germany or the UK, consumers are often ill-informed on issues such as dental cover, and insurers need to explain to them just how high their bills will be if one of their molars ever needs a root canal and a crown; other consumers are fully aware of the price of complicated dental work, but prefer to build up their own contingency fund.

Besides the pull and push sales procedures, we also need to apply another distinction to insurance: **simple** versus **complex** policies. The information needed to take a decisions on products such as professional incapacity insurance, for example, often requires a professional eye: questions about prior health and the meaning of their answers for the offer made are very difficult for the prospective policyholder to weigh up; then there are various types of protection, from full disability through to less comprehensive cover, and then decisions to be taken as to whether to opt for a lump-sum payment or a monthly pension... A car insurance policy, however, is a pretty standard product which can be bought by anyone who is capable of purchasing a car in the first place.

Taken together, all of these considerations can be fed into a simple grid:

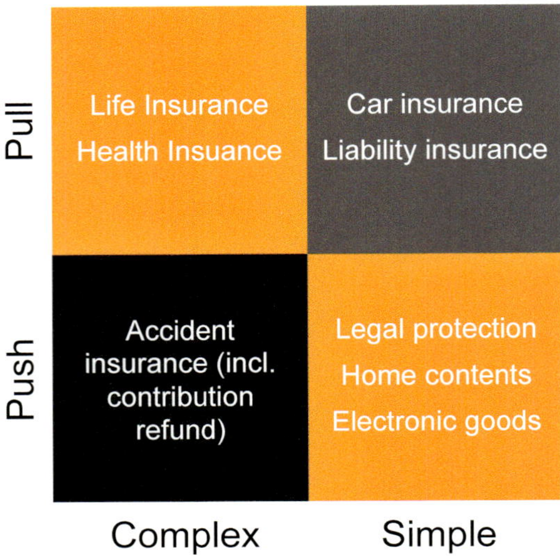

Fig. 4.8: Insurance policies classified by complexity vs. simplicity and pull sales vs. push sales
Source: www.kassenzone.de

The grey area covers policies which are simple in structure and which most consumers require – and, interestingly enough, it is precisely these policies which are already very easy to sell on the internet today. Then again, the results of this shift have not exactly whetted insurers' appetite for expanding online sales into other insurance segments: it is this area in particular in which margins have been wiped out in recent years and in which customers are also increasingly buying from other providers and not directly from insurers. Why, given this precedent, would insurers want to open the sluice gates to areas which have thus far been protected from the flood?

It would, in any case, be no easy matter to start selling products in the orange squares on the internet. Customers do not frequently go online to search for the simple ones such as home contents or legal protection – and those who do are not always the kind of customers insurers want. Someone googling "legal protection cover" identifies themselves as a risk factor to even a rookie actuary. It is customers who get talked into taking out legal protection by their insurance "adviser" (you'll see why we're using scare-quotes here a bit later) who are likely to be better customers because they don't need the product post-haste for a looming court case – and may also forget they even have coverage and never make use of it. So the ideal customer for these types of insurance is not out there on the net; if anything, in fact, any insurer trying to grow this segment too aggressively through online sales channels and by reacting to customer demand may in fact be attracting too high a level of risk.

The issue is completely the reverse when it comes to complex pull products such as compulsory health insurance or life policies: these products are frequently searched for on the internet and there is no reason that this should make insurers wary – in Europe, fit, young, healthy people require compulsory health insurance like anyone else.

But the policies are too complex to be sold on the internet.

The reams of questions which need to be ask to classify the prospective policyholder properly make for a long, complicated booking process or (far worse, both for customers and providers) an erroneous choice of policy. That almost all insurers therefore shy away from offering online policies in the black section – i.e. non-compulsory policies for which there is little demand in any case – is no surprise at all.

It remains to be seen whether these issues can be surmounted by top-quality support hotlines or streamlined booking processes in browsers. There are already several successful direct insurers – i.e. insurers who have never had networks of brokers selling their products – who have internet presences offering information and premium calculators for almost all of their products: CosmosDirekt, for example, is Europe's largest direct insurer, and also offers live webchat support.

Then again, just how many complex policies CosmosDirekt sells directly to consumers on the internet away from its bread-and-butter segment of car insurance and similar is questionable. Anyone aged over 30 and looking for an incapacity insurance quote from their online engine gets a message stating that "Incapacity insurance policies for young professionals can only be offered to customers up until their 30th birthday. We recommend that you take out a standard incapacity insurance policy." The difference between the standard policy and the one for young professionals is not explained; there is also no explanation as to why there is no possibility of taking out a standard policy with the insurer despite it having a heading offering "incapacity insurance". Here, at the very latest, customers are likely to lose patience and head for a professional – who will, of course, use similar or perhaps even then same type of calculator, but who has a better grasp of the issues at hand.

As long as experienced direct sellers are having difficulty explaining the complexity of their products on the internet in a way customers can understand – and as long as customers making these kind of potentially life-changing purchasing decisions get cold feet and, following a preliminary internet search, head for the nearest broker or adviser – some areas of insurance will not be drawn into direct online sales.

Earning money with insurance as a product

What is more, the incumbents in the insurance market have absolutely no motivation to explain and present their more complex products on the internet in such a way as the average consumer can understand and then purchase them. This would make what is currently a very opaque business into a transparent one – and when has the provider of a product ever benefited from more transparency in their markets? (Just look at all those travel agents who've closed since the 90s.)

Depending on their precise positioning, almost all of the established insurance providers have more or less grounds to fear a substantial improvement in customer understanding and of expansion in direct sales. Although their precise definitions and relative importance vary between countries – largely due to differences in their legislative frameworks – there are currently four major types of individuals and organisations selling insurance in most advanced economies:

- Insurance agents (tied to one insurer; directly employed or freelance)
- Insurance brokers (independent of specific insurers)
- Banks (often tied to one or few insurer(s))
- Other outlets (e.g. car dealerships, airlines)

The other outlets tend to simply upsell one-off insurance policies to match their products, making them a lucrative but comparatively one-dimensional channel. A far more complex issue is that of insurance brokers and agents: the latter, above all, will often, depending on what their jurisdiction allows them to get away with, also use a range of words such as "consultant" or "adviser" in more or less brazen attempts to disguise the fact that, whether they are openly tied to one insurance company or working for a bank, they are by definition limited to selling the products of one or, at best, a few select providers – and earn their keep by taking commissions on policies sold. While independent brokers, meanwhile are free to recommend the most suitable product for their clients regardless of which insurer offers it, they too have a vested interested in selling the policies which provide them with the highest rate of commission (indeed, without a basic salary, they may have an even greater interest in so doing).

As such, very little by way of real "advice", "consultancy", or "brokerage" is really taking place.

Simply put, with the commission-based model, which "prices in" (some might say "conceals") the fees due to the agent or broker both on signing and in monthly premiums, anyone selling insurance is incentivised to place the most profitable policy, not the best for the client. The only way round this issue is to redesign the model so that clients pay a fee for consultation, not commission on the product sold. On paper, this approach suits everyone: customers pay up-front for the service they get (advice) and there are no fees hidden in the small print, while the brokers are still paid for their time: what is more, compared to the recurring commission model, the up-front fee should be cheaper for customers because the brokers get paid either way, whereas previously, the hidden fees had to also cover costs for all of the meetings held which didn't lead to a prospect signing up to a policy. So in theory, customers should be clamouring for this model to be introduced so that they can get genuine independent advice, no strings attached, for a fair fee.

So much for the theory. With its system of regulated independent financial advisers who sell life insurance and pensions and may only take up-front fees, the United Kingdom gone the furthest here (although it still allows the more opaque brokerage model for general insurance). The result in practice, however, has been that many customers now avoid the issue entirely and refrain from signing up for the cover they need because they see just how much they would be paying the adviser. Since a society marred by entire generations of insurance-shy, risk-exposed consumers is certainly not the aim of the game, lawmakers elsewhere in advanced economies (Germany and many US states, for example, have been keeping their eye on examples of this kind of reform) will be unlikely to charge into this kind of wholesale shake-up.

So really, everyone involved in insurance has a strong interest in keeping things as they are.

From insurers and their salespeople through to lawmakers and, yes, even customers, who – as far as economic theory goes – should be demanding change but who, when it comes to it, are either also happy to keep the status quo or anything but assiduous in taking advantage of more favourable structures.

The winners of this lack of transparency are the insurers: the whole way insurance companies earn money in usual circumstances is based on informational asymmetry in any case, and the existing market structures guarantee that they will continue to profit from it. After all, the average customer has trouble even understanding all of the provisions of a professional incapacity insurance policy, let alone the tricks of how it is priced; this makes him or her almost unable to compare various offers unaided. Under the current system, however, he or she doesn't even have a chance of knowing what percentage of the salesperson's commission he or she is paying and how much profit the insurer is making on the policy.

Insurers: rabbits in the headlights?

Then again, if there is one thing the internet favours, it is the exchange, collation, and publication of information; e-commerce, meanwhile, offers a structural advantage to new business models. These two simple truths are not good news for those looking to defend the status quo. The overtures of the fight to come are already clear for all to hear: there are price comparison websites specialising in insurance such as Check24 in Germany and the first online-only direct insurers such as Hastings in the UK. Despite its sedate location on the south coast of Sussex, Hastings talks about itself like a Silicon Valley start-up ("agile, data-driven, digital" are the adjectives its PR people use) and it is a thoroughly tech-based approach: customers buy vehicle and home contents insurance from Hastings online and submit claims forms and manage their own data electronically, too.

That this low-cost self-service model helps Hastings keep its processes streamlined and be more efficient than classic insurers is beyond question; what is also certain, however, is that the savings it makes are by no means so impressive that it can afford to offer the kinds of discounts it does. Off the record, industry observers will tell you that the company will, if at all, just about be breaking even; any margin left over will be paper-thin, and so it can only survive through constant growth; this in turn explains its continuing drive to expand. This uncomfortable fact has everyone else on the British market oscillating between occasional bouts of confidence ("Don't worry; at this rate, they'll fold by the end of the year!") and outright panic ("Why is our new business down so sharply? Why are we getting so many terminations of contract?").

*In other European markets,
the established players look on in silent horror
and hope that the contagion doesn't make it over the Channel.*

If the story sounds familiar, that's because it is. Hastings is to insurance now what Amazon was to retail in the mid-2000s: its growth rates are impressive, its margins non-existent – and so everyone else is frozen like a rabbit in the beam of an approaching headlamp, hoping that the blinding light goes out soon. We all know what happens to rabbits in that situation, though.

Nevertheless, it's easy to understand why the board rooms of major insurance companies are paralysed: no-one wants to go down in company history as the guy who swapped a business with 10% margins for one in which, if you're lucky, you break even. It's not that the insurance bosses are stupid: they know that the future doesn't look good and that the rabbit needs to get off the road. Yet the result is much the same as in retail a decade back: "task forces" get set up to examine how the company can "turn the risks of the internet into opportunities". Yet many of these initiatives fail at the first hurdle by misconstruing the internet as simply another sales channel and ignoring the uncomfortable, fundamental questions: "Will customers still accept our business model as it is in 10 years?" Until this kind of analysis is permitted, all of the "project groups" and "think-tanks" will be prevented from actually getting to results which make sense.

Once again, it's not that insurers aren't trying. They're even going a step further and financing hip external "incubators": retail never got to this stage. In Germany, for example, Allianz has set up its very own "digital accelerator" with the aim of finding new business models for the group and anchoring them within its structures. Yet the whole thing is kept near to Allianz headquarters and while it does look like a relatively independent part of the group, a part of the group it remains: both the location itself (in Munich rather than, say, Berlin) and the fact that this location is right next to HQ would tend to disconnect the operation from truly revolutionary thinking. Call it what you will: an incubator, an accelerator, a start-up builder – it takes more than a cool name and free snacks to produce real innovation.

With its AXA Lab in San Francisco, the AXA Group has upped the ante.

Similarly to many other heritage companies, the corporate monolith has decided to make its pilgrimage to within spitting distance of Silicon Valley in the hope of being closer to the real action and then relaying what it overhears back to home base. It's certainly the more promising of the two approaches, but will also turn out to be ultimately futile unless members of the board with real say in the organisation's affairs make frequent visits and get their hands dirty pushing the change. Moreover, it's often not a lack of new ideas that is the issue, but transplanting them successfully back into the core of the business and stopping them being rejected in HQ. That's why stories of mail order companies who have made a real success of the internet are few and far between; why out of the big three in Germany, for example, only Otto managed to make the leap while Quelle and Neckermann (and countless smaller operators) got caught in the headlights. They were in the majority then and remain in the majority now – in the graveyard of dead business roadkill. That means that simply in terms of sheer statistics, it is unlikely that a majority of today's insurance companies will move early and decisively enough to avoid the advancing wheels.

What is more, if retailers have been failing due to dangerous insouciance, internal inertia, and the forlorn hope that things will stay as familiar and as profitable as ever in the face of obvious indications to the contrary, what hope is there for insurers? After all, the business is still very profitable as it is, there are almost no serious competitors in sight, and insurance executives are, it is probably safe to say, some of the world's least risk-happy businesspeople.

In view of this, companies in the insurance sector will avoid transforming their nicely profitable legacy business into one determined by value-for-money-based competition on the internet until they have no other choice: after all, switching too early would destroy both their own margins and those of the competition. Therefore, all of the existing players have every reason to keep things exactly as they are, and it is unlikely that any of them will act until Amazon, Google, or perhaps Facebook start to develop their own products. If that sounds unlikely, it is worth remembering just how much these companies, with their treasure troves of personal data, know about their customers; they can certainly find out more of relevance to risk classifications than any insurance company out there and are also (and this is perhaps of equal pertinence) some of the only potential participants who can handle the regulatory issues in various markets simultaneously. For the GAFA companies, the challenge of getting accreditation in several territories concurrently is one that their legal departments would be able to manage very well – and one that would, in terms of cost, be itemised next to petty cash on their balance sheets. Start-ups, meanwhile, face an uphill regulatory and financial slog in advanced markets where licences are difficult to obtain and without considerable sums successfully invested, there can be no cross-financing from capital gains in the early years. It's a tough start, but one which is, if you ask industry insiders, by no means impossible and could probably succeed in a major European economy with €20 to €50 million of investment (Rocket Internet, by way of comparison, regularly ploughs €20 million into companies which sell furniture on the net, see 4.3). There is no shortage of examples from online retail of just how quickly a game-changing concept can come out of nowhere.

If the fact that there still hasn't been an internet revolution in the insurance industry would seem odd to a time traveller from the recent past, it would probably seem even stranger to one from the near future.

4.5 Tech: the magic bullet and the gun

One of the key reasons why legacy insurers, or established companies in whichever other segments will be the next to feel the heat from hungry internet start-ups, have real difficulty responding to the newcomers is not just the (justified) fear of jeopardising previously profitable business models. Besides their ability as young, agile, fast-growing companies to sacrifice margin today for, well, whatever in the future (see above, 4.1),

the other thing that makes digital attackers so dangerous is their relationship to technology.

Essentially, for the most successful challengers in all sectors, the tech is actually more important than the business. Look at Uber, whose ambition is not – whatever taxi drivers may fear – to become the biggest and best cab service ever: rather, Uber's ambition is learn as much as possible about which journeys people want to make and when. Today, this does indeed enable it to become a formidable competitor for taxis' business; tomorrow, it will allow it to take on everyone from public transport authorities to car manufacturers. Uber's business model will change to match what its technical possibilities become. Rather than a teleological approach to tech – i.e. stating a goal for the business and then building the technical and technological means to achieve whatever that goal is – Uber and others have a tech-led approach, full stop. The technology takes them wherever it is it goes.

This fact shouldn't be, and probably isn't, a surprise – there's a reason these companies are called "tech start-ups" in the media, after all. Yet it's a fact that seems to be at once universally acknowledged but barely understood, by everyone from established businesses to policymakers, who see tech as a magic bullet which, depending on their viewpoint, can either save or destroy their business/legislative frameworks, rather than as what it actually is: the gun which fires the bullets.

Established businesses and IT systems

E-commerce is an area which highlights this category error. There are still retailers out there who think that unparalleled success in selling things online is still just around the corner: all they need to do is install the new shop system that their IT department has been talking about and, hey presto, sales will rocket! That this is by no means the case has yet to dawn on many.

In a way, it's easy to understand how this misconception came about. In the early years of e-commerce, the e-commerce systems deployed by large retailers were essentially extensions to existing ERP programs – a catalogue turned into a website with a shopping basket function. These bolt-ons allowed them to start selling on the internet, often with passable results. As a first step, this was entirely logical, but soon reached its limits inasmuch as a system based on selling things to customers in-store is not much use for responding to competition on the internet. Enterprise systems like Hybris, ATG, and Intershop never purported to be much else except a shop-window on the internet and most larger retailers grasped this around the turn of the Millennium, switching to a next generation of systems which was, to a large extent, decoupled from existing ERPs: from 2003 onwards, internet-focussed shop systems such as Demandware, Magento, and GSI did the running. This development had several effects, the principal one of which was to divide up companies internally: many retailers had to establish a kind of E-Commerce/IT super-department which span away from existing activities. While this allowed increased freedom of movement in the e-commerce environment, it often led to double or triple sets of customer data, marketing infrastructure, and even product information: many companies are now faced with increasing costs in maintaining both an ERP environment and an online shop infrastructure (and have a very powerful IT department which, oddly enough, doesn't see the problem with having lots of money and resources pass through it...). Attempts to link the two to avoid costly manual work and typical multichannel mess-ups are proving challenging – so much so that it is quite understandable that many such companies are looking to start afresh with a third generation which is neither ERP-centric or shop-centric, but customer-centric.

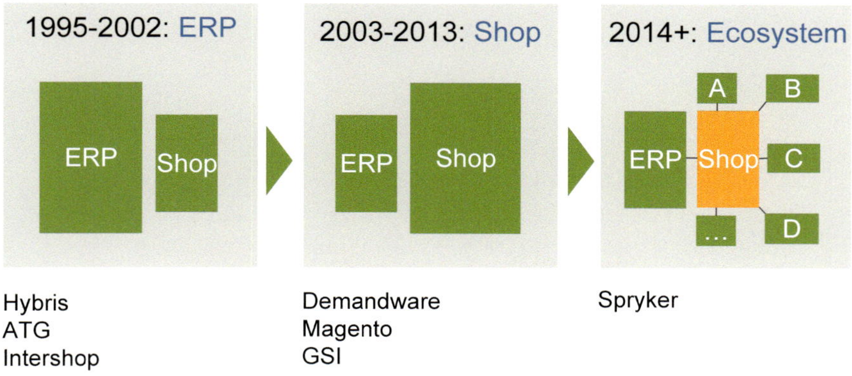

Fig. 4.9: Evolution of e-commerce technology
Source: www.kassenzone.de

Full-blooded e-commerce companies, of course, have always had customer-focussed systems: obviously, they have ERP to manage their inventories, but it is utterly subordinate to the shop, from which everything else stems. What is more, their shops are often custom-built from the start: Asos, Wayfair, Zalando... Take an e-commerce pure-play and it will very frequently be based on proprietary software into which it has poured investment over the years. We're not talking about "shop systems" here, either, but software which happens to be very good at serving a shop – and at doing plenty of other things that give these companies their competitive edge. These platforms are the cores of entire ecosystems composed, besides the shop, of OMS, CMS, PIM, BI, CRM, and various apps for multiple devices. This allows them not just to respond to market movements, but to devise and add new services by developing what they have and thus move the market.

Companies aware of the importance of a tech-centred approach and yet lacking the resources, in-house expertise, or simply the time to start on the green field have a new option in the form of **Spryker**.

This commerce framework is the first commercially available solution based on the experience of successful technology-driven approaches. Spryker was designed by the developers behind hundreds of Rocket Internet and Project A Ventures start-ups and the best practices around agile development, testing environments, and scalability are part of the foundations of Spryker. With a powerful, yet lean and highly customizable framework, Spryker offers two main advantages for its clients:

1. The established technology stack offers the security of tried-and-tested standard software, which **reduces the risk** of building a similar setup in-house. Pure in-house builds à la Wayfair or Zalando require tremendous amounts of investment, are time-intensive and carry very high risks, especially in terms of software architecture. Spryker reduces precisely these risks to a minimum, while offering full control over the technology and giving clients the flexibility of a genuine, pure-breed tech stack.
2. Spryker is 100% developer friendly and geared towards maximizing **developer productivity** in ambitious commerce projects. Based on PHP architecture and with a modular approach, Spryker enables agile teams to grow faster in a cheaper, more productive way. Individual requirements can easily be integrated, including data-driven approaches in the fields of business intelligence, CRM, and online marketing.

Spryker is the next-generation e-commerce platform, catering to market players which value execution speed and see technology as a value driver for their business.

Author Alex Graf launched **Spryker** with Project A Ventures and Nils Seebach in 2014.

In view of this, discussions about the failed Magento 2 and the increasing popularity of Shopware are sideshows, as are the merits of the various enterprise systems still in use such as Hybris. The real issue is that legacy companies are still engaged in what Donald Ferguson, the man behind IBM's popular Websphere platform, has called "the endgame fallacy": attempting to adapt existing IT infrastructure so that it can deal with all of the challenges now and soon to be facing the company in the digital world. As Ferguson's mantra has it, IT departments in large companies spend around three quarters of their budget just on maintaining operational systems; trying to change these systems – and change them so fundamentally that they are ready for the "endgame" – in an existing environment is folly.

The conclusions which follow from this are, of course, deeply uncomfortable. Organisations who are really serious about e-commerce success in the future (and indeed organisations in any other number of sectors soon to get the "GAFA treatment") will have to look at writing off two to three decades of IT development and starting afresh: the first step for many will, counterintuitively perhaps, be taking this restart out of the hands of the existing IT and e-commerce departments in order to make sure that new development is as far away from the thought patterns of the old systems as possible; software development will need to grow from being something one department does to being the centrepiece of the company and the area where it sees itself creating value. Any company which says e-commerce is now its central plank and yet still doesn't have at least one executive with a genuine understanding of the technology on the board is not putting its money where its mouth is and will not be rewarded with success.

In other words, rather than trying to develop the magic bullet, companies would be better off looking to invent a new kind of gun.

"Woke up this morning ..."

There is some debate as to how companies can best go about starting afresh. IT advisory Gartner coined the term "bi-model IT" for a strategy in which big legacy operators use the profit they can still draw from existing structures to finance their own digital start-ups inside their organisations. In other words, the flow of cash which is slowly starting to ebb away gets used to build the next business model before it dries up completely; by that stage, new reserves should have come on stream and the company will have managed the transition.

While this sounds like a reasonable approach and some successes may yet be achieved applying it, with a view to the rules of GAFAnomics (see 4.1 above), we see this way of doing things as far riskier than it appears. To repeat Mark Zuckerberg's quotation, "the only strategy that is guaranteed to fail is not taking risks." Starting up a few digital units inside an existing structure is not in any way risky – and the people working in them will not feel like they are taking risks – or, looking at their payslips and thinking about the next meeting with management, feel like taking risks either.

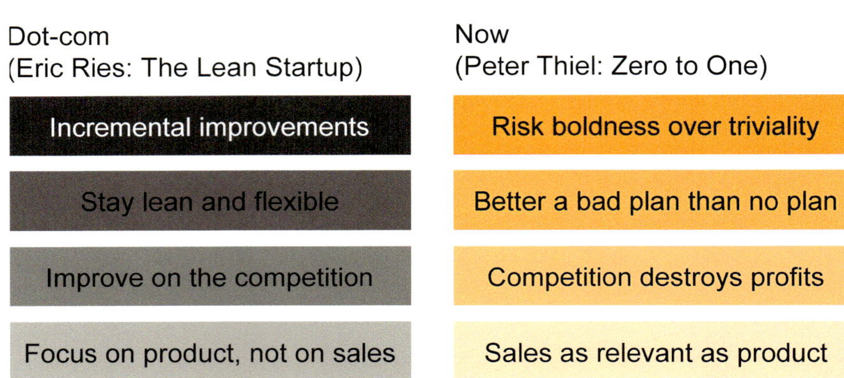

Dot-com
(Eric Ries: The Lean Startup)
Incremental improvements
Stay lean and flexible
Improve on the competition
Focus on product, not on sales
Now
(Peter Thiel: Zero to One)
Risk boldness over triviality
Better a bad plan than no plan
Competition destroys profits
Sales as relevant as product

Fig. 4.10: Founder Advice 2005 vs. 2015

Source: www.kassenzone.de (based on the books of Eric Ries and Peter Thiel)

Real risk-taking is not behaving like insurance companies with their trendy incubators (see 4.4 above), but behaving like Google, which is restructuring itself as Alphabet as we speak so that the changes in its technology and its business are reflected in the company structure. Can you imagine a legacy company in any other industry which is worth billions annually changing everything from its departmental organigram to its name, pretty much overnight? No, us either.

Not that things even need to go that far: in Germany, former mail order company Otto and heritage print publisher Axel Springer have both shown that it can be enough to simply take digital innovation seriously and finance it on the green field away from the prying eyes of established parts of the business. Otto has been rewarded by being able to hold its own as an online retailer while Springer's once button-down executives have – beyond enjoying the Californian sun and growing beards – reaped the benefits as ever higher portions of their turnover are generated by bits, not sheets of paper. By the same token, simply being a young, tech-led attacker is no guarantee of lasting success, either: however agile companies try to keep themselves, all the hot-desking and scrumming and microservices in the world cannot keep large organisations from slowing somewhat – and, crucially, do not slow the pace of the market down, either. Even Amazon (stress on "even") is not able to respond at lightning speed in all of its manifold business areas: Netflix is definitely offering better service in streaming (Amazon competes primarily on price, i.e. by throwing its services into Prime packages), and retail market segments which by rights should belong to the Giant from Seattle already by now may well yet escape it (see furniture, 4.3, above).

Then again, in most segments,
Amazon is a disrupter and not the disrupted.

And this is likely, given how seriously the company takes investment in research and development, to continue to be the case for quite some time. It may be beaten back on one or two fronts, but the Giant is able to sustain continuous advances on many others while, in the background, it develops ever newer and ever more lethal weaponry capable of reshaping the battlefield. For their competitors, it may look like the GAFA companies are shooting magic bullets – and, to a certain extent, they are – but that's not the real point. They're preparing to fight the next war while others are only just realising that they need to get themselves a new gun.

5 Opinions from practice

5.1 Interview with Dr. Florian Heinemann

Dr. Florian Heinemann is a serial entrepreneur and investor with unparalleled experience in the start-up scene: he was, for instance, a co-founder of JustBooks/Abebooks, which was bought by Amazon in 2008, and spent more than four years as managing director at Rocket Internet, where he was particularly involved with Zalando and edarling. Today, Heinemann is managing director of an early-phase investor and company builder he co-founded in Berlin, Project A Ventures, where he is primarily responsible for performance marketing, CRM, and business intelligence. Project A invests in digital business models and offers its operational expertise to young businesses in the e-commerce/marketplace, digital infrastructure/AdTech, and SaaS segments. The portfolio includes companies such as World Remit, nu3, Contorion and Glow. Florian Heinemann also works as a business angel. He did degrees in business studies at the WHU Otto Beisheim School of Management and Entrepreneurship/Innovation management at RWTH Aachen, going on to complete his doctorate at the Wharton School of the University of Pennsylvania.

When you look back at the first project set up around the Millennium, in what ways was e-commerce different at that time as compared to today? What has changed since?

It's been 15 years, so there's been an enormous amount of change. I think the best way to describe was has happened is to look at things in various dimensions:

1. Back then, there simply wasn't the widespread availability of various product ranges that there is today. This meant that simply making specific goods or product mixes available on the internet was much more of a unique selling proposition than it is today – and promised more success.

2. In all areas of value creation, the technological foundations in the early years were still quite rudimentary; there was also a lot less by way of know-how and systems in areas such as customer acquisition, online marketing, and e-commerce infrastructure. Far fewer service providers were active in the market and they only offered limited product ranges.

3. Back then, a lot of the experience we have today and much of the stock of best practices we can apply to e-commerce projects was still missing. That means that those of us setting up businesses in the early years had far less knowledge than today's entrepreneurs. What is more, many of the earliest online retailers had been working in the mail order sector for years beforehand and were simply putting their catalogues on the internet. While they certainly had a head-start in distance selling and logistics as disciplines, they didn't have any specific e-commerce experts – because there weren't any around. It was enough to be a fast learner and you'd already be streaks ahead of the rest. Today, of course, the situation is different: many of the experts have 10 to 15 years of experience behind them and, as a result, need make their profiles distinctive in other ways.

4. Consumers have changed a lot too. In the last 15 years, it's not just companies, but customers who have gained experience in e-commerce. Today's consumers know how to find, compare, and order products on the internet; what is more, the spectrum of products they are buying on the internet is a lot broader. Customers have also become more comfortable than they once were with sharing their personal data as part of the ordering process.

5. The logistics companies, too, have made big improvements to their processes; they are better adapted than they ever have been before to the requirements of e-commerce.

This means that, overall, the conditions are more favourable than ever to operating successfully in e-commerce. The market has grown up – but then again, standards have matured to match, and companies need to do a lot more to be successful in e-commerce.

Your own area of expertise is online marketing more than anything: have developments here been the same? Have the technologies and challenges in this area changed as much as e-commerce overall?

Yes, without a shadow of a doubt. Many of the methods anchored in online marketing today were simply non-existent back then. When we started, Google Adwords was still a long way off; price comparison sites had much less reach, too, and the availability of banner adverts was also comparatively limited.

In fact, it was often enough to simply have a better grasp of the methods of online marketing than the competition and you already had an advantage in acquiring customers. Nowadays, of course, the number of customer acquisition channels has gone up by quite some margin and, what is more, simply being "a bit better" at a single channel such as, say, Google Adwords is no longer enough to make you more successful than your competitors. Then there are the various challenges of actively managing relationships with existing customers: back then, hardly anyone was doing that. Amazon is perhaps one of the few who concentrated on long-term customer relationship management early on; the others were mainly trying to make sure that every single order turned a profit. Nowadays, there is no way you can work like that; the perspective has broadened from orders to relationships. This, of course, makes online marketing more complicated.

Another "new" area of online marketing are the various disciplines such as business intelligence, tracking, and controlling. Back at the turn of Millennium, the customer journey, for example, was of almost no importance at all. Yet in order to be successful on the market today, you've of course got to have a very high level of business intelligence. It is simply no longer enough to have well-positioned customer acquisition structures; you need CRM and BI systems to match. This has made the set of requirements more technology-laden overall: data management and system-side support are much more relevant to marketing activities than they used to be. The same developments can be seen in shop systems, too: anyone looking to play in the big leagues here needs to implement a far higher level of technical sophistication.

This is where the development towards specialised technology service providers has taken on completely new dimensions since then: there is specific software for almost all online marketing disciplines now, each of which offers good or very good performance. What this means, however, is that system architects are needed within organisations who are able to integrate of all of these external software components and tool-sets the best way possible; but at the moment, not many organisations have this kind of expert on board. The new way in which companies gain the upper hand today is therefore by employing good in-house architects or other sources of know-how in this area who are able to orchestrate all of the relevant technologies and the vast amounts of knowledge companies have accrued in e-commerce in order to produce real value. Finding this kind of architecture expert is one of the biggest challenges facing many companies today – especially since there is no check-list to run through when interviewing candidates. It's more or less about employing people who look like they have the potential to become this kind of architecture expert, and many companies have trouble gauging potential. This will change in a few years' time once more of this type of expert with the relevant experience is around on the market. The good news, however, is that companies don't need whole cohorts of architects: one or two are often enough.

There is more and more talk about a shift in power in online marketing from away from Google and towards Facebook, Amazon, and other established e-commerce businesses who are increasingly selling advertising to third parties. Is this a development you too see happening and, if so, what do you make of it?

This development is very clearly visible on platforms which have a) a broad reach and b) get a lot of people in this reach to log in. That means Google, Facebook, Amazon, and Ebay, although Apple and Alibaba of course also have potential here. These companies have an enormous advantage over traditional advertising platforms such as media companies, who are set to lose much of their relevance as a result of these trends. The question is which of these strong log-in platforms will win out, and it is, in my view, beyond question that Google will see a lot of its power ebb away to other players. The digital advertising market overall is still growing very strongly and is currently experiencing a strong expansion into video and moving images as viewing patterns transfer to the internet and, above all, YouTube; this is drawing media budgets – which of course follow the users – away from traditional media into digital advertising and, in my opinion, Facebook and Amazon are in a good position in comparison with Google as they can use their valuable data about the demography, interests, and (especially Amazon) transactions of their users to create profiles. For traditional advertising formats which concentrate on target groups, Facebook is probably the best platform; in performance and transaction marketing, it is more likely to be Amazon which can offer the better data. While there is no doubt that Google too is going to be very successful here, there will be some evening out of power. Nevertheless, if you ask me, the real question is not "What will become of Google?" but more "What is going to happen to all the others?" What I am seeing is a haemorrhaging of influence from traditional advertising platforms and media agencies towards log-in platforms: if 90% of advertising budgets will soon be being spent on only 4 to 5 major portals, then there is no reason that companies can't take care of that themselves, and this robs agencies of their role. This is precisely what the big platforms want, too, and they are working to make sure there is as little room as possible for any intermediaries looking to add value. The winners will be the handful of platforms while most other participants will be among the clear losers on the market,

What would be your advice to an entrepreneur looking to build up an e-commerce business? Is there even any point to setting up in e-commerce today?

It's mainly a question of goals here: what is our entrepreneur looking to achieve? If he or she is looking to build a profitable business selling goods on the internet, then there is nothing to stop them. At the same time, they ought to bear in mind that the larger the share of the product mix on which they are competing with the big e-commerce platforms, the harder it will be for them to grow above the market. I can imagine almost no case in which it would be advisable to try and beat established shops using tools such as performance marketing; the better way for newcomers is to see how they can compile a product mix which gives them a unique advantage over established players – i.e. by offering attractive own-brand goods or an exhaustive depth of niche products.

As long as we're talking about seven-figure turnover here, there is no reason all of this can't work. If, however, the stated aim is to become an e-commerce player in the big leagues turning over more than 100 million Euros and thus attract investors, then the requirements are really rather different. It's a steep gradient. There needs to be a significant capital investment to be competitive in shop systems, performance marketing, and business intelligence; by "significant", I mean seven-to-eight-digit Euro sums. The product mix, too, needs to be clearly distinguishable from others in order to win market share and make it to eight-or-nine-digit turnover. At Project A, we view this as an increasingly tough, and indeed increasingly unrealistic, challenge. If your definition of success is still building a 100-million-a-year business with start-up capital of 1 million within five years, then I think you are probably doomed to fail. I think a more accurate rule-of-thumb here is that, in the medium term, an entrepreneur can expect to earn two-to-three Euros for every one he or she invests. Then we get to the next question, which is whether a company can work profitably or not. Anyone competing closely with Amazon in terms of their product mix will be working against a business model which doesn't even have to turn a profit on the goods it sells because it has access to secondary revenue streams which people setting up a new business do not.

In my view, there are two areas in which entrepreneurs today can build a profitable e-commerce business:

1. Brand differentiation: this means creating and pushing an attractive own brand which can command a price premium and therefore assures profitability on a structural level.
2. Platform model: the possibility of making your own infrastructure available to third parties and earning additional turnover in so doing.

Besides working with a niche product mix which, by definition, limits turnover to a relatively small figure, these two approaches offer the opportunity to build up a successful e-commerce business model. Of course there are exceptions here, but in my view, it is clear that this is where the journey is going.

In your view, which e-commerce models are best equipped to deal with the future of online shopping? What are the prospects for retailers, intermediaries, marketplaces, mail order companies, and manufacturers?

The worst equipped are, beyond a doubt, the retailers and mail order companies: they are facing a very difficult future. Marketplace business models work fine if the market is big and complex enough to allow them to occupy a distinct territory in the long term. Manufacturers of attractive products are, as far as I can see, in a far stronger position as they can keep control of margins; then again, what manufacturers cannot do is keep 100% control of the medium-term direction a brand takes and how its price develops, and this leads to some uncertainty. In my view, those in the strongest position are well-placed intermediaries (Google, Facebook): these platforms can build up a long-lasting competitive advantage and are, at the same time, less affected by external, uncontrollable factors than brand manufacturers.

5.2 Interview with René Köhler

René Marius Köhler is the founder and CEO of internetstores GmbH, known in Germany for successful e-commerce portals such as fahrrad.de. Even as a teenager, René was never in any doubt that he would one day go into business for himself – and aged 20, he had already set up fahrrad.de ("bicycle.de"), launching himself into an entrepreneurial career with no prior training. Self-taught to this day, René is not just a convincing and knowledgeable e-commerce professional, but has the gift of being able to inspire those around him: in short, he is a natural business leader with a uniquely reliable nose for trends and the proficiency to draw the right conclusions for his internetstores business. In 2010, René won the German Gründerpreis for start-up entrepreneurs.

It was 2003 when you started fahrrad.de. In your view, how has the market changed since then?

Back then, the market was a lot narrower and far less complex: shop systems, enterprise resource planning, marketing channels – there was only a limited number of each, and none was hard to get a hold and implement. At the beginning, for us, performance marketing was a bit of SEO and some SEA; then the price comparison engines came along. Stuff like retargeting or TV adverts for online businesses didn't start until later, though. What is more, there was little by way of BI and CRM software to measure effects. All of this meant that, in the early years, you didn't need whole teams of specialists and, overall, you didn't need much money either. Nowadays, young tech companies need a considerably higher amount of start-up capital to get to the same place; anyone looking to catch up to established online shops in terms of customer numbers and turnover figures is facing high investment costs and long periods of losses until they reach profitability.

Indeed. Developments in the consumer electronics segment online show just how much money is being spent nowadays to by e-commerce growth. For start-ups, every Euro of target turnover costs almost one Euro of investment: is this where e-commerce as an industry is headed overall?

Yes, there is a tendency towards expensive growth, but overall, there is a strong correlation between the amount of competition in the product ranges in question and the costs of expansion. In my experience, you need to invest an absolute minimum a third of your target turnover – i.e. one Euro to make three – to get anywhere; paying one Euro to make one Euro would be the maximum. Depending on the product category you're operating in and how you implement your concept, you'll be somewhere between the 1:3 and 1:1 ratios. Of course, we'd need more precise definitions of business details such as whether inventory is part of the equation or if we are simply putting figures on what it costs to get the business up and running: but, by and large, that's how things look for e-commerce start-ups.

So success is getting ever more expensive, but have the rules for how to be successful changed fundamentally since those early days?

No, the basic principles remain very much the same: it has simply become a lot more difficult to implement them. Given the increase in complexity, the standard required in all areas of e-commerce today is far higher. High-powered data analysis and business intelligence offer completely new possibilities – and impose completely new requirements. When we launched fahrrad.de in 2003, our metrics were so rudimentary that in many cases, advertising campaign successes were measured double or triple across channels: if a customer had clicked on a banner advert above the Google search results, both Google The Search Engine and the Google The Advertiser would report as a conversion; this, of course, led to the cumulative turnover measured from conversions being many times our actual sales. In other words, our metrics were almost meaningless. Today, we measure clear differences based on the point in time at which the customer decides to buy, as well as the length and depth of their interaction in the channel in question, allowing us to be far more precise about which channel contributed what to each conversion.

All these sorts of things have only developed in recent years. Before, you would employ someone to "do online marketing" – i.e. all of it. Now that companies have whole departments or at least teams for each single channel, there has been a high degree of specialisation into channels and even areas of channels: it's a completely different environment. SEO, for example, has become so much more complex, and now you need experts for development, architecture, press relations, and content.

What is more, the proportion of consumer sales which is happening on the net is getting bigger and bigger; as the overall volume of the market grows, so too does its complexity. So the rules and the functionality of e-commerce are still very much as they were ten years ago, but, in order to be a successful player in the market, you've got to make a far larger investment than ten years ago: anyone unwilling or unable to upfront this kind of capital is unlikely to make it to critical mass.

How has, in your view, the balance of power in e-commerce changed since then? And what do manufacturers make of online retailers? A few years back, fahrrad.de had made you quite unpopular among brand manufacturers and you had to develop your own brands to keep the business going. Have things changed?

Yes, they have. Back then, manufacturers viewed online retailers with a lot of suspicion. When we started fahrrad.de, a lot of manufacturers saw us as the bad guys, as disruptive internet types out to take the food off of traditional businesses' plates. This was back in the days when no-one in Germany had heard of Alibaba and Amazon was still very much a bookseller; then you had the old mail order people who were using the internet as a kind of Catalogue 2.0. Then there was us, a pure player in the bicycle industry: lots of people saw us as a threat. Many manufacturers thought there was a fundamental decision to be made about whether to deliver to online retailers or not, and it was a big challenge for us trying to get established brands to sell in our shop back then. We got refusal after refusal stating quite bluntly that purely online outfits would not be supplied; established in-store retailers with existing relationships to manufacturers were in a better position, able to transfer their offline range onto the internet without actually having to ask the brands concerned for permission.

In recent years, however, this state of affairs has changed quite significantly. The industry has seen which online retailers have solid business models – i.e. who serves customers well, provides good service levels, sells at a price fair to the brand (avoiding an online price war), and adheres to legal standards. Slowly but surely, retailers running this kind of business have become recognised partners; it took several years, as manufacturers were facing a lot of pressure from retailers, but soon enough, pressure started to come from customers who wanted to order their bicycles online, too, and the manufacturers changed their position. This means that, today, were are set up as a specialist dealer who works with brands – but on the internet, allowing us to join up supply and demand in an efficient way and deliver products across Europe. In contrast to us, it is the Amazons and Ebays of this world who have come into focus as ruthless, greedy players who pit retailers against each other and try to exercise control over the market by means of price wars.

When competing with Amazon, we at fahrrad.de are of course far more specialised: our expert understanding of the products we sell, our ability to assemble bikes and use specially-designed logistics processes to deliver them, is something Amazon cannot replicate; neither customers nor manufacturers see Amazon as a specialist. Amazon's strength lies quite obviously in the enormous well of customer demand it generates, and it varies as an entity from industry to industry. For customers, Amazon delivers amazing performance, but its uncompromising dealings with brand manufacturers are making it increasingly unpopular among them.

What are your tips for newcomers to the industry and anyone looking to set up a business in e-commerce?

The very first question that anyone setting up an internet-based business should ask themselves is whether they really want to concentrate solely on e-commerce. Today, it's a very challenging area: lots of start-ups fail on product issues – purchasing, inventory management, and delivery to customers. Today's market environment is deeply complex, with a very high level of competition and growing investment requirements. Many who set up in e-commerce struggle to become and stay sufficiently profitable, and entrepreneurs should be prepared for that. Then again, successes are still there to be had.

So if people do decide to set up in e-commerce, the second important issue is, to my mind, choosing the right industry. My experience is that there are some industries which, from an e-commerce point of view, are almost impossible to earn money in. Sometimes it's to do with fundamental business issues such as low margins or high rates of return, or there may already be too much competition in the category in question. Yet another online shoe shop, for example, would probably not be a great idea because, on the one hand, rates of return are high and, on the other, strong players such as Zalando are already active in the market.

We closed our portal fitness.de, for instance, due partly to strong competition in the market: Amazon and heritage mail order companies such as Otto and Neckermann were already selling fitness equipment and machines, as were a large number of specialist stores, large and small. The market is not structurally attractive: customer relationships are less important than in other sectors as the frequency with which people buy fitness equipment is just too low for a valuable customer loyalty to build up; bikes offer far more opportunity to develop a connection to customers based on accessories or children's bikes (which need to be replaced with larger models every couple of years). I see a lot of companies who have great teams and implement their idea very well, but who aren't successful because the industry or the country they're in is wrong. So it really is essential to settle on the right product category.

The third crucial question is about how the business model is set up: is it about serving a niche market, growing slowly, staying independent, and not aiming sky-high in terms of turnover? Or is the idea to aim astronomical, working with an investor-driven model and planning a successful exit at some point?

Once entrepreneurs have answered these three questions as well as they can, it is about actually building the business, and this is where the way the teams are put together becomes decisive. I would recommend dishing out shares in the company to the first employees to make sure that a first-class team is formed quickly at the beginning.

In terms of setting up, there should be an overall focus on building structures and designing processes as efficiently and economically as possible, aiming for a tightly-defined target group. The product range doesn't need to be gigantic right from the start: what is more important is that the products which are on sale are well presented and fully described. Overall, setting up today requires a clearer focus than in the early years.

The technical and staffing complexity of e-commerce has gone up steeply in recent years: in your opinion, which new issues are likely to change the market over the coming years? Are there any tectonic shifts coming up for which you are already preparing?

In the coming years, I expect a wave of consolidation in e-commerce: I doubt we will retain the number of shops we have at the present moment in the industry. Many online shops without a clear profile, lacking in customer loyalty, and operating on turnover of between 2 and 25 million Euros annually, will have to shut down.

Other issues I see developing are as follows.

- Increased verticalisation: more and more brands are now attempting to sell directly to end-consumers on the internet.
- Customer experience: this is going to become a central area as shops which do not offer a special experience of some kind or other will have an increasingly rough ride in the future. Look at the number of online shops today which do not have a clear unique selling point, but which still get really rather good results using SEO: there's a lot of them. Many, however, will need to adapt in the near future or face extinction further down the line.
- Low margins: this is another issue which the industry is going to have to solve. Many online shops run on extremely thin margins and investors are becoming increasingly unwilling to invest in growth with no perspective towards profitability. Even big companies listed on the stock exchange such as Amazon are starting to feel the shift, and I think this will lead to an end to the current situation in which online shops are judged on turnover alone: investors are going to want to start seeing more profitability.

In your view, which e-commerce models are well-prepared for the future of online shopping? Is your position as an online retailer secure or will marketplaces, intermediaries, and manufacturers win in future?

My belief is that a retailer counts as well-positioned if it has a good handle on processes and generates repeat sales from satisfied customers. Getting new business is becoming increasingly expensive for retailers, and many acquisitions do not cover their costs. Another issue for retailers to consider is own brands, which may well be advisable for players in certain industries.

To generate high levels of customer demand, meanwhile, manufacturers need very strong brands. In the future, they will face important decisions about whether to sell directly to customers or not, whether to undertake to work exclusively with retailers or to run a parallel end-consumer strategy. At present, manufacturers often decide against selling directly to consumers in order to maintain solid existing partnerships – especially with traditional in-store retailers. This, however, comes with the risk that the brand will lose customers to those competitors who have decided to sell straight to consumers. Beyond this, Amazon is already upping the pressure on manufacturers, and I think it will get even stronger – and that other large retailers will behave in a similar fashion in the future.

One topic we're hearing a lot about at the moment is the idea of "clicks" retailers expanding onto the high street and into shopping centres: are "bricks" an option for fahrrad.de?

No, that's not something we would consider. Companies running store networks have completely different structures to ours and deal with challenges wholly different to those facing the online shopping sector. In order to be successful on the web, sellers have to concentrate fully on internet processes: as soon as you connect online with offline sales, you multiply complexity, and I can only advise against it. This is, however, only a problem for purely internet-based companies – and might not hold true in every single sector.

For online companies, the more inviting prospects lie, in my view, in fast international expansion. You've got to make sure that logistics costs and the situation vis-à-vis competitors are manageable, but it's a better way to go about growing than expanding into physical stores.

Which e-commerce business model is currently the most interesting in your view?

I think the Chinese YY approach (http://www.yy.com/) is particularly exciting: the platform live-streams karaoke and, in so doing, has brought a very new, very authentic idea onto the market. In my opinion, the model suits Chinese culture very well – and offers access to young adults. In 2014, the platform increased both turnover and profits by 100% and kept margins stable. You might not have thought that you can earn money streaming karaoke, but it turns out you can.

5.3 Stephan Schambach

Photo credit: fotostudio charlottenburg/New Store

Stephan Schambach is a pioneer in e-commerce technology and the founder of three major e-commerce platforms: Intershop, Demandware, and NewStore.

With Intershop, Stephan launched the first standard commerce software for online shopping in 1995, bringing it to IPO in Germany on the Neuer Markt in 1998 and the NASDAQ in 2000.

In 2004, he founded Demandware, which offered the first SaaS e-commerce platform for the enterprise market. Demandware was listed on the NYSE in 2012. In 2015, Stephan founded his third e-commerce venture, NewStore. NewStore is the first of its kind mobile retail platform that provides an elegant end-to-end experience for shoppers and store associates, while making one-touch purchase and on-demand delivery standard.

As the retail industry shifts to mobile, NewStore is helping brands create closer, more profitable relationships with consumers through apps.

Schambach is also involved as an investor and board member at various e-commerce start-ups. In addition to his work as an entrepreneur, Schambach is committed to improving the environment for start-ups and high-growth companies in Germany. This includes improving funding practices and exit opportunities. Furthermore, he and the Intershop Foundation are major sponsors of the e-commerce chair at the University of Applied Sciences in Jena (Germany).

Between 2012 and 2014, Schambach completed the Owner/President Management Program (OPM) successfully at Harvard Business School.

Let's look at e-commerce circa 1998, the year in which you put Intershop on the stock market, as against e-commerce in 2016. What have been the biggest changes?

It's been a long journey from e-commerce in 1998 to e-commerce today – one that has passed through many different stages. When Intershop went public in 1998, e-commerce was first and foremost seen as an environment for new companies; it wasn't until two or three years later that existing retailers and major players started to take an interest in online shopping. Working with Enfinity, Intershop delivered a software solution that was also suitable for larger organisations. What has become crystal clear in the intervening 20 years is the companies that can earn money on the internet and the companies that can'tt. In the segment of retailers and marketplaces selling everyday products that are not somehow unique, there are few winners; i.e., only Amazon, and to a certain extent Ebay, can make money selling standard merchandise. Brands, however, have done very well out of e-commerce. It has allowed them to enter into direct customer relationships rather than relying exclusively on brick and mortar middlemen as was so often the case prior to the internet. Brands selling directly to consumers is something thatreally only took off in the last two decades and e-commerce was the catalyst in this reaction.

The changes we're now seeing are far more revolutionary than anything we have seen in the last 20 years. Amazon came about relatively early, as did direct online sales for several brands. Currently, everything is being completely re-ordered as mobile technology upends consumer behaviour. Potential customers are now continuously online and I think this will lead to the equivalent of a re-start in e-commerce as sales increasingly take place in apps rather than in web browsers. Moreover, it is not just consumers, but also sales associates in brick & mortar stores who can use mobile devices, which in turn will lead to completely new business models. Omnichannel hasn't actually been practicable until now. In 2016 brands can, for the first time, offer genuine omnichannel experiences.

In the advanced economies, there doesn't seem to be anything which can halt Amazon's growth, while in China, the Alibaba group has profited the most from e-commerce. Even in less centralised markets, a small group of marketplaces is dominating the sector (Rakuten, Namshi, etc.). Is there any space left at all for newcomers in this retail market?

Whether retailers today even have a shot is an interesting question. My view is that brand owners have a real opportunity, while resellers most often don't. It really is important to distinguish between makers and merchants. While a new retail concept coming onto the market today needs to find a very specific, thus far untapped niche, consumers still do not want Amazon products in high-end segments such as gentlemen's suits or cars; thus, I really don't think we'll end up with a market dominated entirely by Amazon own-brand products. People are still attracted by good design and branding as markers of identity. This means that there will always be a place for lots of different brands. Moreover, on marketplaces, brands have difficulty showing their products the way they want to: often, they'll be placed right next to competing products, which in turn triggers a struggle for the best price. This runs counter to the strategy of brands such as Hugo Boss and Prada, whose business models are simply not built to factor in price competition. These kind of labels can get a pair of trousers made for a few dollars, but want to sell them for upwards of 100 dollars. How can this mark-up be justified? Through marketing, the brand promise and experience. You can't do that with a no-name pair of slacks listed on Amazon: the brand experience can only be created elsewhere – in shops, in adverts. Customers will actually pay more money for this kind of marketing and brand experience, because they associate themselves with the brand. They don't, however, make marketplaces part of their identity. This means that there will always be a path past dependency on Amazon: desirable brands will certainly be able to sell on the platform, but won't be dragged into its orbit.

To be very clear: high-end e-commerce can only work away from marketplaces. I really do not buy this idea that Amazon is going to gobble up everything. Amazon is certainly a great choice for basic products; customers can compare 10 to 15 offers using the reviews. This, in turn, means that retailers not selling their own-brand products are in competition with other retailers – and with Amazon. In the long term, they have absolutely no prospect of profitable growth. Retailers in very specific product groups in which Amazon can't amass the relevant know-how – e.g. fishing equipment – might be able to buck this trend; but wherever Amazon is able to cover the segment, there will be no margins left.

So would you say that retailers will have to, in the long run, adapt the Amazon model?

They can't. No-one is able invest as much as Amazon, so other retailers can do nothing except compete on the Amazon marketplace; they can't set up their own. That doesn't mean that it's easy street for them, though. Quite the contrary, actually. Any retailer without the vertical integration to offer own-brand products for which there is a natural consumer demand, without heavy price competition, now doesn't have a business model.

As a SaaS solution, Demandware's main advantage is that brand manufacturers get to outsource parts of e-commerce and save IT resources. Yet what chance do these companies have in the long term if they want to stand out from the pack, especially as technology leaders are handling their e-commerce activities in house?

Firstly, Demandware clients post online growth rates that are twice as fast as companies that do not use Demandware: that's an accepted figure and analysts can confirm it. If you ask me, the reasons behind this are as follows: Demandware's biggest advantage is that it allows brands to concentrate on their core business, delivering them tools that give a small merchandising team the resources to manage a very complex website with a range of analytics applications, automatic recommendation engines, etc. If you're trying to develop all of this in-house, you'll end up asking yourself if you are a brand manufacturer of toys or clothes or a tech company. What Demandware does is offer organisations that know they are not tech start-ups a far better model than they could ever make themselves.

The way Demandware customers stand out from the competition is through their websites: there is no "typical Demandware site" as it can always be adapted to provide the user experience the company in question wants to offer. In other words, brands differentiate themselves with the products they produce and the design of their websites, not in the programming language used to build their stores.

Design is where the differentiation is?

Exactly, and design is a matter of the brand itself. Demandware allows brands complete freedom when it comes to implementing their brand design on the internet, and remains the only provider that allows the e-commerce websites of large-scale organisations to hit a balance between SaaS and adaptability. The system can be modified and reprogrammed at any point, but still receives automatic updates; this is why such a high proportion of top brands use Demandware.

In your view, what are the biggest mistakes companies make when they approach e-commerce?

My observations are as follows:

1. Brands: It will always be possible to develop successful online shops if the underlying concept is solid; the price tags, however, are getting higher and higher. ost new shops will not work without own-brand products. The era of ambitious new start-ups like Zalando is definitely history. It will be very difficult to build up any new retail concepts; today's newcomers are based on own-brand merchandise and the accompanying concepts.
2. Channels: Warby Parker is an exciting example of how channels can be joined. The concept started with a website and then three stores in New York came along. What we're seeing is that purely online models are actually becoming more rare, and new brands with successful end-consumer operations often need at least one flagship store. Combining online and offline sales is often the most promising approach – and the most capital intensive at the present moment.
3. Catalogues: There is a whole ward full of dying catalogue operators right now, and the only question is how long it will take until they are pronounced dead. Today's successful concepts are targeted at Millennials, i.e. folks under thirty in the broadest sense, and this is the generation which grew up with mobile phones and the Internet. Manyof them don't even use e-mail anymore – and especially dislike filling out forms; they use apps. This generation is impatient and values speed; companies that manage to win over this demographic are the success stories.
4. Mobile commerce: This is where the future is, and I don't think e-commerce today can any longer meaningfully be understood in isolation. What's actually happening is that retail as a whole is being digitised: mobile technology is melding online and offline channels into one user experience. Lots of people still haven't grasped the concept, but luxury labels are quite far along. Concepts that work in the luxury segment can usually be applied to mass-market concepts like H&M. Some services like instant exchange will of course remain premium, but the rest is pretty transferable. This means that the luxury end of the market is an area with enough by way of margins and freedom of movement for experimentation.

What we're seeing is a complete breakdown in customer loyalty. Research shows that customers couldn't care one iota whether they used to shop at Target: when they get online, they go to Amazon, not Target.com, or compare products on Google Shopping first. Is this something you too have noticed?

Yes, I would completely agree with this assessment. There is no customer loyalty to marketplaces or retailers competing for customers on convenience, price, and service; these models have little chance to develop any sort of customer relationship. Amazon is the exception here as it has managed to use Prime to build up customer loyalty (although we shouldn't forget just how much effort and outlay this has taken). At the end of the day, marketplace customers decide on service and price.

What mobile does is offer brands and retailers the weaponry to start shooting back at Amazon. New payment options such as Apple Pay and Android Pay are replacing annoying registration on small smartphone screens. On mobiles devices, other shops have now caught up to Amazon in terms of the sheer convenience of buying: fingerprint payment using touch ID and the new customer is registered and paid up. This means that Amazon's monopoly on easy payment – which it uses its patent on one-click check-out to jealously defend – has now been neutralised. Mobile is reshuffling the cards – and at NewStore, we're looking to deal them out.

You've built your last two businesses in the USA: do you think the US market remains the leading force in e-commerce?

The U.S. is a very good market for us. What makes it most attractive is the good combination of venture capital and a large, homogenous market that is happy to try new things. In addition, a lot of luxury brands have their headquarters here and, more often than not, their largest market. This makes it an excellent environment for NewStore.

Compared to Europe, the USA remains far more innovative. Partly, that's the result of the amount of venture capital available for the experimentation and roll-out phase; the stock market, too, is here and highly fluid. In fact, the stock market is what guarantees the presence of venture capital in the U.S .market. There is nowhere outside of America that can compete with that, except China.

The U.S. market is not hemmed in by too much red tape. In Germany, for example, lots of good ideas get killed by regulation – look at what happened when Uber set up there. It's a fantastic business model, but Germany put the brakes on it and brought it to a standstill. While the U.S. is, in general, a very open economy that adds regulation later, Germany is very quick to forbid things in the first instance and then loosen the legal restrictions later. This is what makes the German market unsuited to new ideas. So while we are expanding into Germany, we're doing so after we saturate the U.S. market, We've set up a large office in Berlin and are developing most of our software there. Within Europe, our first port of call is the UK, which is partly a function of its legislative framework and partly due to the retail infrastructure. The British are, compared to other European nations, that little bit more aggressive and willing to experiment; the Greater London area, especially, offers lots of good foundations for e-commerce innovation such as delivery services which act free of rules and regulations.

If, however, I were a Chinese tech developer and I had the choice, then I'd stay in China before I went to America. The sheer size of the market is attractive, and there is plenty of access to venture capital and to two stock exchanges on which a new company can later be placed.

Which e-commerce business models do you think are the most exciting at the present moment? Do you see something like jet.com coming along any time soon and nabbing market share from Amazon?

What Jet is doing takes a lot of guts – and makes a lot of sense. The strategy is interesting and very much the opposite of how Amazon works. Amazon doesn't place the emphasis on treating the vendors and sellers active on its platform well: as far as it's concerned, there's always plenty more where they came from. Jet, on the other hand, wants to make sure its partners can make enough money to get by and that is a very sensible approach to differentiating itself from Amazon. We won't know for a while whether it will work out for them or not, but if there is any way of grabbing some market share from Amazon, then it is with a completely different business model like the one Jet is using.

In terms of new brands, I think companies like Warby Parker are interesting. It differentiates itself from competitors such as Mr. Spex based on design and production depth. In my view, this kind of hybrid model focussing on Millennials, building its own brand, and using multiple channels is destined for success. We're also going to be hearing a lot about mobile-only concepts which completely sidestep desktop e-commerce.

If you had to bet on one thing for the future of e-commerce, what would you bet on?

That's easy: apps. Brands and retailers that develop branded native apps and provide a beautiful, easy way for consumers to shop the way they want to shop will thrive.

6 Benchmark

6.1 Overview

This e-commerce benchmark helps online business models assess their performance regarding the most important e-commerce competences. You can find the up-to-date version at www.ebench.de.

This page allows you to compile an overview of all the points from the 17 detailed entries on various e-commerce competences.

Competence	Content (short)	Points			
Platform		**0**	**1**	**2**	**3**
Front end	user-friendly webshop				
New verticals	building specialised online shops				
Speed	speed, adding new features to the platform				
Interfaces	integrating all applications				
Tracking	evaluating all user interactions in the webshop				
Service	customer-focussed platform				
Business intelligence					
Obtaining data	collecting data from internal and external sources				
Maintaining data	integrated data management				
Applying data	data-supported decision-making				
Online marketing					
SEO	organic search engine traffic				
SEA	paid-for search engine traffic				
Affiliate marketing	commission-based marketers and sellers				
Display	banner and video advertising				
CRM					
Obtaining customer data	tracking customers, requesting data				
Customer data quality	correct, comprehensive customer data				
Applying customer data	operative and strategic value of customer data				
Social media	social media as an element of CRM strategy				
Overall total					

6.2 Platform

A. Front end

The benchmark for front ends describes the extent to which the site in question is easy for online shoppers to use. Besides a professional look and feel, a user-friendly shop offers all of the information customers need and makes processes (especially placing an order) child's play. A user-friendly shop also offers extra functions which either save time, entertain, or add value in another way. Regardless of what a range of studies may claim, front-end usability is difficult to measure quantitatively: a best-case scenario is when customers receive smooth service and none of their questions are left unanswered.

Scale		Evaluation
0	– Navigation structure is complicated/opaque – Design is unattractive and overworked/too generic – Little product information on offer – Complicated orders process leads to high levels of shopping basket abandonment	Points: Comments:
1	– Design, structure, and navigation are coordinated – Navigation is intuitive and logically structured – Page loads quickly – Customers find plenty of up-to-date information	
2	– Shop structured and designed specifically to suit customer needs – Some personalisation in upper layers of shop – Functions are intuitive and offer genuine added value – Products are presented in an attractive, informative way	
3	– Personalised content and promotions, intelligent recommendation engine – Functions such as search and product view are intelligent and adapt to customer requirements in real-time – Shop is optimised for mobile and tablet devices – Customers get a shopping experience in its own right; no complications, difficulties, or boredom	

Best practice: online giant Amazon

The Amazon webshop is wholly orientated to high speed, a broad selection, and unbeatable user-friendliness. Amazon offers a consistent shopping experience across devices with one-click check-out, copious amounts of information, informative product viewing (often including video content) and frequent customer evaluations. (By the same token, however, Amazon's shopping experience is neither particularly emotional or inspiring.)

B. New verticals

New verticals are additional platforms such as shopping clubs or specialised online-shops. What is benchmarked is the ability to add this kind of new vertical at high speed, at low cost, and without errors. It is important not to lose sight of the specific characteristics of the vertical in question.

Scale		Evaluation
0	– Any new verticals need to be built from scratch – New software, new team, new processes, and new business case	Points: Comments:
1	– New verticals are developed more or less independently of the existing platform – New verticals can be set up in roughly two months	
2	– New verticals are developed on the basis of the existing platform – New verticals can be set up in roughly two weeks	
3	– New platforms are created at speed; new ways of reaching customers (e.g. shopping clubs) can be tested successfully in a short time frame for a low outlay – New verticals and similar issues are part of day-to-day business	

Best practice: fashion shopping on Aboutyou.de and Edited.de

The Edited.de fashion store for youth style was implemented on the Aboutyou.de structure, going live fully functional within three weeks. Edited is the first vertical created wholly on the basis of Aboutyou.de, whose back-end processes it uses while presenting itself to the end consumer as an independent company. This allows for a maximum level of personalisation.

C. Speed

Speed describes the agility of processes, i.e. the ability the platform has to integrate new features. More than anything, this metric evaluates the length of time which elapses until simple to medium-complexity features (e.g. new payment options, new shopping baskets, additional service features such as chat solutions) are implemented. At the same time, all these developments should ideally take place in an experimental learning environment which allows continuous testing and optimisation.

Scale		Evaluation
0	– Waterfall-planning hinders progress – Long lead times for new functions and features (e.g. it takes six months or more to introduce a new payment option)	Points: Comments:
1	– Little effort made to effectively test functions – Implementing new functions on the platform takes several weeks	
2	– Test processes are used to implement new functions error-free – New features can be implemented in a matter of weeks	
3	– Agile structures (lean start-up) – New functions are tested autonomously and implemented fast in a data-driven process – New features are implemented within days	

Best practice: Etsy implements 30 innovations every day

Since 2010, Etsy has been following a strategy of optimising the website with multiple small-scale updates on a daily basis, making 30 code improvements every day (that's over 10,000 annually). The changes are supported by data-driven monitoring and automated testing while decision-making paths have been drastically shortened: members of staff do not have to get managerial sign-off on changes if the alterations in question have been previously discussed and successfully tested. Etsy planning thinks in fortnightly intervals for small-to-medium scale features.

D. Interfaces

Interfaces allow for communication between a range of applications in businesses processes. Important interfaces for a smooth transfer of information within processes include the connections between user-facing front ends and the back-end machine room of the shop system, payment processing, and inventory, fulfilment, and PIM systems, as well as CRM or third-party site integration.

Scale		Evaluation
0	– Minimal exchange of data between only the most important systems – Divergent data structures lead to errors	Points: Comments:
1	– ERP as a good foundation – Crucial APIs used and provided – Internal and external systems integrated	
2	– Fully-functional connections to third-party systems (payment, CRM, social media) – Optimised data structure and integrated modules allow for error-free exchange of data – Real-time data-fidelity (e.g. availability, delivery times)	
3	– Interfaces are optimised to the performance level and speed of the webshop and internal processes – Interfaces such as parcel tracking offer customer value – Ideal mix of in-house and third-party solutions	

Best practice: Aboutyou.de app centre

This developer platform allows coders to add their own applications with webshop functions to Aboutyou.de. In a way similar to Zapier functionality (i.e. automated web application integration), the additions are connected to the shop using meta-interfaces, meaning that apps can be dove-tailed into the Aboutyou.de environment. The background is that external developers can currently access the Aboutyou ecosystem in a way which, to date, was the preserve of the Facebook Developer Center; the motivation behind this is that the Aboutyou wants to offer optimal access for creative ideas which can then be launched on the platform and all of the verticals connected to it.

E. Tracking

The ability to track all interactions in a webshop is a prerequisite to gathering and analysing data, which is then used to measure performance, take decisions, and contact various target groups specifically. Intelligent monitoring systems allow for continuous optimisation of usability, marketing channels, conversion, and shop design (e.g. using A/B testing). The quality, relevance, and the extent to which data is actually used are the specific subjects of benchmarking here.

Scale		Evaluation
0	– Tracking is limited to transactions – Neither internal nor external systems used to track customer behaviour – Each customer is treated like a new customer	Points: Comments:
1	– Traffic and conversions are recorded and evaluated using Google Analytics or a similar solution – Sources of traffic are analysed and optimised – KPIs used to measure levels of success	
2	– A/B testing and usability studies carried out – Aggregated click-streams used to optimise shop – Complete customer journey tracked for every customer (pre-sale, purchase process, and post-sale) and used in marketing and CRM (customer loyalty, cross-selling, support, etc.)	
3	– Additional metrics such as geo-location, sentiment (Facebook Likes, Twitter data, product evaluations, etc.), mobile click-streams, etc. included in tracking – Content and landing pages are real-time adapted to individual customers and their preferences – All available value is squeezed from all information collected	

Best practice: Shoes and fashion retailer Zalando

Zalando uses tracking data to continually optimise marketing measures, product mixes, and page composition; in order to do so, the platform integrates a full range of services (including 36yield, adscale, appnexus, ATMDT, Atemda, Crited, Demdex, Doubleclick, Facebook, Metrigo, OpenX, Pubmatic, Adserver, Sociomantic, YieldLab and Yieldmanager).

Tracking is also something Zalando has established for its television advertising using a Google plug-in which measures additional traffic against the baseline following commercial broadcasts: the results show that Zalando's mobile sales triple when its adverts appear on TV.

F. Service

The sum of all functions which improve the customer shopping experience: benchmarking applies specifically to focus on customers, benefits to customers, and quality of the function.

Scale		Evaluation
0	– Customer service is difficult to find and/or contact – Complaints frequently go unanswered – Service lags behind levels of offered by competitors	Points: Comments:
1	– Basic services such as informative at-a-glance order confirmation and returns policies are offered – Complaints management in place (including strategy and guidelines) – Comprehensive, easily-located information (product pages, newsletters, attractive how-to content and FAQs)	
2	– Customer-friendly service and advice available on all relevant channels (online, telephone, e-mail, social media) – Service offering includes a comprehensive range of payment options, stored shopping baskets, product support, etc. – Excellent, speedy dispatch and shipping at attractive prices/ free of charge, with live parcel tracking	
3	– Live-chat and call-back service available 24/7 – Customer feedback is successfully implemented – Strategic decision that customer service must seek not only to fulfil, but always to exceed customer expectations	

Best practice: "A service company which also happens to sell shoes" Zappos.com

Zappos is famed for its strong focus on world-beating customer service, contactable 24/7 by telephone and live-chat. The strategy behind this is not to "sort customers out" as quickly possible, but rather to support customers at all points and answer all questions much in the same way as a hotel concierge. Zappo's telephone service regularly garners the company a positive PR resonance and the result is that 70-75% of all purchases are made by returning customers.

6.3 Business Intelligence

G. Obtaining data

Obtaining data is the process of gathering data from internal and external sources such as customer behaviour, company activities, market trends, and competitor initiatives. What is important here is the relevance, quality, and applicability of the data. A good system for obtaining data collects information automatically at an ideal point of compromise between depth, quantity, and frequency.

Scale		Evaluation
0	– Low amount of data gathered – Data is patchy – No strategy for prioritising data in terms of importance	Points: Comments:
1	– Structured (e.g. click-stream) and unstructured at (e.g. contents of customer e-mails) are collected – Data sources are limited to internal sources	
2	– Systems for obtaining and analysing data are adapted to the website and other operative applications – Historical relationships are precision-identified and presented – External data (traffic, GPS, social, etc.) is captured – Data protection is a key part of company procedure; this policy is communicated to customers	
3	– Data depth, quantity, and frequency are fully matched to optimum results and are costs efficient – Semantic data is collected internally and externally – External data is collected in the temporal field (customer journey, competition, market developments) – Data is collected in the long term to provide long-term cycle and trend mapping.	

Best practice: Hertz car rentals

Hertz collects semantic, unstructured data from customer surveys, texts and e-mails from customers, and from third-party pages such as ratings sites. This data is centrally processed in real-time with linguistic analysis programs and then used both in planning and operations in order to improve the overall company strategy and optimise offerings on a local level.

H. Maintaining data

Managing all of the data obtained from a range of channels (online, offline, internal, external) is a challenge. Data may be stored on proprietary servers or in the cloud, but legal standards must always be adhered to. A good collection of data features as many links as possible between data sets, automatically archiving and backing up contents to guard against data loss.

Scale		Evaluation
0	– Data is stored in text and XML form – Data silos make it difficult to access and evaluate data – Separate systems lead to data loss	Points: Comments:
1	– Data is integrated using a data warehousing solution – Data is cleansed and standardised – Legal standards are upheld	
2	– Job management systems automate data integration – Safe, cost-optimised archiving and back-up procedures in place – Large amount of storage enables big data approach – Data silos are joined up to make a complete database, eliminating redundant file systems	
3	– Servers are trimmed to high levels of performance und safety – A data scientist (internal or external) is on hand to apply BI in such a way as all systems are ideally integrated – Data-marts form targeted, high-performance units within the overall data warehouse	

Best practice: Streaming platform Netflix

The Netflix data engine has been running in the Cloud since 2009: Netflix uses Amazon's S3 technology in order to record and then suitably depict every "event" generated by the roughly 50 million strong subscriber base. Further systems within Netflix' data management armoury are Hadoop (the underlying database), Hive (which allows for aggregated requests), and Lipstick (for visualisation).

I. Using the data

When BI is linked to company goals, it can be a valuable tool in the decision-making process. Precise predictions can be used to derive recommendations for further action and offer effective advice to various areas of the business. Steering the product mix, managing staff time, targeting marketing campaigns, fixing budgets, and planning strategically are all areas in which data is of use. The goal must be to have automated systems for reporting and, if necessary, triggering alarms in case of excessive deviation.

Scale		Evaluation
0	– Standardised spreadsheet reporting – Lack of individualisation in data requests – Data access limited to few employees, preventing others from getting the information they need, when they need it	Points: Comments:
1	– Data mining allows for evaluations and forecasts – Sales forecasts used to optimise processes and customer orientation – Operative processes are orientated towards data analysis – Multi-user data portal allows for personalisation and distribution of data	
2	– BI as a decision-making support system for operative and strategic management – Multi-dimensional analyses permit precision requests – Applications can access live data – Forecasts link internal and external data	
3	– BI is linked to company goals and BI analyses are integrated into all business processes – As well as process intelligence, comprehensive KPIs offer information about competitors and networks – Decision engineering is used to deliver forecasts and recommendations automatically – Machine learning and special analyses (e.g. linguistic programs) are used to maximise the insight value of the data collected	

Best practice: Streaming platform Netflix

By tracking user behaviour, Netflix is able to analyse, depict, and predict its' subscribers streaming consumption. From examining their preferences, Netflix reached the decision to invest $100m in its first self-produced series, *House of Cards*. The Netflix data philosophy is: 1.) to make data available to all members of staff; 2.) to visualise both small and large quantities of data in order to make it easy to grasp ramifications; 3) the longer it takes to find data, the less value it will have.

6.4 Online Marketing

J. SEO

SEO competence is principally a matter of a platform's ability to channel organic content out of the standard search engines and into its sphere. The goal is to reach first place in the organic search rankings for target keywords on engines such as Google; a range of measures both on and off-site is used to achieve this goal.

Scale		Evaluation
0	– Website hard to read for crawlers – No/few backlinks – Lack of text content on the website – Poor URL structure	Points: Comments:
1	– HTML rules are followed – Lots of content pages online – Backlinks are structured – No flash used	
2	– SEO is already a key element of platform strategy – Site is optimised for universal search (optimised images) – URL designations communicate structure	
3	– Site runs its own networks of backlinks – Landing page created dynamically according to results of internal search – High-value content marketing using proprietary blog/forums	

Best practice: Thomann.de, musical instruments

Detailed content pages such as Thoman's lexicon of advice for the musical instruments it sells in its online shop mean that Thomann.de maintains top positioning in the Google ranks. The whole website is filled with SEO-relevant keywords and has an excellent URL structure: anyone searching Google.de for electric guitar strings ("*Saiten für E-Gitarre*") will see Thomann listed both a s the first and second organic result – ahead of image results and Wikipedia; the lexicon page on which Thomann decribes electric guitar strings ahead of the site on which Thomann sells them.

K. SEA

The aim of search engine marketing is to used paid search results to reach prospects in the most targeted way possible and draw them onto the platform. Search engine advertising space is sold off per keyword (i.e. search terms) by auction: the more relevant and specific the keyword book is, the better the quality of the traffic drawn onto the platform. The goal is to generate relevance and therefore sales and to place the platform as well as possible in the search engine adverts.

Scale		Evaluation
0	– Generic keywords lead to poor quality traffic and a high bounce rate – Landing pages are not optimised and lead back to the generic homepage	Points: Comments:
1	– Click-through rate is the only KPI in the SEA strategy – Focus on Google traffic to the exclusion of other search engines (Bing, Yahoo, etc.) – Landing pages produced for each keyword advertised	
2	– Principle target is conversion (with stages of success defined from page views to sign-up and purchase, etc.) – Continuous keyword optimisation ups traffic quality (conversion tracking, keyword grouping, using negative search terms) – Landing pages optimised for mobile traffic – At least one expert taking care of budgeting, bid management, and SEA strategy execution	
3	– Strategy for product listing ads (Google Shopping) – Holistic strategy encompasses all key search engines – Intelligent optimisation system makes continuous improvements to cost-per-click and traffic quality – Strong focus on customers of all SEA makes adverts attractive to relevant target groups	

Best practice: Shoe and fashion retailer Zalando.de

In all the relevant fashion shopping SEA keywords, Zalando is right at the top. SEA experts in the company bid for around 100 million keywords on Google; the aim of the campaigns is to make sure that the SEA costs per new customer are recouped within six months.

L. Affiliate marketing

Affiliates are third-party marketers and sellers who earn commission on sales. Choosing the right affiliates is essential as they can have both a positive and a negative effect on the image of a brand and influence customers for the better or for the worse. Good affiliates can generate substantial amounts of new business and relationship management with these earners is an important issue.

Scale		Evaluation
0	– Poor choice of affiliates poses risk to brand image (unprofessional, negative associations, etc.) – Bad tracking system demotivates affiliate partners – Lack of relevance or connection to topic	Points: Comments:
1	– Most of the tasks are handled by affiliate networks – Sufficient staff capacity to plan and administer partner programmes – Lack of personal contact to affiliates	
2	– An in-house affiliate management system is set up offering partners personal communication, joint planning for sales initiatives, and access to product information, special prices, and advertising material – Attractive incentives and remuneration systems draw in the best affiliates – Integrated strategy for pricing; targeted, relevant landing pages set up to receive clicks from affiliates	
3	– Comprehensive data analysis with the aim of optimising the choice of affiliate partners and activities – Innovative advertising formats make it easier for affiliates to gain customers – Partner portals, newsletters, personalised strategies depending on the type of affiliate: excellent relationship management – High-value affiliates add to the sheen of the brand	

Best practice: Office outfitters Shoplet.com

Shoplet works with two affiliate networks: Commission Junction and Google Affiliate Network. It places a particular emphasis on taking care of its top-performing affiliates, providing them with exclusive content and special offers. These well-maintained contacts with its best affiliates mean that control of the contents and timing of its sales initiatives remains with Shoplet.

M. Display

Advertising on third-party sites is generally visual, either static, animated, or full video. The goal of display advertising is to increase both brand awareness and product sales, and here too, there should be a focus on optimising costs and conversions as well as on making sure that adverts are placed in the most relevant environments possible. Due to internet users' increasing "banner blindness", good design and creative approaches are a must if display adverts are to have any real effect.

Scale		Evaluation
0	– Poor choice of publisher damages brand image – Tracking not used effectively – Display advertising strategy is not integrated in the overall online marketing strategy	Points: Comments:
1	– Publishers chosen according to target groups – Relevant landing pages selected specifically for campaigns – "Banner blindness" blunts effect of campaigns – Limited quality control of publisher sites	
2	– Strategy takes account of several goals: brand awareness, leads, and conversions – Choice of content and publisher always trimmed to relevance – Fees model optimised from a costs perspective – Optimum choice of message, timing, and environment for each campaign – Video strategy makes efficient use of YouTube	
3	– Mobile strategy adapts to customers – Creative (esp. video) content and attractive formats (e.g. native advertising) increase levels of customer interest and interaction – Optimised behavioural targeting adapts intelligently to the customer (location, browsing, social, search, etc.) without customers feeling annoyed – Landing pages are optimised and personalised	

Best practice: Nissan dealer in Dubai

Nissan uses target-group specific banner advertising on a Dubai property website. The banner adapts automatically to the property searched for: depending on the area, family size, and budget entered, a suitable Nissan vehicle drives into the banner on the website. When customers register for a viewing, there are offered an integrated test-drive – including pick-up and drop-off at the property they are interested in. 1,200 test drives were completed within just a few weeks from campaign launch.

6.5 CRM

N. Obtaining customer data

Data is gathered by asking customers (e.g. for their delivery address) and by automatic tracking (e.g. search and click behaviour on the site). Direct requests to customers must be made simply and in a way which does not elicit undue suspicion; tracking (i.e. behavioural data) is something which should be carried out as comprehensively as possible and linked to customer IDs in order to compile customer profiles rich in information.

Scale		Evaluation
0	– Frequently, tracking cannot be assigned to customer profiles and is therefore less valuable (only aggregated) – Only internal website data is captured	Points: Comments:
1	– Multichannel data is pooled in one system – Internal and external data is recorded – Cookies allow for longer-term tracking	
2	– Detailed, informative customer profiles are generated as tracking data is combined with customer IDs – Tracking software used is scalable – Direct requests to customers for their data are well-designed and only target data whose use customers understand	
3	– Optimised tracking across a range of user devices (multiple PCs, tablet, smartphone) – Intelligent tracking allows for targeted, real-time communication with customers – Soft factors such as customer satisfaction and loyalty are documented using relational indicators	

Best practice: American retail giant Target.com

Target connects all the data from its in-store business with all of the information it can glean from the browsing and purchasing behaviour of its customers. This connection between online and offline CRM data gives Target a high degree of insight when it comes to optimising its product mix online and offline, predicting customer behaviour, and preventing customer loss with targeted measures.

O. Customer data quality

The primary issue here is the reliability of the CRM system and hooking up customer data and customer IDs accurately and comprehensively. This means that data integration from all systems concerned is important, as are checks (e.g. address cleansing on log-in) and updates at regular intervals. The secondary issue to be benchmarked is the relevance, applicability, and informational content of the data.

Scale		Evaluation
0	– Data is incomplete – Data is poorly structured – Data is difficult to integrate and frequently redundant	Points: Comments:
1	– Online and offline data is joined up – ERP integration is uses to prevent data redundancy and data loss – All key data is available	
2	– Customer data is complete, featuring customer history, grouping, demographics, transaction status, etc. – Data is reliable due to frequent e-mail address checks, address cleansing, accurate records of changes to names, etc.	
3	– Customer data can be integrated fully – Soft factors such as customer interests and behavioural data are also featured	

Best practice: The Body Shop natural cosmetics store

Customers who sign up to the loyalty programme offline are asked at the POS whether their e-mail address is correct, guaranteeing data quality from the first point of contact on. New members go on to receive a welcome e-mail which allows the Body Shop to track all further clicks from the e-mail and assign the data gathered to the right customer ID.

P. Applying customer data

Customer data is used both in operational and planning contexts. Operatively, data is used to optimise customer service, target marketing campaigns (both onsite and in other channels), and improve integration of fulfilment processes; strategically, data is applied to product and process optimisation.

Scale		Evaluation
0	– Full potential use of data not exploited – Patchy/incomplete compliance with data protection regulations	Points: Comments:
1	– Data is integrated in customer-facing processes (marketing, customer care, dispatching, etc.) – Aggregated data allows for a more customer-orientated webshop – Marketing campaigns use data	
2	– Customers are divided into segments for targeted marketing – Optimised customer service features swift, personal responses, up-to-the-minute information, product support, etc. – Customer-friendly up and cross-selling; intelligent recommendation engine rather than spam	
3	– Intelligent customer loyalty measures to increase satisfaction, principally due to high-quality, responsive service – Making considered use of customer communication channels in real time – Using data to ensure continuous product improvement – Integrating data into BI to optimise business processes	

Best practice: Rebuy.de, buyer and seller of used goods

Rebuy.de offers its customers an individualised newsletter, while the basis of its recommendation engine is a blend of probability predictions, search requests, socio-demographic data, navigation behaviour, shopping basket contents, buying history, and the CRM profile of each customer. The newsletter is sent, but the personal recommendations are not loaded until it is opened by the recipient.

Q. Social Media

Social platforms can be used for customer loyalty, service, and complaints management as well as recommendation marketing and new customer acquisition. The goal here is to accrue visibility and credibility as well as to include the relevant user communities in the whole buying cycle both on social media and the platform itself.

Scale		Evaluation
0	– Potential in the networks is barely recognised – Networks are used as simply another delivery channel for one-way display adverts – Lack of social media strategy	Points: Comments:
1	– Customer relationship at the centre – Social media management system for planning and distributing content – Potential of the various networks is not being fully exploited	
2	– Social media is part of customer service and integrated into CRM – Viral, authentic campaigns win valuable followers – Social advertising is integrated into the marketing strategy (e.g. Facebook B2C, LinkedIn B2B) – Social media policy formulated – Group buying strategy used to tap full potential of networks	
3	– Pro-actives complaints management – Profiles develop a community with a life of its own – Recommendation marketing from integrating social media into the webshop (OpenGraph) – Social media is included in the whole buying cycle (creating demand on networks, customer service, customer loyalty, recommendation marketing, etc.)	

Best practice: Social CRM at low-cost airline JetBlue

With the promise of "bringing humanity back to air travel", JetBlue sells itself as a particularly customer-friendly and service-orientated airline. The company's Twitter account is personally tended to by social media staff and its tailored to the target group. First and foremost, Twitter is used as a channel for customer care which is always contactable and offers fast answers to all kinds of questions as well, as required, competent complaints management.

Thank you Mareike & Brian!

This is the place where the authors usually thank their families for the ongoing support they have provided during the many sleepless nights invested to create such a book. But, for Holger and myself it was a different story. For one thing, the publisher took on absolutely all of the work necessary to actually produce the book and for another, the two colleagues we had on board with us, Mareike Stobbe (San Francisco) and Brian Melican (Hamburg), spared us the sleepless nights!

Brian was able to piece together a countless number of incomplete texts to create a coherent overall picture and he took care of the translation aspect. Mareike was the driving force behind the content, creating endless case studies, coordinating everything and basically completing the book almost singlehandedly. Holger and I receive all the glory but that isn't really fair. Mareike and Brian are certainly every bit as important to this book as we are.

Without you, this book would never have taken the shape or form that it has done. Thank you very much to you both!

Karl Bischoff also earned huge kudos during our "special" China research for this book. Thanks Karl!

About the authors

Alexander Graf

Alexander Graf is a serial entrepreneur with 10+ years experience in the digital sector and the CEO of *Spryker Systems*, a commerce-technology company which he founded together with Nils Seebach in cooperation with the early-stage investor *Project A Ventures* in 2014.

In 2011, Alexander started the management consulting firm *eTribes*, which supports companies in building and executing digital strategies. Within this practice, he has formed a prestigious expert, entrepreneur and client network, including publishing houses such as *Gruner + Jahr*, manufacturers like *Vitra*, as well as corporations like the *Otto Group*. From 2011, he was also managing director of the agency group *NetImpact Framework*, which he founded together with Nils Seebach and Tarek Müller. It was acquired by the *Otto Group* in 2013 as the starting point of the much acclaimed venture *Collins*. Prior to that, Alexander was senior advisor for the *Otto Group* and in charge of the conception, evaluation and M&A of digital business models.

Alexander publishes the e-commerce specialist blog "Kassenzone" as well as numerous industry studies and books. His latest work "Das E-Commerce Buch" ("The E-Commerce Book") is now published in English. Alexander Graf, born 1980, has studied economics and computer sciences with a focus on innovation and marketing at *Kiel University* in Germany and the *Autónoma* in Madrid, Spain.

alexander.graf@etribes.de, alexander.graf@spryker.com
+49 (40) 3289 29690
www.kassenzone.de, www.etribes.de, www.spryker.com
twitter.com/supergraf
www.linkedin.com/in/alexandergraf
www.xing.com/profile/Alexander_Graf8

Prof. Dr. Holger Schneider

Holger Schneider runs the bachelor's and master's degree courses at the *Wedel University of Applied Sciences* (near Hamburg, Germany), teaching both the strategic and operative issues of e-commerce. He is also a member of the board of the *Digital Analytics Association Germany* with the remit for supporting and developing young data scientists. As a partner in the *eTribes* consultancy company, he advises manufacturers, retailers, and media organisations on digital business issues; working with Alexander Graf, he curates the annual *Digital Commerce Day*.

Previously, Holger Schneider worked as head of business development in new media for the *Otto Group*, where the focus of his activities was on analysing e-commerce business models and their relevancy to the Otto Group. Building on this, he contributed to the development of the Otto Group's e-commerce strategy and made recommendations with regard to setting up or buying in e-commerce business models both on the domestic and international markets.

Holger Schneider read business studies and management at the *WHU Otto Beisheim School of Management* (Vallendar), where he came into contact with e-commerce and digital business at an early stage. He then completed a doctorate in pricing models in digital businesses at the *Christian Albrecht University of Kiel*; Holger Schneider has experience of international markets gathered during a range of hands-on projects and research stays abroad, including at *HEC Montréal* (Canada), *KEIO Business School* (Japan), and the *Center for Digital Business* at *MIT Sloan School of Management* (USA).

hos@fh-wedel.de
+49 (4103) 8048–55
www.fh-wedel.de/mitarbeiter/hos
www.de.linkedin.com/in/holgerschneider/
www.xing.com/profile/Holger_Schneider2

Glossary[1]

Chapter 1

- **Cadabra:** Amazon.com was very nearly called "Cadabra," as in "abracadabra." Founder Jeff Bezos rapidly rethought the name when his lawyer misheard the word as "cadaver."
- **Intermediary:** Intermediaries bring buyers and sellers together without taking ownership of the product, service or property.
- **Pure player:** Also referred to as a **pure-play**, a pure player is a company that invests its resources solely in one channel, usually e-commerce
- **E-tailer:** A retailer selling goods via electronic transactions on the internet (popular at the turn of the Millennium, now somewhat dated)
- **IPO:** An **initial public offering** (IPO) or stock market launch is a type of public offering in which shares of a company sold, usually to institutional investors
- **Price comparison engine:** A comparison shopping website, sometimes called a *price comparison website*, is a vertical search engine that shoppers use to filter and compare products based on price, features, and other criteria.
- **Dot-Com Bubble:** The Dot-Com Bubble was a speculative bubble in the valuations of young internet companies, beginning in the late 1990s and bursting in 2002 with disastrous results.
- **Alibaba:** → See company profile chapter 3
- **Taobao:** → See company profile chapter 3
- **Alipay:** The Alibaba Group's proprietary payment service.
- **Escrow service:** In this model of payment, a third party receives funds for goods or services from the buyer, disbursing them only to the seller on delivery or completion.
- **Tmall:** Alibaba's B2C website in the Chinese market.
- **JD:** → See company profile chapter 3

1 Terms are in order of appearance.

- **Tencent:** → See company profile chapter 3
- **WeChat:** → See company profile chapter 3
- **Black Friday:** Black Friday is the day following Thanksgiving in the United States and has been regarded as the beginning of the Christmas shopping season since 1932.
- **Cyber Monday:** Cyber Monday is a marketing term for the Monday after the Thanksgiving holiday in the United States; it was created by marketing companies to persuade people to shop online

Chapter 2

- **B2C:** Business to consumer
- **B2B:** Business to business
- **C2C:** Consumer to consumer
- **Short tail:** Few products, traded at high volume
- **Long tail:** Many products, traded at low volume
- **SEO:** Search engine optimisation
- **SEA:** Search engine advertising
- **Affiliates:** Affiliate marketing is a type of performance-based marketing in which a business rewards one or more affiliates for each visitor or customer brought by the affiliate's own marketing efforts
- **OTTO:** German mail-order company
- **DPD:** Parcels service
- **DHL:** Parcels service
- **CIC:** Customer interaction centre

Chapter 3

- **Open commerce:** A strategy to open e-commerce websites up and let external developers work with the website assets
- **Omnichannel:** Also known as **multichannel retailing**, omnichannel is a cross-channel business model that companies use with the aim of improving customer experience (NB: The authors of this book have never seen a successful omnichannel business).

- **Flash sale:** This is an ecommerce business model in which a website offers a single product for sale for a period of 24 to 36 hours
- **EBITDA:** A company's earnings before interest, taxes, depreciation, and amortization, used an accounting metric to calculate a company's net earnings
- **Dropshipping:** Drop shipping is a supply chain management technique in which the retailer does not keep goods in stock but instead transfers customer orders and shipment details to either the manufacturer, another retailer, or a wholesaler, who then ships the goods directly to the customer.
- **Dynamic pricing:** Dynamic pricing, also referred to as **surge pricing** or **demand pricing**, is a pricing strategy in which businesses set flexible rates for products or services based on current market demands
- **Curated shopping:** Curated commerce uses shoppers' personal preferences to introduce them to new products they might not have otherwise found.
- **Shopping club:** An online private shopping club is a members only shopping club, where members can buy goods at high discounts

Chapter 4

- **GAFA:** An acronym composed of Google, Apple, Facebook, Amazon
- **Prisoner's Dilemma:** The prisoner's dilemma is a canonical example of a game theory analysis. It shoes how two purely "rational" individuals might not cooperate, even if it appears that it is in their best interests to do so
- **GPO:** Group purchasing organisations
- **Cat content:** Content – often of an inane or banal sort – in which users of social networks post pictures and videos with their cats or in which felines are photoshopped for quote-unquote humourous purposes.

Sources

Chapter 1

1 See "A CLOSER LOOK: The Dot-Com Bubble Bursts" for a few examples.
2 http://www.huffingtonpost.com/michaellevin/the-everything-store-jeff_b_5332348.html
3 https://www.internetretailer.com/2009/02/26/the-history-of-e-commerce
4 Brad Stone, The Everything Store, Little, Brown and Company, 2013
5 http://www.referenceforbusiness.com/history2/44/Ebay-Inc.html
6 http://www.wikinvest.com/stock/Amazon.com_(AMZN)/Data/Revenue_Growth/1998
7 http://www.encyclopedia.com/topic/Initial_public_offerings.aspx
8 http://news.cnet.com/Amazon,-BN-settle-lawsuit/2100-1023_3-204480.html
9 http://www.handelsblatt.com/technologie/it-tk/it-internet/gruendergeist-am-couchtisch-reich-werden-mit-ebay/2428146.html
10 http://www.businessinsider.com.au/nick-swinmurn-zappos-rnkd-2011-11
11 http://www.statista.com/statistics/283165/online-retail-expenditure-in-the-united-kingdom-uk/
12 http://de.statista.com/statistik/daten/studie/3979/umfrage/e-commerce-umsatz-in-deutschland-seit-1999/
13 See "A CLOSER LOOK: The Dot-Com Bubble Bursts"
14 http://www.zappos.com/self-service-return-instructions
15 http://www.presseportal.de/pm/70464/2133143/falsche-preispolitik-neue-media-markt-strategie-geht-an-realitaet-vorbei-batten-company
16 Brad Stone, The Everything Store, Little, Brown and Company, 2013
17 http://etailment.de/thema/marketing/Das-Ende-der-Milieus---und-was-das-fuer-Collins-bedeutet-1638
18 http://www.wikinvest.com/stock/Amazon.com_(AMZN)/Data/Revenue/2002
19 http://www.deutsche-startups.de/2008/06/06/leguidecom-schluckt-dooyoo/
20 http://www.google.com/about/company/history/
21 http://www.heise.de/newsticker/meldung/Otto-Versand-steigert-Online-Umsatz-56941.html
22 http://www.ecckoeln.de/News/Tchibo---Gelungenes-Multi-Channel-Marketing
23 http://www.internethandel.de/vnl/Adidas_Schuhe
24 http://www.investopedia.com/features/crashes/crashes8.asp
* http://www.nasdaq.com/markets/ipos/filing.ashx?filingid=965526, https://www.gartner.com/doc/334368/webvans-collapse-delivers-hard-lesson, http://blogs.wsj.com/venturecapital/2009/11/02/10-years-ago-today-when-online-groceries-were-all-the-rage/ and http://money.cnn.com/2001/07/09/technology/webvan/
** http://money.cnn.com/galleries/2010/technology/1003/gallery.dot_com_busts/index.html, http://www.businessinsider.com/petscom-ceo-julie-wainwright-2011-2, http://www.cnet.com/news/pets-com-latest-high-profile-dot-com-disaster/
*** http://www.businessinsider.com/petscom-ceo-julie-wainwright-2011-2

25 http://de.statista.com/statistik/daten/studie/3979/umfrage/e-commerce-umatz-in-deutschland-seit-1999/
26 http://www.wsj.com/articles/SB10001424052702303277704579347942836197338
27 https://www.internetretailer.com/2015/02/17/us-annual-e-retail-sales-surpass-300-billion-first-ti
28 http://www.statista.com/statistics/283165/online-retail-expenditure-in-the-united-kingdom-uk/
29 http://de.statista.com/statistik/daten/studie/3979/umfrage/e-commerce-umsatz-in-deutschland-seit-1999/
30 Based on German market statistics
31 Brad Stone, The Everything Store, Little, Brown and Company, 2013
32 https://www.internetretailer.com/2015/03/18/amazon-shutter-its-webstore-e-commerce-platform-service
33 Brad Stone, The Everything Store, Little, Brown and Company, 2013
34 http://www.deutsche-startups.de/2008/06/06/leguidecom-schluckt-dooyoo/
35 http://www.wsj.com/articles/SB111766137860748552
36 http://www.golem.de/0710/55405.html
37 http://www.mediamarkt.de/static/pressemitteilung/120116_media_markt_deutschland_start_onlineshop_2012.pdf
38 http://www.inc.com/magazine/20060901/hidi-hsieh.html
39 https://www.internetretailer.com/2007/08/01/repeat-customers-walk-all-over-zappos-com
40 http://www.newyorker.com/magazine/2009/09/14/happy-feet
41 http://www.brickmeetsclick.com/the-multi-channel-future-of-retail-1
42 http://www.forbes.com/forbes/2010/0830/entrepreneurs-groupon-facebook-twitter-next-web-phenom.html?lc=int_mb_1001
43 http://www.businessinsider.com/inside-groupon-the-truth-about-the-worlds-most-controversial-company-2011-10
44 https://www.entrepreneur.com/article/230081
45 http://www.businessinsider.com/rise-and-fall-of-fab-2014-5
46 https://www.internetretailer.com/2014/10/22/fabcoms-founder-describes-its-rise-and-fall
47 http://www.businessinsider.com/declining-site-visits-at-fab-2013-10
48 http://www.nytimes.com/2009/10/23/books/23price.html?_r=0
49 http://www.bevh.org/presse/pressemitteilungen/details/artikel/umsatzzahlen-des-interaktiven-handels-im-2-quartal-2013-die-positive-branchenentwicklung-setzt-sic/
50 http://www.ecckoeln.de/PDFs/2013/de__de_de__smarter_commerce__crosschannel_einkaufserlebnis.pdf
51 z.B. OC&C, Wenn zwei sich streiten... entscheidet der Kunde (https://www.springerprofessional.de/vertriebskanaele/handel/stationaere-haendler-lassen-online-potenzial-ungenutzt/6603660?redirect=1)
52 https://excitingcommerce.de/2013/07/19/zalando-2013-2/
53 http://www.internetworld.de/e-commerce/online-marktplatz/kartellamt-stoppt-asics-marktplatzverbot-1005475.html
54 http://www.welt.de/wirtschaft/article109571946/Neckermann-ist-nun-offiziell-pleite.html
55 http://www.dallasnews.com/business/headlines/20091117-J-C-Penney-is-turning-3244.ece
56 https://excitingcommerce.de/2009/06/10/versandhandelszukunft/
57 Caruso Affliated is one of the largest owners of US retail real estate
58 http://www.prnewswire.com/news-releases/rick-j-caruso-opens-national-retail-federations-2014-big-show-with-keynote-address-the-traditional-mall-is-dead-retail-is-timeless-239823051.html
59 http://www.bloomberg.com/gadfly/articles/2015-11-16/retail-earnings-slowing-internet-sales-aren-t-helping
60 See chapter 4 why we believe the growth will actually be accelerated, bringing the e-commerce share to 30% by 2020.
61 As percentage of the non-food retail, excluding groceries, automotive sales and gasoline.

62 http://www.wiwo.de/unternehmen/handel/details-aus-insolvenzakten-warum-neckermann-nicht-zu-retten-war/8786524.html
63 http://retailgeek.com/jason-scot-show-episode-7-big-amazon-really/
64 http://www.kassenzone.de/2015/11/05/wie-gross-ist-amazon-de/
65 http://www.bloomberg.com/news/articles/2015-12-16/amazon-is-capturing-bigger-slice-of-u-s-online-holiday-spending
66 https://www.internetretailer.com/2015/08/25/best-buys-web-sales-climb-17
67 http://www.marketwatch.com/investing/stock/bby/financials
68 http://mashable.com/2012/11/06/ecommerce-statistics/
69 http://www.kassenzone.de/2014/01/23/otto-find-ich-gut/
70 http://www.cnbc.com/2014/09/30/ebay-and-paypal-to-split-into-two-separately-traded-companies.html
71 http://www.wiwo.de/unternehmen/handel/e-commerce-90-prozent-aller-reinen-online-shops-werden-nicht-ueberleben/9893008.html
72 http://www.nytimes.com/2014/12/05/business/sears-q3-earnings.html
73 http://www.marketwatch.com/story/jc-penney-is-resurrecting-its-catalog-2015-01-19-144852655
74 http://www.bloomberg.com/gadfly/articles/2015-11-11/macy-s-sales-fall-as-competition-heats-up
75 http://www.buchreport.de/nachrichten/handel/handel_nachricht/datum/2013/05/28/multichannel-ist-dringend-notwendig.htm?no_cache=1
76 www.multichannelmerchant.com
77 http://www.bundeskartellamt.de/SharedDocs/Meldung/DE/Pressemitteilungen/2014/02_07_2014_adidas.html
78 http://www.handelsblatt.com/unternehmen/handel-dienstleister/kampf-mit-online-haendlern-kartellamt-setzt-adidas-unter-druck/10136662.html
79 http://etailment.de/news/media/1/Whitepa-Wie-Mar-den-Kontrollverl-bei-Direktvertr-i-9345.pdf (Alexander Graf & Nils Seebach, Knut geht baden (www.etailment.de))
80 http://www.statista.com/statistics/287950/leading-e-retailers-worldwide-based-on-revenue/
81 See Chapter 3 Alibaba, AliExpress, JD.com, Tmall, Xiaomi, Vipshop
82 http://www.ecommercetimes.com/story/420.html
83 http://theconversation.com/two-decades-of-chinese-economic-policy-prepared-the-way-for-jd-com-and-alibaba-26735
84 USA International Business Publications, China E-Commerce Business and Investment Opportunity Handbook, 2009, Page 185f
85 http://www.indexmundi.com/united_states/internet-users.html
86 http://technode.com/2009/01/22/a-brief-history-and-future-of-alibabacom/
87 Taobao translates to "digging for treasures"
88 http://businessideaslab.com/taobao-a-short-story/
89 http://www.forbes.com/2010/01/18/china-internet-commerce-markets-equities-alibaba.html
90 http://www.chinainternetwatch.com/tag/jingdong/
91 http://multichannelmerchant.com/must-reads/difference-chinas-biggest-b2c-platforms-06082014/#_
92 http://www.investopedia.com/articles/investing/062315/understanding-alibabas-business-model.asp
93 http://multichannelmerchant.com/must-reads/difference-chinas-biggest-b2c-platforms-06082014/#_
94 https://www.techinasia.com/talk/online-payment-provider-alipay-chinese-equivalent-paypal
95 http://www.forbes.com/sites/ryanmac/2014/09/22/alibaba-claims-title-for-largest-global-ipo-ever-with-extra-share-sales/#21611f4a7c26
96 http://www.nytimes.com/2015/01/27/business/international/jdcom-chinas-other-e-commerce-giant-follows-its-own-path.html?_r=0
97 http://www.chinainternetwatch.com/tag/jingdong/
98 http://phys.org/news/2015-05-fakes-chinese-e-commerce-giant.html#jCp
99 http://www.chinainternetwatch.com/6031/tencent-rising-of-penguin-empire/
100 http://www.tencent.com/en-us/content/ir/news/2016/attachments/20160317.pdf
101 http://investor.fb.com/releasedetail.cfm?ReleaseID=952040

102 http://fortune.com/2015/07/22/tencent-chinese-e-commerce/
103 http://www.bloomberg.com/news/articles/2014-03-10/tencent-agrees-to-buy-15-stake-in-jd-com-for-214-7-million
104 http://recode.net/2015/10/08/facebooks-david-marcus-the-asian-paradigm-has-shown-messaging-is-the-next-frontier/
105 http://walkthechat.com/wechat-payment-5-reasons-tencent-might-kill-alipay/
106 http://www.investopedia.com/articles/investing/062315/understanding-alibabas-business-model.asp
107 http://techcrunch.com/2015/11/10/tencents-wechat-messaging-app-reaches-200m-users-on-its-payments-service/
108 http://www.chinainternetwatch.com/15957/chinas-b2c-sales-q3-2015/
109 http://asia.nikkei.com/magazine/20151119-SOMETHING-TO-PROVE/Business/Foreign-brands-dive-into-China-s-online-retail-market-on-Singles-Day
110 http://edition.cnn.com/2015/12/15/asia/wuzhen-china-internet-xi-jinping/
111 http://www.businessinsider.de/demand-report-on-chinas-middle-class-2015-11?r=US&IR=T
112 https://www.techinasia.com/chinas-singles-day-crushed-black-friday-offering-lessons-ecommerce
113 http://www.practicalecommerce.com/articles/94777-Sales-Report-2015-Thanksgiving-Day-Black-Friday-Cyber-Monday
114 http://asia.nikkei.com/magazine/20151119-SOMETHING-TO-PROVE/Business/Foreign-brands-dive-into-China-s-online-retail-market-on-Singles-Day
115 http://corporate.windeln.de/wp-content/themes/spacious-child/reports/q3%202015/EN/4_press_release/20151125_windeln.de_9m_Press_release.pdf
116 http://www.freshfields.com/uploadedFiles/SiteWide/Knowledge/33482(1).pdf
117 https://www.techinasia.com/china-embed-police-internet-company-offices
118 http://technode.com/2012/04/21/the-best-and-the-brightest/ and http://technode.com/2014/09/17/the-coming-out-of-china-tech-companies-part-1/

Chapter 2

1 Chris Anderson, The Long Tail, DTV, 2009
2 Marco Hassler, Web Analytics: Metriken auswerten, Besucherverhalten verstehen, Website optimieren, MITP, 2012, Seite 183ff.
3 Ulrich Müller, Kundenbindung im E-Commerce: Personalisierung als Instrument des Customer Relationship Marketing, Deutscher Universitätsverlag, 2005
4 http://t3n.de/news/produktbeschreibungen-vermeidest-532847
5 http://www.looklet.com
6 https://www.socialfresh.com/old-spice-viral-videos/
7 Ralf T. Kreutzer, Praxisorientiertes Online-Marketing: Konzepte - Instrumente - Checklisten, Springer Gabler, 2014, Seite 256
8 Erwin Lammenett, Praxiswissen Online-Marketing: Affiliate- und E-Mail-Marketing, Suchmaschinenmarketing, Online-Werbung, Social Media, Online-PR, Springer, 2013, Seite 124ff.
9 Ralf T. Kreutzer, Praxisorientiertes Online-Marketing: Konzepte - Instrumente - Checklisten, Springer Gabler, 2014, Seite 175ff.
10 http://www.emarketer.com/Article/Pinterest-Really-Leading-Product-Purchases/1009083
11 ECC / IFH Köln (2013) „Cross-Channel beim Kauf von Markenartikeln – Wie Konsumenten Kanäle kombinieren" zu beziehen unter http://shop.ecc-handel.de/de/ECC-SHOP/Themen/Multi-Channel-Management/Cross-Channel-beim-Kauf-von-Markenartikeln-Wie-Konsumenten-Kanaele-kombinieren

12 Björn Schäfers in G. Heinemann & A. Haug (2010), Web-Exzellenz im E-Commerce
13 See also Chapter 1.1 for market development overview
14 Sources: US: Placeable (digital marketing consultancy); Germany: BEVH (Federation of E-Commerce and Mail Order Companies)
15 Gerrit Heinemann, No-Line-Handel: Höchste Evolutionsstufe im Multi-Channeling, Springer, 2013, Seite 52f.
16 Gerrit Heinemann, No-Line-Handel: Höchste Evolutionsstufe im Multi-Channeling, Springer, 2013, Seite 150ff.
17 http://phx.corporate-ir.net/phoenix.zhtml?c=176060&p=irol-newsArticle&ID=2130275
18 http://baymard.com/lists/cart-abandonment-rate (abgerufen März 2015)
19 http://seewhy.com/wp-content/uploads/SeeWhy_eBook_The_Science_of_Shopping_Cart_Abandonment.pdf
20 http://seewhy.com/wp-content/uploads/SeeWhy_eBook_The_Science_of_Shopping_Cart_Abandonment.pdf
21 http://www.konversionskraft.de/conversion-optimierung/infografik-perfekte-warenkorb.html
22 https://www.forrester.com/Understanding+Shopping+Cart+Abandonment/fulltext/-/E-RES56827
23 http://docplayer.org/383481-Payment-im-e-commerce-der-internetzahlungsverkehr-aus-sicht-der-haendler-und-der-verbraucher-iz-2013.html
24 http://docplayer.org/383481-Payment-im-e-commerce-der-internetzahlungsverkehr-aus-sicht-der-haendler-und-der-verbraucher-iz-2013.html
25 EHI Retail Institute (2014), Online-Payment-Studie
26 http://www.ecckoeln.de/Downloads/Themen/Payment/PaymentimE-CommerceDerInternetzahlungsverkehrausSichtderHndlerundderVerbraucherIZ2013.pdf
27 EHI Retail Institute (2014), Online-Payment-Studie
28 http://www.ibi.de/files/ibi_research_Gesamtkosten_von_Zahlungsverfahren.pdf
29 www.internetworld.de
30 http://www.wiwo.de/unternehmen/handel/versandriese-sieben-gruende-warum-amazon-so-maechtig-ist-seite-all/9951552-all.html
31 www.estrategy-magazin.de , http://www.estrategy-magazin.de/versand-fulfillment-anbieter.html
32 http://www.moneysavingexpert.com/news/shopping/2014/01/yodel-named-worst-parcel-delivery-service-again
33 http://www.zeit.de/2014/15/retouren-onlinehandel-umweltbilanz (abgerufen März 2015)
34 Jan Thieme, Versandhandelsmanagement: Grundlagen, Prozesse und Erfolgsstrategien für die Praxis, Gabler, 2013, Seite 318ff.
35 http://www.focus.de/finanzen/paketkopter-im-test-dhl-drohne-bringt-paeckchen-auf-die-insel-juist_id_4156737.html

Chapter 3

1 M.E. Porter, Strategy & Internet, Harvard Business Review 03/2001
2 Alexander Osterwalder, Business Model Generation, John Wiley and Sons, 2010
3 www.businessmodelgeneration.com/canvas
4 https://startupweekend.org/attendees/resources
5 With reference to Finne & Sivonen (2009), The Retail Value Chain
6 http://www.ecckoeln.de/News/Erfolgsfaktoren-im-E-Commerce -
7 https://www.bcgperspectives.com/content/articles/supply_chain_management_-sourcing_procurement_omnichannel_retail_still_about_detail/
8 http://www.wsj.com/articles/peter-thiel-competition-is-for-losers-1410535536

9 http://www.economist.com/news/briefing/21635077-online-businesses-can-grow-very-large-very-fastit-what-makes-them-exciting-does-it-also-make

Kapitel 3.1

1 http://www.handelsblatt.com/unternehmen/handel-konsumgueter/about-you-chef-tarek-mueller-bei-mode-sind-wir-besser-als-zalando-oder-amazon/12460390.html
2 http://www.internetworld.de/e-commerce/e-commerce-trends/about-you-startet-massive-tv-kampagne-1022230.html
3 http://www.internetworld.de/e-commerce/otto-group/e-commerce-start-up-collins-verdreifacht-umsatz-1034459.html
4 http://t3n.de/magazin/collins-e-commerce-labor-239063/
* http://etailment.de/thema/player/Tarek-Mueller-About-You-Wir-haben-ein-ueberraschendes-Potenzial-der-Apps-entdeckt-2726
5 www.chinainternetwatch.com/7695/alibaba-group/
6 https://evigo.com/16165-report-whats-behind-global-success-alibabas-aliexpress/
7 www.internetretailer.com/commentary/2014/09/09/alibaba-tops-e-commerce-sites-russia-well-china
8 http://www.bloomberg.com/news/articles/2015-10-20/alibaba-s-marketplace-adds-russian-merchants-to-boost-expansion
9 https://www.internetretailer.com/2015/06/23/alibaba-says-its-aliexpresscom-leading-retail-site-ru
10 www.chinacheckup.com/kb/questions/what-is-aliexpress
11 https://www.internetretailer.com/2015/06/23/alibaba-says-its-aliexpresscom-leading-retail-site-ru
12 http://www.businesswire.com/news/home/20160128005635/en/Alibaba-Group-Announces-December-Quarter-2015-Results
13 Fiscal year ends March 31st, 2016
14 http://www.statista.com/statistics/225614/net-revenue-of-alibaba/
15 Per company definition, "China retail marketplaces" are Taobao Marketplace, Tmall and Juhuasuan.
16 http://www.marketwatch.com/investing/stock/amzn/financials
17 http://www.alibabagroup.com/en/news/press_pdf/p160505.pdf
18 https://www.techinasia.com/alibaba-biggest-investments-2015
19 http://digitalkaufmann.de/es-ist-still-geworden-um-die-40-raeuber/
20 http://www.reuters.com/article/us-amazon-com-alibaba-group-store-idUSKBN0M205Q20150306
21 http://phx.corporate-ir.net/phoenix.zhtml?c=97664&p=irol-reportsannual
22 http://www.statista.com/statistics/237810/number-of-active-amazon-customer-accounts-worldwide/
23 http://www.usatoday.com/story/tech/news/2016/01/25/amazon-prime-54-million-one-in-five-prime-grew-35-2015/79306470/
24 http://www.mwpvl.com/html/amazon_com.html
25 http://www.cnet.com/news/amazon-business-bolts-and-beakers-boom/
26 http://phx.corporate-ir.net/phoenix.zhtml?c=97664&p=irol-reportsannual
27 http://www.shopanbieter.de/news/archives/8594-amazon-marketplace-haendler-unterbieten-immer-haeufiger-den-markt.html
28 http://www.prosiebensat1.com/files/download/uploads/2015/11/13/p7s1_q3_2015_Bericht_d.pdf
29 http://www.amorelie.de/media/wysiwyg/presse/AMORELIE_Factsheet.pdf
30 http://t3n.de/magazin/amorelie-lea-sophie-cramer-238318/
31 https://excitingcommerce.de/2016/01/05/amorelie-hat-in-den-ersten-9-monaten-133-mio-euro-erzielt/
32 http://ao.com/corporate/wp-content/uploads/2015/11/AO-Results-Presentation-24-November-2015.pdf
33 https://excitingcommerce.de/2016/03/04/ao-erwartet-deutschland-umsatze-von-60-mio-e-im-1-jahr/

34 https://www.insidermedia.com/insider/northwest/uk-revenues-and-earnings-beat-expectations-at-ao.com
35 http://neuhandeln.de/analyse-warum-es-ao-in-deutschland-nicht-einfach-hat/
36 http://neuhandeln.de/elektronik-handel-ao-com-beziffert-deutschland-umsaetze/
37 https://www.insidermedia.com/insider/northwest/uk-revenues-and-earnings-beat-expectations-at-ao.com
38 http://www.bloomberg.com/news/articles/2015-07-20/apple-said-to-lease-office-space-in-seattle-tower
39 http://de.statista.com/statistik/daten/studie/39388/umfrage/umsatz-von-apple-seit-2004/
40 http://www.forbes.com/pictures/mli45fdhfm/1-apple/
41 https://www.internetretailer.com/top500/#!/
42 http://www.apple.com/choose-your-country/
43 https://www.fool.de/2015/09/23/tim-cook-apple-findet-reisenden-absatz-in-china/
44 http://images.apple.com/de/pr/pdf/q4fy15datasum.pdf
45 http://www.wikinvest.com/stock/Apple_%28AAPL%29/Data/Operating_Margin
46 http://www.asosplc.com/~/media/Files/A/ASOS/results-archive/pdf/2015-annual-report.pdf
47 http://www.kassenzone.de/2013/06/17/projekt-collins-warum-otto-so-handelt/
48 http://uk.reuters.com/article/uk-asos-results-idUKKCN0SE0IW20151020
49 http://www.bloomberg.com/news/articles/2014-06-05/asos-cuts-full-year-margin-forecast-as-pound-strengthens
50 http://www.businessoffashion.com/community/companies/asos
51 https://news.markets/shares/asos-big-opportunity-brand-fashions-says-berenberg-6631/
52 http://www.asosplc.com
53 http://www.businessoffashion.com/community/companies/asos
54 https://www.onlinehaendler-news.de/handel/allgemein/5340-asos-deutschland-schnittmenge-zalando.html
55 http://www.asosplc.com/~/media/Files/A/ASOS/results-archive/pdf/2015-annual-report.pdf
56 http://www.forbes.com/sites/alexkonrad/2015/10/14/inside-blue-apron-and-the-meal-kit-rush/
57 http://www.forbes.com/sites/alexkonrad/2015/10/14/inside-blue-apron-and-the-meal-kit-rush/#780c25b77af9
58 http://www.fastcompany.com/3047254/fast-feed/with-new-135-million-series-d-blue-apron-takes-the-lead-in-funding-for-meal-kit-st
59 http://www.businessinsider.com/blue-apron-plated-hello-fresh-difference-2015-4?IR=T
60 https://www.mobilestrategies360.com/2016/04/14/blue-aprons-app-its-secret-sauce-engaging-customers
61 http://www.fastcompany.com/3051332/fast-feed/you-can-now-have-wine-delivered-with-your-blue-apron-dinner
62 https://www.blueapron.com/pages/mission
63 http://www.businessinsider.com/blue-apron-plated-hello-fresh-difference-2015-4?IR=T
64 http://www.stockpup.com/companies/NILE/10-K.html
65 http://investor.bluenile.com/releasedetail.cfm?ReleaseID=954457
66 http://www.bluenile.com/inside-blue-nile
67 https://www.internetretailer.com/2015/12/10/blue-nile-braces-late-holiday-rush
68 http://www.bluenile.com/de/policies/shipping/where-we-ship
69 http://investor.bluenile.com/releasedetail.cfm?ReleaseID=940841
70 http://investor.bluenile.com/releasedetail.cfm?ReleaseID=954457
71 http://www.fool.com/investing/general/2016/02/11/shares-plunge-as-blue-nile-inc-reins-in-its-growth.aspx
72 https://www.internetretailer.com/2015/11/06/blue-niles-q3-revenue-increases-4
73 https://www.internetretailer.com/2015/06/05/leading-jewelry-e-retailer-blue-nile-opens-its-first-showroom
74 http://www.businessinsider.com/how-bonobos-is-maturing-into-a-major-brand-2015-8?IR=T

75 http://www.huffingtonpost.com/entry/casper-mattress-startup_us_564c9928e4b06037734bd61d
76 https://casper.com
77 http://www.conrad.com/ce/en/content/cms_au_company/Unternehmen?WT.ac=-footer_unternehmen
78 http://neuhandeln.de/geschaeftsjahr-2014-conrad-kratzt-an-der-umsatzmilliarde/
79 https://www.conrad.de/de/ueber-conrad/unternehmen/geschichte.html
80 http://www.elektroniknet.de/distribution/strategie-trends/artikel/101111/
81 http://www.channelpartner.de/a/wir-wollen-zu-einem-e-commerce-unternehmen-werden,3043921
82 https://www.conrad.de/de/filialen/filialservice/bringservice.html
83 http://www.logistra.de/news-nachrichten/nfz-fuhrpark-lagerlogistik-intralogistik/6735/maerkte-amp-trends/conrad-electronic-das-wachstum-bewaeltigen-mit
84 http://neuhandeln.de/offiziell-conrad-gruppe-beerdigt-hoh-und-getgoods-de/
85 http://www.cognitivepricing.com/uploads/3/0/2/8/30281035/occ_messers-schneide_pricing-2013.pdf
86 http://www.deliveryhero.com/deliveryherolaunchespremiumbrandurbantasteingermany/
87 http://www.welt.de/wirtschaft/webwelt/article152432009/DasgrosseGeschaeftmitdemEssen-aus-demInternet.html
88 http://www.deliveryhero.com/about/
89 http://www.gruenderszene.de/allgemein/deliveryherostreichttechstellen
90 http://www.welt.de/wirtschaft/webwelt/article152432009/DasgrosseGeschaeftmitdemEssen-aus-demInternet.html
91 http://www.internetworld.de/ecommerce/ecommercetrends/deliveryheroboersengangim-vierten-quartal1073248.html
92 http://www.welt.de/wirtschaft/webwelt/article151733093/AufderJagdnachDeutschlands-Einhoernern.html
93 https://investors.ebayinc.com/annuals.cfm
94 Primarily as a result of the weak Euro
95 http://www.ebay.com/s/valet
96 http://presse.ebay.de/pressrelease/ebay-feiert-20-jahre-und-startet-ebay-plus-deutschland
97 https://investors.ebayinc.com/annuals.cfm
98 Primarily as a result of the weak Euro
99 https://investors.ebayinc.com/annuals.cfm
100 http://www.ebay.com/s/valet
101 http://presse.ebay.de/pressrelease/ebayfeiert20jahreundstartetebayplusdeutschland
102 http://excitingcommerce.de/2016/01/23/dieinternetstoresmit10mioeebitdabei140mioe-umsatz/
103 http://www.internetstores.de/portfolio.html:
104 http://www.internetstores.de/ueberuns/auszeichnungen.html
105 http://de.statista.com/statistik/daten/studie/311751/umfrage/umsatzvoninternetstoresfahrradde/
106 http://www.internetstores.de/presse/detailansichtnews/article//internetstoresholdinggmbh-starkeswachstumbeiumsatzundebitdazum30062015.html
107 http://excitingcommerce.de/2016/01/23/dieinternetstoresmit10mioeebitdabei140mioe-umsatz/
108 http://www.internetstores.de/presse/detailansichtnews/article//internetstoresholdinggmbh-starkeswachstumbeiumsatzundebitdazum30062015.html
109 https://www.deutschergruenderpreis.de/preistraeger/2010/internetstores/
110 http://www.internetstores.de
111 http://www.internetstores.de/portfolio/bike/bikester.html
112 http://www.recode.net/2015/3/16/11560292/giltgroupesverycloudyfuture
113 http://www.orckestra.com/en/ideas/blog/2015/january/flashsalesinomnichannelretailecommerce
114 http://www.forbes.com/sites/clareoconnor/2016/01/07/saksparenthudsonsbaybuysgiltgroupe-in-250millioncashdealwillfoldintosaksofffifth/#17f1ceeb635d
115 http://www.businessinsider.com/giltgroupestory20152?IR=T
116 http://phx.corporate-ir.net/External.File?item=UGFyZW50SUQ9NTc1NjUxfENoaWxkSUQ9Mjc5MjkyfFR5cGU9MQ==&t=1

117 http://www.inddist.com/news/2016/01/graingerclose55branches2016q4salesprofitdip
118 http://phx.corporate-ir.net/External.File?item=UGFyZW50SUQ9NjA5MjgyfENoaWxkSUQ9MzIzMDE5fFR5cGU9MQ==&t=1
119 https://www.internetretailer.com/2015/04/16/wwgraingerclosescapturing40salesonline
120 http://www.inddist.com/news/2016/01/graingerclose55branches2016q4salesprofitdip
121 https://www.internetretailer.com/2015/04/16/wwgraingerclosescapturing40salesonline
122 http://www.businessinsider.de/harrysceosexplainhowtheyacquiredamillioncustomersin2years2015-12?r=US&IR=T
123 http://www.forbes.com/sites/stevenbertoni/2015/07/07/razorwarsharrysraises75milliontofight-gilletteanddollarshaveclub/#5c08d25f346a
124 http://www.businessinsider.de/harrysceosexplainhowtheyacquiredamillioncustomersin2years2015-12?r=US&IR=T
125 http://www.businessinsider.de/harrysceosexplainhowtheyacquiredamillioncustomersin2years2015-12?r=US&IR=T
126 http://www.welt.de/print/die_welt/wirtschaft/article151745098/AufderSuchenachEinhoernern.html
127 https://excitingcommerce.de/2015/12/17/furhellofreshhatdergeplatzteborsengangkaumfolgen/
128 https://excitingcommerce.de/2015/12/17/furhellofreshhatdergeplatzteborsengangkaumfolgen/
129 http://www.hellofreshgroup.com/hellofreshfactsandfigures/
130 https://excitingcommerce.de/2015/10/29/hellofreshgewonnenekundenrechnensichnach2quartalen/
131 https://excitingcommerce.de/2015/07/23/wiehellofreshdieumsatzeauf250mioeexplodieren-lasst/
132 http://ir.homedepot.com/phoenix.zhtml?c=63646&p=irolnewsArticle&ID=1735130
133 https://www.internetretailer.com/2016/02/24/mobilesparksq4saleshomedepot
134 https://www.internetretailer.com/2015/06/04/homedepotwinsinternetretailersfirstexcellence-awards
135 https://www.internetretailer.com/2016/01/20/homedepothammersawayonlinegrowth
136 http://www.bloomberg.com/gadfly/columnists/ASkbVJ3fYAA/shellybanjo/articles/20151209/home-depotshareholdermeetingnonewstores
137 http://cdn.home24.net/static/media/om/cms/presse/151110pressemitteilunghome24uebernimmt-fashionforhome.pdf
138 https://www.rocketinternet.com/sites/default/files/investors/20150930_Rocket_CMD_Presentation_Part2.pdf
139 http://cdn.home24.net/static/media/om/cms/presse/151215pressemitteilunghome24app-auszeichnung.pdf
140 http://cdn.home24.net/static/media/om/cms/presse/151110pressemitteilunghome24uebernimmt-fashionforhome.pdf
141 http://cdn.home24.net/static/media/om/cms/presse/151110pressemitteilunghome24uebernimmt-fashionforhome.pdf
142 http://excitingcommerce.de/2015/10/15/ikeawachstonlineauf190mioehome24kann-vorbeiziehen/
143 http://www.berlinerzeitung.de/berlin/interviewmitberlinerhome24chefderklassische-moebelhandelistnichtmehrzeitgemaess,10809148,32695232.html
144 http://kinnevik.se/Documents/Capital%20Markets%20Day%20September%202014/12.%20 2014_09_18_Home24@KCMD.pdf
145 http://www.berlinerzeitung.de/berlin/interviewmitberlinerhome24chefderklassische-moebelhandelistnichtmehrzeitgemaess,10809148,32695232.html
* http://meedia.de/2014/11/03/vier-jahre-im-moebelmarkt-verschollen-wie-sich-home24-ueber-ikea-lustig-macht/
146 http://www.ikea.com/ms/de_DE/thisisikea/abouttheikeagroup/index.html
147 http://www.ikea.com/ms/de_DE/thisisikea/abouttheikeagroup/index.html:
148 http://www.ikea.com/ms/de_DE/thisisikea/abouttheikeagroup/index.html:
149 http://www.ikea.com/ms/de_DE/pdf/yearly_summary/ikeagroupyearlysummaryfy15.pdf
150 http://www.bloomberg.com/news/articles/20151210/ikeaceoseesonlineaccountingfor10of-revenue-by2020

151 http://www.applianceretailer.com.au/2015/10/retailtrendswatchoutikeapushesbuttononecommerce/#.VrD8CM7igc
152 http://ecommercenews.eu/ikeaplanstosignificantlygrowitsecommercebusiness/
153 https://www.onlinehaendlernews.de/handel/allgemein/22303ikeaerlaeutertomnichannel-ausrichtung.html
154 http://www.stern.de/wirtschaft/news/ikeamoebelshoppenimnetzkoennenkundenbeidiesen-unternehmenbesser6303502.html
155 http://fortune.com/ikeaworlddomination/
156 http://www.ikea.com/ms/de_DE/pdf/yearly_summary/ikeagroupyearlysummaryfy15.pdf
157 http://cx-commerce.de/2013/01/warum-ikea-online-nicht-abhebt/
158 https://globenewswire.com/news-release/2016/03/01/815658/0/en/JD-com-Announces-Fourth-Quarter-and-Full-Year-2015-Results.html
159 According to EUR-USD rates on 31/12/2015 (1,0859)
160 JD is China's second largest online retailer as measured by GMV, but the largest as measured by revenue.
161 The Alibaba Group figures also contain those of Alibaba.com, Tmall, Taobao, Alipay and Juhuasuan
162 http://ir.jd.com/phoenix.zhtml?c=253315&p=irol-reportsOther
163 http://ir.jd.com/phoenix.zhtml?c=253315&p=irol-homeProfile
164 See chapter 1.2 for more on cooperation between JA and Tencent
165 Applies to customers who have entered their credit card details on WeChat and already used other paid services
166 http://venturebeat.com/2015/11/16/amazons-other-china-rival-jd-com-hits-double-the-revenue-of-market-leader-alibaba-in-q3/
167 http://www.china-briefing.com/news/2015/09/15/tmall-yihaodian-and-jd-a-comparison-of-chinas-top-e-commerce-platforms-for-foreign-enterprises.html
168 http://www.newsslash.com/n/7444-jet-com-erwirtschaftet-eine-milliarde-us-dollar
169 https://www.internetretailer.com/2016/04/15/jetcom-predicts-its-sales-will-total-1-billion-may
170 http://www.investors.com/news/technology/how-e-tail-startup-jet-com-plans-to-take-on-amazon/
171 http://vator.tv/news/20150512whatsitliketobeaunicorn
172 http://www.buzzfeed.com/sapna/justfabfableticstarget675millioninsalesthisyear#.da3BJkA1V
173 http://www.presseportal.de/pm/109549/3131226
174 http://corp.justfab.com/?action=about
175 http://www.buzzfeed.com/sapna/justfabfableticstarget675millioninsalesthisyear#.da3BJkA1V
176 https://www.internetretailer.com/2015/11/02/amidcomplaintsjustfabwillreviewitsvipprogram
177 http://www.ottogroup.com/de/die-otto-group/konzernfirmen/limango.php
178 http://www.kassenzone.de/2016/03/08/limango-shopping-club-2-0/
179 http://www.ottogroup.com/media/docs/de/download/meldungen/2016/pm_jahresbericht2015_limango_final.pdf
180 www.limango.de and www.ottogroup.com
181 http://www.internetworld.de/e-commerce/internet/es-bleibt-in-familie-287227.html
182 http://a3.cdn.limango-media.de/raw/upload/v1/media/presse/info/limango-Unternehmensprofil.pdf
183 http://www.ottogroup.com/media/docs/de/download/meldungen/2016/pm_jahresbericht2015_limango_final.pdf
184 http://www.internetworld.de/e-commerce/online-handel/limango-vorne-mitspielen-1092455.html
185 http://www.internetworld.de/e-commerce/online-handel/limango-vorne-mitspielen-1092455.html
186 Cf. Vente Privée company profile
187 http://www.ottogroup.com/media/docs/de/download/meldungen/2016/pm_jahresbericht2015_limango_final.pdf
* http://www.onetoone.de/Limango-geht-nach-Polen-und-in-die-Niederlande-20188.html
188 http://www.metrogroup.de/~/assets/mag/documents/reports/metrogroupgeschaeftsbericht-201415_de.pdf?la=dede

189 http://www.channelpartner.de/a/befindetsichredcooninderrueckwaertsbewegung,3046763
190 http://www.heise.de/newsticker/meldung/NachAmazonstartetauchMediaSaturnLieferungam-Tag-derBestellung2969484.html
191 http://www.metrogroup.de/~/assets/mag/documents/investorrelations/resultspresentationfy-201415_en.pdf?la=en
192 http://www.metrogroup.de/~/assets/mag/documents/reports/metrogroupgeschaeftsbericht-201415_de.pdf?la=dede
193 http://www.channelpartner.de/a/online-wachstum-von-media-saturn-faengt-station-aeren-rueckgang-nicht-auf,3044105
194 http://investor.nordstrom.com/phoenix.zhtml?c=93295&p=irol-newsArticle&ID=2140704
195 http://investor.nordstrom.com/phoenix.zhtml?c=93295&p=irol-newsArticle&ID=2140704
196 https://www.internetretailer.com/2015/11/17/online-accounts-nearly-20-nordstroms-sales
197 https://www.trunkclub.com/help/what-is-trunk-club-s-affiliation-with-nordstrom
198 https://www.cbinsights.com/blog/nordstrom-e-commerce-case-study
199 https://www.internetretailer.com/2016/03/10/e-commerce-eats-nordstroms-profits-and-s-ok
200 http://www.businessinsider.de/you-can-return-nordstrom-rack-to-nordstrom-2016-2?r=US&IR=T
201 https://www.internetretailer.com/2015/08/14/nordstrom-e-commerce-sales-jump-24-q2
202 http://www.businessinsider.de/you-can-return-nordstrom-rack-to-nordstrom-2016-2?r=US&IR=T
203 https://www.otto.de/unternehmen/de/unternehmen/kennzahlen.php
204 https://www.otto.de/unternehmen/de/unternehmen/kennzahlen.php
205 http://www.wiwo.de/unternehmen/handel/ottogroupumsatzwaechstwieder-kraeftig/13385602.html
206 http://www.ottogroup.com/de/newsroom/meldungen/PartnerschaftmitPowaTagOttoGrouptreibt-AusbaudesweltweitenMobileGeschaeftsB2Cweitervoran.php
207 http://www.ottogroup.com/de/newsroom/meldungen/AufWachstumskursMYTOYSGROUPzieht-positiveJahresbilanz201516.php
208 https://www.otto.de/shoppages/service/
209 http://www.overstock.com/81690/static.html?TID=ABOUT:History
210 http://www.overstock.com/81690/static.html?TID=ABOUT:History
211 http://www.overstock.com/81690/static.html?TID=ABOUT:History
212 https://help.overstock.com/app/answers/detail/a_id/1505
213 http://www.furnituretoday.com/article/528604insideoverstockcometailerpreachescustomer-vendorworkercare
214 https://www.internetretailer.com/2016/02/10/overstockcomssalesgrow21q4107year
215 http://www.wired.com/2016/02/whybitcoinwillthrivefirstinthedevelopingworld/
216 http://www.overstock.com/85771/static.html?TID=WORLDRDSP_FAIRTRADE
217 http://global.rakuten.com/corp/about/overview.html
218 http://techcrunch.com/2016/02/12/raktrenchment/
219 https://newsroom.rakuten.de/unternehmensprofil/rakuten_inc/
220 https://newsroom.rakuten.de/unternehmensprofil/rakutenglobal/
221 https://newsroom.rakuten.de/unternehmensprofil/rakuten_inc/
222 http://www.kassenzone.de/2013/06/11/rakutengewinnt/
223 http://excitingcommerce.de/2012/02/12/rakutenalsalternativezuamazonundebay/
224 http://techcrunch.com/2014/10/22/japansrakutenrampsupgloballylauchesrakutencouk-marketplaceanddropsplaycom/
225 http://excitingcommerce.de/2016/01/03/rakutenbleibtnocheinjahrumanamazon-vorbeizuziehen/
226 http://techcrunch.com/2016/02/12/raktrenchment/
227 www.global.rakuten.com
* https://www.internetretailer.com/2013/05/17/rakuten-kicks-its-fifth-european-e-marketplace
228 http://investor.staples.com/phoenix.zhtml?c=96244&p=irolnewsArticle&ID=2137064
229 http://www.computerweekly.com/news/2240226743/CIOinterviewDaveUbachsCIOStaples-Europe
230 http://www.staplesadvantage.de/warum_staples/ausdehnung/globale_ausdehnung/
231 http://www.pymnts.com/news/2014/stapleslaunchesecommercemarketplace/#.VKAe6cACA

232 http://investor.staples.com/phoenix.zhtml?c=96244&p=irolnewsArticle&ID=2137064
*http://investor.staples.com/phoenix.zhtml?c=96244&p=irol-reportsannual
233 http://www.computerworld.com/article/3067264/artificialintelligence/atstitchfixdatascientistsand-aibecomepersonalstylists.html
234 http://www.recode.net/2016/2/24/11588184/stitchfixtheonlinepersonalstylingstartuptolaunch-mensbusiness
235 http://www.computerworld.com/article/3067264/artificialintelligence/atstitchfixdatascientistsand-aibecomepersonalstylists.html
236 http://modernmrsdarcy.com/bets-stitch-fix-tips/
237 http://www.mystatesman.com/news/lifestyles/fashion-style/how-stitch-fixs-katrina-lake-is-changing-the-retai/nrLYd/
238 http://www.mcall.com/news/breaking/mc-stitch-fix-coming-to-lower-nazareth-20160421-story.html
239 http://www.statista.com/statistics/225614/net-revenue-of-alibaba/
240 We can assume that Tmall has booked most of these sales for itself
241 http://www.chinadaily.com.cn/business/2015-11/12/content_22439883.htm
242 http://pressroom.venteprivee.com/sitecore/content/PR/PressReleases/2016/Le%20Verone.aspx
243 http://de.fashionmag.com/news/NachzweistelligemWachstumgonntsichVenteriveeeinneues-Burogebaude,614554.html#.VrNYYc7igc
244 http://pressroom.venteprivee.com/sitecore/content/PR/PressReleases/2016/Le%20Verone.aspx
245 http://www.businessinsider.com/granjoninterview20115?IR=T
246 http://fortune.com/2014/10/27/ventepriveeusatoshutdown/
247 http://de.fashionmag.com/news/NachzweistelligemWachstumgonntsichVenteriveeeinneues-Burogebaude,614554.html#.VrNYYc7igc
248 http://www.textilwirtschaft.de/business/VentePriveeruestetsichfuerdieExpansion_100571.html
249 https://www.macroaxis.com/invest/ratio/VIPS--Number-of-Employees
250 http://ir.vip.com/phoenix.zhtml?c=250900&p=irol-newsArticle&ID=2142850
251 http://www.reuters.com/finance/stocks/companyProfile?symbol=VIPS.K
252 http://www.bloomberg.com/news/articles/2015-11-24/hedge-funds-focus-on-vipshop-in-shift-away-from-china-e-commerce
253 http://ir.jd.com/phoenix.zhtml?c=253315&p=irol-reportsOther
254 http://ar.alibabagroup.com/2015/assets/pdf/20-F.PDF
255 https://excitingcommerce.de/2015/10/20/showroomprive-vipshop-will-beim-ipo-anteile-fur-30-mio-e/comment-page-1/
256 Financial year ends on 31/01/2016
257 http://corporate.walmart.com/our-story/our-history
258 https://www.internetretailer.com/2016/01/15/wal-marts-e-commerce-focus-will-grow-stores-close
259 http://corporate.walmart.com/our-story/our-history
260 http://s2.q4cdn.com/056532643/files/doc_financials/2015/annual/2015-annual-report.pdf
261 http://corporate.walmart.com/our-story/our-business
262 https://www.internetretailer.com/2016/02/18/wal-marts-online-sales-growth-slows-year
263 https://www.internetretailer.com/2016/02/18/wal-marts-online-sales-growth-slows-year
264 http://fortune.com/2015/12/22/retail-ecommerce-2015-amazon-walmart/
265 https://www.internetretailer.com/2016/04/14/walmartcom-invites-more-merchants-sell-its-marketplace
266 https://wanelo.com/about
267 http://blog.wanelo.com/post/105275701075/news-shopify-merchants-can-now-sell-directly-to
* https://wanelo.com/about/shopify
268 http://techcrunch.com/2015/11/16/wary-of-the-next-warby/?utm_content=buffer5a060&utm_medium=social&utm_source=linkedin.com&utm_campaign=buffer#.vv9bta:gpYA
269 https://ca.warbyparker.com/region-select
270 https://ca.warbyparker.com/retail
271 http://fashionista.com/2015/08/warby-parker-nordstrom

272 https://www.warbyparker.com/terms-of-use
273 http://s2.q4cdn.com/848638248/files/doc_presentations/2015/W.Presentation_Q4-2015_FINALv2.pdf
274 http://www.businessinsider.com/the-story-behind-wayfair-2014-10?IR=T
275 http://www.forbes.com/sites/abrambrown/2014/04/16/how-wayfair-sells-nearly-1-billion-worth-of-sofas-patio-chairs-and-cat-playgrounds/#2dcc894035de
276 https://www.internetretailer.com/2016/02/26/wayfairs-direct-consumer-sales-nearly-double-q4
277 https://excitingcommerce.de/2016/02/29/wayfair-wachst-2015-um-931-mio-auf-225-mrd-71/
278 http://investor.wayfair.com/investor-relations/press-releases/press-releases-details/2015/Wayfair-Sells-its-Australian-based-Business-to-Australias-1-Online-Furniture--Homewares-Retailer-Temple--Webster/default.aspx
279 http://ir.williams-sonomainc.com/sites/williams-sonomainc.investorhq.businesswire.com/files/doc_library/file/WS_15AR.pdf
280 http://ir.williams-sonomainc.com/press-release/corporate-and-brand-announcements/minted-partners-pottery-barn-kids-and-pbteen-exclusi
281 http://multichannelmerchant.com/marketing/williams-sonoma-finds-success-digital-age-06102014/
282 https://www.internetretailer.com/2016/03/18/williams-sonomas-online-sales-increase-64-year
283 https://www.internetretailer.com/2016/03/18/williams-sonomas-online-sales-increase-64-year
284 http://multichannelmerchant.com/marketing/williams-sonoma-finds-success-digital-age-06102014/
285 http://corporate.windeln.de/?page_id=111
286 http://corporate.windeln.de/?page_id=43
287 http://www.finanznachrichten.de/nachrichten-2016-05/37476751-dgap-news-windeln-de-ag-windeln-de-setzt-wachstum-im-ersten-quartal-fort-china-geschaeft-belastet-ausblick-deutsch-0-16.htm
288 http://neuhandeln.de/neocom-warum-windeln-de-kein-abo-modell-anbietet/
289 http://www.internetworld.de/e-commerce/start-up/windeln.de-schwaechelt-1104750.html
290 http://www.recode.net/2015/12/28/11621724/meetwishthe3billionappthatcouldbethenext-walmart
291 http://www.recode.net/2015/12/28/11621724/meetwishthe3billionappthatcouldbethenext-walmart
292 http://www.bloomberg.com/news/videos/b/8db04ddf7815467298fd581cc4b0d1da
293 http://www.recode.net/2015/12/28/11621724/meetwishthe3billionappthatcouldbethenext-walmart
294 http://techcrunch.com/2016/03/01/thehotecommerceappwishhashundreds-ofmillionsofusersplus-otherfascinatingstats/
295 http://www.recode.net/2015/12/28/11621724/meetwishthe3billionappthatcouldbethenext-walmart
296 http://www.forbes.com/sites/melanieleest/2016/01/15/why-chinas-xiaomi-sold-a-disappointing-70-million-smartphones-in-2015/#3ceb0b0531fe
297 https://stratechery.com/2015/xiaomis-ambition/
298 http://fortune.com/2016/01/15/xiaomi-smartphone-sales-fall-short/
299 http://www.businessinsider.de/xiaomi-ceo-backs-off-2015-sales-targets-2015-12?amp?r=US&IR=T
300 http://www.forbes.com/sites/melanieleest/2016/01/15/why-chinas-xiaomi-sold-a-disappointing-70-million-smartphones-in-2015/#3ceb0b0531fe
301 https://corporate.zalando.de/de/ir
302 https://excitingcommerce.de/2016/03/22/zalandokundigtfulfilmentbyzalandoservicean/
303 The strategy behind the Movmnt app
304 https://excitingcommerce.de/2016/03/01/zalandowachstimdachraumauf158mrdeuro28/
305 http://www.businessinsider.de/zappos-ceo-tony-hsieh-on-misconception-about-holacracy-2016-2?r=US&IR=T
306 http://www.zappos.com/shoes
307 http://www.forbes.com/sites/danpontefract/2015/05/11/what-is-happening-at-zappos/#29fbfb0f31b3
308 http://www.zappos.com/d/about-zappos
309 http://www.forbes.com/sites/danpontefract/2015/05/11/what-is-happening-at-zappos/#29fbfb0f31b3

310 http://www.zappos.com/canada
311 http://www.zappos.com/blogs/zclt-stories-the-8-hour-call/
312 http://investors.zooplus.com/downloads/zooplus_Geschaeftsbericht_2014.pdf
313 http://investors.zooplus.com/downloads/d_CN_zooplus_PrelimsFY2015_160128.pdf
314 http://de.statista.com/statistik/daten/studie/151133/umfrage/onlineumsatzvonzooplusag/
315 http://investors.zooplus.com/downloads/d_CN_zooplus_PrelimsFY2015_160128.pdf
316 http://investors.zooplus.com/downloads/d_zooplus_CN%209M_151118.pdf
317 https://www.internetretailer.com/europe500/
318 http://www.finanzen.net/nachricht/aktien/GeldanlageReportZooplusDasunterschaetzteE-CommercePowerhouse3991674
319 http://www.haufe.de/marketingvertrieb/onlinemarketing/ecommercezooplushatbeidenkunden-die-nasevorne_132_218054.html
* http://investors.zooplus.com/downloads/IR-Presentation_November2014.pdf
320 http://mcdn.zulilyinc.com/images/press-room/apple_pay_0825_2015.pdf
321 http://www.zulily.com/faq
322 http://www.wsj.com/articles/zulily-nips-business-model-in-the-bud-1427165209
323 https://excitingcommerce.de/2015/08/23/als-zulily-merkte-dass-es-auf-die-falschen-kunden-gesetzt-hat/

About Spryker

Spryker Systems develops e-commerce software based on the principles which have brought success to the international leaders in internet retail. Spryker is a modular shop technology for companies who consider data and intelligent service as integral to the product, offering them a genuine alternative to costly, risky proprietary development. Supporting agile, high-productivity processes, Spryker stands for a new generation of software, making it possible to build customer-focused business models which are continually evolved by data as it is acquired. The Spryker Systems team is located in Berlin and Hamburg. Find out more at https://spryker.com/ or on Twitter: @sprysys.

How Spryker impacts your Business

Productivity

More rollouts, better code, tailored features

- Data-driven technology with all data (incl. secondary) in one place
- PHP based with highest development standards for maximum development speed
- Consequent use of the SOLID principles to avoid interdependences between components and guarantee maintainability and expandability

Performance

Front-end speed, unlimited products, TV traffic-ready

- Separation of front end and back end
- Slimline front-end application (Yves) without full page cache to allow continious updates and avoid outdated content
- Powerful back end (Zed) for complex business logics such as cart calculations and payments

Flexibility

Modular system, atomic upgrades, easy connectors

- Every component can be customized or replaced by a client-developed feature
- Easy optimization for local markets due to multiple layers in the system that address different aspects of the internationalization
- Easy integration of different IT systems involved in order processing, e.g. stock, CRM or order management

Technology

Spryker's architecture is based on a separation of front-end and back-end applications. The front end (Yves) delivers ultra-fast performance to the customer, the back end (Zed) provides the user's combined business logic - all data is stored in one place (data hub) to deliver secure and reliable data sets. Spryker is a framework and not a limited standard system. All components, even core elements such as the catalogue, can either be built upon or replaced if a more customized component proves to be beneficial for the company's business model. This concept is totally new to an e-commerce world in which shop systems are still built as applications.

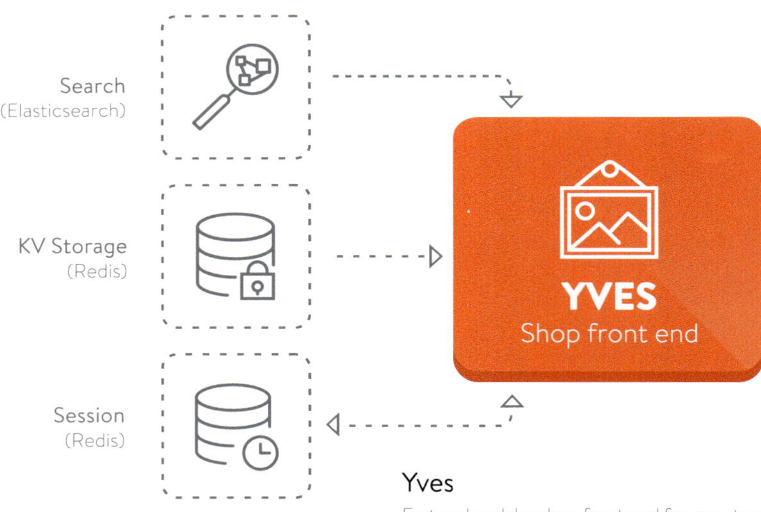

Open Code

Although the core of Spryker is a commercial product, the source code is open to the public. This is a new approach of software distribution which is called "Open Code": Developers can retrieve the source code on Github and evaluate the framework if it fits to their needs. Spryker even has a contribution agreement. The difference to open source is the license that only allows evaluation. So if you want to use Spryker for your project, we would be more than happy to talk with you.

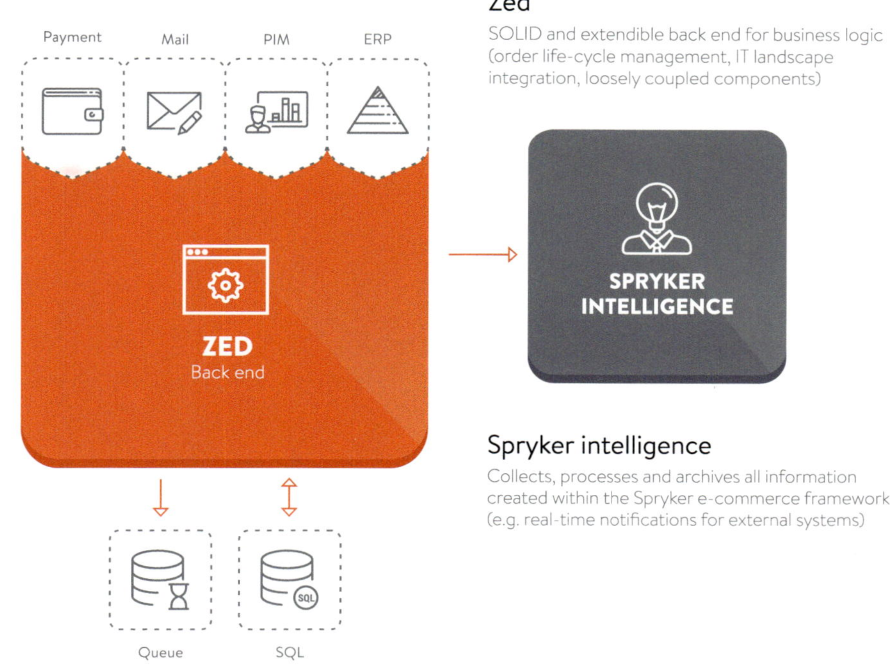

Zed

SOLID and extendible back end for business logic (order life-cycle management, IT landscape integration, loosely coupled components)

Spryker intelligence

Collects, processes and archives all information created within the Spryker e-commerce framework (e.g. real-time notifications for external systems)